The Hong Kong–Guangdong Link

Hong Kong Becoming China: The Transition to 1997

Ming K. Chan and Gerard A. Postiglione
Series General Editors

Because of Hong Kong's remarkable development under British rule for the past 150 years and its contemporary importance as a world economic and communications center on the Pacific Rim, and due to Hong Kong's future status as a Special Administrative Region of the People's Republic of China from 1997 well into the mid-twenty-first century, M.E. Sharpe has inaugurated this new multi-volume series. Published for an international readership, this series aims at providing both expert analysis and the documentary basis for a more informed understanding of Hong Kong's transition as a free society and capitalist economy toward socialist Chinese sovereignty under the "One Country, Two Systems" formula.

This series explores various crucial dimensions of Hong Kong's current development in this transition process and their implications for the international community. Individual volumes in this series will focus on key areas and issues ranging from China's Basic Law for Hong Kong, education and social change, the existing common law legal system, the historical relationship between Britain, China, and Hong Kong, urban growth and infrastructural development, the control of the media, social movements and popular mobilization, the cultural identity of Hong Kong Chinese, to economic linkages with mainland China, the Beijing–Hong Kong–Taipei triangle, "brain drain" and migration overseas, as well as the internationalization of Hong Kong.

The books in this series so far are: *The Hong Kong Basic Law: Blueprint for "Stability and Prosperity" under Chinese Sovereignty?* edited by Ming K. Chan and David Clark; *Education and Society in Hong Kong: Toward One Country and Two Systems*, edited by Gerard A. Postiglione; *The Common Law System in Chinese Context: Hong Kong in Transition,* by Berry Hsu; *Precarious Balance: Hong Kong between China and Britain, 1842–1992,* edited by Ming K. Chan; *Reluctant Exiles? Migration from Hong Kong and the New Overseas Chinese,* edited by Ronald Skeldon; and *The Hong Kong–Guangdong Link: Partnership in Flux,* edited by Reginald Yin-Wang Kwok and Alvin Y. So.

Ming K. Chan is a member of the History Department, University of Hong Kong, and Executive Coordinator of the Hong Kong Documentary Archives, Hoover Institution, Stanford University.

Gerard A. Postiglione is Senior Lecturer in Sociology of Education, University of Hong Kong, and Director of its Education and National Integration Program.

Hong Kong Becoming China:
The Transition to 1997

The Hong Kong–Guangdong Link

Partnership in Flux

**Reginald Yin-Wang Kwok
and Alvin Y. So, editors**

An East Gate Book

M.E. Sharpe
Armonk, New York
London, England

An East Gate Book

Library of Congress Cataloging-in-Publication Data

The Hong Kong–Guangdong Link: Partnership in Flux /
Reginald Yin-Wang Kwok and Alvin Y. So, editors.
p. cm.—(Hong Kong becoming China: the transition to 1997)
"An East Gate book."
Includes bibliographical references and index.
ISBN 1–56324–620–1 (hardcover: alk. paper)
1. Hong Kong—Economic conditions.
2. Hong Kong—Politics and government.
3. Kwangtung Province (China)—Economic conditions.
I. Kwok, R. Yin-Wang. II. So, Alvin Y., 1953–
III. Series: Hong Kong becoming China.
HC470.3.H666 1995
337.5125051'275—dc20
95–15378
CIP

Printed in the United States of America

The paper used in this publication meets the minimum requirements of
American National Standard for Information Sciences—
Permanence of Paper for Printed Library Materials,
ANSI Z 39.48-1984.

BM (c) 10   9   8   7   6   5   4   3   2   1
BM (p) 10   9   8   7   6   5   4   3   2   1

———— Contents

Contributors

Roger T. Ames	Department of Philosophy, University of Hawaii at Manoa.
Ming K. Chan	Department of History, University of Hong Kong. Hong Kong Documentary Archives, Hoover Institution, Stanford University.
Gregory Guldin	Department of Anthropology, Pacific Lutheran University.
Graham Johnson	Department of Anthropology and Sociology, University of British Columbia.
Reginald Yin-Wang Kwok	Asian Studies Programs, and Department of Urban and Regional Planning, University of Hawaii at Manoa.
Ming-kwan Lee	Department of Applied Social Studies, Hong Kong Polytechnic University.
Lixun Li	Centre for Urban and Regional Studies, Zhongshan University.
Alvin Y. So	Department of Sociology, University of Hawaii at Manoa.
Ian Scott	School of Social Sciences, Murdoch University.

Victor Sit

Department of Geography and Geology, University of Hong Kong

Xiaopei Yan

Centre for Urban and Regional Studies, Zhongshan University.

Yun-Wing Sung

Department of Economics, Chinese University of Hong Kong.

Xueqiang Xu

Centre for Urban and Regional Studies, Zhongshan University.

Series General Editor's Foreword

Indeed, Hong Kong has little future without Guangdong. The days when Guangdong was considered Hong Kong's hinterland of farms and fields are long over. Economic reforms have transformed South China. This has had an enormous impact on Hong Kong, which has moved much of its manufacturing over the border and now employs more than three million industrial workers in Guangdong. This is contributing to a "Manhattan-ization" of Hong Kong.

Yet, Guangdong's economy still pales in comparison to that of Hong Kong. With a tenth of the population of Guangdong, Hong Kong is the world's eighth largest trading economy. Does the Hong Kong tail wag the Guangdong dog? Or will Hong Kong soon be swallowed up by Guangdong? The plot thickens as four new international airports all within a radius of fifty miles in the southern tip of the Pearl River Delta, one each in Hong Kong and Macau and one in each of China's Special Economic Zones, Shenzhen and Zhuhai, compete with one another. But make no mistake about it, behind Guangdong's dependency on Hong Kong is, in fact, a growing dependency on the world economy. This will continue to be the case, though in the process, Hong Kong's growing dependency on Guangdong may reshape its own internationalism.

The PRC's policy of reform and opening has permitted Guangdong to be more like Hong Kong. But Hong Kong is also becoming part of China by 1997. The reality is that as South China has become more like Hong Kong, Hong Kong has continued to develop in its own way. After 1997, Hong Kong is supposed to continue to go its own way according to the "one country, two systems" formula. Yet, the growing interdependency that is the focus of this book confronts Hong Kong with an interesting challenge. Can it continue to develop its own way while increasing functional integration with Guangdong? The answer will depend on what limitations are imposed on Guangdong's future course by the central government, because Guangdong may become as much like Hong Kong as it is permitted by Beijing.

Though their partnership is and will continue to be in flux, their economies are, and will remain, inseparable. Economic linkages between the two may act to shape Hong Kong's future development. But will Hong Kong remain in its own image? How long will it be before the Hong Kong tide is turned back? Herein lies the contradiction. It will be impossible for Guangdong to turn back the tide of Hong Kong influence until it possesses comparable economic strength and external clout.

Guangdong has more than its fledgling economy, however, to interact with Hong Kong; it also has the PRC's full economic might behind it. Hong Kong's economic miracle, in a similar manner, has the support of a global economy. The loyalties of that global economy, nevertheless, are pragmatic and would just as soon move north as Hong Kong sheds its "little tiger" image and becomes increasingly overshadowed by the dragon.

As two separate points on a flat plane, the upward progress of Hong Kong and Guangdong could meet to form an isosceles triangle. More accurately, however, Hong Kong's path is upward and direct, and while Guangdong may move more rapidly than Hong Kong, its upward path will be more obliquely upward and in the direction of Hong Kong, resulting in a right triangle. The base of that right triangle will be angled to support a similar direction of the development of the market economy in other regions of China north of Guangdong.

The editors of this volume have chosen the approach of center-periphery, rather than triangles. The Hong Kong–Guangdong nexus does not exist in a vacuum, but in a global relationship rooted in the Asia-Pacific belt of economic prosperity. Hong Kong has much to offer its cousins from the mainland, not the least of which is access to its global network. At the same time, Hong Kong will reveal more about its cultural roots and identity to the global community. This will require a psycho-cultural adjustment, oriented more toward the mainland, that will test its current internationalism.

Future scenarios for the Hong Kong–Guangdong nexus are many and complex. There are no better experts on the subject than the contributors to this volume. The various dimensions and implications of the partnership between the two have been carefully considered by chapter authors and volume editors; many of them have the advantage of personal roots in Guangdong, as well as years of active research on the Hong Kong–Guangdong relationship, from both the regional and Pan-Pacific perspectives. Their collective efforts contribute to an informed and in-depth understanding of the dynamics of growth and development in this Hong Kong–Guangdong region as it become a rising economic core on the Pacific Rim toward the twenty-first century. If the Hong Kong–Guangdong links work well, there will be even more ground for optimism for the larger PRC-HK integration.

Gerard A. Postiglione
Hong Kong, June 1995

Acknowledgments

This volume consists of some extensively revised and updated papers stemming from a conference in November 1991 at the University of Hawaii at Manoa under the auspices of the Hawaii Committee for the Humanities and the Center for Chinese Studies. Some chapters were commissioned after that conference for this book. The past and present directors of the center, Daniel Kwok and Roger Ames, have given this project continuous encouragement and support. The Louise and Y.T. Lum Foundation, Priscilla K.T. Chung, Panda Travel, Inc., Spaces, AM Partners Inc., the law office of Alan W.C. Ma, and Daniel Leung donated generously to bring scholars from the continental United States and abroad to the conference. The School of Hawaiian, Asian, and Pacific Studies and the Department of Sociology provided the financial support for manuscript preparation. To all of them, we are most grateful.

In editing the volume, the comments and suggestions of Ming K. Chan and Gerry Postiglione were immensely helpful and much appreciated. Brian Daly, Sylvia Donati, Martin Leicht, and Kim Mar formed an effective team for computer formatting, manuscript typing, and the painstaking task of reference checking. We are particularly appreciative of the thankless but meticulous production work done by Angela Piliouras and the M.E. Sharpe staff.

Alvin Y. So is especially thankful to Don Topping, the director of the Social Science Research Institute at the University of Hawaii, for the release time to edit this publication. Finally, the editors would like to take this opportunity to show their gratitude to their teachers—Professors Chester Rapkin, Carl Riskin, and Lucie Cheng—for their introduction and guidance in the fields of political economy and contemporary China.

Reginald Yin-Wang Kwok and Alvin Y. So

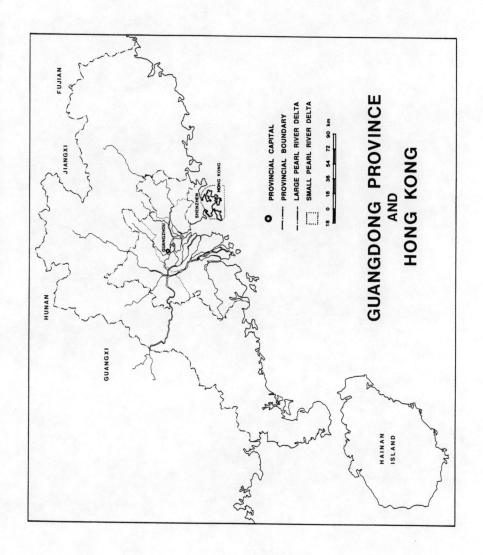

GUANGDONG PROVINCE
AND
HONG KONG

The Hong Kong–Guangdong Link

1

A Framework for Exploring the Hong Kong–Guangdong Link

Reginald Yin-Wang Kwok and Roger T. Ames

On July 1, 1997, Hong Kong will formally be returned to the People's Republic of China (China). The territories most directly involved in this transfer are Hong Kong and the adjacent Chinese province of Guangdong. These two territories have had a continuous, though at times interrupted, cultural and economic relationship since Hong Kong was ceded to Britain in 1842. Following China's adoption of the Open-door Policy in 1978 as part of its Economic Reform, the links joining Hong Kong and Guangdong have intensified and flourished.

Before examining the various dimensions of this ongoing integration process, we shall first review recent interactions between Hong Kong and Guangdong since Economic Reform, in particular the effects of direct Hong Kong investment. In the years following 1978, Beijing gradually opened its door to international production and business, with Guangdong designated as the province for such experimentation (Xu, 1991). The Chinese Open-door Policy came at a time when Hong Kong's export production had reached a point where Hong Kong was seeking to expand its production to offshore territories. China in general, and Guangdong in particular, provided the production advantages that had been steadily eroding in the *de facto* city state. Moreover, China offered the geographic advantages of proximity and convenient transportation, as well as the cultural advantages of a common language and family ties. Hong Kong seized the opportunity, becoming the first and largest investor in China.

Since then, Hong Kong has progressed from an export manufacturing base to a postindustrial information economy. Moreover, as a thriving international metropolis, it has regained its original function of entrepôt lost after 1950, and now serves as the trade middleman between China and the outside world.

More important, it has quickly grown into a financial and investment center comprised of transnational firms whose investments are directed outward to other territories—over three-quarters of Hong Kong's offshore investment is in China, with the remaining amount committed primarily to Southeast Asia (Hongkong Bank, 11–1990). Hong Kong has thus been able to establish itself as a world city with a complex of transnational connections in the Asia-Pacific region (Taylor and Kwok, 1989).

In the process of Hong Kong's emergence as a world city, its economy has become progressively tied to that of China through its Guangdong connection, and vice versa (Kwok, R., 1986). Trade with China has grown spectacularly. During the seventeen-year period since the Open-door Policy came into effect, imports from China have grown by more than eighteen times to constitute over one-third of Hong Kong's total imports in 1989. Exports to China have grown by over 540 times, amounting to more than 19 percent of Hong Kong's total exports in 1989 (Kwok, R., 1992a). Hong Kong has been the source of two-thirds of the total foreign investment in China, contributing greatly to its foreign-exchange income and providing expertise in management, marketing, information, and advisory services for China (Hongkong Bank, 6–7–1989). China and Hong Kong, despite their different economic and institutional systems, have become close economic partners.

This collaborative production has accelerated both Hong Kong's postindustrial development and Guangdong's industrial takeoff. In the future, their respective production roles are generally expected to continue basically unchanged. International commerce, finance, transportation, and services remain Hong Kong's primary functions, while Guangdong is expected to initiate a program of technological enhancement, labor training, and product upgrading within its industrial development (Tong and Wu, 1992). This strategy is a natural extension of the present trend, but it seeks to do more than merely preserve the status quo.

Hong Kong–Guangdong integration is a crucial turning point in Chinese history and has profound meaning for its socialist transformation to a mixed economy. The process of integration is having a major impact on the future institutional forms of both territories, as their governments, societies, and political groups maneuver for positions of influence on the outcome of the 1997 unification project. The 1997 issue has appeared frequently in newspaper headlines and has been reported on in international, national, and local mass media. It has already occasioned comprehensive economic and cultural transformations in both Guangdong and Hong Kong, leading to massive changes in industrial infrastructure, population concentrations, structure of management, and land use. There have also been significant changes in personal values and world views, ethics and etiquette, institutional behavior and ideology. Within households and organizations, conflicts have emerged among the generations. As a result, individuals, families (both nuclear and extended), neighborhoods, communities, enterprises, and governments have all been forced to respond by adjusting their internal and external relationships, their modes of expression, and their decision-making procedures. Historically, practically all accepted norms and dictums have been openly challenged (Kwok and So, 1991).

The principal purpose of this introductory chapter is to suggest a method for investigating the Hong Kong and Guangdong connection, with the intention of applying this method to appraise the present course of development and forecast a possible future outcome. There are three levels of discussion in this chapter. First, we propose an analytic framework that might be useful for reviewing and interpreting the economic, social, political, and cultural dimensions in the Hong Kong–Guangdong link. Second, we examine, in general, the present relationship between Hong Kong–Guangdong and the global community through patterns of population migration. Third, related to the framework of analysis and the relationship between the region and the world beyond, we present four research issues addressed by scholars in the humanities and social sciences who have been studying various aspects of this integration process, and here offer their assessments of the territory's future.

Although the integration process is having greatest impact on Hong Kong and Guangdong, there are altogether five players who continue to influence and be influenced by this process. Apart from the two contiguous areas—Hong Kong and Guangdong—Britain (London) and China (Beijing) have also participated in the negotiating process. Less obvious and more remote is the fifth population affected—the migrants from Hong Kong who have established residence in Canada, Australia, Britain, the United States, and parts of southeast Asia, adding greatly to the numbers of overseas Chinese (*Huaqiao*).

There are many perspectives in this complex and conflicting interaction. In a broad sense, the integration is a process of societal changes within the context of large-scale development. We would suggest that the societal evolution in the Hong Kong–Guangdong region is essentially subject to three major forces: *political and cultural forces, institutional structure,* and *development.* The fast-paced transformation in this south China region can be construed as a contention among different political and cultural forces. There is a historical dynamic between national unity and diversity, and a continuing philosophical dialectic between the center and the periphery—Beijing vs. the Hong Kong–Guangdong region. Institutionally, integration is the blending of socialism and capitalism, the determination of a territorial organization for managing the process of change, and the delineation of the level and limit of the fusion—Beijing vs. Hong Kong. Developmentally, the process of integration maneuvers between economic growth and political control—Hong Kong–Guangdong and Beijing. These three interdisciplinary perspectives are by no means mutually exclusive; they frequently overlap and interact with each other. To study and understand the interaction toward territorial integration, it is necessary to construct an analytical framework that incorporates these three perspectives. Of the players, Hong Kong, Guangdong, and Beijing are the chief constituents and hence are the bases of the analytic grid.

Before we can discuss Hong Kong's possible transnational future, we must first examine the symbiotic relationship between Hong Kong and Guangdong, their economic restructuring since Economic Reform, and their domestic and international connections. One of the most noted trends is the continuous in-migration from other parts of China to Guangdong, and the out-migration of Hong Kong's population. This floating-population phenomenon may well cause social and political imbalance in the province. The "brain drain," it is argued, will deplete the crucial economic resource—skilled labor and tested entrepreneurial talent. The loss of Hong Kong's most productive labor is expected to decrease productive capability and impair economic growth. Hence, the human exodus is seen as detrimental to the region's future (for further discussion on Hong Kong population movement, see the recent publication of Skeldon, 1994).

Projections of the Hong Kong–Guangdong future are often contradictory and always controversial. Beijing sees the process as a positive development, ideologically controllable and economically beneficial. Hong Kong will continue to be Beijing's window on Western technology and its bridge to the capitalist world. The Western press is far more reserved. A perusal of the *Asian Wall Street Journal* or the *Far Eastern Economic Review* since 1984 should give the reader sufficient pause about the assumed efficacy of Chinese-style management in the future economic, political, and social development of Hong Kong. This same debate rages within academic circles with equal heat and diversity of opinion. The Hong Kong–Guangdong connection is fluid and changeable, and its possible future is the theme that occupies all of the authors in this anthology.

A Framework with Three Perspectives

Let us elaborate briefly the theoretical framework of the three perspectives outlined above. From these vantage points, we will attempt to analyze broadly events in Hong Kong, Guangdong, and Beijing—the most immediate players.

The Political and Cultural Forces

Looking at the process of integration from the political-cultural perspective, periods of national unity and disintegration have never been conceived of as contradictory or mutually exclusive events. Rather, they are complementary aspects of the dynastic cycle, reflecting as they do the two sides of the political dynamics of the state. The sequential alternation between unity and disunity within the Chinese state is its normal process of development (Kwok, D., 1991). In the Hong Kong/China relationship, the British colonization of Hong Kong has been perceived by Beijing as a dynastic incident. In historical terms, Hong Kong's return to China is not only legally justifiable by appeal to international law; it is inevitable. The separation of Hong Kong from China has been nothing more than a temporary arrangement, and its reintegration is the natural course of things.

Unity runs deep in Chinese historical consciousness. Expressed through cultural mediums such as novels, poetry, operas, and the dynastic histories themselves, this historical consciousness informs us of the Chinese commitment to political unity and cultural continuity. Chinese culture simply does not question either the desirability or the inevitability of eventual reunion. The cultural ideal of a unified China tends to produce a prescriptive and didactic scholarship that at times pays greater attention to how things should be than to how things really are. Whatever the final shape of the Hong Kong–Guangdong integration in 1997, there may be some lessons to be learned about the distance between the ideal and the reality in the Chinese experience of dynastic unification and division (Kwok, D., 1991).

Anticipating 1997, Beijing has proclaimed the "One Country, Two Systems" (*yiguo liangzhi*) policy (Zhou and Shi, 1988: 60–61), providing the institutional instrument under which unification will take place. Hong Kong will retain its free market system, whereas Beijing will continue with its own brand of socialist development. This will ensure Hong Kong's continuous economic role in China's transformation as the "window" to the outside world and instigator of China's growth through its uninterrupted supply of investment. Neither entity will interfere with nor impose itself upon the other (*Huaqiao ribao*, 12–24–1991). Implied in this policy is the acceptance of diversity within unity. In reality, diversity in China has always existed through the preservation of regional culture traditions, ethnicity, dialects, and localized growth.

Since the Economic Reform of 1978, economic diversity has become increasingly apparent among the coastal, central, and interior regions of China. Even more pronounced is the difference between the economic system prevailing in the south, particularly in Guangdong, and that of the north (*Far Eastern Economic Review*, 4–4–1991: 21–24). The south is more open to the free market system and overseas trade and has adopted many free market practices, especially in its enterprise structure, trade, and production. The north, on the other hand, retains much more of the orthodox state socialist practice. Beijing has generally accepted and tolerated economic regionalism, but often has been disturbed by the prospect that such diversification may lead to chaotic political conditions. Political opinions vacillate between encouragement and suspicion, although official policy has not closed down such experiments. Whenever the state feels that diversity may threaten its legitimacy, it reacts swiftly and with decision to reinforce uniformity and centralization. The Tiananmen Incident in 1989 is a recent reminder of such tactics. The uncertainty of the Hong Kong–Guangdong role in the Chinese Economic Reform is simply a reflection of the unpredictability of the dynamics of state politics.

Unity with diversity is a critical historical issue. In Beijing and Hong Kong, there are both believers and doubters with respect to the outcome and possible benefits of the 1997 integration. The present popular posture is one of "wait and see" without any firm commitment: Let the unfolding of events confirm or refute the historical phenomenon, and meanwhile put the Hong Kong–Guangdong future on hold.

Philosophically, the dynastic Chinese state has been structured as a hierarchical spire with power emitting from the center and with tribute drawn in from the periphery. This cultural model is not a concept but a practical guide for political distribution. Yu Ying-shih uses the "five zones" (*wufu*) of submission as a device for describing the dynamics of the Han world order, tracing the concentric circles from the court at the center to the "wild zone" at the frontier (Yu, 1986: 379–80). This hierarchical, radial scheme also describes the descending degree of tribute that was provided to the court at the center, not only in the form of local products and services, but also in the form of political and cultural influence. When the center is strong, tribute moves in to reinforce it, with the greatest degree of influence on the center being exerted from elements close to the center itself: the court officials, the aristocracy, the wealthy merchants, the military leaders, the population of the capital. The center commands control during periods of stability and strength, maintaining its centripetal relationship with the diverse political elements that together constituted the aggregate called China. Through the accumulation of both cultural power and political power, the court rules from the center by appeal to a unifying ideology.

As the center weakens, however, incidental elements that were on the periphery have the potential to exert an increasing amount of influence in the gradual process of reshaping, and in some instances, subverting the center. To the extent they do so, they move inward and cease to be marginal.

This "inner-outer" concentric-circle model of hierarchical, overlapping centers articulating a central focus through patterns of deference seems pervasive in the peculiarly Chinese world view, and has explanatory force in delineating the genetic structure of most of China's formal institutions—for example, the traditional sense of polity with the emperor at the center. Concrete, functioning patterns of deference contribute in varying degrees, and are constitutive of the authority at the center, articulating and bringing into focus the character of the social and political entity—its standards and values. The attraction of the core is such that, when it is strong enough, it draws into its field and suspends the disparate and diverse centers that constitute its field of influence. But when the core weakens, what had been contribution to the center becomes the energy of contest. What was a tightening spire becomes a gyre, disgorging itself of its now disassociated contents. Politically, the welter of disparate organizational structures—clans, municipalities, religious associations, tribal affiliations, warlords, regional identities, and so on— with their original diversity in some degree having been concealed within the previously existing harmony, precipitate out and reestablish their independence.

Traditionally, those who fell from favor were exiled to the periphery—the more undesirable, the farther from the center. The periphery represented the uncivilized and the weak, whereas political strength and cultural sagacity were concentrated in the state capital.

Contemporary China still retains this commitment to centripetal harmony. A real argument can be made that the China of our own day seen from within the Chinese experience itself is not a radical disjunction with its past. The present-day socialist state, founded after a half-century interregnum, has all of the trappings of a new dynasty. Some contemporary historians have gone so far as to describe the People's Republic of China as an *imperium redivivum*:

> The Chinese Communist state displayed all the characteristics of the Empire: a highly centralized, hierarchically organized bureaucracy with a coherent view of the world; a socio-administrative structure into which all parts of the population fitted and which fitted all parts of the population; and an ideology that provided a basis for the conceptual unification of the entire society. (Mancall, 1984: 337)

Political order is a hierarchical system with the pattern of authority radiating outward from the center to the periphery. Beijing can be seen as the inner region relative to the outer regions (such as Guangdong) of the barbarians, just as the royal domain was, relative to the outer lords' zones, an inner zone. Whatever constitutes the authority at the center derives its authority from having implicated within it the order of its field of influence. During these times of instability, when the center has weakened, what was peripheral moves inward. The weakness in the center provides the opportunity for the periphery to take on a stronger political and cultural role. Ultimately, the periphery is in the position to affect and transform the center. Whenever state policy is indecisive and speculative, and administration is decentralized, the locality is increasingly able to deviate from the norm, and to exert its influence on the central government.

The political and cultural situation is complex. With London relinquishing political sovereignty and assenting to Hong Kong's merger with China in 1997, the political and cultural transition will follow the now familiar path of "decolonization." The laments of abandonment and the complaints of betrayal increase in intensity from Hong Kong's local communities. Decline in the identification with and the importance of things British will, in the days ahead, be complemented with a rise in the importance of and interest in things Chinese. Externally, the flight of capital and the emigration of well-off and skilled people are phenomena accompanied by a growing internal consciousness of ethnicity and cultural identity. As the authority of London erodes, the assertiveness of Beijing moves in to fill the void (*South China Morning Post*, 6–20–1992).

The opposite is true in Guangdong. In its openness to overseas markets and influences, it embraces all things international as they are filtered through Hong Kong, and foreign culture takes on growing significance. The adoption and imitation of Hong Kong and overseas technologies and values becomes the norm, replacing those that are more traditionally Chinese. In commercial and production practices as well as in social behavior, the trend of internationalization prevails. The twin processes of Hong Kong decolonization and Guangdong internationalization will lead either to an integrated culture or to direct confrontation. Whatever the outcome, the Hong Kong–Guangdong culture will be the most powerful peripheral influence in reshaping the center.

In contemporary China, periphery–center interaction has certainly been acknowledged, and has regularly been adopted as a developmental strategy. For example, the commune movement of 1958 and the Dazhai and Daqing models of 1964 were introduced for national adoption only after experimentation on the periphery (Kwok, R., 1981). The ability of the periphery to offer viable alternatives for the formation of policy confirms the center's legitimacy and its creditability, and serves to fortify and invigorate it. Thus, Beijing's acceptance of Hong Kong–Guangdong integration depends on whether it is assessed as a workable, acceptable, and vital possibility for China's future development, or, alternatively, is viewed as a threat to the prevailing policy of "socialism with Chinese characteristics" (for further discussion of core–periphery dynamics, see the recent publication of Chan, 1994).

Institutional Structure

From the institutional perspective, Economic Reform led the nation from state socialism to open-ended market socialism. The Beijing leaders deemed the time ripe to move upward from a primitive stage to a more advanced stage of socialism (*Beijing Review*, 1981: 35–39). The state socialism in force since liberation had served to move China out of a situation of underdevelopment and abject poverty, propelling it to a high level of independence and stability, and thus preparing the nation for a more diverse and complex form of development.

The critical factor in this institutional change is the perceived opportunity for greater economic growth and efficiency. The state socialist strategy fostered extensive growth by widening the economy (Szelenyi, 1989), but it also brought with it inflation, stagnation, inefficiency, and inflexibility (Kwok, R., 1992b). The market system is seen as a disciplinary mechanism for cost-saving production, for reducing waste and hoarding, for increasing responsiveness to demand, and for improving quality. These are the important characteristics of production that state socialism fails to promote (Kornai, 1989). Market socialism, with the adoption of appropriate market instruments, is viewed as an effective way to overcome the deficiencies of state socialism and to combine the benefits of the socialist and capitalist systems (Brus, 1989).

Market socialism is also considered as a method to increase producers and consumers, to diversify decision makers, to enhance flexibility and fluidity in the exchange system, to adopt innovative and advanced technology, and to multiply the economic effects of these several developments. As the market brings forth competitive producers, they respond to demand efficiently, produce a variety of goods quickly and in abundance, and improve the technology used in production and, consequently, the quality of the goods. These various improvements can overcome immobility in production and many of the difficulties inherent in the present stage of Chinese state socialism (Kwok, R., 1992b). These are the necessary innovations to stimulate the economy and raise it to a higher level in order to achieve real growth and a better standard of living. Implied in the Economic Reform program are the diversification of economic decision making, a reliance on entrepreneurship, and, with Beijing still acting to resist it, the decentralization of concomitant political power (Kwok, R., 1992b). Capitalism is cautiously being adopted for China's socialist modernization (*Beijing Review*, 1992: 12).

Institutional transition, nevertheless, is heavily determined by the relative strength of ideological postures. The penchant for change characteristic of reformers who advocate market socialism is countered by the orthodox adherence of the state socialist to strong statist rule and centralized development. The market system is considered to be "capitalistic" and "dependent" by those holding the orthodox state socialist position, taking the maintenance of ideological authoritarianism as their prime task. In contrast, economic acceleration and prosperity come first on the reformist agenda, and restraint on private entrepreneurship is viewed as conservative and obstructive. These positions have been periodically challenged and defended within the state bureaucracy. Often, ideological struggles emerge and subside unpredictably, as the fluid patterns of party politics and the lineaments of leadership take shape at some distance from the public. The reformist position gained ground in the early 1990s (*Far Eastern Economic Review*, 3–26–1992: 10; and *Asian Wall Street Journal Weekly*, 3–23–1992), a development that is likely to usher in some institutional changes. The orthodox position, however, remains in the background, and it is still more than capable of reasserting its political influence (*Far Eastern Economic Review*, 4–2–1992: 13).

The current movement toward market socialist reform has been fed by the momentum of nonstate development. The growth of the collective and private sectors has been steady and spectacular. In comparison, the growth of the state sector has been much slower. In particular, industries directly under central government control have continued to sustain losses, are frequently delinquent in tax payments, and tend to stockpile an inventory for which there is little demand (*Asian Wall Street Journal Weekly*, 3–9–1992). The nonstate sectors that operate in the market system have been expanding; they now produce almost half of the nation's industrial output and can no longer be ignored. Capitalist development, though not explicitly acknowledged, is practiced in earnest. In the foreseeable future, this heavy dependency of the economy on the market sector is expected to continue its dramatic growth.

In territorial terms, the constant refrain, "socialism with Chinese characteristics," refers to a desirable mix of things Western and things indigenous to the Chinese tradition. From dynastic times to the present, Beijing has insisted on the need to maintain Chinese independence and cultural uniqueness in the face of the constant threat of losing its territorial and cultural sovereignty to powers beyond its borders. To protect the nation from excessive dependency on foreign culture and to limit the penetration of overseas influence, a historically familiar policy of "territorial containment" was invoked to open up selected frontier zones for foreign systems of development. These open zones are for experimentation and observation, and serve to shelter the rest of China from alien influences. Other less-well-defined areas tolerate a foreign presence, but do so unwillingly. As overseas elements are allowed only in these clearly demarcated and guarded areas, their absorption can be controlled and their impact contained by keeping them at a distance (Chu and Zheng, 1992).

Treaty ports in imperial times served the same function as devices for territorial containment. The Special Economic Zones (SEZs) are all in south China, with three out of the four in Guangdong. Out of the fourteen Open Coastal Cities, two are located in the province. One of the three Open Regions, the Pearl River Delta, is also in Guangdong. These then are the present-day territorial containment areas that control international capital flow and cultural penetration. There has been a deliberate effort on the part of Beijing to maintain the lines of this territorial containment, so that foreign elements remain primarily in the outpost, Hong Kong, thus keeping mainland Guangdong relatively free from excessive influence. The aggressive entry of overseas-Chinese capital from Hong Kong, later joined by large capital investment from Taiwan and Singapore, however, has successfully integrated southern Guangdong into the world economy, and has accelerated the rapid growth of this province (Chu and Zheng, 1992).

To Beijing, Hong Kong's market system clearly has economic advantages. It not only represents a successful demonstration of how market capitalism can be adapted into a culturally Chinese world, but also has been an effective catalyst for the dramatic economic growth of south China. Chinese socialist leaders are convinced that the Hong Kong experience has been effective, that its policies, management strategies, and techniques are adaptable to China, and that the model can be adopted selectively for China's future development. Hong Kong is therefore a model as well as a potential engine for rapid and constant growth. So long as Beijing is moving toward market socialism, Hong Kong will continue to have a major functional role.

Hong Kong also serves as a contemporary experiment in territorial reunification. The process is viewed as a prelude to similar integration of Macao and hopefully Taiwan in the future. China will benefit from the experience, and will have the opportunity to make whatever adjustments are deemed necessary. If it is ultimately successful, it will demonstrate Beijing's capability and willingness to practice "One Country, Two Systems." Success in the reunification process may possibly give Taiwan an incentive to rejoin the mainland.

The present system in Hong Kong, however, has presented China with many political problems: the open demonstrations in Hong Kong following the Tiananmen Incident and its aftermath, the growing movement toward democratization, and the constant challenge to Beijing's intervention in Hong Kong's affairs by the elected representatives. These are signals of the political changes that come with successful economic growth, changes that are necessary for the working of the market. The demands of the community directly challenge central authority and require accommodation from the state. Beijing's reluctance to make the necessary administrative changes and to pay the political price suggests that the present Hong Kong system is unlikely to be adopted unaltered.

Development

From the developmental perspective, the Hong Kong–Guangdong connection resides within the Asia-Pacific regional economic network. With the postmodern orientation of the capitalist West, the transformation from a Fordist to post-Fordist mode of production has initiated a series of technological and institutional adjustments (Harvey, 1990). The transformation of the production process is not yet complete, and both regimes are currently in place. Post-Fordist production requires small, constantly changing, low-skill, and labor-intensive operations as essential parts of the process. The industrialized economies have discovered that models of this kind of production exist in abundance in the Asia-Pacific region, and have found these plants to be suitable economic partners. The new production process has thus accelerated the process of industrialization in the Asia-Pacific region.

Fed by the globalization of the industrial process and the new division of labor, capital investment from the industrialized economies of the United States and Japan has flowed in a hierarchical pattern to Asia's four Newly Industrializing Economies, or NIEs (Hong Kong, Singapore, South Korea, and Taiwan). The four Asian NIEs have been found to be suitable offshore locations for production for several reasons: Their economies are adaptable to the international market, they hold a cooperative and efficient labor pool, and they have globally oriented governments. Flexibility in entrepreneurial response and fast action in an ever-changing international market have ensured rapid and sustained growth in the economies of the NIEs.

As the Asian NIEs have developed, they have raised their investment capability and upgraded their labor skills. Their need for their own investment market for an overaccumulation of capital, and their need for alternative sources of manual labor to offset a domestic labor shortage have forced these economies to decentralize their production to other Asia-Pacific locations—locations that are necessarily at a lower level of economic development. The transnational economic system has thus extended farther downward in seeking out alternative production opportunities and advantages. When the Open-door Policy for foreign investment was adopted under China's Economic Reform, the Asian NIEs found a receptive partner in China as a location for offshore production (Kim and Kwok, 1991). As Guangdong has historically been the most accessible region, has the best entrepreneurial capability, and has been willing and eager to join the global market, the transnational economic network quickly embraced south China as its new member.

The growth patterns in the Asia-Pacific region are being interpreted as new and successful models of development, implying that there are fundamental commonalities among the different developmental strategies employed by the Asian NIEs. There is also the assumption that the Asia-Pacific economies form a pyramidal hierarchy with Japan at the summit, capping sequential lower layers comprised of the Asian NIEs, the ASEAN 4 (Indonesia, Malaysia, Philippines, and Thailand), and China at the base. Growth effects are postulated to filter down through a descending flow of transnational capital.

This v-shaped pattern of regional economic interdependence is described also as the "Flying Geese" pattern. It is held together primarily by direct foreign investment from the economically more advanced locations to the less advanced ones (Chen, 1991). The international network of interdependence is necessary because of the globalization of the industrial process under the post-Fordist regime. Corporations seek production advantages by breaking up the production process and establishing subprocesses in locations that provide the most conducive environment. As labor is one of the essential factors in production, subprocesses are often situated in those territories that supply an optimal labor force. Social stability and hospitable political climates are local conditions vital to ensure the confidence of foreign businessmen. Responding to the code for direct foreign investment, many developing economies have set up export-processing zones that satisfy all of these requirements, and that offer special privileges and financial incentives to foreign investors (Kim and Kwok, 1991).

The Asia-Pacific region has proved to be the geographical area that provides investors with substantial production advantages, and as a consequence it has been attracting a substantial share of direct foreign capital. This infusion of foreign monies for industrialization has been a major stimulus for economic growth. As recipients of this foreign confidence, the Asian NIEs have been able not only to mount and sustain their development program, but also to export investment to less developed economies (Kim and Kwok, 1991). All four Asian NIEs are actively investing in China, and among them Hong Kong continues to be the clear leader and the most important partner (Sung, 1992).

Beijing's Open-door Policy for international trade and its establishment of Special Economic Zones demonstrate clearly that it welcomes direct foreign investment as a legitimate mode of development. Enabling China to enter and entrench herself in the Asia-Pacific transnational capital network, these policies and instruments have ensured Hong Kong's pivotal role and Guangdong's important position in China's future growth.

In reviewing the Hong Kong–Guangdong relationship, these three perspectives—political and cultural forces, institutional structure, and development—suggest very different trajectories for the future of the Hong Kong–Guangdong region, although the weight assigned them necessarily varies as they are factored into different integration issues. Projections for 1997 and after are further complicated by the often contradictory conditions that define each of these perspectives, leaving us with no simple prognosis.

Let us summarize the general conditions with respect to the three interdisciplinary perspectives. In terms of political and cultural forces, the present economic diversity reflects a kind of regionalism that has been and continues to be tolerated by the central powers, with Guangdong leading the way in experimentation with the market system (Vogel, 1989). However, the orthodox Chinese concept of the socialist state and the party has stressed the importance of unity. Philosophically, the acceptance of more localized decision making and greater autonomy for regionally based enterprises indicates the willingness of the center to be shaped at least in some degree by its periphery. This practice does not conform to party principle, which recommends strongly that lower-level administration abide by decisions from above. So far, there has been no strong ideological resistance to the actual pattern of development, but ideological rigidity does surface from time to time, particularly when the state comes under challenge. The Tiananmen Incident was a clear reminder of the fragility of the existing situation, the abruptness with which it can change, and the unpredictability of the future whenever pragmatism and orthodoxy come into conflict.

The institutional commitment to transform into market socialism seems well established. The instrument, the method, and the actual process that will effect this transformation have not been specifically detailed. The open-endedness of the policy invites speculation and confusion. If the market component can grow and lead the way, the future of Hong Kong–Guangdong is guaranteed. If the market component has a secondary and supplementary function only, the region's development will be constrained. Opening to transnational capital development has facilitated China's growth and has given it new momentum. Rationally, the current direction is consistent with world trends and seems inevitable. However, the continuing impact of foreign forces is at times at odds with socialist morality, and periodically xenophobia erupts and hampers development.

The combination of all three perspectives suggests that Beijing's commitment to market socialism and an open economy would favor Hong Kong–Guangdong integration. As long as the economy of the region continues to perform better than the economies of the other domestic regions, the Hong Kong system will have an interregional impact through its investment in, production linkages with, and multiplier effects on other parts of China. At the very least, Hong Kong's market system serves as a model for China's development, giving it some economic legitimacy to survive and flourish. The economic role of the future Hong Kong–Guangdong region seems clear. It stands between the international market and China proper as a facilitator and a buffer for market experimentation, as a laboratory for the selection and adaptation of management techniques and production technologies, and as a periscope for examining foreign market possibilities.

In order to pave the way for economic changes, the political and cultural systems will, by necessity, also transform. That Beijing is willing to concede and to accommodate this transformation is less clear, since at present it still assumes that these attendant changes are ideologically undesirable and unnecessary. The political role of Hong Kong in China's future can also be problematic. It is often considered to be a haven of capitalist transgression and a breeding ground for political subversion (Chan, 1991). It must be carefully watched. The territory may need to be disciplined and controlled if its civic actions continue to challenge the authority and legitimacy of the state. These social, cultural, and political consequences will lead to a direct confrontation with the orthodox ideology and morality. Whatever the outcome, this confrontation will create disorder, disintegration, and disincentive for the region's economy.

We now have identified some of the key factors that will have a determinative force on the development of the Hong Kong–Guangdong connection and the process of integration, and that must be taken into account in any discussion of future events. The uncertainties remain, partly because of the speculative nature of futuristic studies, and partly because of the many perspectives that must enter into any assessment or projection.

Transnational Relationship Through Migration

In the intersectoral analysis of the dualist Third World, the modern capitalist sector absorbs surplus labor from the traditional indigenous sector for industrial production. With a relatively limitless supply of labor from the traditional indigenous sector, the modern capitalist sector accumulates wealth and continues to grow. The less developed sector, by reducing its surplus human resource, becomes more efficient in production and gradually improves its technology and income. As the more developed sector continues to industrialize, both sectors grow in a symbiotic relationship (Meier, 1989). This simple model reflects one aspect of the Hong Kong–Guangdong pattern of growth. What it shares in common with the south China experience is the transfer of labor through migration to Hong Kong (the more developed sector) and job creation in Guangdong (the less developed sector). More significantly, this model asserts that labor mobility plays a key part in development.

Hong Kong and Guangdong are not isolated entities, and they have had a shared history. From imperial times, Guangdong—particularly the Pearl River Delta, which is one of the three most populous river delta regions in China—has had a very high man–land ratio. The high population density has been resolved in two ways: by intensive cash-crop farming to increase production and income, and by emigration to reduce labor surplus and consumption. Emigration has been directed primarily to overseas countries, with Southeast Asia and North America being the favored targets. Hong Kong traditionally has been the transit point for migration abroad. Waiting for opportunities, negotiating for immigration, and taking jobs in the colony often waylaid the intended migrants, transforming them into Hong Kong residents. Many would-be migrants have stayed on, especially during periods of economic growth when employment was plentiful. In the post– World War II period, Hong Kong witnessed a continuous and spectacular growth. The escalating job opportunities and living standards created a migration magnet for Guangdong's population.

As most of the residents in Hong Kong are originally from its hinterland, Guangdong province, kinship ties have always been strong between the two territories, and the populations have shared in the same geographical and cultural heritage. Ever since Hong Kong was ceded to Great Britain as a colony in 1842, there have always been intense political, economic, and sociocultural linkages between Hong Kong and Guangdong. Even when China turned socialist and closed its door in the 1950s and the 1960s, there were still substantial informal economic and sociocultural interactions between capitalist Hong Kong and socialist Guangdong through kinship ties. When China reopened its door in 1978, the process of integration between the province and the colonial metropolis accelerated. This integration dynamic was further intensified after the signing in 1984 of the Sino-British Joint Declaration, in which London promised to return the sovereignty of Hong Kong to Beijing in 1997. Both events have given further impulse to invigorate the enduring ties of kinship.

Those emigrants who took up residence overseas similarly continued ties with their families and clans in their native places, not infrequently by sponsoring new emigrants from the same village and by sending remittances back to families and relatives (Nee and de Bary, 1972). Village or native-place associations and the perceived obligation of the emigrants to aid the residents of their native places have been characteristic of overseas Chinese communities, and continue in modern times. It also strengthens an international network of cultural, social, political, and economic ties that last for many generations.

Before the 1978 Economic Reform, remittances to China were controlled, predominantly through nonluxury personal goods such as clothing. Traveling in China, for both nonresidents and residents, was restricted. Visits to one's home village by overseas Chinese, including those from Hong Kong, were not easy and not customarily attempted. Communications between native-place associations and the native place were limited. Since 1978, the flow of Hong Kong travelers to China has rapidly and steadily increased. By 1990, the annual per capita trips to China had reached close to three, and projections have it continuing to increase in the years ahead (Kwok, R., 1992a). At present, the internal population movement within the region, particularly between Hong Kong and Guangdong, is increasing.

Most of the trips between Hong Kong and Guangdong are business-related, but there is a significant proportion of family visits, and journeys to native places usually are accompanied by abundant gifts of household electronics and other durable luxuries for relatives and friends. Increasingly, remittances take the form of donations for civic and social services. Schools, hospitals, old-age homes, roads, and bridges are built and maintained by those who are financially well off (Kwok, R., 1986). One very successful businessman in Hong Kong donated a university to his home city of Shantou in Guangdong. In addition to providing income subsidies and social service capital, the remittances also contribute to Guangdong's balance of payments. The native-place association is a strong cultural institution that continues to aid development through remittance and to foster international ties through social affiliation.

With the spectacular industrial growth in south China since Economic Reform, Guangdong has become a magnet for migration from other provinces. Industrialization led by Hong Kong investment not only absorbed Guangdong's surplus rural labor, but further attracted the existing agricultural labor as well. Migrant workers initially were contracted for agricultural work in order to replace the depleted labor. As foreign investment continued to grow, the new labor-intensive plants swallowed up the local labor and demanded still more; manufacturing firms began to employ laborers from other provinces. The same conditions exist in other sectors, and now migrant workers are engaged in all sectors, including transportation, service, and security, often filling those undesirable (dirty, difficult, and dangerous) jobs left vacant by the availability of better-paid manufacturing positions (Zhou, 1992).

With the pending 1997 reunion, there has been a steady exodus of middle-class Hong Kong residents, who feel insecure about the uncertain economic and political future. International migration from Hong Kong has been increasing since 1986. Although the increase has fluctuated, the number held steady at about sixty thousand per year in the early 1990s. The migrants are typically professionals, managers, skilled workers, and the wealthy. This "brain drain" is projected to be as high as "a quarter of a million of Hong Kong's best and brightest before the Chinese takeover" (Skeldon, 1990). The depletion of the critical white-collar workers and entrepreneurs is generally considered to be a major problem for Hong Kong's growth. This migration is not an isolated phenomenon, but is part of the general pattern of increasing mobility of the Asia-Pacific and Chinese populations (Skeldon, 1990).

The continuous flow of migrants to North America, Australia, Britain, and Southeast Asia has also meant the establishment of a new and expanding network of native-place associations now with the native place being Hong Kong itself. Since the new overseas Chinese are modern, educated, and skilled, their social ties and exchanges are often transferred into the arenas of business and production (for example, the Hong Kong–Canada Business Association). The new role of the native-place associations as economic institutions will further strengthen the international capital system.

As the Hong Kong–Guangdong region develops, there are three major kinds of population movements. Internal to the region, there is an intensive and continuous population interaction between the colonial metropolis and the province, consolidating the region economically, socially, culturally, and, in due course, politically. External to the region, there is the migration to the province from other parts of China, supplying the region with low-level inexpensive labor, while allowing the provincial work force to upgrade economically and technically. Other provinces provide an additional reserve labor pool for further regional development. There is also a strong out-migration of educated laborers from Hong Kong to overseas destinations, leaving a vacuum to be filled by an expanding professional work force. These emerging white-collar employment opportunities replace the blue-collar jobs previously available in the metropolis's manufacturing sector, which has now been relocated to the province.

These three population movements are interlinked by industrial production. They are also instrumental in the region's industrial restructuring and the process of population relocation. Migration allows for labor substitution and upgrading in the region. With the rise in numbers of Hong Kong–originated overseas Chinese, industrial labor in the metropolis is reduced, causing the relocation of plants to the Guangdong area. The provincial laborers, in taking up industrial employment, have to be replaced by workers from other provinces. The migrant workers from the rest of China, by filling the lower range of Guangdong's labor market, provide an unlimited labor pool. This pool constitutes a base for the division of labor and supports the transnational production process. With this network of production spanning the Pacific and linking up with North America and Europe, the Hong Kong–Guangdong region becomes the transmittal point for information between China and the outside world. This new transnational economic network further reinforces the region's crucial role in China's development, and will propel the south China metropolitan region into a new stage of development. Thus, migration need not be considered totally detrimental to Hong Kong's future: it has the potential to make the entire region more enterprising, innovative, and vital.

Just as Beijing must be seen in a way continuous with its past, we can use the Chinese sense of centripetal harmony to trace the "Hong Kong–overseas Chinese" phenomenon back into history. As an outpost on the frontier of Chinese culture mediating overseas influences and translating them into something acceptable to prevailing values, "Hong Kong–overseas Chinese" is a familiar enough phenomenon.

We begin from the classical Chinese assumption that there is only one world, with the Chinese states at the center. It is important to observe that the term, *zhongguo*, a self-designation for China that is generally translated as "the Middle Kingdom," originated in preimperial times and referred to the collection of disparate polities that made up the "central states." It was not one, but many. These states, however, were conjoined by standing in closer proximity to the shifting cultural center than did the *waiguo*, also a term of classical vintage referring to the relatively more foreign states. Human civilization was ordered through a pattern of tributary relationships that drew the plethora of outlying political spheres into the centripetal center at the Chinese court—a peculiarly Chinese kind of ritually constituted political and cultural harmony.

It is important to observe that China was traditionally a "stay-at-home" civilization where its control over its extended regions was derived from its wealth and culture. The goal was one of self-sufficiency rather than expansionist designs prosecuted through trade initiatives and military conquest. This notion of parochial self-sufficiency seems to be the pattern at the local level as well as on a national scale; even today, a town qualifies as a "city" (*shi*) on the basis of its complete and self-sufficient complement of industries and services. Historically, when expansionism was necessary, it was usually in an effort to preserve the imperial order of China and defend it against incursions of hostile intruders. Frequently the Chinese court would pursue the policy of "using barbarians to control barbarians" (*yi-yi zhi yi*), employing the "inner border-guarding (*baosai*) barbarians" as a buffer against the "outer barbarians." The "barbarians" that belonged to the Chinese world as "dependent states" (*shuguo*) would be divided into "inner" (Hong Kong as the modern counterpart) and "outer" (overseas Chinese as the modern counterpart) on the basis of taxation and tribute; they were generally allowed to follow their own traditional ways and customs.

In this border hinterland, there were many different kinds of markets—*junshi* markets within garrisoned cities, and *guanshi* or *hushi* "frontier" markets— where the much-desired Chinese products could be used to vent aggression and manipulate the border peoples into a relationship with China that required a minimum of direct control. The Han dynasty Confucian Jia Yi describes these commercial centers on the borders of China:

> The fact that the border market often swarmed with the *Xiongnu* (a northern nationality in classical China) was not only because it was a place for the exchange of commodities, but also because it was a place where fine Chinese food and wine could always be obtained. (Cited in Yu, 1967:101.)

Taking this kind of an internal perspective and looking over the broad sweep of Chinese history, analogies to Hong Kong might include Guzang, the capital of Wuwei province in the Heshi of the northwestern frontier; certainly Jiaozhi (now Tonkin in present-day Vietnam) when it served as a seaport in the later Han, known for its pearls, ivory, incense, and tortoise shells; and Panyu in Guangdong, which served as a traditional port of entry.

Hong Kong is unquestionably a place where fine Chinese food and wine can always be obtained. But such analogies in treating Hong Kong as just one more satellite mediating overseas Chinese and foreign access to Chinese markets and culture might understate the importance of Hong Kong and its potential influence on China's future. Applying this centripetal model, the growing influence of Hong Kong on the periphery has to be measured in the *degree* of difference it introduces into the Chinese world order. Hong Kong's territory and population are insignificant in the Chinese world. Its land area is less than 1/10,000th of China, and its population is less than one half of 1 percent. Yet tiny Hong Kong might well have the potential and the opportunity to alter the future course of Chinese history in a significant if not truly dramatic way (Ames, 1991).

Research Issues

In the recent literature, researchers have been interested in foreseeing what will happen in 1997. Will the merger of capitalist Hong Kong and socialist China work? If so, to whose benefit? Will capitalist Hong Kong be transformed into a semisocialist colony? Or will socialist Guangdong be turned into a branch of the international bourgeoisie?

Many researchers on the Hong Kong–Guangdong integration process are attracted to the study of short-term episodes that are major news concerns (*Jidutu xianggang shouwangshe*, 1988; Mushkat, 1990; Zheng, 1989), rather than to the task of delineating and articulating the complex and long-term structural transformations in the region. Also, these existing studies tend to focus narrowly on either Hong Kong or Guangdong (Jao et al., 1985; Vogel, 1989; Xu et al., 1988; Yee, 1989), thus ignoring the intricate linkages and dynamic calculus of forces that conjoin the two territories. Furthermore, the literature concentrates almost exclusively on either political or economic topics (Chen, Y., 1991; Segal, 1993; Zhou, Chen, and Qu, 1992), without providing an interdisciplinary approach to trace the interactions among these factors on Hong Kong's and Guangdong's future development. Finally, focusing on short-term fluctuations, the literature often promotes a one-sided pessimistic perspective, insisting that the merger of the market capitalism of Hong Kong with the state socialism of Guangdong will lead to economic breakdown and political disintegration. There is a decided absence of a comprehensive investigation of the nature, the rate, and the long-term impact of the process of transformation that is overtaking the two territories as they move toward 1997.

Obviously, this unprecedented process of integration that will define the future of Hong Kong and Guangdong offers an opportunity for various disciplines to interact in an effort to document and analyze the restructuring that has already been set in motion. Although the present literature on integration has been mainly produced by economists and political scientists, other scholars have responded to the situation to provide different interpretations and perspectives. In fact, the process of integration is advancing with such speed and complexity that it requires an interdisciplinary approach to examine its origins, the constantly changing configuration of economic, political, and cultural forces, and the prospects for future development.

We believe that the combination of disciplines represented in this volume can shed new light on the major changes in the Guangdong–Hong Kong relationship since 1978. The need for a more comprehensive approach invites this dialogue between the humanities and the social sciences to examine those pertinent issues that will have a bearing on this historical example of quantum societal transformation.

In addition to the disciplines of economics and political science, the chapters in this volume include philosophy, history, sociology, anthropology, and geography. Scholars who have been researching and writing in these areas collaborate to share their findings and analyses. By bringing humanities and social science researchers together, new insights are revealed, challenging questions are raised, and diverse viewpoints are proffered. The contributors to this volume, after a period of initial consultation, gathered together in November 1991 at the University of Hawaii to exchange information, compare views, and discuss and comment on findings. Coordination, revision, and update of papers took place during the first half of 1992. The contents represent the collective thought on the subject up to that date.

Some major integration issues emerge in this collaborative study, and can be identified. The societal transformation in the two territories is at once discrete and reciprocal, and, at the same time, it is convergent. Specific analyses of this transformation can only be pursued by reference to the overreaching conditions that are determining the character of change in the region. The force for this change in the Hong Kong–Guangdong link is undeniably economic development as it is driven by the industrial base. Development, however, is not an abstract process. It has the vitality to mold and be molded by the society in which it occurs, affecting especially the perceived cultural identity and the values of the people in the region. Cultural change must be taken into account as a factor that has enormous explanatory force in understanding the course that this development takes. Finally, there is some real curiosity about the process and the eventual outcome of the melding of two major political and economic systems—capitalism and socialism—coming together from opposite directions and amalgamating into a novel, hybrid entity. Thus, in the following chapters, we discuss the changing dynamics of the historical linkage between Hong Kong and Guangdong province, examine the unrelenting industrial restructuring of the region, study the cultural transformation of the people as massive changes overtake them, and anticipate a possible future for south China.

In reviewing the Hong Kong–Guangdong link, we attempt to define the nature and parameters of the relationship. Is the historic political and cultural press toward unity a sufficient force to consolidate the two territories, or has a century and a half of division left too many institutional, political, and cultural barriers to allow for reunion? In looking back over the historical accounts of the relationship, Ming Chan rehearses the unifying, reinforcing, and dividing attitudes, events, and movements that have shaped our present moment, and recounts the various ways in which the two territories have interacted. In 1997 and beyond, can these historically established ties be expanded, and how will they influence the region? Based on similar concerns about political culture, Graham Johnson explores the link through the ties of transnational migration. How does the native-place association as an enduring institution work to bond Guangdong and Hong Kong together, and how has it helped to extend the region to the outside world? How have these ties regulated Guangdong's geographical pattern? And what are the prospects for continued growth of the region's expanding global economy? Preparing for the future, Beijing and London have been regulating the transition of Hong Kong.

From the standpoint of the developmental perspective, industrial restructuring reveals how the two territories operate in and respond to a global economy. How will they respond to each other as the institutional differences begin to fade? Xueqiang Xu, R. Yin-Wang Kwok, Lixun Li, and Xiaopei Yan study industrialization in Guangdong. What kind of production adjustments have been made? What has Hong Kong's role been in this development? Moreover, what are the possibilities for future economic partnership? Turning to Hong Kong, Victor Sit considers the core–hinterland relationship between Hong Kong the metropolis and the provinces as the basis for their growth and development. How has Hong Kong's economy been transformed after incorporating Guangdong in its modes of production? What has caused the growth of the information sector and the associated structural changes? Given the new economic advantages and benefits apparent in Guangdong that have been introduced directly by Hong Kong, will these developments be persuasive to the authorities in Beijing, facilitating greater institutional accommodation for the Hong Kong system?

Cultural transformation calls attention to the fact that the region's development is subject to and shaped by specifically southern Chinese political and cultural forces. Adjustments to anticipated institutional changes are, however, not necessarily mutual or reciprocal in the two societies; they may affect the economic and class structures in the two sites differently. Gregory Guldin looks at Guangdong and investigates the developmental impact on civil society. How is the emerging Guangdong culture related to that of Hong Kong? Is the differential in development a determining factor in the new culture, and if so, in what way? Furthermore, how does the movement toward the market system affect popular arts and human behavior? Surveying the transnational migration in Hong Kong, Ming-kwan Lee interprets the population movement as the behavioral manifestation of a series of cultural awakenings raised by the anticipated events of 1997. What are the consequences of changing social conditions and psychological insecurity that have been brought on by the progress toward integration? How does Hong Kong society diagnose and assess its future economic conditions? With the increasing social awareness of the metropolis as an entity, what are the causes of an identity crisis that is intensifying with time?

Lastly, we search to understand and project the possible future of integration. In this section, we analyze the region in the coming years from two perspectives.

From the development perspective, Yun-wing Sung argues that Hong Kong's role as a catalyst for substantial development is obvious to Beijing. He demonstrates that Guangdong's economic gains are derived directly from its link with Hong Kong, and will increase further after integration. However, will Beijing regard institutional concession as either essential or worthwhile in order to sustain these gains? Ian Scott challenges certain basic presuppositions that underlie the prevailing interpretation of Hong Kong's political culture. As Hong Kong has already existed as its own specific polity, its political culture, he insists, is markedly different from that of Beijing, which presumes that the natural state is one of unity. Since the future has been negotiated and determined between London and Beijing, what are the circumstances under which the Hong Kong government can retain its legitimacy? As each of the three players—Hong Kong, Beijing, and London—attempts to establish an institutional system consistent with its own interests, what are the likely political maneuvers that will lead us up to 1997? With the near future so obscure, the ultimate outcome of the integration process is in doubt.

In this volume, the research findings of the various authors do not provide a single conclusion to these questions about the present and future of the Hong Kong–Guangdong reunification, nor is this the aim of our efforts. The purpose here is to identify a consensus, to distinguish differences in informed scholarly views on and interpretations of these integration issues, and to provide an opportunity for continued discussion and debate. By presenting the broadest view of the ongoing economic and sociocultural transformation, the discussions and analyses demonstrate the complexity and the indeterminate nature of the Hong Kong–Guangdong link. There are no easy answers here. The goal is both to inform and to invite readers to think, to draw on our appraisals, and to develop their own conclusions.

References

Ames, Roger T. (1991), "Hong Kong: From Here to Dynasty," paper presented at the international workshop Historical Changes in Hong Kong and South China: Sociocultural Integration Toward 1997, Center for Chinese Studies, University of Hawaii at Manoa, Honolulu, November 15–16, 1991.

Asian Wall Street Journal Weekly, March 9, 1992; March 23, 1992.

Beijing Review, Vol. 24, No. 27, July 6, 1981; Vol. 35, No. 12, March 23–29, 1992.

Brus, Wlodzimierz (1989), "Evolution of the Communist Economic System: Scope and Limits," in *Remaking the Economic Institutions of Socialism: China and Eastern Europe*, ed. Victor Nee and David Stark, Stanford: Stanford University Press.

Chan, Ming K. (1991), "Hong Kong–Guangdong Linkages in Historical Perspective," paper presented at the international workshop Historical Changes in Hong Kong and South China: Sociocultural Integration Toward 1997, Center for Chinese Studies, University of Hawaii at Manoa, Honolulu, November 15–16, 1991.

Chan, Ming K., with John D. Young, ed. (1994), *Precarious Balance: Hong Kong Between China and Britain,* Armonk, NY: M.E. Sharpe.

Chen, Edward K.T. (1991), "Recent Developments in Hong Kong and Its Relationship with China," paper presented in "China and Hong Kong" panel, International Symposium on Pacific Asian Business, Pacific Asian Management Institute and College of Business Administration, University of Hawaii at Manoa, Honolulu, January 8, 1991.
Chen, Yuxiang (1991), *Jiuqi lantu* (Blueprint for '97), Hong Kong: Guangjiaojing chubanshe (Wide Angle Press).
Chu, David K.Y., and X. Zheng (1992), "Fuzhou, the Capital City of a Frontier Province, Fujian," in *China's Coastal Cities: Catalysts for Modernization*, ed. Y.M. Yeung and X. Hu, Honolulu: University of Hawaii Press.
Far Eastern Economic Review, April 4, 1991; March 26, 1992; April 2, 1992.
Harvey, David (1990), *The Condition of Postmodernity: An Enquiry into the Origins of Cultural Change*, Cambridge, MA: Basil Blackwell.
Hongkong Bank, *Economic Report*, June/July 1989; November 1990; June 7, 1989.
Huaqiao Ribao (*Wah Kiu Yat Po*; Overseas Chinese Daily), December 24, 1991.
Jao, Y.C. et al., eds. (1985), *Hong Kong and 1997: Strategies for the Future*, Hong Kong: Centre of Asian Studies, University of Hong Kong.
Jidutu xianggang shouwangshe (Christian Sentinels for Hong Kong) (1988), *Guoduqide xianggang: zhengzhi, jingji, shehui* (Hong Kong in transition: politics, economy, and society), Hong Kong: Guangjiaojing chubanshe (Wide Angle Press).
Kim, Won Bae, and R. Yin-Wang Kwok (1991), "Restructuring for Foreign Investment in Asia Pacific," *Southeast Asian Journal of Social Science*, Vol. 19, Nos. 1, 2.
Kornai, Janos (1989), "The Hungarian Reform Process: Visions, Hopes, and Reality," in *Remaking the Economic Institutions of Socialism: China and Eastern Europe*, ed. Victor Nee and David Stark, Stanford: Stanford University Press.
Kwok, Daniel W.Y. (1991), "Unification and Division in the Chinese Historical Experience," paper presented at the international workshop Historical Changes in Hong Kong and South China: Sociocultural Integration Toward 1997, Center for Chinese Studies, University of Hawaii at Manoa, Honolulu, November 15–16, 1991.
Kwok, R. Yin-Wang (1981), "Trends in Urban Planning and Development in China," in *Urban Development in Modern China*, ed. Lawrence Ma and Edward Hanten, Boulder, CO: Westview Press.
———— (1986), "Regional Relationship and Interaction Between Hong Kong and China," in *Planning and Development of Coastal Open Cities: Part II Hong Kong Section*, ed. P.L. Choi, P.K. Fong, and R.Y. Kwok, Hong Kong: Center of Urban Studies and Urban Planning, University of Hong Kong.
———— (1992a), "Hong Kong–Guangdong Interaction: Joint Enterprise of Market Capitalism and State Socialism," paper presented at the workshop Hong Kong and its Hinterland, University of Toronto, York University, Joint Center for Asian Pacific Studies, University of British Columbia, Vancouver, January 1992.
———— (1992b), "Urbanization under Economic Reform," in *Urbanizing China*, ed. Gregory Guldin, Westport, CT: Greenwood Press.
Kwok, R. Yin-Wang, and Alvin Y. So, eds. (1991), *Historical Changes in Hong Kong and South China: Sociocultural Integration Toward 1997*, Monograph, Center for Chinese Studies, University of Hawaii at Manoa.
Lu, Ping (1992), "Fahui gezi youshi, baochi gezi tese, gongtong changzao fanrong" (Exploit local advantages, preserve local characteristics, jointly create prosperity), paper presented at the Conference on Pearl River Delta Economic Development: Review and Prospect, Research Center of Pearl River Delta Economic Development and Management, Zhongshan University, Zhongshan, May 7–11, 1992.
Mancall, Mark (1984), *China at the Center: 300 Years of Foreign Policy*, New York: Free Press.

Meier, Gerald M. (1989), *Leading Issues in Economic Development*, 5th ed., New York: Oxford University Press.

Mushkat, Miron (1990), *The Economic Future of Hong Kong*, Boulder, CO: Lynne Rienner.

Nee, Victor G., and Brett de Bary (1972), *Longtime Californ': A Documentary Study of American Chinatown*, New York: Random House.

Segal, Gerald (1993), *The Fate of Hong Kong*, London: Simon & Schuster.

Skeldon, Ronald (1990), "Emigration and the Future of Hong Kong," *Pacific Affairs*, Vol. 63, No. 4.

———, ed. (1994), *Reluctant Exiles? Migration from Hong Kong and the New Overseas Chinese*, Armonk, NY: M.E. Sharpe.

South China Morning Post, June 20, 1992.

Sung, Yun-wing (1991), *The China–Hong Kong Connection: The Key to China's Opendoor Policy*, New York: Cambridge University Press.

——— (1992), "The Economic Integration of Hong Kong with China in the 1990s: The Impact on Hong Kong," paper presented at the workshop Hong Kong and its Hinterland, University of Toronto, York University, Joint Center for Asian Pacific Studies, University of British Columbia, Vancouver, January 1992.

Szelenyi, Ivan (1989), "Eastern Europe in an Epoch of Transition: Toward a Socialist Mixed Economy?" in *Remaking the Economic Institutions of Socialism: China and Eastern Europe*, ed. Victor Nee and David Stark, Stanford: Stanford University Press.

Taylor, Bruce, and R. Yin-Wang Kwok (1989), "From Export Center to World City: Planning for the Transformation of Hong Kong," *American Planning Association Journal*, Vol. 55, No. 3.

Tong, Dalin, and Mingyu Wu (1992), "Xianggang–Zhujiang sanjuezhou: xinde jingji lianmeng" (Hong Kong–Pearl River Delta: new economic alliance), paper presented at the Conference on Pearl River Delta Economic Development: Review and Prospects, Research Center of Pearl River Delta Economic Development and Management, Zhongshan University, Zhongshan, May 7–11, 1992.

Vogel, Ezra F. (1989), *One Step Ahead in China: Guangdong under Reform*, Cambridge, MA: Harvard University Press.

Wu, Wai Man (1990), "China's Shenzhen Special Economic Zone: A Social Benefit–Cost Analysis," Ph.D. diss., University of Hawaii at Manoa.

Xu, Xueqiang (1991), "Economic Transformation in Guangdong," paper presented at the international workshop Historical Changes in Hong Kong and South China: Sociocultural Integration Toward 1997, Center for Chinese Studies, University of Hawaii at Manoa, Honolulu, November 15–16, 1991.

———, et al. (1988), *Zhujiang sanjiao zhoude fazhan yu chengshihua* (Development and urbanization of Pearl River Delta), Guangzhou: Zhongshan daxue chubanshe (Zhongshan University Press).

Yee, Albert H. (1989), *A People Misruled: Hong Kong and the Chinese Stepping Stone Syndrome*, Hong Kong: API Press.

Yu, Ying-shih (1967), *Trade and Expansion in Han China*, Berkeley: University of California Press.

——— (1986), "Han Foreign Relations," in *The Cambridge History of China*, Vol. 1, *The Ch'in and Han Empires 221 B.C.–A.D. 220*, ed. Denis Twitchett and John Fairbank, Cambridge: Cambridge University Press, pp. 377–462.

Zheng, Yushuo (1989), *Guoduqide xianggang* (Hong Kong in transition), Hong Kong: Sanlian shudian (Joint Publishing Co.).

Zhou, Bajun, Wei Chen, and Wei Qu (1992), *Xianggang: bansui zhengzhi guodude jingji guodu* (Hong Kong: the economic transition that accompanies the political transition), Hong Kong: Sanlian shudian (Joint Publishing Co.).

Zhou, Daming (1992), "Zhujiang sanjuezhou weilai renkou fenbu tezheng ji yidong qushi fenxi" (Analysis of migrant labor in Pearl River Delta: characteristics and trend of population movement), paper presented at the Conference on Pearl River Delta Economic Development: Review and Prospect, Research Center of Pearl River Delta Economic Development and Management, Zhongshan University, Zhongshan, May 7–11, 1992.

Zhou, Yizhi, and Hanrong Shi (1988), *Xianggang yu yiguo liangzhi* (Hong Kong and "One Country, Two Systems"), Beijing: Zhongguo shehui kexue chubanshe (China Social Science Press).

Part I
Hong Kong–Guangdong Link: A Review

2

All in the Family: The Hong Kong–Guangdong Link in Historical Perspective

Ming K. Chan

Geographically, Hong Kong is part of China and, economically, it was part of China with Guangdong Province as its immediate hinterland. While administratively a British colony since 1842, Hong Kong has been populated overwhelmingly by Chinese, with the great majority coming from the Pearl River Delta. Indeed, to many Chinese residents in Hong Kong, particularly in the pre-1949 days, "China" meant Guangdong while "homeland" referred to the ancestral villages in the Pearl River Delta. Since the opening and modernization of China in 1978, a popular cliché emerged from the other side of the border: "Shenzhen is Hongkongized, Guangdong is Shenzhenized, and the whole country is Guangdongized" (*Kaifang shidai* [Open Times], 1989: 13–14). Both are vivid reflections of the intimate relationship between Hong Kong and Guangdong from historical and contemporary contexts.

This chapter aims at a brief delineation and preliminary assessment of some of the basic features and specific issues for both positive collaboration and stressful confrontation in the dynamic and organic linkages between Hong Kong as a British colony and Guangdong as the vanguard province in south China. While viewing major developments during the past one and a half centuries through a historical perspective, this chapter will also draw reference from the more recent trends in this bilateral relationship. Using the 1949 Communist takeover of the Chinese mainland as an analytical demarcation, this chapter will try to compare and contrast the Hong Kong–Guangdong link in the pre- and post-1949 periods. It will also illuminate the implications of this Hong Kong–Guangdong nexus for the Chinese nation and the international community in Hong Kong's current transition toward 1997 when it will become a Special Administrative Region of China.

Hong Kong–Guangdong Relations, 1842–1949

The sense of community and belonging between the people of Hong Kong and Guangdong has been so strong and pervasive in human, cultural, social, and economic terms that an old saying, "the province and Hong Kong as one family" (*XiangGang yijia*), is a very apt characterization of their many overlapping ties and multiple linkages despite their divergent developmental paths and different political jurisdictions. This kind of intimate relationship stemmed from the historical and demographic reality underlining Hong Kong's growth and development as a geographic part of Guangdong populated mainly by immigrants from the province and their descendants, whose mother tongue is for the most part still Cantonese (Guangzhou dialect).

While mutual interests and shared benefits have helped to cement their close collaborative linkage in economic terms during most of the twentieth century, Hong Kong and Guangzhou, the provincial capital and economic hub of Guangdong, were once rival port cities competing for dominance in international trade and regional traffic in the late nineteenth century. Eventually they became so closely integrated in economic activities with a division of labor that there was a real case of functional interdependence between the two, with Hong Kong and Guangzhou being two halves of a single economic core encompassing the entire Pearl River Delta region (Murphey, 1977: 250). However, prior to reaching such a state of economic interdependence, relations between Hong Kong and Guangdong were stormy. Many Guangdong natives never really "forgave" Hong Kong as a British colonial creation whose prosperity was achieved at the expense of Guangzhou's preeminence as the economic hub of south China. In view of British Hong Kong's early development in the context of Sino-British relations and Sino-international trade, such Guangdong sentiments are not without justification.

Hong Kong's Birth and Guangdong's Decline

Besides the issue of opium imports into China, British dissatisfaction with the Guangzhou system, whereby foreign trade with Guangzhou could be handled only by the Cohong merchants there, was the major cause behind the 1839–42 Opium War between China and Britain. China's defeat enabled the British to abolish Guangzhou's monopoly on foreign trade with two particular provisions in the Treaty of Nanking (1842). One was the opening of five ports along the

China coast to foreign trade—Xiamen, Fuzhou, Ningbo, Shanghai, and Guangzhou, thus inaugurating the "treaty port system." The other provision ceded the island of Hong Kong to the British Crown in perpetuity (Wakeman, 1978: 163–212).

As such, the birth of Hong Kong as a British Crown colony was a direct result of China's first humiliating defeat by foreigners in modern times. Guangzhou lost its monopoly of China's maritime international trade to the treaty port system. Worse still to Guangdong's pride, Hong Kong was deliberately acquired as "a British rival to the Chinese-controlled trade at Guangzhou" (Murphey, 1953: 53).

The Treaty of Nanking created an economic crisis in Guangdong as the four newly opened treaty ports competed vigorously with the much-diminished Guangzhou. A drastic geographic shift occurred in the trade of tea and silk, the two major items of Chinese export. The end of Guangzhou's monopoly in foreign trade meant that goods for export from Central China were no longer obliged to move along a difficult route over the mountains to reach Guangzhou. Instead, they could be transported along more natural and less expensive routes to the nearest treaty port. Thus tea leaves produced in Zhejiang, Jiangxi, and Anhui began to move through Shanghai once it was opened as a treaty port in 1843. Its tea exports rose from 1 million pounds in 1844 to 80 million pounds in 1855, which accounted for 58 percent of China's total tea exports (Murphey, 1953: 103–9). The southern tea leaves produced in Fujian were shipped through Fuzhou. Only the Hubei and Hunan leaves were still brought to and sold in Guangzhou, and even then, what Guangzhou managed to retain of the tea trade was further ravaged by the Taiping Movement of 1850–64 (Morse, 1910: 363–66; Wakeman, 1965: 98–100; Polachek, 1992).

Guangzhou also lost the important raw silk trade after 1853. Of the four silk-producing areas in China, the two lower Yangzi provinces of Jiangsu and Zhejiang together accounted for about half of the total production, while the Guangzhou region accounted for about 20 percent. The silk produced in the Yangzi region naturally gravitated to Shanghai, which became the new exchange center for Chinese silk. By 1855, over 60 percent of China's total silk exports passed through Shanghai. Guangzhou was left with only the locally produced silk to deal with. Far away from the major centers of production, Guangzhou was soon replaced by Shanghai as the greatest port in the emerging "treaty port system" in China (Murphey, 1953: 109–11; Wakeman, 1965: 100).

"Direct dependents" of the once prosperous foreign trade in Guangzhou—porters, dockhands, warehousemen, and crewmen of Chinese junks—immediately felt the pinch with the shift in the tea and silk traffic. The Guangzhou junk crews further suffered from the competition of foreign vessels that entered the coastal trade after 1842. The foreign-trade merchant community in Guangzhou was also deeply affected by trade dislocation (Wakeman, 1965: 100–101). Furthermore, there was a significant increase in the quantities of British cotton goods imported to China, mainly due to the new lower-rate tariff introduced by the Treaty of Nanking (Yan, 1955: 59–64; Cooke, 1858: 169; Fairbank, 1953: 350–56). The impact of this almost unrestricted influx of British cotton goods on Guangdong's textile industry was devastating. Spinning machines almost disappeared from Panyu and Nanhai, the two counties bordering on Guangzhou city, where British yarn displaced native yarn. A drastic decline also occurred in the weaving and dyeing industries in Panyu and Shunde counties, where more than half of the female work force was idled (Peng, 1957: 486; Liang, 1874: 36–37; Chen, 1959: 17–38).

The Treaty of Nanking created mass unemployment and a host of other social and economic problems in Guangdong. Jobless textile workers, porters, boatmen, craftsmen, and dislocated peasants formed a large pool of surplus labor. Wage rates decreased while geographic and occupational mobility became higher. It was no accident that a great many porters and boatmen in Shanghai during its early treaty port days were Guangdong people (Bridgeman and Williams, 1848: 473). Hundreds of sailors and boatmen thrown out of work turned to piracy, while many of the unemployed joined secret societies or bandit gangs, and still others formed a highly mobile urban fraternity of beggars and thieves. Coastal piracy and local uprisings in Guangdong rose sharply after the Opium War. Amid urban disorder and rural unrest, business declined and unemployment increased (Wakeman, 1965: 100–101; Lie Dao, 1958: 124–25; Peng, 1957: 515–16; Chesneaux, 1972: 1–21; Shi, 1879: 50: 31, 82: 12).

It is understandable that the Guangdong people blamed their sufferings on the British, who started the Opium War, opened other ports, brought on a variety of misfortune, and took Hong Kong and turned it into a challenge to Guangzhou. Thus, the popular anti-British sentiments among the Guangdong people were rooted in both their protonationalism and economic self-interest. Hong Kong, the newly acquired British stronghold in south China, became deeply involved in the crossfire of Sino-British conflicts that turned even more violent during the Second Anglo-Chinese War of 1856–60.

The war broke out over the immediate pretext of the Arrow Incident in Hong Kong, but it had as its real cause British dissatisfaction with their inability to enter Guangzhou city and the desire to gain further concessions from China (Hurd, 1967).[1] Hostilities commenced when a joint British-French force attacked Guangzhou in October 1856. By early January 1858, Guangzhou was occupied by foreign troops, who stayed for almost four years until October 1861. Once again, China was defeated. This time the Anglo-French troops even reached Beijing, the imperial capital. Finally, peace was restored in 1860 with the Treaty of Peking. Among other provisions, the treaty added to British Hong Kong the peninsula of Kowloon on the mainland directly across the harbor. The permanent cession of Kowloon was indeed a fulfillment of the British desire for additional territory in Hong Kong and it laid the foundation for the colony's spectacular growth. In one stroke, the colony's problem of overcrowding was lessened with room for easy expansion over the peninsula's flat land, and its harbor became well secured with control over the whole marine area (Collins, 1952: 99–101). As for Shanghai, the opening of six new treaty ports along the coast greatly enhanced its position as the geographically most central point for coastal trade. At the same time, the right of inland navigation along the Yangzi for foreign vessels, and the opening of Hankou and two other Yangzi ports confirmed Shanghai's role as the commercial apex of the entire Yangzi region.[2]

These twin developments assured the commercial ascendancy of Shanghai and the corresponding decline of Guangzhou as China's preeminent port of trade. The rapid rise of Hong Kong as an entrepôt also seemed to seal the economic fate of Guangzhou, whose remaining role in the south China trade was being challenged by the colony. An early sign of Guangzhou's apparent demise occurred, ironically, amid the boycott against the British and Hong Kong during the Arrow War. As a prominent foreign merchant recalled: "Up to 1856, Guangzhou was the chief place of business in China, and all the mercantile firms had their headquarters [there] with the exception of the two leading English houses (Jardine, Matheson and Co., and Dent and Co.), whose heads were in Hong Kong. But with the destruction of the [foreign] factories [in Guangzhou], all were driven there [Hong Kong]."[3] So it seemed that Guangzhou's loss was Hong Kong's gain.

Many factors were thus combined to undermine Guangzhou's position in foreign trade in the 1860s. The combined total value of its imports and exports fell from $34,600,000 (Mexican silver dollars) in 1860 to $21,400,000 in 1865. When compared with other newly opened treaty ports in customs duties collected, Guangzhou fell behind Shanghai, Fuzhou, and Hankou during the mid-1860s (Hao, 1970: 50; Tables 3 and 4). However, a decade later, Guangzhou recovered partially, and from 1870 to the 1890s it ranked second only to Shanghai in gross value of foreign and domestic trade as recorded by the Chinese Maritime Customs (Murphey, 1953: 121). In terms of Guangzhou's external trade, there was a fairly steady leveling for two decades, with only minor ups and downs in the total value of import and export from 16,584,833 taels in 1867 to 16,206,606 taels in 1885. A significant upward increase was registered from the 1886 figure of 22,196,613 taels to 29,519,629 taels in 1894, on the eve of the Sino-Japanese War (Cheng, 1985: 101–2). This recovery was due in part, paradoxically, to Hong Kong's rise.

Following the end of the Arrow War and the Taiping Movement, Hong Kong enjoyed almost uninterrupted growth and the colony rapidly developed from a small outpost of the British empire into a major international entrepôt. With its spacious, deepwater harbor, Hong Kong was able to challenge and eventually displace Guangzhou as the international port of south China catering to coastal as well as oceangoing vessels. The total number and tonnage of ships engaged in foreign trade that entered and cleared Hong Kong harbor increased steadily: from 1,975 ships of 1,354,173 tons in 1858, to 4,791 ships of 2,640,347 tons in 1869 (one year after the Suez Canal was opened), to 21,867 ships of 22,939,134 tons in 1913, the eve of World War I; by 1930, 28,374 ships of 37,909,385 tons were recorded by the port authorities (Hong Kong, 1932: 2–9). When native Chinese junks and steamers engaged in inland and coastal trade are included, the figures for Hong Kong's total shipping tonnage increase from 35 percent to 40 percent.

The prosperity in Hong Kong whetted the British appetite for an extension of the colonial domain. The calls for moving the boundaries farther north from Kowloon peninsula became most intense in 1894 when China was at war with Japan. Taking advantage of China's defeat and the Western powers' subsequent "scramble for concessions," the British demanded further territorial concessions from China. Parallel to the Japanese gain of Taiwan island in the 1895 Treaty of Shimonoseki and the establishment of Russian, German, and French spheres of influence in Manchuria, Shandong, and southwest China respectively, the British obtained from China a ninety-nine-year lease of the New Territories (NTs) under the Convention of 1898. Extending from Mirs Bay to Deep Bay, running along the Shenzhen River in Baoan county, this leased territory represents some 93 percent of present Hong Kong's landmass.

The British took formal possession of the New Territories on April 17, 1899, coincidentally the fourth anniversary of the signing of the Shimonoseki Treaty. Although a public holiday was declared in the colony, the native population of the new British domain was less enthusiastic about the takeover, which changed their status overnight from residents of Baoan, Guangdong, to colonial subjects. The long delay between the effective day of the lease on July 1, 1898, and the assumption of British jurisdiction was due in part to local Chinese resistance against British occupation. In April 1898, hostilities against the British in the New Territories caused much damage to property. Chinese men from both sides of the new border were involved, including regular Guangdong soldiers. At the end, the British forces prevailed, but only at a considerable loss of prestige and with a bitter aftermath (Wesley-Smith, 1980: 11–60). The futility of further resistance was recognized by the officialdom and people of Guangdong, who by then had to accept the reality of an increasingly close functional relationship with British Hong Kong, now substantially enlarged by the annexation of a big slice of Guangdong.

Interdependence and Rivalry

A clear indicator of Hong Kong's growth is its phenomenal population increase. Its Chinese population (which accounts for 98 percent or more of the colonial total), 92,441 in 1860, doubled to 187,770 in 1890, increased even more rapidly to 415,180 in 1910 and 615,625 in 1920, and reached 849,751 in 1931.[4] These increases were mainly the result of massive migration from the Pearl River Delta and other parts of Guangdong. The composition changed considerably during the post-1911 republican era, with one-third born locally, but still half were born in the delta and less than 20 percent were born in other parts of the province. Those born outside of Guangdong and Hong Kong constituted less than 5 percent in both periods (*Hong Kong Census Report,* 1891, 1897, 1901, 1906, 1911, 1921, and 1931).

The massive influx from Guangdong provided Hong Kong with an abundant supply of labor that was relatively inexpensive but not totally unskilled. This is a commonly acknowledged key factor responsible for Hong Kong's remarkable development then and since 1949 (Rabushka, 1973: 12; Szczepanik, 1958: 4–12). At the same time, Hong Kong's growth offered much-needed employment opportunities to the Guangdong people. Besides absorbing the surplus manpower of the province, Hong Kong's superior harbor facilities and its strategic location as the hub of British Far East and Pacific shipping facilitated massive international migration from Guangdong, especially to British domains.

The magnitude of this human traffic through Hong Kong grew with time. In 1855, 14,683 Chinese left the port, in 1872, 27,721 left and 23,773 returned; in 1881, 70,625 left and 52,983 returned; the great majority of these transients were natives of Guangdong (Endacott, 1958: 126–30, 196–97, 255–56). By the turn of the twentieth century, more than one hundred boardinghouses and numerous labor agencies were set up in the colony to service this "coolie trade," shipping about one hundred thousand laborers per year to southeast Asia, Australia, and the Americas. Sometimes agents were sent into the Guangdong hinterland to recruit overseas laborers, while many prospective emigrants from the province came to Hong Kong on their own (Chan, 1975: 96). In their emigration path, workers from the hinterland often came to Guangzhou before proceeding to Hong Kong, where they might find employment and stay on or migrate overseas from the colony. Thus, Guangzhou and Hong Kong formed a partnership in this migration traffic and their relationship was that of division of labor and cooperation. Guangzhou functioned as the central collection and transshipment center, while Hong Kong served as the international clearinghouse and port of sail as well as an economic center that could actually absorb and employ some migrants from Guangdong (Chan, 1975: 81, 99–100).

Thriving on Guangdong emigration traffic, Hong Kong also functioned as a supply center to provision overseas Chinese communities, which are often "Guangzhoutowns" (Cantontowns) to all practical intents and purposes. The colony also worked in the reverse direction as the principal clearinghouse for remittances from Guangdong natives abroad. According to C.F. Remer's estimates, total overseas remittances into China exceeded $150 million Chinese silver dollars by the turn of the century and averaged more than $280 million between 1914 and 1930 (Remer, 1933). A survey of provincial banks finds that total overseas remittances into Guangdong reached $295 million (Guangdong dollars) in 1928, right before the Great Depression that reduced the inflow to $180 million in 1936 (Lin, 1989: 600–601). This significant capital inflow was vital to the economic life of the province; besides supporting the family dependents of the overseas workers, it helped to finance many new businesses and industries in Hong Kong and throughout the delta. Hong Kong's essential function in this regard can be reflected in the Chinese name "abundance of remittance" (*Huifeng*) of the Hong Kong and Shanghai Banking Corporation (HKSB), which is still the largest bank in the colony and was the foremost foreign bank in China before 1949.[5] Headquartered in Hong Kong, the Hong Kong and Shanghai Banking Corporation issued the local banknotes, which were widely circulated in Guangdong. Adding to the Guangdong economic clout in the Chinese national market was the fact that the international currency exchange rate for China as a whole was set by the bank's Shanghai branch until 1935.

A near "monetary union" existed between Hong Kong and Guangdong, as their currencies often circulated freely as common and accepted media of transaction in each other's domains. Before 1950, Hong Kong banknotes were used extensively in Guangdong, whose people had much less trust in the value of their own provincial notes. Guangdong coins were accepted in Hong Kong for daily use until they were prohibited by the Hong Kong government in November 1912. This official ban provoked a tramway boycott until February 1913 among the local Chinese grassroots population, who interpreted the British measure as an unfriendly act disrespectful toward the new Chinese republic (Chan, 1993). Despite this incident, the close economic ties and intensive human and cargo traffic between the province and the colony necessitated Hong Kong's monetary synchronization with the Chinese mainland. Therefore, when China removed its currency from the silver standard on October 5, 1935, and inaugurated a new managed currency system, Hong Kong followed suit by banning the export of silver on November 9, 1935. Then, on December 5, 1935, Hong Kong also introduced a new managed currency system and recalled all the silver coins in circulation. The Hong Kong government admitted that this reform had to be made as China had changed its system (Tom, 1957: 71–75; Hong Kong Government, 1936: A20). The functional symbiosis of Hong Kong and Guangzhou in external trade can further illustrate their interdependence. Despite the ascendancy of Hong Kong, Guangzhou as a port of trade did not lapse into absolute decline. By the last decades of the nineteenth century, Guangzhou had lost out to Hong Kong as the most important port in south China. Yet it retained its old advantages as the hub of an extensive inland waterway system and the center of domestic commerce for the Guangdong–Guangxi region. In foreign trade Guangzhou still had important assets as the real administrative, social, and economic hub of south China, notwithstanding Hong Kong's prominence and proximity.

Hong Kong, despite its Chinese population, is a British colony with an almost offshore location; while transactions can be conducted through its facilities, it is not itself the China market. Even after Hong Kong had become the foreign trade "counter" for south China, Guangzhou remained south China's central "department" for the purchase and collection of Chinese exports as well as the distribution "department" for foreign imports; these were functions Hong Kong did not and perhaps could not easily perform (Endacott, 1958: 194). To a large extent, Hong Kong dealt with the foreign markets on behalf of Guangdong, which was the real supplier of exports and buyer of imports; Hong Kong's role as an entrepôt is exactly that of a middleman. As such, Hong Kong has always been Guangdong's largest trading partner, even though Hong Kong's own capacity both as consumer of Chinese products and manufacturer of goods exported to China was relatively small before 1949. It was Hong Kong's role as a transshipment point that accounted for its large share in Guangdong's external trade (*Guangzhou nianjian*, 1935: 401–10). With the exception of a few Japanese vessels, there were normally no oceangoing ships operating directly from Guangdong to foreign ports exclusive of Hong Kong. Thus, most of Guangdong's exports went first to Hong Kong and then were transshipped to various points abroad, while most of the foreign imports into Guangdong were also transshipped through the colony (Arnold, 1926: 52). Undoubtedly, a very large portion of Guangdong's share in China's total foreign trade involved items transshipped through Hong Kong, which had superior harbor facilities and more direct and extensive international shipping routes. By performing certain functions that Guangdong could not perform satisfactorily or efficiently, Hong Kong became Guangdong's outer harbor for foreign trade, while Guangdong was the colony's immediate and indispensable economic hinterland.

The closeness of their integration was revealed clearly in the circulation of goods and individuals between the colony and the province. The size and magnitude of this human traffic can be seen in the 1921 Hong Kong Government census, even with its significant margin for error. This census was conducted during the Qing Ming Festival when a sizable part of the local Chinese community returned to the province to perform their traditional duties of paying respect to their ancestral graves. As a result, the tabulated census total was underreported by at least 5.3 percent, or 35,000 persons out of a normal population of some 660,000 (*Hong Kong Census Report*, 1921: 155–56). The waterborne traffic between Hong Kong and Guangzhou and other Pearl River Delta ports was among the busiest in the world, with frequent scheduled ferry services. For instance, in 1936 the average daily passenger arrival in Hong Kong from Guangzhou alone was 2,422 by rail and 2,033 by ferry as against 2,303 departures by rail and 2,169 by ferry (Hong Kong Government, 1939: 108). As one geographer has suggested, "At least in commercial terms, Hong Kong and Guangzhou are best regarded as closely integrated parts of a single city in which Hong Kong acted as the wholesaling and shipping center" (Murphey, 1977: 250 n. 7). Their relationship was one of interdependence and division of labor. Many Guangdong people, however, did not share this view but considered it a case of British Hong Kong domination and Guangdong subordination (Hong Kong, 1938: 121).

Guangdong's resentments against Hong Kong's supremacy in shipping and trade grew increasingly strong in the republican era. Various schemes were suggested to regain Guangzhou's lost prominence as the leading port of south China. Among his many plans for the reconstruction of China, Sun Yat-sen advocated the development of Whampoa in the outskirts of Guangzhou into a great, first-rate, deepwater international port to compete with or even displace Hong Kong (Sun, 1920: 49–56). During the 1925–26 General Strike–Boycott, some of the strikers constructed the twenty-five-mile-long Sun Yat-sen Highway from Guangzhou to Whampoa as the first step toward the realization of this dream.

In sharp contrast to the economic devastation in Hong Kong (where shipping fell almost 50 percent to 310,361 vessels totaling 36.8 million tons in 1926), the Strike–Boycott brought unusual growth and unexpected prosperity to Guangzhou. Vessels that had previously docked at Hong Kong came instead to Guangzhou, where an average of forty vessels called every day. The inauguration of direct shipping service (by forty-five oceangoing steamers) on a regular schedule between Guangzhou and other ports, coupled with the suspension of the Guangzhou–Hong Kong traffic, contributed much to the increase in Guangzhou's overall trade. Because Hong Kong was boycotted, many of its former trading partners turned naturally to Guangzhou, where foreign and Chinese goods went directly. All these seemed to substantiate the traditional argument that Hong Kong's prosperity was achieved at Guangdong's expense (Chan, 1975: chap. 11).

On the whole, the economic growth of Hong Kong was not without redeeming value for Guangzhou and the province. Of positive significance for the economic modernization of Guangdong, as well as for Guangdong's economic clout elsewhere in China, was Hong Kong's legal status as a British territory. It enabled Guangdong native-owned enterprises registered in Hong Kong to expand into other British strongholds in the treaty ports with special privileges accorded to foreign firms under the unequal treaties. For instance, the four largest modern department stores in Shanghai before the war were all Guangdong native-owned and -managed businesses headquartered in Hong Kong.

Furthermore, because of their longer, more extensive contacts with the Guangdong people in their Hong Kong main offices and Pearl River Delta branches, major British banks and corporations in Shanghai and other treaty ports very often relied on the services of Guangdong compradores and technicians. Prior experience in foreign trade and the depressed Guangdong economy accounted for the fact that a majority of the compradores in the newly opened treaty ports were from Guangdong, recruited by major British firms in Hong Kong. Noted examples include Tong Jingxing (Jardine, Matheson) and Zheng Quanying (Butterfield, Swire) (Hao, 1970: 48–54). It was through such Hong Kong connections and riding on the coattails of the British imperialist economic machine, that Guangdong natives managed to establish themselves as the second most powerful regional economic bloc in Shanghai, rivaling the local Ningbo gang for dominance. Indeed there is much substance to the old cliché *"wuguang bucheng tie"* ("without Guangdong, there is no iron," meaning railways, modern industry, machinery, mining, and shipping), as British economic penetration from Hong Kong into hinterland China opened up opportunities for a modern Guangdong economic network of merchants, compradores, foremen, and skilled laborers supplementing the already influential Guangdong guilds and labor gangs in traditional regional trade.

Within the regional context, the Guangdong–Hong Kong commercial network could be seen in the large number of Guangzhou firms that set up branches and agencies in Hong Kong, while the local merchants, for their part, sent buyers into the province to make purchases and arrange for supplies. In fact, a number of well-known business concerns in Hong Kong today still carry the prefix of "Guangzhou and Hong Kong" (ShengGang) in their titles or trademarks. Both merchant guilds and labor unions in Hong Kong were often branches or affiliates of high-level general guilds or labor federations in Guangzhou, which were the highest provincial bodies in the trade or profession. An exceptional case in reverse was the Chinese Seamen's Union founded in 1921, with its national and international headquarters located in Hong Kong. This reflected the strategic position of the colony in both coastal and international shipping throughout south China and its vital function as recruitment point for Guangdong seamen (Chan, 1975: chap. 6).

In fact, the economic and functional intimacy between the province and the colony has been well recognized by both sides since the turn of the twentieth century. By the 1930s, when political relations between the two were at their historic best, even the Hong Kong government openly acknowledged that it was economically part of China. Its Economic Commission reported in 1935 that "Hong Kong's economic value is more closely related to south China and that such industrialization as may be possible in the Colony should be a part of the economic development of south China as a whole" (Hong Kong Government, 1935: 86). Meanwhile, a contemporary business guidebook published in Guangzhou stated that "Guangzhou's business relations with Hong Kong and Macau are so extensive that the authors feel this book would be incomplete without certain information on these cities being included" (Canton Advertising and Commission Agency, 1971: "Foreword").

Despite such seemingly parallel perceptions of their closely linked economic fate, there was still considerable rivalry between the business communities of Hong Kong and Guangdong. One major issue was the high Chinese tariff on Hong Kong goods. Another concerned the construction of a loopline linking the Guangzhou–Kowloon and Guangzhou–Hankou railways. These issues revealed the fierce competition between the two communities, with Guangdong businessmen resorting to a protectionist stance. While Hong Kong merchants were appealing for a reduction of Guangdong tariffs on Hong Kong products in 1934, manufacturers of rubber shoes, cigarettes, glass, and matches in Guangzhou also petitioned the Social Bureau not to grant Hong Kong's request. Both the Chambers of Commerce and the municipal authorities in Guangzhou supported the local manufacturers and issued public declarations against special treatment for Hong Kong imports (Guangzhoushi shehuiju, 1934: 9; *Kungshang Ribao*, 6–23–1934).

In settling the 1925–26 General Strike–Boycott, the British offered a $10 million loan to develop Whampoa Port, conditional upon the chief engineer and accountant being British, and upon the construction of the loopline. The Guangdong authorities rejected this offer as a thinly disguised British attempt at economic domination, since this loopline would have allowed through rail traffic from Hong Kong to Hankou, bypassing Guangzhou and thus making the new Whampoa Port superfluous (Chan, 1975: 350). In the mid-1930s, Hong Kong again appealed for the linking of the two railways, but this was rejected by the Guangdong authorities who thought Guangzhou's interest would be adversely affected. The Guangzhou Chamber of Commerce argued that through train service with the loopline would enable Hong Kong merchants to evade the tariffs besides bypassing Guangzhou in trading directly with central and north China (*Huazi Ribao*, 2–10–1936; *Kungshang Ribao*, 6–19, 23–1934). Right before the Japanese attack in north China in July 1937, the loopline was built by the Chinese government. From then on, until the fall of Guangzhou in October 1938, Hong Kong served as the main supply center for China's war effort against the Japanese, supplying more than 1 million tons of strategic materials to the mainland through the Guangzhou–Kowloon Railway as linked with central China via the loopline (Liu, 1962: 156).

Patriotic Frontline, "Subversive Base," or Two-Way Asylum?

A major part of the strains and stresses underlining the Hong Kong–Guangdong linkage has been the political reality of Hong Kong as the citadel of British imperialism in China at the expense of Chinese national as well as Guangdong provincial interests and pride. After the British occupation of Hong Kong in 1841, thousands of Chinese from the Pearl River Delta flooded the colony, where they found employment and took up residence. The Chinese population in Hong Kong rose from 12,361 in 1842 to 69,251 by 1856 (Hong Kong, 1932: Appendix, 1–2). In view of the depression in Guangdong, Hong Kong's development meant economic opportunities for which the people should have been grateful. Yet, fresh from their humiliating defeat by the British, and still suffering from the subsequent economic disaster, the people of Guangdong were extremely sensitive to further foreign infringements on their interests and assaults on their pride. As Hong Kong was snatched away by the British in revenge for the Guangzhou Cohong System, the colony soon became the symbol of British imperialism and thus the target of patriotic outbursts in Guangdong. In this sense, the frontline of defense for Guangdong started with the Chinese in the colony.

Events in 1849 and 1857 serve as early illustrations. In April 1849, when Hong Kong governor Sir George Bonham, threatening military attack, demanded the right for the British to enter Guangzhou city, a boycott against trade with Hong Kong and the British broke out in Guangdong. People throughout the delta were mobilized and local militia were ready to resist the British at any cost. The determination of the local populace scored a victory, forcing the British to abandon for the moment their effort to enter Guangzhou (Wakeman, 1965: 90–105; Nolde, 1960: 229–315).

During the Arrow War, Chinese workers in Hong Kong responded actively to the call for resistance against the British. In addition to the boycott against Hong Kong, the guilds in Guangzhou declared a general strike against the colony in April 1857. Within a month, more than twenty thousand Chinese workers gave up their jobs in Hong Kong and returned to the mainland. Business came to a standstill and life in the colony became difficult as it was hard to hire help or get food supplies. The attempts of the British to recruit laborers in Guangdong's Baoan county met with stiff resistance from the Baoan people (Morse, 1910: 436; Xia, 1865: 8–9). The same pattern of popular mobilization against the British was repeated time and again, employing economic means for political ends in the confrontations between Guangdong and Hong Kong. This reflected both the economic circumstance of Hong Kong and the peculiar nature of its ties with Guangdong.

The record of grass-roots collective actions against the British in Hong Kong dates from the early days of colonial possession—from the 1857 strike, to the 1884 strike and riot against the British attempt to repair a French warship in a local dockyard during the Sino-French War (Tsai, 1984: 2–14), to the devastating sixteen-month-long 1925–26 Guangzhou–Hong Kong General Strike–Boycott under the Guomindang–Chinese Communist Party United Front against British brutalities in China.[6] In each of these episodes, the loyalty of the majority of Chinese workers in Hong Kong rested with their undoubted Guangdong homeland despite economic opportunities in the British colony.

Such strong displays of patriotic sentiments at the Chinese grass-roots level, transcending political demarcations, had been a hallmark of class solidarity reinforced by local/parochial forces in nationalistic and revolutionary movements in the region. Of course, British colonial rule in Hong Kong and imperialistic aggression toward Guangdong led directly to a strong collective identity among the local populace as natives of Guangdong and as Chinese. Noted cases of British provocation include the 1923–24 Guangzhou Maritime Customs Incident and the 1924 Guangzhou Merchant Corps Revolt. On both occasions, the British governor in Hong Kong advocated armed intervention against Sun Yat-sen's regime in Guangdong in order to secure British interests (Chan, L., 1990: 155–67). In consequence, regional solidarity became intertwined with patriotic pride, while anti-imperialism and popular nationalism found concrete expressions through local/regional cohesion among the Guangdong people. The strong manifestation of popular nationalism among the Chinese grassroots in Hong Kong also stemmed from the economic, social, and legal injustices they experienced under an alien, uncaring, and often arrogant colonial state (Chan, M., 1990: 132–46).

To Chinese people on both sides of the border in times of crisis, Guangdong and Hong Kong often served each other mutually as places of asylum. Noted examples include the warm welcome and full range of hospitality extended by the government and party authorities as well as by labor unions and charitable organizations in Guangzhou to strikers returning from Hong Kong in the 1920 Mechanics' Strike (9,000 strikers) (Chan, 1975: 47–49; 166–72), the 1922 Seamen's Strike (100,000 strikers),[7] and of course the 1925–26 General Strike–Boycott (250,000 strikers). The support and shelter Hong Kong strikers enjoyed in their Guangdong homeland enabled them to escape the repressive measures of the British colonial regime, and to substantially enhance their bargaining position vis-à-vis that regime and big business. Guangdong's sanctuary function for Hong Kong strikers was a crucial factor contributing to their 1920 and 1922 economic strike victories and to the long duration of the General Strike–Boycott. Of equal importance for the close relationship between the workers in both places was the fact that workers on strike in Hong Kong did not have to fear the recruitment of strikebreakers from Guangdong, and vice versa. In fact, the tight institutional links between labor unions on both sides of the border, as reinforced by close personal ties at both the union leadership and membership levels greatly alarmed the British authorities. In the aftermath of the 1925–26 General Strike–Boycott the Hong Kong government enacted a law explicitly prohibiting the use of union funds for purposes outside Hong Kong and the formation of a union in the colony as a branch of any labor union in China (England and Rear, 1981: 129–30).

In reverse, Hong Kong provided a breathing ground for Communist rebels, including Ye Jianying (father of former Guangdong governor Ye Xuanping) in the aftermath of the Chinese Communist Party's (CCP's) 1927 Guangzhou Commune Uprising, Zhou Enlai after the failure of the August 1927 Nanchang Uprising, and Deng Xiaoping in 1931 after the Guomindang (GMD) attack in Jiangxi (Li, 1992: 22–23). When the Guomindang regime's white terror made life impossible for the underground Communists during the late 1920s and 1930s, the Chinese Communist Party's South China Bureau and Guangdong Provincial Committee could no longer operate in Guangzhou but were relocated to Hong Kong in the form of a CCP Hong Kong Working Group.[8] Hierarchically, Hong Kong was classified only at the municipal level but for that period it was the regional and provincial Communist hub. Under the umbrella of British neutrality, the colony offered wartime refuge to mainland Chinese personnel and institutions during the early phase of the Sino-Japanese War (1937–41). After the Pacific war broke out and Hong Kong fell to the Japanese on Christmas Day 1941, the refugee exodus reversed direction. From 1937 to 1938 Hong Kong's population grew from under 1 million to 1,650,000 due to the arrival of refugees from China's southern provinces, mainly Guangdong. But from 1942 until

Japan's surrender in autumn of 1945, Hong Kong's population had dwindled to about 600,000, mainly as a result of the Japanese emigration policy that forced the local Chinese populace to Guangdong (Cameron, 1991: 251). Throughout the Sino-Japanese War of 1937–45, Hong Kong was an extremely important base for Chinese Communist guerrilla activities, especially Guangdong's East River Column, which covered the colony in its operations (Guangdongsheng danganguan, 1984; Gangjiu duli daduishi editorial committee, 1989; Dongjiang zongduishi editorial committee, 1985).

During the 1946–49 Civil War, Hong Kong also served as a safe haven for leftist elements and Guomindang dissidents from Guangdong and the north. In fact, right after the victorious Chinese Communist forces took Guangzhou in October 1949, the new municipal and provincial leadership was formed with political figures who actually took a special northbound train from Hong Kong to take office (Barnett, 1963: 83–95). Meanwhile, a large number of GMD loyalists and past regime officials escaped to Hong Kong, joining the multitude of ordinary people who exited Guangdong for the colony. By the end of 1950, Hong Kong's population was estimated at 2,360,000 (Cameron, 1991: 280). Of course, these are only the more recent examples that have occurred since the late Qing dynasty. With Hong Kong accommodating refugees and migrants from Guangdong during political upheavals, wars, natural disasters, economic depressions, and social unrests, the majority of the influx settled in the colony for good.

More than just a passive or neutral asylum for rebels and dissidents of various political and ideological persuasions, Hong Kong served as a supply depot, propaganda mill, funding source, recruitment ground, and even a fountainhead of modern thought for many a reformist cause (as in the case of Kang Youwei and Liang Qichao, both natives of the Pearl River Delta) and for revolutionary undertakings against the Chinese state, as exemplified by the career of Sun Yat-sen (another native of the delta) (Chan, L., 1990: chaps. 1 and 2). In this sense, the colony has a tradition of being the "base of subversion against the Chinese state" long before its post–June 4, 1989, condemnation by the People's Republic of China and the Chinese Communist Party leadership (Renmin Ribao, 7–21–1989).

One could also argue, however, that if Guangdong is often called "the cradle of Chinese revolution" (Vogel, 1969: 32–37), then Hong Kong's positive role in it should not be overlooked. Furthermore, from 1937 to 1941, when most of coastal China was under Japanese occupation, Hong Kong was the most crucial offshore "patriotic base" for China's resistance efforts. The Chinese in the colony enthusiastically responded to the call for anti-Japanese donations and war bond subscriptions, while local Chinese newspapers (many staffed by Guangdong journalists in exile) served as patriotic mouthpieces even at the risk of British colonial press censorship.[9] Of course, Hong Kong Chinese had traditionally been extremely generous in charitable efforts toward disaster relief in Guangdong, such as the West River floods. Indeed, at the popular level, with or without the blessing of the central Chinese state, the patriotic sentiments of Hong

Kong Chinese toward the province of Guangdong and the Chinese nation should
be beyond doubt.

Observations on the pre-1949 Linkages

Hong Kong—with its world-class free-port facilities, modern commercial and
financial institutions, urban infrastructure and public utilities, Western-style sani-
tation system, common-law legal system, and municipal administration—had
often been regarded by people of Guangdong as a model of Westernized development and a successful example of modernity on Chinese soil. Indeed, Hong
Kong had been an effective channel for the transfer of both hardware (machinery, material goods) and software (technology, mentality, thoughts, and
styles) stimulants for modernization into the Guangdong hinterland. Hong Kong
could be credited with many contributions to the advancement of Guangdong
into its position as one of the most economically developed as well as socioculturally progressive and cosmopolitan provinces in China before 1949.

The remarkable relationship between Hong Kong and Guangdong, based on
mutual benefit and shared values through interlocking human and institutional
ties, functional cooperation, and division of labor in the private sector, seems to
have worked best with little interference from the central governments in Beijing, Nanjing, and London. Indeed, the solidarity between Guangdong people on
the mainland and in the colony could easily feed on its own momentum with
little need for central control or external supervision. Such province–colony
collaboration formed the basis for a very influential regional force vis-à-vis the
Chinese central state in political, military, and economic development. The *de
facto* autonomy of Guangdong under Chen Jitong's reign against the dictates of
the Guomindang central authorities in Nanjing during the period 1929 to 1936 was
due in part to resources from the global Guangdong network through Hong Kong.

A close parallel is the prewar Munich–Berlin linkage, which, despite both
cities being German, was often not as close and harmonious as the Munich–
Innsbruck link, in spite of the border before 1938. One could easily substitute
Guangzhou for Munich and Nanjing for Berlin with Hong Kong (and Macao) as
Innsbruck (and Salzburg), and the Guangdong relationship with the northerners
might take on the same flavor as the Bavarians versus the Prussians. Indeed, the
remarkable development of the Guangdong region, with Guangzhou and Hong
Kong as magnetic nodule points during the period 1842 to 1949, has profound
implications for contemporary south China as the vanguard in the modernization
drive of the People's Republic.

Post-1949 Trends

The post-1949 era saw drastic change in the once intimate relations between the
colony and the province due to fundamental ideological reorientation accompa-

nying the political, economic, and social upheavals on the mainland under the Communist system. The Communist takeover triggered off massive waves of political and economic migration from Guangdong into Hong Kong during the 1950s, 1960s, and 1970s, leading to fundamental differences in Hong Kong's economy and society (Vogel, 1989: chap. 2).

Due to the deterioration on the London–Beijing diplomatic front under the Cold War shadow, Guangdong's external linkages were severely curtailed, including its ties with Hong Kong. The Chinese built a giant fence along the Hong Kong–Guangdong border. Formal documentation was required for border crossing, through train service was suspended, circulation of Hong Kong banknotes and periodicals was prohibited, and direct trade and exchange of services became much restricted. The Chinese Communists' isolation of their southern gateway from the "imperialist-bourgeois evil" influence of colonial Hong Kong was answered by the Western powers' "containment policy" toward the People's Republic of China. Furthermore, Hong Kong's post-1949 strategic function as the Western powers' peep hole through the bamboo curtain for intelligence gathering on the Communist mainland also added to the colony's "subversiveness" in the eyes of the Chinese authorities. Such developments tend to reaffirm the earlier observation that without central government interference or external pressure, Hong Kong–Guangdong collaboration as a fraternal regional core sometimes could work miracles.

Uneasy Neighbors, 1949–1978

When the Chinese Communists took over Guangdong in 1949, they had the capacity to recover Hong Kong as well. But, for strategic and economic reasons and based on their own experience of working there openly or in the underground, Chinese leaders decided to tolerate Hong Kong's continued existence as a British colony with obvious advantage to the People's Republic: Britain's diplomatic recognition of the PRC as the sole legitimate national government of China in early 1950 stemmed in part from its concern for Hong Kong (Tang, 1993). The United Nations mandated embargo against mainland China following the PRC's military involvement in the Korean War in 1951 officially cut off much of the legal trade between the colony and the province (Chan, M., 1991). Overnight, Hong Kong lost its Chinese economic hinterland and much of its regional and entrepôt trade.

This forced the colony to regear itself toward light industrial manufacturing for (non-China-bound) export markets. This industrialization effort was helped substantially by the relocation of production facilities, a skilled work force, and modern entrepreneurship from Guangzhou, Shanghai, and other Chinese cities during the 1948 to 1950 period.[10] The illicit trafficking of goods and supplies from Hong Kong into Guangdong by "patriotic" business elements from 1950 to

1953 provided an underground ensemble to the once thriving intra–Pearl River Delta trade. This massive smuggling network to provision the Chinese motherland evoked the memory of Hong Kong's vital function as wartime China's sole international maritime channel for strategic supplies from abroad during the period 1938 to 1941. Thus, despite political changes, ideological contradictions, and international realpolitik, Hong Kong's unchanged nature as a community of Guangdong natives, with its strategic geography as part of coastal Guangdong, can still yield benefits to itself and to the province.

These natural assets and the undiminished global contacts of Hong Kong eventually helped to restore partially the international economic contacts of Guangdong after 1949, as evident in the semiannual Guangzhou Trade Fair, inaugurated in 1957, which served until the early 1980s as the People's Republic's main trading counter with the West. Perhaps this could be regarded as a Chinese Communist restoration of the pre–Opium War Cohong system under which Guangzhou monopolized China's international maritime trade. (Land trade then was conducted with Russia, and other Asian neighbors like Vietnam and Korea, at other contact points on a different basis. A similar situation occurred during the period of the 1950s through the 1970s.)

Despite sharp difference in their ideopolitical and economic systems, socialist Guangdong and capitalist Hong Kong, even during the Cold War heydays, maintained various linkages in human and trade traffic, though much reduced in intensity and frequency. A carefully regulated trickle of legal immigrants from the province crossed into Hong Kong every day. Before the Cultural Revolution, some "patriotic" youths who graduated from the colony's "leftist" schools went to Guangdong for their university education. The PRC-controlled banks in Hong Kong functioned as a conduit for remittances from local residents as well as from overseas Chinese to their families and relatives in the province. During the early 1960s, in the immediate aftermath of the failure of the Great Leap Forward, many Hong Kong grocery stores started a new service of sending food parcels into individual households in Guangdong. These parcels were paid for by Hong Kong residents who wished to relieve their Guangdong relatives from the effects of bad harvests and the economic downturn by providing them with dried meat, canned food, cooking oil, nuts, and other edibles.

While the lifestyle of Hong Kong was considered to be ideologically "contaminated," material goods and funds from Hong Kong relatives were always welcomed by the people in Guangdong. This was especially true by the early 1970s when human and economic traffic between the province and colony became more frequent and relaxed following the détente between the People's Republic and the West and the gradual decline of ultraleftist fever on the mainland. Since then, both government-to-government contacts and popular-level personal and business exchanges between both ends of the Pearl River Delta have flourished. As a result, the province has been much stimulated toward change by the massive inflow of material goods, capital, technology, expertise, ideas, and styles from the outside world as transmitted through "the window to the south wind," that is, Hong Kong (Vogel, 1989: 44–47, 60–63).

Behind the "stability and prosperity" of Hong Kong during the last four decades, it is easy to identify some of the many direct contributions from Guangdong. The province has been a major supplier of fresh produce, grocery items, livestock, and staple foods that feed the Hong Kong population, many of whom migrated from Guangdong in successive waves during the periods 1948 to 1953, 1962, and 1976 to 1980. On the one hand, the massive influx strained the already critical housing shortage and inadequate infrastructural facilities, and created a host of social problems in the colony. On the other hand, the immigrants provided a pool of useful and inexpensive manpower sharing a common ethnic and cultural background with the local mainstream populace, thus contributing to Hong Kong's industrialization and economic growth.

The shortage of fresh water, aggravated by the colony's population growth and industrial expansion, has been substantially alleviated by water from the East River, supplied through an extensive aquasystem of pumping stations and long-distance pipelines in Guangdong. Of course, Hong Kong has to pay for the water and the construction of the aqua-infrastructure. However, foodstuffs from the mainland have been priced below world market levels, constituting the mainland's indirect subsidy to maintain lower living costs in the colony. Incidentally, the lower price tag of supplies from the People's Republic enhances their domination of the local consumer market and also helps to reduce the cost of raw materials for local industries. In such an exchange relationship, Hong Kong has been a major market for China's exports; together with its entrepôt functions and inflow of overseas remittances, the colony earns 40 percent of China's foreign exchange revenue. Of course, many of these goods and services, as well as tourism traffic, are routed through, originated from, produced by, or processed in the province.

Renewed Partnership since 1979

The major breakthrough in the Guangdong–Hong Kong relationship came in 1979 following the People's Republic's new policy of economic reform and international opening as directed by Deng Xiaoping. A significant aspect of China's quest for the four modernizations in its economic, technological, and infrastructural development has been the pivotal role played by Hong Kong, which serves as a valuable window and bridge to the outside world of modernity and material advance.

Since the 1980s, the creation of three Special Economic Zones (SEZs) in the Pearl River Delta, as a pillar in the People's Republic's drive toward opening and modernization, further testifies to this vital economic dimension of Hong Kong. Indeed, the most successful of the Special Economic Zones, Shenzhen, often prides itself in having been "Hongkongized" in its pace of economic growth and scope of industrial development, much of which is financed by direct investment from Hong Kong. According to a 1992 press report, more than twenty thousand Hong Kong factories had already been relocated to Shenzhen, which is becoming more like Hong Kong, not just in its many new skyscrapers but in everyday life as well—from the hair styles and fashions worn by the residents to their use of Hong Kong currency notes. (It has been estimated that 20 percent of all issued Hong Kong notes are in circulation on the mainland.) From a small border town of thirty thousand, Shenzhen is now home to over 1 million, mainly young workers from Guangdong and farther north who come to earn the highest wage in China, which has increased tenfold over the past decade (*Hong Kong Economic Journal*, 4–3–1992).

The 1984 Sino-British Joint Declaration, which stipulated the People's Republic's resumption of sovereignty over Hong Kong on July 1, 1997, will alter not only Hong Kong's future fate but also its relations with Guangdong, which have become increasingly close since the economic reform and opening in 1979. The era of transition has witnessed intensive and extensive interactions between the colony and the province, including several official visits by the British Hong Kong governor and Guangdong governors to each others' domains as well as working missions and exchange visits by their subordinate officials. The multifold increase in human and goods traffic has been facilitated by simplified border-crossing procedures, the resumption of passenger air flights in 1978, through train service in 1979, and the double-tracking of the railway line between Hong Kong and Guangzhou. By the mid-1980s, long-distance bus, hydrofoil, ferry, Hovercraft, and freight services linked Hong Kong directly with all nearby delta points and major cities in Guangdong. Serious traffic jams at border checkpoints have been part of the daily routine for Hong Kong truck drivers on the Shenzhen run. A direct-dial long-distance telephone network between Hong Kong and the delta has been in operation for several years. A six-lane high-speed highway linking Hong Kong, Shenzhen, and Guangzhou has been constructed by private Hong Kong interests.

The special policies and unusual flexibility in economic matters permitted by the central authorities, reinforced by the direct linkages with and massive inputs from Hong Kong, have indeed reshaped Guangdong's economy over a decade. In speed, style, size, scale, and scope, Guangdong is both the vanguard and the most successful example of marketization, industrialization, and internationalized economic development for China as a whole.

The People's Republic's scheduled resumption of sovereignty in 1997 induces a sharp reorientation of political allegiance and a revival of localism toward the mainland among Hong Kong Chinese elites, many of whom were born and raised in the province but later made their fortune and fame in the colony. No longer casualties of Cold War mentality, Western containment, Maoist radicalism, or rigid administrative constraints, many Guangdong émigrés feel safe to reidentify themselves openly with their homeland after a long absence of three to four decades. Longtime local "patriotic" figures and leftist leaders as well as new social and economic elites in the colony, who became friendly toward Beijing, were appointed members of the National People's Congress/Chinese People's Political Consultative Conference. Interestingly, their appointments came formally under the quota for Guangdong province, as Hong Kong remains under British jurisdiction until 1997 (*Hong Kong Economic Journal*, 5–18–1992).

Donations made by provincial natives residing in Hong Kong for massive charitable and educational undertakings almost parallel their economic investment there. Noted examples include the U.S. $30 million endowment to start a new university in his birthplace (Shantou) by tycoon Li Ka-shing and a new Olympic-standard sports compound in the Tianhe suburb of Guangzhou bankrolled by "patriotic" entrepreneur Henry Y.T. Fok. Indeed, there have been numerous clinics, schools, retirement homes, libraries, and recreational facilities as well as training programs and scholarship funds established throughout delta towns and villages out of the generosity of their Hong Kong kinsmen. And the list is growing fast. These business elites' warm gestures of devotion to their native places, following the "reopening of Guangdong" in the late 1970s, have done more than just renew long-broken contacts; they have helped to win recognition and goodwill as well as, through personal connections, access to the powers that can facilitate business deals and investment projects. By cultivating relationships and gaining trust with Guangdong cadres, Hong Kong investors hope to resolve the inevitable problems in their mainland business operations speedily, without lengthy and legalistic negotiations (Smart and Smart, 1991).

The response among Hong Kong's grassroots people to their "rediscovery of Guangdong" is no less intense, with sheer volume of direct personal contacts making up for their relatively more meager material contributions. Visits to the ancestral homeland by Hong Kong residents become so massive during public holidays as to create international traffic jams in land, sea, and air transport. During the Lunar New Year holidays since the mid-1980s, over 1 million (20 percent) of Hong Kong's population journey into the mainland, with the great majority going to Guangdong destinations for family reunions, bringing as gifts the latest in consumer electronics and fashions as well as other Western delicacies and fancy trinkets. Hong Kong now accounts for some 60 percent of tourist arrivals and 70 percent of tourist expenditures in China, and a major chunk of this traffic is to or through Guangdong. Mainland Chinese tourists visiting Hong Kong have also increased rapidly, mainly from Guangdong, with their trips paid for by relatives and friends in Hong Kong (Sung, 1990: 259).

The massive Hong Kong investment in the Special Economic Zones and other delta cities and towns has created a new kind of industrial process, with more than 3 million Guangdong workers currently employed in Hong Kong–owned and –managed enterprises in the delta, much larger than the total manufacturing work force in Hong Kong itself (about 0.63 million in September 1992) (Hong

Kong Government Information Services, 1993: 97). The change in the delta in outward processing activities for Hong Kong assumed significance after 1985. This new development was in part a response to the official policy of promoting joint ventures, which were given greater autonomy and preferential treatment. Aside from management expertise, these joint ventures brought with them overseas markets and access to the legal and financial infrastructure in Hong Kong, thereby allowing the investors to minimize their reliance on the rudimentary market institutions for doing business in Guangdong. The enormously improved standard of living among the people in Guangdong, stemming from employment in these ventures and expanded external trade and services, in turn creates strong demand for consumer goods and services, part of which can be supplied by or through Hong Kong. Thus, a new pattern of division of labor and intertwined cycles of demand and supply in manpower, goods, and services pull Hong Kong and Guangdong closer in economic integration.

Shadow of Discord

The transfer or relocation of manufacturing plants from Hong Kong into the delta hinterland, however, causes serious problems in unemployment and dislocation among Hong Kong's blue-collar people, of whom a sizable portion are recent migrants from Guangdong. There have been numerous incidents of Hong Kong workers going to work in the morning only to find the premises empty and the management flown, and substantial sums in unpaid salary after moving entire production facilities to the mainland where labor wages are at least 50 percent (in Shenzhen) less than in Hong Kong (*Wen Wei Pao*, 11–11–1991; *Ming Pao*, 12–16, 27–1991).

Such social and psychological side effects of intradelta economic realignment should not be underestimated, since it sometimes pits cousin against cousin over basic rice-bowl issues. In the same light, the Hong Kong government's decision, under pressure from local big business, to import laborers (mainly from Guangdong) has been vocally opposed by the local labor unions, including the leftist Hong Kong Federation of Trade Unions. Their opposition is based on the fact that imported labor would further depress employment opportunities for local Hong Kong workers, who have already suffered from the ill effects of production relocation into the mainland. Furthermore, the importation of mainland labor would lower wages and strain the already inadequate local housing and social infrastructure.[11] These issues also reflect the sometimes less than cordial personal rapport between the Hong Kong people and their "country cousins" across the border in everyday situations.

Proud of their own material wealth, high productivity, international knowledge, and urban sophistication, many Hong Kong residents tend to look down on their relatively less developed and coarser Guangdong neighbors. Many of these provincials, when they first arrived in the colony as migrants, frequently received rough treatment in low-paying menial jobs, and those who came as representatives of mainland business organizations were often taken in by deception and dubious deals. In the transition to 1997, however, "country cousins" and mainland cadres stationed in Hong Kong enjoy considerable counterleverage vis-à-vis their "city cousins," some of whom are trying to curry favor with the new masters who may not even be Cantonese-speaking (Vogel, 1989: 72). Generally speaking, the people of Guangdong are quite sympathetic toward their Hong Kong counterparts' struggle for greater freedom and democracy vis-à-vis Beijing since the mid-1980s, with a clear understanding that a freer and more prosperous Hong Kong would also mean more freedom from central control for Guangdong.

There are also instances of serious Guangdong–Hong Kong discord over specific issues. Sometimes major developments in Guangdong as dictated by the central government may not work to the interest of Hong Kong, thus affecting regional harmony. To a large extent, Beijing still dictates or supervises various major decisions in Guangdong. Despite the many layers of intimate exchanges and collaborations between Hong Kong and Guangdong, Hong Kong must conduct most of its negotiations (often through London) with Beijing, especially on matters relevant to the 1997 transition. Thus, neither the province nor the colony could fully decide its own relationship with its neighbor without reference to central authorities. A particularly notorious case in point is the construction of a nuclear power plant in Daya Bay less than 50 kilometers from settled areas of Hong Kong, where more than 2 million people in the summer of 1986 signed petitions against this Guangdong project.

Another problem causing concern in Hong Kong is lax border control in Guangdong, which enables Vietnamese boat people to make their way through the province to Hong Kong, thus exacerbating Hong Kong's already heavy problem of providing shelter and board to illegal immigrants from Indochina. At one point, the numbers were over 70,000 in the late 1980s and still more than 43,350 by the end of 1992 (Hong Kong Government Information Services, 1993: 386). Of course, Guangdong itself has been the prime source for the massive influx of illegal immigrants wishing to rejoin their families and relatives in the colony. In Guangdong the rise in prosperity "rubbed off" from Hong Kong has in turn attracted tidal waves of mobile elements from the poorer provinces in China's interior. Almost every spring since the late 1980s this "blind current" floods the streets of Guangzhou in search of employment.

Furthermore, bourgeois Hong Kong also means opportunities for crime, vice, corruption, smuggling, and black-marketeering for criminal elements from the province, which is a source of illegal firearms and illicit contacts for local Hong Kong criminals. During the first half of 1992, Hong Kong was besieged by a continuous string of violent robberies in which criminals with heavy firearms such as AK-47 automatic guns and grenades engaged the police in large-scale shoot-outs resulting in some casualties. Another disturbing development on the security front has been the extremely serious problem of high-seas smuggling (on board fast powerboats) of stolen cars (including official sedans used by the colony's top officials) from Hong Kong to the mainland, and of electronic appliances, drugs, and other contraband from the mainland to Hong Kong. A major topic in recent discussions between various Hong Kong official and private delegations and Guangdong–Beijing officialdom concerns the possibility of the People's Republic and Hong Kong joining their police and customs in efforts to combat these cross-border crime waves and smuggling epidemics (*Ta Kung Pao*, 5–17–1992; *South China Morning Post*, 6–17–1992). It seems that the underworld on both sides of the border has availed itself fully of the opportunities for collaborative profitmaking.

Hong Kong–Guangdong Toward 1997 and Beyond

The near magical socioeconomic transformation of Guangdong during the last decade not only sets it a world apart from the rest of China, but integrates it much more intimately with Hong Kong. This has profound implications for the future development of China as a whole. Indeed, the combined inputs from Hong Kong, overseas Chinese from Guangdong, and international sources have advanced Guangdong to the forefront of all China's provinces in profitability, technological adaptation, productivity, industrialization, marketization, and sociocultural modernity, even ahead of Shanghai, which, until the 1980s, was China's foremost economic center and pacesetter of popular culture. Guangdong now contributes 20 percent of its foreign currency earnings to the People's Republic of China's national coffer, rivaling Shanghai's yield (*Hong Kong Economic Journal*, 4–3–1992). There is a certain sense of historical justice behind contemporary Guangdong's Hong Kong–propelled economic takeoff and displacement of Shanghai as the harbinger of China's future.

An important part of the People's Republic's rationale in setting up these Special Economic Zones is to use Hong Kong as a real-life example whose experience in economic management and production technology could be transferred to and practiced in the zones, which might then serve as socialist China's laboratory in the adoption of such capitalistic inputs (Greenwood, 1990: 273). Some scholars suggest that lessons from Hong Kong's developmental experience should be useful for the major cities of China (Donnithorne, 1983: 282–310). However, the essence of the Hong Kong experience lies not just in the techniques of the market economy, but also in the rule of law safeguarding property rights and civil liberty, and especially in the limited role of the state, which sets Hong Kong far apart from the Special Economic Zones and the rest of Guangdong, in addition to the already sharp disparities in levels of material attainment, affluence, and productivity.

In many respects, the case of Hong Kong is unique. By the 1990s, Hong Kong's per capita income had surpassed that of its colonial master Britain, with more investment going from Hong Kong to Britain than the other way around

(Vogel, 1991: 68). The recent acquisition of the Midland Bank by the Hong Kong and Shanghai Banking Corporation demonstrates Hong Kong's global reach as the economically most successful Chinese community today. With less than 10 percent of the provincial total population (65 million) and only 0.5 percent of the province's landmass, Hong Kong's total gross domestic product (about U.S. $71.3 billion in 1990–91 and U.S. $95 billion in 1992–93) is larger than that of Guangdong (U.S. $44.2 billion in 1990) (Hong Kong Government Information Services, 1993: appendix 9: 419; *Hong Kong Economic Journal*, 10–12–1991: 2). Clearly there are lessons to be learned by the mainland from Hong Kong's success, despite the inevitable jealousy and uneasiness due to their sharp differences in levels of material well-being and ideological orientation.

Indeed, the highly internationalized economy, popular culture, social institutions, academic programs, and lifestyle of Hong Kong are having a far-reaching impact on Guangdong, which is often regarded as socioculturally avant-garde and even spiritually "polluted and contaminated"—deviating from orthodox Maoist standards. While this may help to bridge some of the deep gaps in value and culture among people of the delta under different jurisdictions, it only deepens the suspicions and invokes stronger displeasure from the central party/state.

The establishment of the People's Republic's first stock exchange in Shenzhen (with the only other one in Shanghai) and the construction in Canton of a horse-racing track for sport (and gambling) provide further evidence that Guangdong is fast becoming another Hong Kong. In fact, in his now famous and often repeated promise to maintain the "stability and prosperity" of Hong Kong, Deng Xiaoping assured the people of Hong Kong that they could keep on enjoying their present bourgeois lifestyle, specifically, "stock exchange speculation, horse racing, and sing song dancing" for fifty years without change after 1997. Thus, before Hong Kong assumes its Special Administrative Region (SAR) status under the sovereignty of the People's Republic, the breakthrough province of Guangdong seems to have already been "Hongkongized" to some extent.

With a population of close to 6 million, Hong Kong is the largest Cantonese-speaking city in the world (as compared with Guangzhou's 3.6 million) and the core center of an extensive international network of satellite overseas "Guangzhoutowns" (Cantontowns). Since the 1980s, the "1997 syndrome" has triggered a serious crisis of confidence in the future, causing this network to expand rapidly through massive emigration and "brain drain" from Hong Kong to Canada, the United States, Australia, New Zealand, Singapore, and Europe. In a sense, Hong Kong and its overseas "branches and extensions" collectively constitute a very powerful and dynamic international dimension buttressing Guangdong's place in China and in the world arena. As evident in President George Bush's decision to lift economic sanctions against the People's Republic of China and to continue its "most favored nation" (MFN) status, the U.S. government's recognition of Hong Kong and Guangdong as the most open, liberal, and developed region in China can even serve as a convenient official justification for global realpolitik consideration.

On October 5, 1992, the United States government passed special legislation to affirm its commitment to support Hong Kong's continuing status as a free society and open economy after 1997 by treating the Hong Kong Special Administrative Region separately from the People's Republic on such issues as import quotas, tariffs, visas and migration, cultural and educational exchanges, technology transfers, and air traffic rights. This "United States–Hong Kong Policy Act" can be interpreted as U.S. encouragement to further economic liberalization and internationalization of the south China region, with Hong Kong as the dynamic center for positive change. Beijing, however, viewed this as an unwelcome interference in Chinese domestic affairs and detrimental to friendly Sino-U.S. relations (*Hong Kong Economic Journal*, 4–6, 22, 23, 24–1992; *South China Morning Post*, 4–10–1992). Thus, in a far-fetched scenario, it may seem that an internationalized, capitalistic, and even blatantly pro-West Hong Kong has the potential of becoming a treacherous Trojan horse, capturing not just Guangdong through the pocketbook but endangering all China as well.

As reflected in the ongoing controversy over the construction of a new airport in Hong Kong, despite the September 1991 Sino-British Memorandum of Understanding, international confrontation between the two central governments in Beijing and London may obscure the genuine possibilities for creative regional cooperation in long-term large-scale development. In the field of civil aviation, Hong Kong would naturally be the site for the major new international airport, with Shenzhen's new Huangtian airport concentrating on regional and hinterland traffic and Macao's new airport serving as an auxiliary facility to both. In recalling the memories of the pre-1937 disagreements over Guangzhou's railway loopline construction, one can be confident that an eventual solution to such a Sino-British impasse would emerge to serve the true needs of Hong Kong, Guangdong, and above all, China. In the countdown toward colonial sunset, and in the aftermath of the Tiananmen Square Incident of June 4, 1989, realpolitik maneuvers between London and Beijing have led to deep suspicion and distrust, accentuating strains and stresses at the expense of the positive interdependent and collaborative features in the Hong Kong–Guangdong nexus. Despite all this, in the long run, what is good for the south China region should also be beneficial to the entire Chinese nation.

Indeed, the spectacular development of Guangdong catches the attention of the world and strengthens the call for further reform and opening within the People's Republic. Paramount leader Deng Xiaoping, who toured the Special Economic Zones in early 1992, praised Guangdong's prospect as Asia's fifth Little Dragon, putting it in a league with Hong Kong, South Korea, Taiwan, and Singapore. Deng not only urged the cadres to adopt from capitalism to transform China's economic zones into new "Hong Kongs," he also talked of extending the "fifty years' no change" in the social, legal, and economic systems of the Hong

Kong Special Administrative Region to a full one hundred years (*Newsweek*, 2–17–1992: 8). From the perspective of regional realpolitik, Hong Kong is definitely the greatest asset of Guangdong, which enjoys the highest growth rate and living standard in the People's Republic, and is a forum for crucial policy debates on further reform and opening. In this sense, Hong Kong and Guangdong, in their increasingly close and productive socioeconomic integration, have become an issue in national power politics with much at stake.

Riding on the tidal wave generated by the "Deng reformist cyclone," Guangdong in the early 1990s unveiled its new development plans, which include extensive tax incentives to foreign industries and new technologies as well as a massive 1.7 million-square-kilometer development zone along the Pearl River linking all the existing Special Economic Zones, export-processing districts, and technical innovation zones around metropolitan Guangzhou (*Ta Kung Pao*, 6–19–1992). Lu Ruihua, as deputy governor of Guangdong, openly predicted in Hong Kong, with continued efforts at a faster pace, the province's current economic reform will generate enough momentum to elevate Guangdong to the level of a "moderately developed" country and, within twenty years, turn it into Asia's fifth Little Dragon. He fully acknowledged the vital contribution of Hong Kong, which now accounts for 80 percent of Guangdong's investment from external sources while the colony also handles 80 percent of Guangdong's exports (*Hong Kong Economic Journal*, 4–3–1992).

Meanwhile, the provincial government corporation, Guangdong Enterprises (whose shares have been actively traded in Hong Kong's stock exchange), sought to raise HK $1.62 billion in the colony through new shares issued by its locally based subsidiary. The provincial government's Guangdong Development Bank also planned to acquire a local Hong Kong bank in order to utilize fully the colony's financing facilities (*Hong Kong Economic Journal*, 6–1–1992).

During his June 1992 visit to Hong Kong, Guangzhou mayor Li Ziliu announced several major undertakings involving Hong Kong interests: the construction of a seventy-nine-kilometer highway from Guangzhou to Conghua county in Guangdong; the listing and trading on the Hong Kong stock exchange of shares in two subsidiaries of the municipal development corporation; the building of a underground rail transit system in Guangzhou; and the floating of U.S. $1.1 billion worth of municipal bonds denominated in foreign currency. Hong Kong investors are expected to be the major financial facilitators and even underwriters of these new projects, which would enable Guangzhou to catch up with the other four Little Dragons in fifteen years (*Ta Kung Pao*, 6–19–1992; *Wah Kiu Yat Pao*, 6–19–1992).

From these frenzied economic activities, and the fact that almost every county and city government in Guangdong (and many other provinces) has set up an economic office in Hong Kong, the colony has become the most effective shortcut to get funding, technology, skills, and external market access for mainland development. However, more than a decade into the reform and opening of the

People's Republic, there is a significant change in the Beijing–Hong Kong economic relationship. Increasingly, Hong Kong and the mainland have made more use of each other to extend trade with other economies, while trading less with each other as producers and consumers. With greater marketization and industrialization, the mainland may eventually compete with Hong Kong in the international market (Hsueh and Woo, 1991: 89). As Guangdong grows in affluence and economic power, it also wants to change its relationship with Hong Kong from an apprenticeship to a genuine partnership. The provincial government even floated the concept of an "economic union" with Hong Kong as a priority in its current Five-Year Plan (*Far Eastern Economic Review*, 5–16–1991: 64–66). With the 1997 sovereignty transfer looming closer, Hong Kong and Guangdong's interdependence can only grow stronger, while China should have much to gain from their full integration as a cornerstone of its reform and opening.

This kind of sentiment is prevalent among those on the frontline. In an interview with an American journalist, Guangzhou mayor Li Ziliu spoke out with confidence and pride:

> When the sovereign barriers fall between China and Hong Kong in 1997, China will be one country with two systems. Though cooperation between Canton and Hong Kong will increase, they will be like two parallel but separate paths moving in the same direction, bringing parallel development to southern China.
>
> China's central planning has always allowed for natural regional differences. For example, Deng Xiaoping has given the four southern coastal provinces of Guangdong, Hainan, Fujian and Zhejiang—all in close proximity to Hong Kong—the authority to pursue economic development further than the rest of the country.
>
> The past decade has clearly demonstrated that the advantages of opening outweigh the disadvantages. Opening will not mean we will adopt the lifestyles or culture of the outside world. We understand that everything has two sides, but we are committed to the practice of selective development.
>
> Under central direction, our system has allowed Guangzhou to go one step ahead to lead other regions of China along the path to economic prosperity. (*National Political Quarterly*, 1992: 7)

Hopefully, after 1997, without its colonial baggage, imperialistic affront, and problems of alien jurisdiction, Hong Kong can become a net gain to Guangdong and to the entire Chinese nation. By then, a host of very exciting developmental possibilities involving Hong Kong–Guangdong can easily take shape. One blueprint envisions even fuller functional integration between Hong Kong and Guangzhou, as well as with Shenzhen and the other Special Economic Zones and cities in Guangdong, which together will form the nucleus of a new China Economic Community in the south. This community can be further expanded to include the three maritime provinces of Taiwan, Hainan, and Fujian as a highly productive and dynamic stretch of the Pacific Rim in the twenty-first century. In a more immediate context, some local analysts talk openly of the creation of a "Greater Hong Kong" economic power bloc encompassing Hong Kong, Guangzhou, Macao, and other delta points with a total population of 20 million (*Hong Kong Economic Journal*, 6–17–1992).

These scenarios suggest that the remarkable historical and contemporary Hong Kong–Guangdong linkages may have an even more promising future prospect, provided that they develop their collective potential more fully and creatively without undue external political dictates and ideological interference. In looking ahead, one may ask, as a lead article in *Newsweek* does, "Is Guangdong still a province of China, or has it become a colony of Hong Kong?" (*Newsweek*, Asia edition, 2–17–1992: 8–12). Any meaningful answer to this question will illuminate not just the changing nature of the Hong Kong–Guangdong relationship toward 1997 and beyond, but will help to relate the south China experiment to the current drive of the People's Republic of China toward modernization, reunification, and the "building of socialism with Chinese characteristics."

Notes

1. Hurd was the current British Foreign Secretary.
2. For the rise of Shanghai and its superior transport routes, see Murphey (1953), especially chapters 4 and 7. Also see Fairbank.
3. Augustin Heard, Jr., "Old China and New," Heard Collection, Baker Library, Harvard Business School, as quoted in Hao (1970: 49–50).
4. *Historical and Statistical Abstracts of the Colony of Hong Kong, 1841–1930*, Appendix, pp. 2–9. The 1931 figure comes from the *Census Report*, 1931, in *Session Papers* for the year 1931.
5. For the historical development of HKSB, see King (1988–89).
6. On the 1925–26 General Strike–Boycott, see Ho (1985), Motz (1972), Chan (1975: chap. 11), and Chesneaux (1968: chap. 12). The contemporary and post-1949 Chinese publications on this strike–boycott are analyzed in Chan (1981: 95–97).
7. There are several major academic studies on this important strike. The best overall account remains Glick (1969). Also see Chan (1975: chap. 10), and Chan, W.K. (1991: chap. 5).
8. Zhonggong Guangdong shengwei dangshi yanjiu weiyuanhui and Zhonggong Guangdong shengwei dangshi ziliao zhengji weiyuanhui, comps., Zhonggong Guangdong dangshi dashiji (Chronology of the Chinese Communist Party in Guangdong) (Guangzhou, 1984, internal circulation), section 3, same compilers, *Guangdong dangshi ziliao* (Sources on Guangdong Chinese Communist Party History) (Guangzhou: Guangdong renmin chubanshe, 1984), Vol. 3, pp. 25–80.
9. For instance, see the blocked-out wording and even blank spaces due to censorship in the news pages of *Huazi Ribao*, one of the oldest Chinese dailies in Hong Kong, during the 1937 to 1941 period; *Ta Kung Pao*, August 13, 14, 1938.
10. A recent case study of one aspect in this process is in Wong (1988).
11. *Gongyun Yuebao* (Labor Movement Monthly Report, Hong Kong: Labor Education Center); every issue since the late 1980s carries lengthy press clippings on this issue, for instance, No. 96 (March 1992), pp. 31–42.

References

Arnold, Julean (1926), *China: A Commercial and Industrial Handbook*, Washington, D.C.: Government Printing Office.
Barnett, A. Doak (1963), *China on the Eve of Communist Takeover*, New York: Prager.
Bridgeman, E.C., and S. Wells Williams, eds. (1848), *Chinese Repository*, Vol. 17.
Cameron, Nigel (1991), *An Illustrated History of Hong Kong*, Hong Kong: Oxford University Press.
Canton Advertising and Commission Agency (1971), "Foreword," in *Canton, Its Port, Industries and Trade*, Canton: Canton Advertising and Commission Agency, 1932; reprint, Taipei: Cheng Wen Publishing Company.
Chan, Lau Kit-ching (1990), *China, Britain and Hong Kong 1895–1945*, Hong Kong: Chinese University Press.
Chan, Ming K. (1975), "Labor and Empire: The Chinese Labor Movement in the Canton Delta, 1895–1927," Ph.D. diss., Stanford University.
——— (1981), *Historiography of the Chinese Labor Movement, 1895–1949*, Stanford: Hoover Institution Press.
——— (1990), "Labor vs Crown: Aspects of Society–State Interactions in the Hong Kong Labor Movement Before World War II," in *Between East and West: Aspects of Social and Political Developments in Hong Kong*, ed. Elizabeth Sinn, Hong Kong: Centre of Asian Studies, University of Hong Kong, pp. 132–46.
——— (1991), "Consequence of the Korean War and Truman's China Policy: A Forty Years' Retrospective from Hong Kong," paper presented at the Mid-West Conference in Asian Affairs, Iowa City, Iowa, September 1991.
———, ed. (1993), "Hong Kong in Sino-British Conflict: Mass Mobilization and the Crisis of Legitimacy, 1912–1926," in *Precarious Balance*, Armonk, NY: M.E. Sharpe, 1994.
Chan, W.K. (1991), *The Making of Hong Kong Society: Three Studies of Class Formation in Early Hong Kong*, Oxford: Oxford University Press.
Chen, Qizhi (1959), "Jiawu zhanqian Zhongguo nongcun shougong mianfang zhiye de bianhua huo ziben zhuyi de chengzhang" (The evolution of postwar Chinese rural household handicraft and cotton spinning occupations and the growth of capitalism), *Lishi yanjiu* (History Research) No. 2, pp. 17–38.
Cheng, Hao (1985) *Guangzhou kangshi: Jindai bufan* (History of Guangzhou Port: The modern era), Beijing: Haiyang chubanshe (Ocean Press).
Chesneaux, Jean (1968), *The Chinese Labor Movement, 1919–1927*, Stanford: Stanford University Press.
———, ed. (1972), "Secret Societies in China's Historical Evolution," in *Popular Movements and Secret Societies in China, 1840–1950*, Stanford: Stanford University Press, pp. 1–21.
Collins, Sir Charles (1952), *Public Administration in Hong Kong*, London: Royal Institute of International Affairs.
Cooke, George W. (1858), *China*, London: Routledge.
Dongjiang zongduishi Editorial Committee (1985), *Dongjiang zongduishi* (History of the East River Column), Guangzhou: Guangdong renmin chubanshe (Guangdong People's Press).
Donnithorne, Audrey (1983), "Hong Kong as an Economic Model for the Great Cities of China," in *China and Hong Kong: The Economic Nexus*, ed. A.J. Youngson, Hong Kong: Oxford University Press, pp. 282–310.
Endacott, G.B. (1958), *A History of Hong Kong*, London: Oxford University Press.
England, Joe, and John Rear (1981), *Industrial Relations and Law in Hong Kong*, Hong Kong: Oxford University Press.

Fairbank, John K. (1953), *Trade and Diplomacy on the China Coast*, Cambridge, MA: Harvard University Press.

——— (1978), "The Creation of the Treaty System," in *The Cambridge History of China*, Vol. 10, *Late Ch'ing, 1800–1911*,ed. John K. Fairbank, Part I, Cambridge: Cambridge University Press, pp. 213–63.

Far Eastern Economic Review, May 16, 1991.

Gangjiu duli daduishi Editorial Committee (1989), *Gangjiu duli daduishi* (History of the Hong Kong–Kowloon Independent Brigade), Guangzhou: Guangdong renmin chubanshe (Guangzhou People's Press).

Glick, Gary (1969), "The Chinese Seamen's Union and the Hong Kong Seamen's Strike of 1922," M.A. thesis, Columbia University.

Greenwood, John G. (1990), "The Integration of Hong Kong and China," in *Economic Reform in China: Problems and Perspectives*, ed. James A. Dorn and Wang Xi, Chicago: University of Chicago Press, pp. 271–76.

Guangdongsheng danganguan (Guangdong Provincial Archives), ed. (1984), *Dongjiang zongdui shiliao* (Historical sources on the East River Column), Guangzhou: Guangdong renmin chubanshe (Guangdong People's Press).

Guangzhou nianjian 1935 (Canton Yearbook 1935), Canton: Guangzhoushi shehuiju.

Guangzhoushi shehuiju (Guangzhou Municipal Bureau of Social Affairs) (1934), *Yewu baogao, 1934* (Report on Activities, 1934), Canton: Guangzhoushi shehuiju, Vol. 2.

Hao, Yen-p'ing (1970), *The Comprador in Nineteenth-Century China: Bridge Between East and West*, Cambridge, MA: Harvard University Press.

Ho, Virgil K.Y. (1985), "Hong Kong Government's Attitude to the Canton–Hong Kong Strike and Boycott of 1925–1926," M.S. thesis, Oxford University.

Hong Kong (1932), *Historical and Statistical Abstracts of the Colony of Hong Kong, 1841–1930*, Hong Kong: Government Printer.

——— (1938), *Report on the Social and Economic Progress of the People of the Colony of Hong Kong*, Hong Kong: Government Printer.

Hong Kong Census Report, 1891, 1897, 1901, 1906, 1911, 1921, 1931, Hong Kong: Hong Kong Government Printer.

Hong Kong Economic Journal, October 12, 1991; April 3, 1992; April 6, 22, 23, 24, 1992; May 18, 1992; June 1, 1992; June 17, 1992.

Hong Kong Government (1935), *Report of the Economic Commission, 1935*, Hong Kong: Government Printer.

——— (1936), *Administrative Report for the Year 1935*, Hong Kong: Government Printer.

——— (1939), *Report by the Labour Officer Mr. H.R. Butters on Labour Conditions in Hong Kong*, Hong Kong: Government Printer.

Hong Kong Government Information Services (1992), *Hong Kong 1992: A Review of 1991*, Hong Kong: Government Printer.

——— (1993), *Hong Kong 1993: A Review of 1992*, Hong Kong: Government Printer.

Hsueh, Tien-tung, and Tun-oy Woo (1992), "The Development of China's Foreign Trade and the Role of Hong Kong, 1979–1989," in *A Decade of Open-door Economic Development in China, 1979–1989*, ed, Edward K.Y. Chen and Toyojiro Maruya, Hong Kong: Centre of Asian Studies, University of Hong Kong, and Tokyo: Institute of Developing Economies.

Huazi Ribao, February 10, 1936.

Hurd, Douglas (1967), *The Arrow War: An Anglo-Chinese Confusion 1856–1860*, London: Collins.

Kaifang shidai (Open Times), (1989), No. 2, pp. 13–14.

King, Frank H.H. (1988–89), *The History of the Hongkong and Shanghai Banking Corporation*, 4 vols., Cambridge: Cambridge University Press.

Kungshang Ribao, June 19, 23, 1934.

Labor Education Center, comp., *Gongyun yuebao* (Labor Movement Monthly Report), Hong Kong: Labor Education Center.

Li, Gucheng (1992), "Xianggang conglai jiushi aiguo jidi" (Hong Kong has always been a patriotic base), *Dangdai* (Contemporary Magazine), February 15, 1992.

Liang, Dingfen, ed. (1874), *Panyuxian zuzhi* (Panyu County Gazette), Canton, Vol. 12.

Lie Dao, ed. (1958), *Ya Pien Chan Cheng Shih Lun Men Chuan Chi* (Collected essays on the history of the opium war), Peking: Joint Publisher.

Lin, Jinzhi (1989), *Jindai Huaqiao touzi guonei qiyeshi ziliao xuanji: Guangdong quan* (Source materials on the history of overseas Chinese investment in modern China: Guangdong), Fuzhou: Fujian renmin chubanshe (Fujian People's Press).

Liu, F.F. (1962), *A Military History of Modern China*, Princeton: Princeton University Press.

Ming Pao, December 16, 27, 1991.

Morse, Hosea Ballou (1910), *The International Relations of the Chinese Empire, Vol. I*, London: Longmans, Green.

Motz, Earl (1972), "Great Britain, Hong Kong, and Canton: The Canton–Hong Kong Strike and Boycott of 1925–26," Ph.D. diss., Michigan State University.

Murphey, Rhoads (1953), *Shanghai: Key to Modern China*, Cambridge, MA: Harvard University Press.

——— (1977), *The Outsiders: The Western Experience in India and China*, Ann Arbor: University of Michigan Press.

National Political Quarterly, 1992.

Newsweek, February 17, 1992.

Newsweek (Asia edition), February 17, 1992.

Nolde, John (1960), "The False Edict of 1849," *Journal of Asian Studies*, Vol. 20, No. 3, pp. 299–315.

Peng, Zeyi, ed. (1957), *Zhongguo jindai shougongye shi ziliao, 1840–1949* (Source materials on the history of modern Chinese handicraft industry), Beijing: Zhonghua shuju (Chinese Press).

Polachek, James M. (1992), *The Inner Opium War*, Cambridge, MA: Harvard University Press.

Rabushka, Alvin (1973), *The Changing Face of Hong Kong: New Departures in Public Policy*, Stanford: Hoover Institution Press.

Remer, C.F. (1933), *Foreign Investment in China*, New York: Macmillan.

Renmin Ribao (People's Daily), July 21, 1989.

Shi, Cheng (1879), *Guangzhou fuzhi* (Canton County Gazette), Canton.

Smart, Josephine, and Alan Smart (1991), "Personal Relations and Divergent Economies: A Case Study of Hong Kong Investment in South China," *International Journal of Urban and Regional Research*, Vol. 15, No. 2, pp. 216–33.

South China Morning Post, April 10, 1992; June 17, 1992.

Sun Yat-sen (1920), *The International Development of China*, Shanghai: Commercial Press.

Sung, Yun-wing (1990), "The China–Hong Kong Connection," in *Economic Reform in China: Problems and Perspectives*, ed. James A. Dorn and Wang Xi, Chicago: University of Chicago Press, pp. 255–66.

Szczepanik, Edward (1958), *The Economic Growth of Hong Kong*, London: Oxford University Press.

Ta Kung Pao, May 17, 1992; June 19, 1992.

Tang, James T.H. (1993), "World War to Cold War: Hong Kong's Future and Anglo-Chinese Interactions, 1941–1955," in *Precarious Balance*, ed. Ming K. Chan, Armonk, NY: M.E. Sharpe, 1994.

Tom, C.F.J. (1957), *The Entrepôt Trade and the Monetary Standards of Hong Kong, 1842–1941*, Chicago: University of Chicago Press.

Tsai, Jung-fang (1984), "The 1884 Hong Kong Insurrection: Anti-Imperialist Popular Protest During the Sino-French War," *Bulletin of Concerned Asian Scholars*, Vol. 16, No. 1, pp. 2–14.

Vogel, Ezra F. (1969), *Canton under Communism: Programs and Politics in a Provincial Capital, 1949–1968*, Cambridge, MA: Harvard University Press.

———— (1989), *One Step Ahead in China: Guangdong under Reform*, Cambridge, MA: Harvard University Press.

———— (1991), *The Four Little Dragons: The Spread of Industrialization in East Asia*, Cambridge, MA: Harvard University Press.

Wah Kiu Yat Pao, June 19, 1992.

Wakeman, Frederic, Jr. (1965), *Strangers at the Gate: Social Disorder in South China, 1839–1861*, Berkeley: University of California Press.

———— (1978), "The Canton Trade and the Opium War," in *The Cambridge History of China*, Vol. 10, *Late Ch'ing, 1800–1911*, Part I, ed. John K. Fairbank, Cambridge: Cambridge University Press, pp. 163–212.

Wen Wei Pao, November 11, 1991.

Wesley-Smith, Peter (1980), *Unequal Treaty 1898–1997: China, Great Britain and Hong Kong's New Territories*, Hong Kong: Oxford University Press.

Wong, S.L. (1988), *Emigrant Entrepreneurs: Shanghai Industrialists in Hong Kong*, Hong Kong: Oxford University Press.

Xia, Xie (1865), *Zhongxi jishi* (Chronicle of Sino-Western Affairs), (reprinted in Taipei: Wen Hai Publisher, 1967), Vol. 13, pp. 8–9.

Yan, Zhongping (1955), *Zhongguo mianfangzhi shigao, 1889–1937* (Draft history of Chinese cotton textile industry, 1889–1937), Beijing: Kexue chubanshe (Science Press).

Zhonggong Guangdong shengwei dangshi yanjiu weiyuanhui, and Zhonggong Guangdong shengwei dangshi ziliao zhengji weiyuanhui (Guangdong Provincial Chinese Communist Party Committee: Party Affairs Subcommittee and Guangdong Provincial Chinese Communist Party Committee: Information Collection Subcommittee), comps. (1984a), *Guangdong dangshi ziliao* (Sources on Guangdong Chinese Communist Party history), Guangzhou: Guangdong renmin chubanshe (Guangdong People's Press).

———— (1984b), *Zhonggong Guangdong dangshi dashiji* (Chronology of the Chinese Communist Party in Guangdong), Guangzhou, internal circulation, section 3.

3

Continuity and Transformation in the Pearl River Delta: Hong Kong's Impact on Its Hinterland

Graham E. Johnson

In 1997 Hong Kong's political status will change with the resumption of Chinese sovereignty over the territory and a century and a half of British colonial control will come to a formal end. In the late twentieth century, Hong Kong has had a distinctive and major role in the global economy, which, in the decade since reform in China began in 1979, has become central to China's incorporation into the world economic system. One hundred fifty years of British administration in Hong Kong has had a profound impact on the territory. It has created a distinctive social system that cannot readily and expeditiously be incorporated into the existing economic, political, and social structures in China itself. Negotiations between the governments of China and Britain therefore attempted to create a legal and political structure for the Hong Kong region ("the Basic Law") to take into account Hong Kong's historical development and the role that it has come to occupy in China's own economic future.[1]

This chapter will outline some of the features that have made Hong Kong distinctive, especially over the past forty years. It will describe how Hong Kong's fractured links with its hinterland in the period before 1979 had a pronounced effect on its own economic performance. It will further indicate that the links have changed significantly since the period of Economic Reform began in China in 1979 and since the signing of the Anglo-Chinese agreement on the future of the territory. It will discuss some of the issues arising from the connections between Hong Kong and its hinterland through an examination of five localities in the Pearl River Delta. I will indicate that where Hong Kong connections are intense, there has been major structural change as production systems are incorporated into the global economy. The entrepreneurial activities with Hong Kong partners are a key to economic transformation. Where partnership is lacking, structural change is muted. In parts of Hong Kong's hinterland where there are extensive links with overseas Chinese, in contrast to "compatriots" (*tongbao*) in Hong Kong, while the impact of those connections is substantial, especially for the social infrastructure, they have not resulted in fundamental economic restructuring.

Bond between Hong Kong and Pearl River Delta: Responding to Chinese Development Strategies

Hong Kong was created as a consequence of the expansion of European capitalism into East Asia in the mid-nineteenth century, when China's door was forcibly opened to economic processes that it was incapable of incorporating without massive economic, political, and social disruption. China reluctantly became a part of the "world system" and Hong Kong played a key role in Chinese economic history in the century that followed, along with a group of "treaty ports" that were created in the wake of the Anglo-Chinese conflict that ceded part of Hong Kong ("in perpetuity") to the British.[2]

British procedures were dominant in the treaty ports along the China coast and especially in Shanghai, Hong Kong's illustrious twin on the Yangzi, until World War II fundamentally affected global economic and political forces. The British dominated China's two great commercial deltas from the mid-nineteenth century. British merchants (and perhaps other merchants of European origin) found commercial dealings, enforceable in British courts, a more reliable alternative to the older arrangements of the trading season in Guangzhou. Previously, they were subject to the whim of Chinese government officials, and had to make an enforced sojourn to Portuguese Macao, whose government was at best indifferent to the needs of the China traders.

The first phase of Hong Kong's history effectively ended in 1941, the centennial of its creation as a British possession, when it came under Japanese occupation. The occupation of Hong Kong was severe in its impact.[3] In 1945, when it ended, Hong Kong's role in the world economy began to undergo a major transformation. Structural changes in the global economy created the opportunity for an economic transformation in Hong Kong that could scarcely have been imagined at the moment of its liberation from Japanese occupation.

The immediate consequence of civil war in China and the formation of the People's Republic of China was the flight of capital and entrepreneurial skill to Hong Kong. There was also a massive out-migration of people from throughout China, but especially from its Pearl River Delta hinterland. Chinese capital and entrepreneurial skill, ample supplies of cheap and hardworking labor, and an interventionist governmental structure were elements that figured in the creation of the economic system that emerged in the 1950s and the 1960s.

From the early 1950s China moved in a distinctive "state-socialist" direction, and for a complex of reasons it was significantly insulated from the global economy for the next thirty years. As a consequence, Hong Kong's relationship to its hinterland changed. Vogel has suggested that Hong Kong "lost" its hinterland in 1950 after the formation of the People's Republic of China (Vogel, 1989: 44–47).

In late 1978, with Deng Xiaoping firmly in control of the Chinese state, massive tampering with the machinery of economic control that had been in place since the 1950s was attempted. A new Open-door Policy was created. Unlike that of the nineteenth century, the new Open-door Policy was created on China's terms and was not forced by aggressive European commercial intentions. A cautious opening to the forces of the market and the global economy occurred. In the search for a recipe for economic success, the coastal regions of south and southeast China were given a degree of autonomy to develop innovative responses to China's perceived crisis, which was seen, in large part, as a failure to improve the material well-being of the population. Part of the effort was political and resulted in the negotiations to resume sovereignty over Hong Kong and Macao (and also likely the integration of Taiwan, China's "other" Newly Industrializing Economy [NIE], as a long-term goal).

The economic transformations as a consequence of policy initiatives since 1979 have been substantial in all the coastal provinces of China (Yang, 1991: 42–64). They have been especially marked in Guangdong, which has become firmly incorporated into the global economy and has assumed a particular role in the new international division of labor (Thorns, 1989: 68–101).

Major rural economic change has occurred as a consequence of incorporation into the world system. There has been a shift from a relatively insulated, state-dominated economic system to one that is open to outside influences, and in which rural households and rural communities have assumed, or reassumed, control over production activities.

Economic opportunity in nonagricultural production has been expanded throughout rural China with major consequences for peasant households, who can deploy their members into an array of new economic activities. Major changes in China's rural development policies, and their impact in a variety of regional contexts since 1979, have been extensively documented.[4] The Pearl River Delta has been favorably located to take advantage of new directions in policy.

Guangdong, located strategically along China's south coast, is a large province of substantial geographic, economic, and cultural diversity. Its economic core is the Pearl River Delta with Guangzhou as its regional center. The delta also contains Hong Kong and Macao and two of the three Special Economic Zones (SEZs) that were located in Guangdong after the promulgation of the Open-door Policies in 1979. Outside the delta, the province is mountainous and therefore relatively poor, with inadequate communications and a pronounced linguistic diversity.

Aggregate statistics for Guangdong province, although impressive, tend to mask the performance of the delta which, since early 1985, has been designated an "Open Economic Region" (*Jingji kaifang qu*).[5] The delta occupies a commanding position in the Guangdong provincial economy. It has built on its advantageous location, closely proximate to Hong Kong and, through it, to the world economy. Although it was unable to take full advantage of its long tradition of commercialized production before 1978, nonetheless it was the major provincial producer of cash crops such as fish, sugarcane, silk cocoons, fruit, and vegetables. In the wake of rural reform, its agricultural sector has flourished under the newly liberalized policies. While sericulture in the central delta has declined, the production of fish, fruit, and vegetables has expanded dramatically, destined for both the domestic market as well as Hong Kong/Macao and beyond.

The major transformation in the rural sector, however, has not been in agriculture. Rapid economic growth has occurred as the rural sector has shifted to an emphasis on nonagricultural production. Entrepreneurial energies have been released in a flurry of industrial growth. This was concentrated, initially, in certain regions of the delta. The central delta from Guangzhou south to Macao and the Zhuhai Special Economic Zone, and the eastern corridor to Hong Kong and the rapidly expanding Shenzhen area, were the major areas of economic activity at the outset of the reform period. These developments were possible partly because national policy allowed the province considerable autonomy as it pursued new ways to seek capital and retain foreign exchange earnings. The central and eastern Pearl River Delta was also able to mobilize its extensive links with its kinsmen and fellow countrymen living in Hong Kong and Macao. The eastern delta renewed links with its kinsmen and fellow countrymen both in Hong Kong and overseas, especially in North America.

The entire delta has long been an area of out-migration. From the mid-nineteenth century large numbers of émigrés from south and southeast China met some of the developmental needs of the burgeoning global economy and worked as unskilled laborers in the Americas, southern Africa, and Southeast Asia. The western reaches of the delta are the ancestral homeland of the great majority of Americans and Canadians of Chinese origin.

In the 1980s, the entrepreneurial skills and capital of these émigrés were actively sought by their Guangdong kinsmen and fellow countrymen. Kinship connections and local village association loyalties have become a central part of local development initiatives. In the process the delta has become firmly linked to the global economy through its Hong Kong connections. It has thus begun to share with other parts of East and Southeast Asia some of the developmental characteristics that McGee has described as the "desakota process" in which an intense mixture of agricultural and nonagricultural activities stretch along linear corridors between large city cores. The process, McGee indicates, typically oc-

Table 3.1

Pearl River Delta Region: 1990

	Open Economic Region*	Guangzhou (Urban Area)	Zhenzhen SEZ	Zhuhai SEZ	Total	Provincial Per- centage
Population**	16.56	3.94	0.88	0.33	21.71	34.8
Value						
(billion yuan)	69.19	26.02	14.21	3.72	113.14	68.5
Agriculture	7.55	0.41	0.04	0.08	8.08	36.4
Industry	61.63	25.62	14.17	3.64	105.06	73.5
Exports (billion						
U.S. dollars)	3.39	1.23	2.95	0.46	8.13	77.4
Agricultural/ Industrial Output Value (per capita)						
(yuan)	4,178	6,604	16,148	11,272	5,211	2,643

Sources: Guangdong tongji nianjian, 1991, 1991: pp. 40–47. Guangdongsheng Xian (Qu) Guomin Jingji Tongji Ziliao 1980–1990, 1991.

*The Pearl River Delta Open Economic Region is composed of 28 *xian* and municipalities and excludes the "urban" area of Guangzhou and the Shenzhen and Zhuhai Special Economic Zones. Guangzhou's dependent *xian* (Panyu, Zengcheng, Huaxian, and Conghua), as well as Baoan (Shenzhen) and Daomen (Zhuhai), the dependant *xian* of Shenzhen and Zhuhai, are included in the Open Economic Region.
**Includes temporary population without official residence permit.

curs in regions characterized by high population densities that were formerly dominated by wet rice agriculture (McGee, 1989: 93–108; McGee, 1991: 3–26; Johnson, 1992: 185–220). The Pearl River Delta constitutes one of these "desakota" regions (see Table 3.1).

The dramatic growth rates that the Hong Kong economy began to enjoy in the 1980s were due to a renewed relationship with China and especially its Guangdong hinterland. As one consequence, substantial investable funds were generated. Hong Kong entrepreneurs became truly global in their activities and, like other entrepreneurs in East Asia, began to have an impact on economies where they had hitherto been little involved.

Hong Kong entrepreneurs were, however, culturally most comfortable in China and most familiar with their largely Cantonese-speaking hinterland in the Pearl River Delta. While the internal character of Hong Kong's economy changed, Hong Kong entrepreneurs did not relinquish control over profitable production lines—the output from which was in great demand in the affluent societies of the First World. During the 1980s, the conditions of production changed for Hong Kong and rising wage rates compromised the colony's ability to efficiently produce commodities that demanded large amounts of labor. Hong Kong entrepreneurs increasingly shifted certain product lines out of Hong Kong. Some went to Malaysia, Thailand, and other parts of Southeast Asia. A few went to Africa, but most went to China. Some were relocated to the new Shenzhen Special Economic Zone (which was built in Hong Kong's image and resembled the new towns of the Hong Kong New Territories), but most went beyond the zone to the Pearl River Delta itself. Hong Kong entrepreneurs became central to the economic well-being of localities within its hinterland, to which they were often connected by ties of kinship and village association sentiment.

The Pearl River Delta: Five Examples

In a general fashion, I have asserted that since 1979 and the beginnings of reform in China, Hong Kong has exerted a significant economic presence on its hinterland and has assisted in a major way in its transformation. Hong Kong entrepreneurs, in concert with Guangdong officials at various administrative levels, have taken full advantage of the flexibility implicit in the reform measures to begin a process that has fundamentally changed the economy of the Pearl River Delta and by the early 1990s expanded the area of economic transformation beyond the physical limits of the delta proper. The second part of this chapter moves the argument from the general to the specific. I will describe some of the effects of development in rural regions of the Pearl River Delta hinterland since the reforms began. Building on work begun in the 1970s (Johnson and Johnson, 1976), I have looked at developments in five locations across the delta (see Map 3.1).

I chose the locations in the 1970s in different policy circumstances when the links between Hong Kong and its hinterland were still strained and tenuous. Each was administratively a commune and each had some distinguishing characteristics. Duanfen, located in Taishan *xian* in the western delta, is a center of out-migration to North America. Leliu in Shunde *xian*, in the central delta, had a distinctive cash-crop economy and possessed some unique cultural characteristics.[6] Luogang and Renhe are close to Guangzhou, located in Baiyun *qu* (formerly the "Suburban District"). Luogang is mountainous but long famous for its fruit production. Renhe, to the north, a grain specialist area, was known for its radical political character in the Cultural Revolution, when it was called Dongfeng (East Wind) commune, and coincidentally was a major source of migration to Canada. Fucheng, in Dongguan *shi* (formerly, *xian*), is a major source of migrants to Hong Kong, where I worked in the 1960s.[7]

The economies of the five units and the villages that compose them have changed substantially since reform got under way in 1979.[8] One index of the change and the response to the reform initiatives is substantial growth in per capita income (see Table 3.2 on page 71).

The opportunities for economic transformation have been a consequence of internal factors, of which the indigenous economy and leadership are key, and of

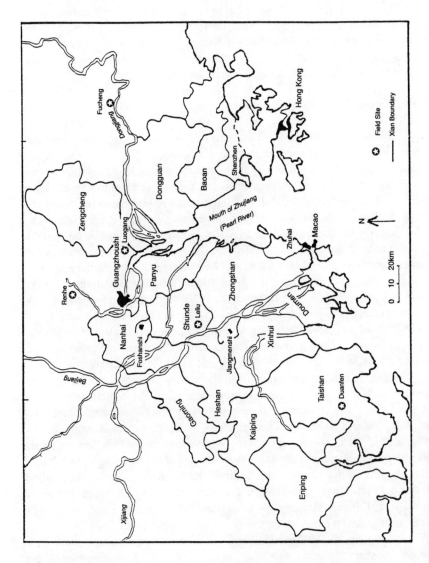

Map 3.1. Field Sites on the Pearl River Delta.

Table 3.2

Per Capita Income of Selected Production Units in the Pearl River Delta: 1979–1990 (yuan)

Unit	1979	1984	1990	Annual Growth (%)
Duanfen	90	494	1,235	127.2
Leliu	180	701	1,857	93.2
Luogang	119	961	2,142	170.0
Renhe	157	448	1,800	104.7
Fucheng	352	865	1,913	44.3

Source: Interviews, 1979–91.

location. Since the reform initiatives got under way linkages with émigrés in Hong Kong or Macao or in overseas Chinese communities have become of increasing importance.

Of the five units, Duanfen, located in southern Taishan, has benefited the least from the opportunities of the reform period. It is distant from Guangzhou and Hong Kong and its prospects for growth and development were, until recently, hampered by inadequate communications. As an overseas Chinese area it suffered disabilities from almost the moment of its incorporation into the People's Republic of China. The overseas connections were political liabilities for much of the three decades from 1949 to 1979, especially during the period of the Cultural Revolution. It remained a subsistence economy with a heavy dependence on remittances from abroad. Annual per capita income in the middle 1970s was below 100 yuan.

After 1979 the overseas links were viewed in a positive light and many of the harsh political judgments that had colored local policy options were reversed. Duanfen has remained an agricultural economy firmly based on grain production but its economic base has diversified. Cash crops, such as fruit and sugarcane, and the raising of poultry have become widespread. Duanfen has prospered since reform but its incorporation into the world system has not occurred on the same scale as other units in central and eastern portions of the Pearl River Delta. It is partly a question of its relatively remote location, but also a question of the particular nature of its non–Hong Kong/Macao overseas links.

Leliu lies in Shunde in the central region of the delta. It enjoyed a distinctive economy based on fish farming, sugarcane, and silk-worm cultivation. There are no rice paddies in Leliu and its commercialized (and export-oriented) agricultural production allowed its peasant cultivators to enjoy relative prosperity even before the reform period. It was an area of extensive out-migration to Hong Kong before 1949 and links were revitalized with its emigrants in the wake of reform. A young and dynamic leadership sought to involve the entrepreneurial energies of Hong Kong in its economic transformation. Its agricultural economy, especially fish farming, has remained buoyant, although sericulture has been eliminated as a consequence of pollution and the low prices for cocoons. Its agriculture has been overwhelmed by dramatic growth in nonagricultural production. The market towns of Shunde have become the centers of light industrial production, which has allowed its households to enjoy some of the highest incomes in rural China.

Luogang is located off the main highway that links Guangzhou to eastern Guangdong at the eastern edge of Baiyun *qu* of Guangzhou municipality.[9] Formerly part of Panyu *xian*, it has a long history of specialization in fruit production. Changes in pricing policies and release from the highly bureaucratic control of the fruit market allowed its peasant cultivators to increase household income substantially throughout much of the 1980s. The region did not have a history of extensive out-migration and the local economy saw little growth in its small-enterprise sector at the outset of the reform period. Its villages remained firmly agricultural and their proximity to major markets (especially Guangzhou) allowed them to take full advantage of new commercial opportunities and to profit from higher prices paid to fruit growers. In the early stages of reform, fruit specialists were extensively recruited throughout the delta to assist other localities in diversifying their grain-based economies to move into highly profitable citrus production, in which the Luogang region had a historic specialization. Grain production also remained important throughout the 1980s. Luogang's proximity to centers of labor demand (especially in construction) allowed villagers to seek employment opportunities outside agriculture. At the end of the 1980s, newly established citrus groves came into production and fruit prices tumbled. The construction boom experienced a downturn and Pearl River Delta labor suffered competition from the enormous influx of outsider migrants. Luogang natives returned to their villages and the local cadres looked to economic diversification as the mechanism to continue their economic success. The enterprise sector began to grow and an export orientation with the Hong Kong connection became central to local success.

Renhe is located at the northern edge of Baiyun *qu*. It has a large and dense population that was mostly engaged in grain production and enjoyed a good deal of success during the "grain-first" policies of the 1970s. It lies beyond the zone of intense vegetable cultivation that has developed to meet the needs of the Guangzhou market and it has relatively little involvement in cash cropping, although it has had some success in raising poultry. Its out-migration was substantial in the past and there are significant numbers of its natives overseas and in Hong Kong. Its industrial capacity at the *zhen*, village, and individual levels has grown since the reform period, often in cooperation with Hong Kong entrepreneurial interests. Yet, the degree of Renhe's incorporation into the broader economy of the delta is less extensive than that of other units in the central delta or units closer to Guangzhou or Hong Kong. The capacity of the local economy to absorb surplus labor is limited. The large numbers of men, especially those under forty years of age, have left the area to seek work in Guangzhou and elsewhere in the delta, leaving the management of the agricultural economy to women and older men and, at the outset of the 1990s, to nonprovincial outsiders due to substantial subcontracting of the land.

Fucheng extends in a wedge to the south and east from Dongguan city. The economic growth of Dongguan since reform got under way has been remarkable. Fucheng has fully shared in the transformation of the entire *shi*.[10] Dongguan has benefited from its close proximity to the Shenzhen Special Economic Zone and Hong Kong. It has fully utilized the investment resources and skills of its émigrés in Hong Kong, who have provided much of the capital for an extensive array of enterprises, both industrial and agricultural, that have transformed the rural economy of Dongguan.

Fucheng has more than four hundred enterprises whose foreign-exchange earnings in 1990 were over HK $100 million. They include plastics, garment manufacture, electronics, and toys, virtually all destined for the world market as subsidiaries of Hong Kong–based manufacturers. They also include large shipments of vegetables for the Hong Kong market and fruit for both Hong Kong and domestic markets throughout China.

The five units are broadly representative of the Pearl River Delta. They extend across the delta representing differing production regimes that are historically influenced but also a consequence of different leadership strategies and different developmental possibilities in the wake of reform. The villages within the five units and their constituent households have responded creatively to the new possibilities. I will first outline the consequences for the central and eastern delta (what Vogel calls "the inner delta"; Vogel, 1989: 56–62), and will then make some comments on developments in the western reaches of the delta, in which connections with overseas Chinese, rather than with Hong Kong, are dominant.

The reform process has turned on "openness," and the external connections that localities possess are often based on kinship. The presence or absence of kinsmen outside of the village and the broad communities that villages form have been decisive for the development process. Kinsmen have become sources of investment and entrepreneurial skill. Yet it is important to distinguish between the effects of kinsmen who are resident in Hong Kong or Macao and those who are overseas Chinese. Unquestionably, the areas in the western delta have benefited in particular ways from extensive overseas Chinese linkages. The substantial (and growing) funds that have flowed into the region from North America and elsewhere (including Hong Kong) have been channeled into projects such as roads, bridges, and public buildings, of which schools and hospitals are most common. In other parts of the delta, investment funds and entrepreneurial energies derived from Hong Kong (and to a lesser degree from Macao), by contrast, have been directed toward the creation of productive enterprises and have had a major and direct effect on local systems of production.

The consequences for economic change in the eastern and central delta, where the presence of Hong Kong– and Macao-based kinsmen is proportionally large, can be readily contrasted with those in the western delta, where the proportion of overseas Chinese kinsmen and overseas Chinese households is larger. Fundamental economic change, as a consequence of the entrepreneurial activities of Hong Kong–based kinsmen, has been greater in the central and eastern delta. The greater the degree of incorporation into the global economy, the greater the effect on the local economy. The extent of change in the Hong Kong hinterland varies from locality to locality, depending on the extent and nature of the émigré involvement in the local economy. For some localities there are no connections at all and fundamental structural change is therefore largely absent. Links are crucial for new economic opportunities and the most critical of them are those that stem from Hong Kong. Localities have to express a willingness to mobilize those links and not all have the capacity or the desire to engage in the process of creating new forms.

The Central and Eastern Delta: The Hong Kong Connection

The central and eastern regions of the Pearl River Delta have been the most advantageously located to exploit the new policy options. The region was historically highly commercialized and open to a variety of external linkages. The assumptions of development policy for much of the thirty years after 1949 compromised these connections and local economies turned inward under intense pressure from the Chinese state.[11] Peasant resistance was substantial but maneuverability was highly constrained.[12] Possibilities for economic innovation changed after 1979.

The large multi-surname village of Wantong in Fucheng, Dongguan, which had been a brigade during the commune period, reacted quickly to the changed circumstances after 1979. The village had responded well to collectivization and a dynamic and highly respected leadership had organized major land reclamation during the Great Leap Forward, which resulted in high grain yields and relatively high per capita incomes even before 1979. Its party secretary was transferred to the commune level shortly before the reforms got under way. Working closely with a *xian* leadership committed to exploring new economic relationships, he argued for mobilization of capital and entrepreneurial resources among the substantial number of local émigrés in Hong Kong, with considerable success. His area was helped by its proximity to the growing Shenzhen Special Economic Zone and the dramatic improvement in road communications with Hong Kong.

The consequences of local economic transformation have been major. There has been little movement of local labor away from Fucheng as the village economies have intensified.[13] Only 34 percent of the indigenous labor force is engaged strictly in household-managed agricultural production. The rest works in enterprises, the bulk of which are run by the village as collective entities. There is no single lineage base to the village (as in neighboring Zengbu)[14] but an intense local loyalty exists. It is a loyalty that was furthered during the period of intense agricultural collectivism in the 1960s and 1970s. It has been heightened with the extensive involvement of Hong Kong–based émigrés in the village economy throughout the 1980s and into the 1990s. The links to the global economy are direct. Much of the production of the village-run enterprises, such as garments and plastics, is destined for Hong Kong and for reexport to Europe and North America. All the former brigades in Fucheng have established industrial estates with new plant and have built dormitory facilities for the largely immigrant work force at a cost far below that which prevails in Hong Kong. The physical dispersion of much of the Hong Kong manufacturing sector to the Pearl River Delta hinterland has been to units of which Fucheng, and the villages that comprise it, is a typical example.[15]

Not all the village-run enterprises in Wantong have been industrial. Vegetables were cultivated year-round for the Hong Kong market by an enterprise that worked jointly with a Hong Kong–based entrepreneur who left the village shortly after 1949. The enterprise employed wage workers, the bulk of whom were villagers. Its operations were much reduced after 1990 as vegetable production in Baoan, attached to Shenzhen municipality, much closer to Hong Kong, became more cost-efficient and as the industrial base of Wantong further expanded with its industrial estate. The village has also moved into tourism in a major way. In concert with another Hong Kong–based native, it has created a "holiday village," complete with villas, a handsome restaurant, and a variety of leisure activities, with the Hong Kong market and the leisure needs of Hong Kong residents clearly in mind. The local economy is thus closely integrated with the world system through Hong Kong, and it has become acutely aware of new consumption patterns in affluent Hong Kong.

Wantong fully demonstrates the potential of Hong Kong connections. By contrast, the fruit-growing village of Tsimkong (in Luogang) has prospered in the reform period but not as a consequence of global incorporation through Hong Kong links. Its major comparative advantage is a long history of growing fruit (oranges, lichee, and pineapple). Reform of the price system and the resurgence of private marketing has caused rapid increases in household income. Economic strategy is less elaborate than in Wantong. It involves maximum allocation of household labor in highly commercialized agricultural production. There is little out-migration and a virtual absence of kin abroad or in Hong Kong or Macao. The Tsimkong economy has therefore responded largely to changes in the domestic market but its opportunities have grown as a consequence of increases in disposable income throughout the region, which are in large measure a consequence of Hong Kong–inspired economic activities. Some of Tsimkong's fruit production, of lichees in particular, is destined for Hong Kong.

At the end of the 1980s, as I noted, the domestic market changed and was no longer as buoyant for the villages of Luogang as it had been for much of the decade. Villagers returned from their temporary sojourns as fruit-growing specialists or as construction workers. Cadres at various levels sought to augment the enterprise base. At the *zhen* level, Hong Kong connections were sought and garment factories have been established. A large and modern pharmaceutical plant has been established, using local sugarcane to produce the base for Chinese herbal "tonics," largely for export. At the village level, two enterprises are notable. One raises a highly desirable black-skinned chicken for export to the markets of Hong Kong and Southeast Asia. It is a joint enterprise with Hong Kong–based interests and a provincial-level marketing organization, located in Guangzhou. A second, employing skilled craftsmen from Zhejiang, manufactures Chinese-style ebony and rosewood furniture, primarily for export to Hong Kong, Taiwan, and overseas Chinese areas. This, once again, represents a geographical dispersion of an economic activity, once well represented in Hong Kong, that has become increasingly difficult to maintain there due to production-cost increases. Traditional Chinese furniture is in high demand in affluent Hong Kong and Taiwan. Collectively organized village enterprises in cooperation with Hong Kong entrepreneurs are beginning to have an impact even in a locality that for much of the 1980s profited only indirectly from the increasing Hong Kong influence over its hinterland. Progress in local economies in the delta increasingly requires access to the Hong Kong market and an involvement with Hong Kong–based entrepreneurial interests.

The Central and Eastern Delta: Lack of Connection

Two villages, although in the eastern and central delta, lack extensive penetration by Hong Kong interests for slightly different reasons, and the consequences of the absence of those links is instructive.

Leliu, like other former communes in Shunde, in the heart of the delta, has benefited very substantially from its Hong Kong links. Naamshui has been less involved in the economic transformation of Leliu than other villages in the region. There has been a persistent inability to develop industrial enterprises and thereby to diversify the village economy. As a consequence, a large portion (40 percent) of the labor force remains in agricultural production. Most of the men under forty have left the village and often Leliu itself. They work as carpenters, decorators, and temporary workers in construction, commerce, and transportation. They regularly return to the village but they have no continuing role in village-based production activities. The village agricultural economy is dominated by women, despite the demise of sericulture, and by older men who have contracted fishponds, either individually or (more commonly) in cooperation with men from other households.

Village households make a steady living, if not spectacular by local standards (per capita income was about 1,400 yuan in 1990, slightly below the level of

Leliu as a whole). One reason for the failure to diversify the village economy is that it is in a remote corner of the *zhen*, although it has been linked by road to the administrative center of Leliu and to Daliang, the county town, for more than a decade. Its Hong Kong émigrés are relatively few in number and the village lacks, or fails to make full use of, its village association (*guanxi*), which has been so critical for the success of other villages in Shunde. There is an intense village solidarity, and the organization of production does not differ dramatically from its practice in the 1960s and 1970s. Fish production is organized around cooperative principles, and income from the contracted fishponds is distributed (*fen hong*) on an annual basis. The collective health care system works well, people receive pensions, and there are only two "five-guarantee" households. Naamshui was extremely successful during the dominance of the Dazhai model, and there is little question that its agricultural economy is efficient and its commitment to collective welfare very strong. There are households in the village (intriguingly, with former "landlord" political status) that have been extraordinarily entrepreneurial and prosperous. They are, however, exceptional, since the village as a collectivity has chosen to remain aloof from the vaster changes that sweep the area around it. In the reform era there is no single model of success that dominates and if a village does not wish to emulate others, it is for the village to decide.

Ngawu, in Renhe, has also changed less dramatically than some other villages in the delta. It, too, is firmly agricultural and has only a small-enterprise sector. In the past it was also deeply committed to certain ideological positions and may not have grasped with wholehearted enthusiasm some of the ideas of the reform period. A significant proportion of its male labor force is working outside the village. Ngawu has a large number of households with relatives abroad. Many of these overseas Chinese reside in Canada. The impact of overseas Chinese kinsmen on local economies is distinctive and does not typically translate into economic transformation of the kind experienced in those parts of the delta where Hong Kong émigrés are most numerous.

Ngawu has not been able to capitalize fully on the opportunities implicit in policies for transforming its system of production. Many households remain in subsistence production. Only a few village households have members working in the *zhen*-managed enterprises, and there are only a few enterprises at the village level to absorb local surplus labor. The out-migration of household labor is therefore substantial but predominantly male. Villagers have sought employment in construction projects—either in Guangzhou or Shenzhen—many of them joint ventures with Hong Kong. The village economy may therefore benefit significantly, but indirectly, from the broader penetration of the delta economy by Hong Kong.

The long-term prospects for continued prosperity in Renhe are somewhat compromised by its failure to expand significantly its export-oriented enterprise sector. In the mid-1980s it created an amusement park with a Hong Kong entrepreneur, who left the region for Hong Kong in the early 1950s. The park has not been a success: Transportation and communications with Guangzhou are poor, and patrons never materialized in sufficient numbers. The leadership in Renhe is well aware that outside investment is central to a strong economic performance in the future. Its difficulties were only furthered when its most industrialized segment separated and formed a smaller *zhen* in 1987. Its speciality was grain farming and this is unlikely to bring gains in the 1990s. The indigenous population is increasingly reluctant to engage in field agriculture and already some four hundred outsider households have subcontracted land in Renhe. The indigenous labor force will be increasingly absent unless major internal economic change persuades them to end their sojourning. And change will be possible only when larger numbers of entrepreneurs, preferably with a Hong Kong or Taiwan base, can be persuaded to invest in the area.[16]

The Western Delta: The Overseas Chinese Connection

The distinctive western Pearl River Delta region is the homeland of many North Americans of Chinese origin.[17] Overseas Chinese have remained fiercely loyal to their ancestral villages of origin. It is such loyalty on the part of Chinese overseas that calls forth a willingness, even after decades abroad, to donate to homeland projects. Understanding this, local leadership in production units throughout the delta has encouraged the involvement of its émigrés in local economic development and other projects since the reform initiatives began in the 1980s. The success in the western delta of overtures to natives resident abroad has been substantial. Its consequences have been markedly different when compared with the central and eastern delta regions. It has not resulted in economic transformation, but it has markedly improved the social infrastructure.

The great majority of households in Duanfen have relatives overseas; they are described as "overseas Chinese dependents" (*qiaojuan*). Only a small proportion of households do not have kinsmen abroad. The closeness of kinship will determine the amount of support that relatives abroad will provide. A close relationship will increase the possibility of obtaining an immigration visa and of joining kinsmen abroad through the programs of family reunification. In the western delta it is, therefore, important to distinguish the proportion of households with relatives abroad and, among these, whether their relatives are directly or more distantly related.

Non-*qiaojuan* households have the fewest resources and are therefore reliant upon their own abilities. *Qiaojuan* households whose kinsmen are distantly related may receive remittances from their relatives abroad but have little opportunity to migrate. They have significant advantages when compared with the non-*qiaojuan* households. Their remittances can become working capital and their connections with relatives abroad can be a source of capital inputs. Since 1979, *qiaojuan* families have been leaving in large numbers as part of family reunification policies in as Canada, the United States, and elsewhere. As a consequence, there is a considerable amount of property standing empty, which is often managed by the remaining (distant) *qiaojuan* kinsmen. Such properties can be used as an economic resource. The access to capital by distant *qiaojuan* households has allowed them to contract formerly collectively managed facilities (such as orchards, general stores, or repair facilities) at the village level and therefore augment their participation in agriculture with private production activities in the tertiary sector. The private sector is much more extensive in the western delta, and the highly collectivized process of rural industrialization is much smaller, particularly at the village level.

Since 1950, the issue of how to attract investment by ethnic Chinese abroad has been an important and troublesome issue in the formulation of overseas Chinese policy (Fitzgerald, 1972: 121–26), and it readily fell victim to conflicting domestic political currents in the past. After 1979, investment was actively sought abroad and the involvement of both overseas Chinese and émigrés from Hong Kong and Macao in the new economic program was regarded as important. In the traditional areas of overseas migration, the willingness of overseas Chinese to commit substantial funds to public projects depended on the resolution of some outstanding grievances. One involved the return of property that had been seized during the land reform and the closely related issue of political status that emerged from the land reform process. Chinese abroad had suffered a good deal of discrimination while living and working in societies that only rarely granted them full participation. They remitted funds from their occupations, which were often either low-status or within the ethnic subeconomy. Such remittances were put into land and housing; at the time of land reform the remitters were often judged to be "landlords" and their properties were confiscated. Many Chinese abroad were clearly "working class" and they bitterly resented what was perceived as a social injustice in the land reform process. Their relatives in China, many of whom were prevented by discriminatory immigration legislation from leaving China, suffered from their political labels for much of the thirty years after land reform. The two issues were substantially resolved by the mid-1980s.

The fate of lineage organizations was another nagging question. The western delta was characterized by a highly elaborate lineage organization before 1949. It was compromised by land reform, in which lineage property was confiscated, and by the time of the Cultural Revolution, if not before, the ancestor cult and all it stood for was emasculated. While the full elaboration of all aspects of the operation of lineages cannot be contemplated, many of them are once again practiced. Graves have been repaired, rituals are performed at the graves of apical ancestors, ancestral halls are being restored, ritual feasts are given in the halls once more, and lineage libraries are being refurbished. Lineage officers have begun to act as agents for members of the lineage, similar to the way the administrators of lineage trusts intervened on behalf of members in the period before 1949.

The restoration work that occurs is made possible by donations that come from local and external contributors. The major donations are from abroad. Funds are remitted through a worldwide network that is maintained by a sophisticated and widespread communications system. A large stream of local publications flows from the western delta, focusing on the importance of the contributions of kinsmen and fellow countrymen overseas in maintaining local integrity. Local history and local tradition are emphasized; economic advances receive careful attention, but they are seen to be in harmony with the local cultural base.

In the areas strongly associated with overseas Chinese, schools and education funded by the relatives overseas speak of upward mobility and lineal integrity. Before 1949 in Taishan, class and kinship were linked to overseas connections. In the thirty years after land reform, those connections were often a liability, although they continued to be of importance. In the past ten years, the liabilities have become advantages and have contributed to a developmental process that reflects national policies, as a consequence of intense and distinctive patterns of overseas linkages. Similarly, the Hong Kong connection is also crucial in the development of the western delta. The remittance funds that flow into the region, substantial though they are, are not put primarily into economic enterprises, as they are in the central and eastern delta. The impact of them, nevertheless, is substantial. The public facilities in the traditional homeland areas of overseas Chinese are superior to those in any other rural region in Guangdong (possibly in China as a whole). The details of social structure in this region differ significantly from other regions because of the long history of migration to an array of overseas locations and a long history of concern with the fate of the homeland by Chinese abroad. That concern was strained by the intemperate policies toward overseas Chinese and their dependents over a thirty-year period, but it was not dissipated. Homeland loyalties have been encouraged in the reform period and overseas Chinese have responded with enthusiasm. Hong Kong has become a global center for an array of economic forces. It has also become the point at which to concentrate and organize homeland sentiments for overseas Chinese and to encourage their involvement, once again, in their points of ancestral origin.

Conclusion

Hong Kong and the participants of Hong Kong's economic success, primarily drawn from the Pearl River Delta, have assumed a key role in innovative policies that were formulated in Guangdong beginning in 1979. Hong Kong became the catalyst that drew the Guangdong provincial economy into the global economy after 1979. Increasingly after 1979 and the formulation of reform policies, Hong Kong rebuilt the entrepôt trade with China. Hong Kong capital and entrepreneurship became key elements in economic change within China as a whole. It was especially significant for Guangdong and its economic core, the Pearl River Delta.

A full appreciation of Hong Kong's prospects after 1997 must take into account its relationship to the broader region of China in which it is now, in the early 1990s, a key part and a key player. Hong Kong has an extensive set of economic and cultural links to its hinterland, particularly the Pearl River Delta, which has been transformed since Economic Reform was initiated in China in 1979. The economic, political, and cultural links between Hong Kong and its hinterland have been critical since the nineteenth century. In the aftermath of the formation of the People's Republic of China they were charged with ambiguity and regarded with suspicion by the central authorities. In the aftermath of reform they have reemerged as the key to the economic and social transformation of Guangdong, which has seen itself firmly incorporated into the global economy.

The role of Hong Kong in the transformation of its hinterland has been examined in this chapter through the experiences of a set of five rural localities in the Pearl River Delta since the reform of China's economic system got under way. These localities occupy varying situations in the delta.

The experiences of the five localities show different aspects of regional transformation in the 1980s. The characteristics of particular local economies indicate distinct responses to the possibilities of reform. A major feature of the Pearl River Delta as a whole in the 1980s, but especially after 1985, has been rapid economic growth. It has been fueled by industrial and tertiary-sector growth in which Hong Kong investment, entrepreneurial skill, and management expertise have been extensively utilized. The entrepreneurial skills that have driven the economic transformation of Hong Kong since the 1950s have been tapped by localities throughout the delta in the 1980s.

No region of China has developed as rapidly as the delta, especially after the middle part of the 1980s. The major stimulus has been Hong Kong. The key figures are Hong Kong–based expatriates who, having left in anticipation of, or shortly after, the formation of the People's Republic of China, responded to calls to return to their native places after the reform initiatives. Their identification with ancestral villages is strong even after a three-decade sojourn in Hong Kong. Equally, however, the appeals from their home areas present economic opportunity as the global economy continues its restructuring and as Hong Kong's economy undergoes change. The eastern and central delta, which includes the Special Economic Zones of Shenzhen and Zhuhai, but which should be seen in a separate light, has benefited most dramatically from the activities of émigrés from Hong Kong (and to a lesser degree, Macao).

The western delta, dominated by the overseas Chinese presence, presents a different scenario. Hong Kong–based natives of the region, along with their kinsmen and fellow countrymen in the overseas Chinese areas of the world (and especially North America), have resumed with great intensity a set of contacts with the homeland that was compromised by government policy toward overseas

Chinese dependents (*qiaojuan*) in the years after land reform in the early 1950s. The Hong Kong connection is no less important for the overseas Chinese areas of the western delta than it is for areas of the central and eastern delta where Hong Kong–based expatriates (*tongbao*) rather than overseas Chinese (*huaqiao* or *huayi*) predominate. The consequences of the two relationships are different, however. There has been massive economic transformation of the central and eastern delta as a consequence of expatriate investment in productive enterprises. The economic effects of the Hong Kong connection for the overseas Chinese areas are less immediately obvious. In the overseas Chinese areas there has been major investment in social infrastructure such as roads, schools, hospitals, and public buildings. They continue a tradition begun in the nineteenth century when natives of the western delta began to migrate in large numbers to Southeast Asia and North America. It was a tradition disrupted first by the Japanese occupation of the homeland and then, after 1950, by government policy.

Hong Kong and its hinterland have changed dramatically since reform was proposed in 1979. Hong Kong has continued to prosper as it has assisted in and benefited from the transformation of the Pearl River Delta of which it is economically and culturally part and to which it will be administratively linked after 1997 in a fashion that is still uncertain.

There is little question that the older cultural ties have been augmented by increasing economic integration throughout the 1980s. Hong Kong has greater economic strength relative to Guangdong than it had in the past. Hong Kong no longer lives under the cultural shadow of Guangzhou and Guangdong as it did until 1949. The separate developmental trajectories of Hong Kong and the delta after 1950 have had major consequences in the 1980s and into the 1990s and will likely remain even after the formal resumption of Chinese sovereignty.

A regional economy that is now emerging, energized by Hong Kong's enormous entrepreneurial capacities, is split across distinct administrative and political systems. After 1997 the political and administrative barriers will be diminished, although it is unlikely that Hong Kong's economic dominance will lessen. There is clearly an important cultural distinctiveness between Hong Kong and its hinterland that only widened in the thirty years after 1950. It is one that has converged substantially since 1980 as Hong Kong and its hinterland have become increasingly integrated. Despite the pundits and their reservations about the fate of Hong Kong's political structures, Hong Kong's domination of its hinterland will likely remain well beyond 1997, and those who lack Hong Kong connections will likely be disadvantaged.

Notes

1. The Draft Agreement in 1984 (Draft Agreement, 1984) specifies the broad mechanisms. A set of annexes that deals with China's policy toward Hong Kong, the nature of the Sino-British liaison group, land leases, and the exchange of memoranda between the

British and Chinese governments can be found in Ching (1985). The Basic Law was approved by the National People's Congress in April 1990 in an atmosphere changed significantly by the events in China, and reaction to them in Hong Kong, during the spring of 1989. A draft of the Basic Law with commentary appears in McGurn (1988). See also Hicks (1989) for views written before June 1989. The perception from Taipei is expressed in Domes and Shaw (1989). A recent Canadian view is Nadeau (1990).

2. For a popular account of the early period, see Collis (1946). The most thorough scholarly analysis is still Fairbank (1953). See also Wakeman (1967).

3. On the Japanese occupation, see Lethbridge (1969: 77–126); Endacott (1978); Luff (1967); Kwan (1984: 178–90).

4. See the essays in Parish (1985); Griffin (1984); Perry and C. Wong (1985: 1–194); Ash (1988: 529–55); Delman et al. (1990); Zweig (1991: 716–41).

5. The core of the delta is composed of the two "municipalities" (shi) of Foshan and Jiangmen, which were created out of the former Foshan prefecture, in the early period of reform. The western part of the delta is composed of Doumen, Heshan, and the four xian—Enping, Taishan, Kaiping, Xinhui—from which the bulk of the North American Chinese population traces its ancestry; the central delta extends from Guangzhou south and includes Nanhai, Punyu, Shunde, and Zhongshan; and also mountainous Gaoming and Sanshui. The eastern delta consists of Dongguan and Baoan, adjacent to the Shenzhen Special Economic Zone and Hong Kong. In 1987 the administrative definition of the "Open Economic Area" was expanded up the West River to include Zhaoqing shi, north of Guangzhou to include Hua xian and Conghua xian, and eastward to include much of what had formerly been Huiyang prefecture. Most of these new additions are not strictly delta, but are mountainous and the residents speak Hakka. They had begun to share in the prosperity of what is known as "the small delta," the original, essentially Cantonese-speaking, core. For a discussion of the "small" and "large" delta, see Guangdong nianjian 1989 (252–53; 492, 496). Official statistics on the delta, large or small, exclude Guangzhou's urban area, which includes still largely rural Baiyun qu, and the two special zones. I have included them.

6. The distinctive ecological features of Shunde (and of Leliu in particular) are described in Ruddle and Zhong (1988).

7. For much of the 1980s I interviewed cadres at a variety of administrative levels associated with the units. In the summer of 1986 I selected five villages from among the units, based on my general knowledge of them. Using the household records I drew random samples of village households and administered a standard questionnaire. The work was funded by a research grant from the Social Sciences and Humanities Research Council of Canada. The Chinese Academy of Social Sciences gave me every assistance. In Guangdong I was greatly helped by the Guangdong Academy of Social Science and by the Department of Sociology at Zhongshan (Sun Yatsen) University. I express my thanks to Li Ruichang and Chen Daojin and to Professor He Zhaofa. Mr. Tan Xiaobing assisted me in collecting the data. His efforts are greatly appreciated.

8. Some general findings are indicated in the following: Johnson (1982: 430–52; 1986: 237–54; 1989: 191–226).

9. For a broad account of Baiyun qu (formerly the "Suburban District"), see Guangzhou nianjian 1991 (1991: 552–54).

10. The performance of Dongguan is detailed in Zhonggong zhongyang bangongting (1989). Fucheng's performance is detailed on pp. 219–20.

11. Siu (1989) describes the consequence of state policies from the 1950s for citrus and fan palm production in Xinhui. Xinhui is on the highly commercialized eastern edge of the western delta. Field sites are in and around the xian city. The arguments Siu makes for Huancheng can appropriately be made for much of the central and eastern delta. Even

where cash cropping was extensive, its development was compromised by the emasculation of peasant marketing after 1956, and especially after the Great Leap Forward.

12. See Zweig (1989: esp. 153–62) for an account of peasant resistance to collectivist policies in the Lower Yangzi region.

13. On the contrary, growth in the number of enterprises in the *zhen* as a whole (there were 346 enterprises in 1987, of which 118 were wholly engaged in processing of materials for the international market [*wailai jiagong*]) has resulted in the recruitment of several thousand workers from outside the area, many of whom are neither Cantonese-speakers nor natives of Guangdong.

14. See Potter and Potter (1990: esp. 251–69). Zengbu is across the river from Wantong, the village in Fucheng that I surveyed, and draws the bulk of its brides from the village.

15. Wantong is the village in Fucheng most familiar to me. It is not necessarily the most dramatic example of change in Fucheng. Tsimtau (Qiantou) is even more astonishing in terms of the number and diversity of its enterprises. See my remarks on this example in Johnson (1989: 206–7). It now distributes 100 yuan per month from enterprise profits to all indigenous members of the village.

16. In the summer of 1991, a delegation from Renhe visited North America and organized meetings with émigrés from the region. They brought well-produced brochures explaining regulations for investment in Renhe and the possibilities for both assisting the native place and also turning a profit. See the comment on some of the efforts by the Renhe government to deal with the poorer villages by helping them establish export-processing facilities in *Guangzhou nianjian 1991* (1991: 554).

17. I have benefited from numerous conversations with Dr. Woon Yuen-fong of the University of Victoria about the western delta. She has generously shared her findings from Chikan in neighboring Kaiping *xian*. See Woon (1989: 324–44; 1990: 139–72; 1–1991: 139–69).

References

Ash, Robert F. (1988), "The Evolution of Agricultural Policy," *China Quarterly*, No. 116, pp. 529–55.

Ching, F. (1985), *Hong Kong and China: For Better or Worse*, New York: China Council of the Asia Society and the Foreign Policy Association.

Collis, M. (1946), *Foreign Mud*, London: Faber and Faber.

Delman, Jørgen, Clemens S. Ostergaard, and Flemming Christiansen, eds. (1990), *Remaking Peasant China: Problems of Rural Development and Institutions at the Start of the 1990s*, Aarhus: Aarhus University Press.

Domes, Jurgen, and Yu-ming Shaw (1989), *Hong Kong: A Chinese and International Concern*, Boulder, CO: Westview Press.

Draft Agreement Between the Government of the United Kingdom and Britain and Northern Island and the Government of the People's Republic of China on the Future of Hong Kong (1984), Hong Kong: Government Printer.

Endacott, G.B., ed., with additional material by A. Birch (1978), *Hong Kong Eclipse*, Hong Kong: Oxford University Press.

Fairbank, J.K. (1953), *Trade and Diplomacy on the South China Coast*, Cambridge, MA: Harvard University Press.

Fitzgerald, Stephen (1972), *China and the Overseas Chinese*, Cambridge: Cambridge University Press.

Griffin, K., ed. (1984), *Institutional Reform and Economic Development in the Chinese Countryside*, London: Macmillan.

Guangdong nianjian 1989 (Guangdong Yearbook 1989) (1989), Guangzhou: Renmin chubanshe (People's Press).

Guangdong tongji nianjian 1991 (Guangdong Statistical Yearbook 1991) (1991), Guangzhou: Guangdong Tongjiju.

Guangdongsheng Xian (Qu) Guomin Jingji Tongji Ziliao, 1980–1990 (Statistical materials on the national economy at the county (district) level, 1980–1990) (1991), Guangzhou: Guangdong Tongjiju.

Guangzhou nianjian 1991 (Guangzhou Yearbook 1991) (1991), Guangzhou: Renmin chubanshe (People's Press).

Hicks, G. (1989), *Hong Kong Countdown*, Hong Kong: Writers and Publishers Cooperative.

Johnson, Elizabeth, and Graham Johnson (1976), *Walking on Two Legs: Rural Development in South China*, Ottawa: International Development Research Center.

Johnson, G.E. (1982), "The Production Responsibility System in Chinese Agriculture: Some Examples from Guangdong," *Pacific Affairs*, Vol. 55, No. 3, pp. 430–52.

——— (1986), "1997 and After: Will Hong Kong Survive? A Personal View," *Pacific Affairs*, Vol. 59, No. 2, pp. 237–54.

——— (1989), "Rural Transformation in South China? Views from the Locality," *Revue Européene des Sciences Sociales*, Vol. 27, No. 84, pp. 191–226.

——— (1992), "The Political Economy of Chinese Urbanization: Guangdong and the Pearl River Delta," in *Urbanizing China*, ed. Gregory Guldin, Westport, CT: Greenwood Press, pp. 185–220.

Kamm, John (1989), "Reforming Foreign Trade," in *One Step Ahead in China: Guangdong under Reform*, ed. Ezra Vogel, Cambridge, MA: Harvard University Press, pp. 338–92.

Kwan, Lai-Hung (1984), "The Charitable Activities of Local Chinese Organizations During the Japanese Occupation of Hong Kong, December 1941–August 1945," in *From Village to City*, ed. D. Faure, J. Hayes, and A. Birch, Hong Kong: Centre of Asian Studies, University of Hong Kong, pp. 178–90.

Lethbridge, H.J. (1969), "Hong Kong under Japanese Occupation: Changes in Social Structure," in *Hong Kong: A Society in Transition*, ed. I.C. Jarvie in consultation with J. Agassi, London: Routledge and Kegan Paul, pp. 77–126.

Luff, L. (1967), *Hong Kong: The Hidden Years*, Hong Kong: South China Morning Post.

McGee, T.G. (1989), "Urbanasasi or Kotadesasi? Evolving Patterns of Urbanization in Asia," in *Urbanization in Asia*, ed. L. Ma, A. Noble, and A. Dutt, Honolulu: University of Hawaii Press, pp. 93–108.

——— (1991), "The Emergence of *Desakota* Regions in Asia: Expanding a Hypothesis," in *The Extended Metropolis: Settlement Transition in Asia*, ed. N. Ginsburg, B. Koppel and T.G. McGee, Honolulu: University of Hawaii Press, pp. 3–26.

McGurn, William, ed. (1988), *Basic Law, Basic Questions*, Hong Kong: Review Publishing Company.

Nadeau, Jules (1990), *Hong Kong 1997: Dans la Gueule du Dragon Rouge*, Montreal: Editions Québéc/Amerique.

Parish, W.L. (1985), *Chinese Rural Development: The Great Transformation*, Armonk, NY, and London: M.E. Sharpe.

Perry, E., and C. Wong (1985), *The Political Economy of Reform in Post-Mao China*, Cambridge, MA: Council on East Asian Studies, Harvard University, Harvard University Press.

Potter, S.H., and J.M. Potter (1990), *China's Peasants: The Anthropology of a Revolution*, New York: Cambridge University Press.

Ruddle, Kenneth, and Zhong Gongfu (1988), *Integrated Agriculture–Aquaculture in*

South China: The Dyke–Pond System of the Zhujiang Delta, Cambridge and New York: Cambridge University Press.

Siu, Helen (1989), *Agents and Victims in South China: Accomplices in Rural Revolution*, New Haven: Yale University Press.

Thorns, David (1989), "The New International Division of Labor and Urban Change: A New Zealand Case Study," in *Pacific Rim Cities in the World Economy*, ed. M.P. Smith, New Brunswick and Oxford: Transaction Books, pp. 68–101.

Vogel, Ezra (1989), "Guangdong's Dynamic Inner Delta," *The China Business Review*, September–October, pp. 56–62.

——— (1989), *One Step Ahead in China: Guangdong under Reform*, Cambridge, MA: Harvard University Press.

Wakeman, F. (1967), *Strangers at the Gates*, Berkeley: University of California Press.

Woon, Yuen-fong (1989), "Social Change and Continuity in South China: Overseas Chinese and the Guan Lineage of Kaiping County, 1949–1987," *China Quarterly*, No. 118, pp. 324–44.

——— (1990), "International Links and Socio-economic Development of Modern China: an Emigrant Community in Guangdong," *Modern China*, Vol. 16, No. 2, pp. 139–72.

——— (1991), "From Mao to Deng: Life Satisfaction among Rural Women in an Emigrant Community in South China," *Australian Journal of Chinese Affairs*, No. 25, pp. 139–69.

Yang, Dali (1991), "China Adjusts to the World Economy: The Political Economy of China's Coastal Development Strategy," *Pacific Affairs*, Vol. 65, No.1, pp. 42–64.

Zhonggong zhongyang bangongting (Chinese Central Office) (1989), *Dongguan shinian: 1979–1988* (Dongguan ten years: 1979–1988), Shanghai: Shanghai renmin chubanshe (Shanghai People's Press).

Zweig, David (1989), "Struggling over Land in China: Peasant Resistance After Collectivization, 1966–1986," in *Everyday Forms of Peasant Resistance*, ed. Forrest D. Colburn, Armonk, NY: M.E. Sharpe: pp. 153–62.

——— (1991), "Internationalizing China's Countryside: The Political Economy of Exports from Rural Industry," *China Quarterly*, No. 128, pp. 716–41.

Part II
Cultural Tranformation

—————————————————————— **4**

Toward a Greater Guangdong: Hong Kong's Sociocultural Impact on the Pearl River Delta and Beyond

Gregory Eliyu Guldin

As 1997 approaches, scholars and others must finally confront the reality of the integrated nature of southern Guangdong, an integration that has come about despite the political boundaries and blinders of the past thirty-odd years. As a reflection of Cold War myopia, academics in both the People's Republic of China (PRC) and Hong Kong have consistently analyzed Guangdong and Hong Kong as if they existed *sui generis* and in isolation from each other (Zheng, 1989: 253–54). Now, fortunately, our viewpoints are broadening.

Key to this visionary expansion has been the truly historic reconnection of ties between Hong Kong and Guangdong.[1] As was the case prior to the Chinese Revolution of 1949, the Pearl River Delta (*Zhujiang sanjiaozhou*) can now once again refer not only to the geographical delta area but also to Guangzhou, Hong Kong, and Macao (Chan, 1988; Leeming, 1989). Such a linguistic shift symbolizes the renewed ties between the colonial territories of Hong Kong and Macao on the one hand, and the region's territorial majority, the province of Guangdong, on the other. Most analysts of the process have charted the economic aspects of this reintegration and have fairly ignored the sociocultural. This chapter seeks to help redress the balance.

The Thirty Years' Warp

Hong Kong emerged as a major location in the delta in the wake of British warships firing on delta shorelines during the Opium Wars. The British imperialists set loose processes that revolutionized life in the delta. The region became the locus of foreign capital, and provincial development tipped in the delta's favor. Furthermore, whereas Guangzhou had long developed as the preeminent provincial center and the locus of international trade in the centuries preceding the invasion, now Hong Kong began to usurp that position while Guangzhou slipped increasingly into a semicolonial and dependent status (Luk, 1989: 202).

During the century leading up to the triumph of Communist revolutionary forces in 1949, Hong Kong and Guangzhou served as the dual poles of the Cantonese world, with the British Crown colony clearly possessing a greater valence. The outbreak of the Korean War in June 1950, however, radically changed things in the delta. With the United States–led and United Nations–endorsed blockade against China, trade with the newly proclaimed People's Republic of China came to a near standstill. The old entrepôt trade, whereby Hong Kong profited as the transshipment point for goods into and out of China, collapsed (Vogel, 1989: 45).

All contact between Hong Kong and Guangdong, though, did not stop. Especially during the early 1950s, the border was far from "sealed" and substantial smuggling of goods occurred. Many workers from Hong Kong returned to Guangzhou during this period, since the living standards of the two cities were not very different (Zhu, 1991). During China's "Three Bad Years" following the Great Leap Forward, Hong Kong's donations of oil, rice, and other foodstuffs played a crucial role in aiding Guangdong relatives and *tongxiang* (countymates) to weather the tough times.[2] Even during the decade of the Cultural Revolution, from 1966 to 1978, people and goods flowed back and forth across the border; at no time could we say that *all* contact was cut off, that China was totally isolated. In the three decades after the outbreak of the Korean War, immigrants continued to trickle into the colony—both legally and illegally—thereby contributing to the surplus labor pool that helped fuel Hong Kong's early industrialization in the 1950s and 1960s.

Hong Kong also served as an escape valve for Guangdong and especially for the delta. Whenever the situation in China deteriorated, thousands would make the crossing, as they did during the early 1960s, and then again during the periods of economic stagnation in the 1970s (Chan et al., 1984: 235, 266). Such a flow of people into Hong Kong meant that ties with the surrounding counties of the delta were repeatedly renewed and that there was a constant stream of Hong Kong people back to the delta. For if thousands were making it to Hong Kong each year, tens of thousands of Hong Kong residents were making the return trip. On annual holidays the Chinese border guards would allow travelers to visit their native villages, and many took advantage of these opportunities to maintain family and village ties (Vogel, 1989: 46).

Trade between Hong Kong and Guangdong continued as well throughout the period 1949 to 1978. Guangdong not only provided the bulk of Hong Kong's water supply but also most of its produce. Considering that Guangdong thus supplied Hong Kong with cheap labor, cheap food, and other basic necessities during the takeoff period of Hong Kong's move to light industrialization, one could legitimately conclude that Guangdong in effect subsidized Hong Kong's economic rise (Guldin, 1989: 29–34; Vogel, 1989: 46; Xu et al., 1989: 224).[3]

Industrialization and urbanization, meanwhile, were also proceeding in Guangdong, but at a much slower pace. Like cities throughout China, the emphasis was on changing Guangzhou from a "city of consumption" to a "city of production." Heavy industry was emphasized while commerce, foreign trade, and consumer-oriented industries were allowed to deteriorate (Xu et al., 1988: 78–79). Thus, despite their different political orientations, both Hong Kong and Guangzhou were industrializing, though with different emphases and different social results.

One key difference was that the Guangdong side of the border was operating according to socialist principles of balanced regional growth. Consciously seeking to avoid extremes of development and underdevelopment as had been growing throughout the century proceeding the Communist takeover in Guangdong, the government pursued a deliberate policy aimed at stimulating the northern and noncoastal areas of the province rather than the delta and coastal areas (Luk, 1989: 203). It is thus likely that even if there had not been a Cold War–inspired blockade of China, trade between Hong Kong and the delta would have decreased. As it was, the trade that did continue now flowed through state corporations in Guangzhou; the freewheeling trade that had tied the delta to Hong Kong prior to 1949 was no more. Even within the province (as well as in the rest of China), the emphasis was on self-reliance and central planning, so that horizontal linkages were suppressed. To a degree unimaginable before 1949, the delta was simultaneously isolated from Guangzhou as well as from Hong Kong (Chan, 1988: 4–5; Leeming, 1989: 263).

This was a relative isolation, for contacts did continue, as we have seen. Yet, with the construction of this new socialist society in China, people began to see Hong Kong in a new light. Many Chinese cultural conservatives had long seen Hong Kong (and the treaty ports in general) as the source of most Chinese ills, but now the anti–Hong Kong attitudes were given a new charge—that of socialist morality (Wickberg, 1992). Especially given the enthusiasm with which many viewed the changes of the 1950s, it was quite common for people in Guangdong to feel pride in China's achievements and many people came to accept the government's portrayal of Hong Kong as:

> a city where there were few values beyond wealth and where sexual immorality, crime, corruption, and lavish waste were rampant . . . where colonialists and capitalists oppressed the common workers, where many had no place but to sleep but on the streets, and where workers were perpetually insecure about their future. (Vogel, 1989: 62)

Nevertheless, all the capitalist horror stories told about Hong Kong were not able to filter out the contrary stories of visiting relatives. Ever since the Hong Kong boom began in the early 1960s, reports had filtered in about Hong Kong's prosperity, adding to a pent-up demand to go to Hong Kong. The post-1978 "opening to the outside" policies of the post-Mao reformers, furthermore, only exacerbated the desire to be and live like those in Hong Kong, as delta people realized the true depth of the developmental gap separating them from their compatriots in Hong Kong. When the Maoist world view collapsed in the late 1970s, a Hong Kong vision of the good life rushed in to take its place.

Reconnecting: The Greater Pearl River Delta Returns

That Hong Kong vision entered Guangdong during the 1980s with a rolling wave of Hong Kong people, ideas, and lifestyles as it became increasingly convenient to cross the border. By 1987 an incredible 30,100,000 cross-border trips by Hong Kong residents were recorded (Zheng, 1989: 257),[4] indicating that trips to visit relatives and to do business were far in excess of what the delta had ever seen, even when we consider the pre-1949 period. One cadre in a small town in Nanhai county told me that, even there, thousands of Hong Kong people come to visit every year.

The new attitude in Beijing toward increasing contacts with the world beyond the borders of the People's Republic has enabled the Hong Kong-to-Guangzhou journey to be quickened from the all-day affair of the pre-1978 period to the three-hour express train journey from Hung Hom terminal in Kowloon to Guangzhou's rail station. Hydrofoil and airplane services ferrying people between the metropolises have also been boosted, while ferry and freight service has likewise been greatly expanded. Telephone calls no longer need be booked hours in advance; direct dialing is now possible between Hong Kong and most delta locations (Vogel, 1989: 60–61), as are international direct-dial calls. The increase in the ease of telephone communication has been truly phenomenal; between 1982 and 1985 alone, the number of minutes spent on phone lines between the delta and Hong Kong more than doubled (Zheng, 1989: 258). Yet even with such a dramatic rate of growth, the demand for telephone communication far outstrips the capacity of Guangdong's anemic system to satisfy it. Cellular phones began to bridge the gap in 1988 and 1989 and have spread very rapidly since then.[5]

The year 1988 also saw the beginning of officially approved tourism between the People's Republic and Hong Kong, so that now delta residents can satisfy their curiosity about the prosperous society to their south without emigrating permanently.[6] Even before then, however, many PRC residents had received permission from both governments for visits to Hong Kong, and 174,100 PRC residents were recorded to have visited Hong Kong in 1987. The overwhelming majority of these visitors go to see relatives; one village head in Nanhai county reported to me that about half of the families in his village with relatives in Hong Kong had visited Hong Kong between 1980 and 1985.

Not all these trips from the People's Republic to Hong Kong, however, were family affairs. Many of the visitors were sent by their *danwei* (work units) to live in Hong Kong, learn Hong Kong ways, and transfer such knowledge to their home bases (Vogel, 1989: 63–65). Zheng (1989: 273) reports that an equal number (10,000 or so) of Hong Kong people have gone in the opposite direction; these managers and like personnel have accompanied their firms' relocation to delta sites to oversee their operations. Such Hong Kong personnel on both short- and long-term assignment in the towns and villages of the delta represent a continuing locus of Hong Kong managerial innovation and cultural modeling.

The economic reforms made possible the transferal of Hong Kong business operations to the delta, but it was Hong Kong's shortage of cheap labor that made it an economic imperative for Hong Kong capitalists. By mutual agreement and effort of the British and Chinese, after 1980 the constant and often heavy flow of illegal migrants into the colony was mostly choked off. Whereas tens of thousands made it to Hong Kong each year during the 1960s and 1970s, most migrants now arrive legally, with 27,300 recorded in 1987 (Zheng, 1989: 257).

The expanding Hong Kong economy, having nearly exhausted its local labor supply (with an unemployment rate under 2 percent), simply expanded into Guangdong to take advantage of lower labor and land costs (Vogel, 1989: 68–69). Between 1 and 2 million Guangdong workers are estimated to be working for Hong Kong firms (Leeming, 1989: 273; Vogel, 1989: 442) and this, more than anything else, has worked to integrate the region. Furthermore, the impact of this expansion is felt far beyond the counties immediately north of the Shenzhen Special Economic Zone border. In a cascading series of migratory, social, and cultural reactions, the livelihood and life chances of entire communities and regions have been transformed by these developments. As male workers have left the farms in the delta to work in the Hong Kong and locally established new manufacturing enterprises, they have left behind a mostly elderly and female work force in their wake. Often even this remnant work force is inadequate to fulfill agricultural contract responsibilities, so that workers from as far away as Hunan, Jiangxi, and Guangxi provinces (dubbed *xin kejiaren*, "the new Hakka") are subcontracted to till the land. Entrepreneurs from all over the country, furthermore, now feel it imperative to have business ties, in person or at a distance, with Guangdong. The Hong Kong economic expansion occurring in the delta thus has ramifications that extend far beyond the old colonial borders.[7]

One mostly unnoticed result of the opening to the outside is the increase in the number of Hong Kong–delta marriages. Marital ties to wealthy outsiders, whether true *Huaqiao* (overseas Chinese) or Hong Kong compatriots, have long been the goal of many a delta family (e.g., Chan et al., 1984: 211). Recently, though, such arrangements have once again become more common; an increasing number of young Hong Kong men believe that setting up and maintaining an apartment in Hong Kong is just too expensive. Far preferable is finding a Guangdong *lo por* ("old lady"; wife) and visiting her on occasion. For the wives and their families, however, the goal of the marriage is to get the wife (and her relatives) to Hong Kong themselves. In an effort to restrict this bridal flow, the Hong Kong government has established quotas and bureaucratic hurdles that usually take five years past the submission of an immigration petition to surmount.

Remittances and gifts from Hong Kong kinfolk are also important factors in transforming the delta. Chan et al. (1984: 273–74) report how even in the first few years of the economic reforms money from Hong Kong relatives was immediately put to work to take advantage of the new opportunities, often resulting in annual incomes double or triple that of those who, lacking such sources of outside capital, simply remained in the fields. Johnson and Woon (n.d.: 16) likewise report that the more Hong Kong–connected central and eastern sections of the delta have been far more successful in attracting investment and entrepreneurial skills from the outside. Such Hong Kong money, when combined with that of the *Huaqiao*, is estimated to supply over 90 percent of all the start-up capital in the delta for private enterprises (Xu et al., 1988: 118).

Some truly spectacular investments from wealthy Hong Kong businessmen seeking prestige and/or influence in China have also been made. Li Ka-shing and Henry Fok, both billionaires, have donated substantial sums for the construction of universities in Guangdong while other businessmen have set up a *peiHua* ("Cultivate China") foundation to support modernization efforts, particularly personnel training, in China (Vogel, 1989: 63–64; Zhu, 1991). Others donate to rebuild libraries, build basketball courts, or repair the local temple.

Social welfare in the delta also gets a healthy boost from Hong Kong donors. They help to fund the educational, medical, physical, and entertainment costs of various town activities and projects while their free-spending style also helps boost the local tourist and restaurant industries. Such displays of conspicuous wealth could not help but influence people's thinking and lifestyles (Xu et al., 1988: 118).

The Hong Kong Cultural Model

The 1980s in China were the decade when the old orthodoxies that had guided the People's Republic for decades were tossed aside by both officials and the public alike. The Maoist slogan "Serve the People" was replaced by "Getting Rich Is Glorious!" as the seesaw political battles of the first three decades of the People's Republic took their toll in the wavering ideological allegiance of the population. Disillusionment and alienation was the national mood by the late 1970s when the new economic reforms began, and the pragmatism of the new era left people looking for new goals and world views by which to organize their lives.

Hong Kong's consumerist vision of modernity soon filled the ideological vacuum. People in Guangdong repeatedly came into contact with their wealthier relatives in Hong Kong and read and saw on TV how well Hong Kongers were doing. They asked at first, "Why them?" but pretty soon they were saying, "Why not us? If other Cantonese could make the leap into prosperity, we can too." Thus began a painful but spirited rethinking of their way of life. The model of how to behave, though, was increasingly before them, for Hong Kong was no longer a politically distant other world. Visiting relatives, newspapers, radio, videos, and television brought Hong Kong into their homes every night.

Vogel (1989: 53), while discussing the origins of the Hong Kong way of life, perceptively compares Hong Kong to other Chinese societies and points out that Hong Kong did not have an explicitly articulated system of public values. Unlike the People's Republic with its socialist ideology and Taiwan with the Nationalists' blending of Sun Yat-sen's Three Principles and Confucianism, Hong Kong's public values were keyed to the acquisition of wealth and the pursuit of business. I would add, however, that Hong Kong *did* acquire public values, but they were not Chinese values. As a colony, the prestige forms in Hong Kong have always been British/Western and not Chinese of any variety.[8] Only in the run-up to 1997, and due to the civic maturation of Hong Kong society, has this xenocentrism begun to be challenged (see Guldin, 1992b).

Hong Kong's position vis-à-vis its Guangdong hinterland is thus more complicated than simply being a wealthier version of Guangzhou. Hong Kong represents not only prosperity but also a Westernized version of prosperity; or most accurately, a *sinicized* version of Western prosperity. The "south wind"[9] that blows into Guangdong and the People's Republic from Hong Kong thus brings with it a model of modernity that is already adjusted for local tastes. It is such a combination of elements that makes the model so appealing.

Information

As a world-class information center, Hong Kong offers Guangdong a variety of services and connections that make the colony invaluable for the province's development. Along with the economic and popular ties between the two spheres, the flow of information has swelled considerably during the last decade. From computer links to academic conferences to trade exhibitions, the Hong Kong model has established itself firmly across the Shenzhen border and throughout much of the province (Zheng, 1989: 258).

In the world of business and commerce, Hong Kong's management style, its access to world information networks, and its well-developed commercial and financial sectors (Vogel, 1989: 67, 436) have all helped to stamp the Hong Kong business style on the minds of the People's Republic's Cantonese (Guldin, 1992a: 172). Even those not directly in contact with Hong Kong businesses or their Hong Kong managers could get a powerful feel of the Hong Kong style of life (or what is just as important, a feel of the *perceived* Hong Kong lifestyle) just by entering one of the grand hotels in Guangzhou and elsewhere that are jointly owned and/or managed by Hong Kong people. With their glittering and spacious entrances, their white-uniformed and -gloved door-boys, their fountains, indoor pools, and courteous service personnel, such hotels set a standard of opulence, wealth, and efficiency that could not fail to impress people accustomed to far lower levels of public accommodation.

A surprising locus of Hong Kong influence in the Guangdong countryside, especially in the delta, is the government's own network of cultural centers in the villages and towns of the delta and beyond. Each provincial *qu* (district) has set up its own *wenhua zhan* ("culture station") that in turn coordinates the activities of the local *wenhua zhongxin* ("culture centers"). Funded by the *qu* governments with contributions from Hong Kong *tongbao* (compatriots), these *zhongxin* have helped disseminate Hong Kong cultural influences in the decade or so since they began to spread throughout the province.[10]

The staff at one *wenhua zhongxin* in Nanhai county told me that many of the most popular recreational activities for young people have to do with Hong Kong. Video games from Hong Kong, for example, were the rage throughout the mid-1980s, as were dance halls ("discos") and videotapes. For all of these activities, the local *wenhua zhongxin* were actively arranging for the game machines and equipment to arrive from Hong Kong. These officials were quite proud of these activities, for they showed how open Guangdong was. Many provinces will not allow dances but in Guangdong even senior county officials show their sophistication by taking animated twirls on the dance floor.[11]

The Mass Media as Modes of Transmission

Reaching far greater numbers of people and spreading the Hong Kong model beyond those with Hong Kong relatives or those who work or visit Hong Kong–managed or Hong Kong–managed/connected firms, Hong Kong's mass-communications network is perhaps the strongest and most broadly felt outside influence on the Pearl River Delta and beyond. Videos, radio, and television are conduits for the penetration of Hong Kong culture into nearly all towns and villages of the delta. Newspapers and magazines also find their way into the delta, but Chinese customs officials are often zealous in keeping out foreign periodicals and papers, and so relatively few Hong Kong Chinese bring them in.[12] All the greater the influence, then, of those media that do make it in, whether by illegal smuggling (often the case with videotapes) or by wireless communication (radio and television).[13]

In the past, the government was vigilant about jamming outside broadcasts, but even if they had not been, the influence of television and radio would have been limited, since few people had the machines to receive the signals. The prosperity of the 1980s enabled large numbers of people in the towns and villages of the Guangdong countryside to receive such sounds and images for the first time. Higher incomes have made more leisure time possible and encouraged the growth of a "household culture" with its requisite televisions, tape decks, radios, telephones, motorcycles, and newspaper subscriptions. Zhou (1990: 39) reports that 59.33 percent of Guangzhou households had radios in 1988, followed by Foshan with 55 percent and Dongguan county with 46 percent. Television sets were even more ubiquitous, with comparable figures of 72.69, 67, and 64 percent, respectively, for *color* televisions. The numbers for stereo tape decks run from 42.33, to 59, to 56 percent, respectively. According to a separate investigation, ownership of VCRs in the late 1980s was approaching 10 percent of delta households.

All of these objects of common desire serve to widen the horizons of their owners; it is no wonder that these horizons have extended south, for Hong Kong provides readymade and linguistically compatible broadcast programs, tapes, and printed matter. Cassette tapes and videotapes, for example, are quite popular, and Cantonese language videos from Hong Kong are ubiquitous both within and without the culture stations. So great is the demand for such tapes, that a new industry has arisen around the private rerecording and sale of the tapes.

Radio, too, is important, with Hong Kong's Commercial Radio Stations One and Two (*Shangye yi tai, liang tai*) and the new *Liang you* being the most popular. These stations are on the air nearly around the clock and have strong broadcasting signals that reach hundreds of kilometers into Guangdong. One survey revealed that 53 percent of the delta listened to the Commercial Radio stations regularly while only 10 percent listened to the *Zhongyang renmin* (Central People's) Broadcasting Service (Zhou, 1990: 39–40).

Nevertheless, it is television that rules as the premier avenue of outside cultural penetration. A count of black-and-white as well as color televisions reveals that 83.2 percent of delta households have television. And the stations they are tuned to are mostly Hong Kong ones. Surveys indicate that only 17 percent of respondents regularly watched the Central Broadcasting Station, the national network outlet of the People's Republic in Guangzhou. By contrast, fully 79 percent of viewers reported that they regularly watched Hong Kong television. The most popular channels in the delta are Hong Kong's Jade, followed by ATV's Chinese language service, and the *Zhujiang* (Pearl River) Station run by Shenzhen Television (Zhou, 1990: 39–40).

When asked what people liked so much about Hong Kong television, two chief responses were repeated both to me and to other surveyors (Guldin, 1992a: 169–70; Zhou, 1989: 236; Zhou, 1990: 40). People in the delta especially appreciated the greater speed and reliability of Hong Kong news and the lively content of Hong Kong programming—including the commercials and their catchy jingles. Surveys reveal that dramatic series, the news, and Cantonese-language movies are the top choices with the Guangdong audience.

Until recently, not all of the delta could directly receive Hong Kong television without erecting large "fish-bone" antennae to capture the coveted signals, although most of the southern delta could, while the southernmost counties (Zhuhai, Zhongshan, Shenzhen, Baoan, Dongguan, and others) had a hard time receiving Guangzhou television (Zhou, 1990: 40). Satellite dishes have now largely replaced those unsightly antennae, and by the early 1990s Hong Kong television reception was quite common, not only in the counties adjoining the Hong Kong–Shenzhen border, but in Guangzhou as well. In the past, only the large joint-venture hotels could offer Hong Kong television programming. Now it is available to regular people and *danwei* (political cadres) by cable connection.

Faced with such stiff competition, the television stations in Guangzhou, and especially those that broadcast somewhat in Cantonese, have seen fit to alter their programming to meet a more demanding public. Sometimes the Guangzhou stations will purchase foreign and Hong Kong movies and series for rebroadcast on Guangzhou frequencies, but more thoroughgoing reform is also being attempted: more detailed news reporting, more entertainment and sports specials, and the introduction of more contemporary (that is, more Hong Kong–like) styles of acting and broadcasting. The Zhujiang station has thus recently introduced a late-night variety program—*Foon Luk Gum Siu* ("Enjoy Yourself Tonight")—in clear imitation of Hong Kong's long-running and immensely popular *Huanle jian xiao*, which is itself a takeoff on the American "Tonight Show."

Zhou Daming has extensively analyzed the role of the mass media in the delta and he believes that its influence is pervasive (Zhou, 1990: 41–44). It makes the delta more accepting of the outside world, and thereby accelerates cultural change. He reports a slogan popular in the delta, *Pai wu, bu pai wai* ("Discard the polluted aspects, but don't discard the outside"), which reflects an attitude of selective admission of Hong Kong cultural elements.[14]

Commercialization—although not caused solely by Hong Kong contact—is certainly reinforced by the reception of Hong Kong media. Whether through television, radio, or in publications, the delta's population has become increasingly familiar with product brand names and with the promotion of consumer goods by advertising. Market surveying has begun as well. The post-1978 consumerist trend of PRC society has thus swelled in tandem with Hong Kong influence. Receipt of the colony's advertisements, furthermore, has also fostered a strong demand for foreign goods ranging from cigarettes to alcohol, to designer neckties, to Nike sneakers, to cosmetics. The prices for such items can range from between a few times to dozens of times the price for comparable PRC-made products. This has created a great demand for products so expensive that people cannot afford them; some have been led to theft or suicide as a way to deal with the frustrations of an increasingly competitive consumer society (Zhou, 1990: 43).

The Hong Kong mass media are also held responsible for introducing some other not so salubrious elements into the delta. Hong Kong pornographic videos, magazines, and movies, as well as other suspect and banned books and magazines, are all smuggled into the country and are held responsible for corrupting the people's morals, especially among the young. The openness to the outside has also seen a revival of "feudalistic superstition," as people imitate popular Hong Kong religious practices such as consulting fortune-tellers, burning incense, and going to temples. Sweeping the graves (*sou mou*) and consulting *fengshui* (geomancy) specialists have likewise become popular once again as Hong Kong operates as a source for a Chinese and Cantonese cultural revival. New religious organizations have also sprung up, with many, such as the *Shangdide Nuer* (God's Daughter) organization, being denounced as fronts for criminal activities (Zhou, 1990: 44).

The media, as well as increased people-to-people contact, have brought about still other changes. The very way people speak has begun to show the influence of greater exposure to Hong Kong Cantonese. Although the delta was an integrated Cantonese cultural and linguistic area prior to 1949, the thirty years' warp in their relationship meant that different varieties of Cantonese developed. In Hong Kong, English and foreign influences predominated, while in Guangzhou and the rest of the delta, the influences were Chinese and mostly from *putonghua* (Mandarin). Renewed contact in the 1980s has meant the spread of Hong Kong speech styles not only in the delta but often in areas of China far removed from the southern coast.

Prior to Liberation, standard Cantonese was based on the dialect spoken in Guangzhou's wealthy suburb of Xiguan, with no major differences in vocabulary or pronunciation from the speech of Hong Kong other than those deriving from Hong Kong's precolonial origin as a part of Baoan county and thus its linguistic orbit. In the 1950s, however, Guangzhou began to use many new political words that were borrowed from *putonghua*. Linguists at Guangdong's College of Nationalities believe that the last few decades have also seen the emergence of new tonal and phonemic differences between the two Cantonese speech varieties.

Reform has reversed this process of linguistic bifurcation as English loan-words common in Hong Kong Cantonese—such as *bye-bye*, *dik-see* (taxi), and *ah Sir* (Sir)—have come into more widespread use in the delta. Significantly, people report as well the public use of the loan-words, as words like *see-daw* (store) now appear on shop signs. Local officials also report that more and more people are referring to the local police according to the Hong Kong fashion as *chai lo* (Hong Kong slang for police) rather than as *min jing* or *jing cha* (people's police). The Hong Kong term has neither the political nor *putonghua* (Mandarin) flavor of the earlier Guangzhou terms it is replacing.

Furthermore, despite repeated campaigns to popularize the speaking of *putonghua*, capability in Mandarin is declining in Guangdong. Rural cadres report that in the 1970s most people under thirty-five could speak *putonghua*, but in the 1990s, even this group is seeing a falloff in the ability to master the national tongue. Many primary schools no longer bother to have even minimal exposure to the *putonghua* language. Broad exposure to Cantonese-language media thus is clearly making an impact.[15] This in turn is helped by a general societal reemphasis on Cantonese as even national television programs are dubbed into Cantonese and Cantonese songs and drama climb in popularity.

Local commentators have remarked that delta youth often use Hong Kong speech to impart an air of sophistication, and foreign reporters have noted that this is a national trend (Kristof, 1991a). Throughout the People's Republic, certain English terms that have become part of Hong Kong speech have spread nationwide. *Bye-bye, party, de-shi* (from the Cantonese *dik-see* for "taxi"), have become hot slang terms on the streets of China. Here the impact of Hong Kong blends with that of Taiwan (Kristof, 1991b), as their joint model of modern ways of being Chinese catches people's attention. Hence the increasing use of traditional characters (as opposed to the simplified script used in the People's Republic for the past thirty-odd years), and the trend for shop names to follow Hong Kong and Taiwan fashions. In Guangzhou, visitors from Hong Kong now chuckle when they see local eateries dubbing themselves with the name Ah Yee Leng Tong (Cantonese for "Mother's Younger Sister's Delicious Soup"). The mention of "sister-in-law's" cooking is a delicate reference to what draws a husband to seek the company of a woman younger than his wife, for *ah yee* (Cantonese for *a yi*) is also slang for "concubine." Such a slightly bawdy reference we could expect in Hong Kong, but in socialist China? Things *have* changed!

Changing Lifestyles

All of these changes have made the Pearl River Delta of the 1990s far different from the delta of only fifteen years ago. Life has changed in many ways, some fundamental, some minor, and Hong Kong has been intimately involved with both varieties of change. The spread of tipping may be a minor example of Hong Kong's influence, while the changed economic landscape has been the source of far-reaching changes in people's lives. The reforms have allowed some villages to sell agricultural produce directly to Hong Kong and thus make huge profits while other households have become filled with the gifts and remittance-bought goods provided by their Hong Kong relatives. All in all, the lifestyle changes were dramatic:

> Families that only half a decade earlier had been obliged to participate frequently in nighttime political meetings now instead spent their evenings glued to TV showings of Hong Kong's soap operas, kungfu movies, and variety shows. (Chan et al., 1984: 274)

At the level of governments and bureaucracies, there were joint discussions of transportation, energy, communications, and infrastructural needs between Hong

Kong and Guangdong representatives (Vogel, 1989: 443). Schools on both sides of the borders began to connect actively, with Hong Kong University and the Chinese University of Hong Kong establishing and maintaining contact with colleagues in a wide array of Guangdong education institutes from Zhongshan University to South China Normal College. Thus researchers from Zhongshan University's Anthropology Department came to Hong Kong to work with colleagues there on an archaeological excavation on Lantau Island (*Daiyusan*, Cantonese for *Dayu shan*) during the autumn of 1990, while Hong Kong scholars have attended numerous panels and conferences in Guangzhou. This indicates that the connections among the Hong Kong educational, athletic, and entertainment worlds have become nearly as strong as the economic and demographic ties. To highlight this aspect of the Hong Kong influence on Guangdong, let us focus on a seemingly peripheral aspect of the sociocultural scene, Guangdong's Cantonese opera.

Yuet kek (*Yueju*): Reflections of a Changing Guangdong[16]

The history of the Cantonese opera (*Yuet kek*, Cantonese for *Yueju*) as performed in Guangdong and Hong Kong over the previous decades very much reflects the shared and disparate fates of the two. Like the societies in which they were and are embedded, the opera scenes were closely integrated in the pre-1949 period, only to separate with the Cold War isolation of Guangdong from Hong Kong. Although both suffered popular decline during the postwar years, the circumstances, causes, and effects of such reversals were quite different. As we now move toward the end of the second decade of post-Mao reform, their trajectories are yet again heading toward convergence, as similarities begin once more to outweigh differences.

Yuet kek was long the most popular entertainment form of the province, with appeal to rich and poor alike. Although its primary audience has always been the three-quarters or so of the province's population that understand Cantonese, large numbers of Cantonese speakers in Guangxi as well as Hong Kong, Macao, and overseas have also been numbered among its enthusiastic adherents. With as long a history of artistic development as Beijing opera, *Yuet kek* has come to be emblematic of Cantonese cultural identity, and as such it serves well as a marker of sociocultural change and adaptation.

During the 1950s, for example, *Yuet kek* began to fall out of favor in both Hong Kong and Guangdong. In both societies the opera was seen as "too traditional." In colonial Hong Kong *Yuet kek* was unfavorably contrasted with the "modern" and "more sophisticated" art forms of the West, and its falloff in popularity was precipitous, especially among the elite. In the People's Republic also *Yuet kek* was also seen to be "too traditional," but there the evaluation rested on the opera's seeming lack of congruence with the revolutionary changes that had transformed Chinese culture. With its repertoire based on feudal characters, themes, and values, the opera was politically suspect. As most political campaigns began in the cultural realm, those professionally involved with *Yuet kek* always felt vulnerable to harassment and persecution.

People on both sides of the Shenzhen border, then, had ideological reasons to be suspicious of the opera. In addition, in both societies socioeconomic changes (earlier in Hong Kong, more recently in the People's Republic) have brought about increased competition from other entertainment forms and demands on people's time. Little wonder, then, that the populations of Guangdong and Hong Kong turned away from *Yuet kek* and toward "new things."

Challenges *to* Yuet kek

The recent decline in *Yuet kek* popularity is not the first time it has hit a "slack wind." Wang (1986: 64) points out that even in the late Qing era, *Yuet kek* experienced political problems when the performer Li Wenmao led an anti-Qing uprising and the government banned the opera. In the late 1920s and early 1930s *Yuet kek* once again fell on hard times with the advent of the sound movies.

The boom in "talkies" hit Guangzhou forcefully: the city had twice as many movie theaters by 1933 as theaters given over to *Yuet kek* performances, with the movie theaters taking in 1.6 times the income of the opera-based theaters. In response to the fall-off in attendance[17] many troupes folded and many *Yuet kek* people joined the Depression jobless. "Why did the movies beat out *Yuet kek*? Because their artistic methods were more advanced than the old opera's" (Wang 1986: 65). Others claim that movies were more popular because they dealt with a wide variety of themes and because they were shorter than opera performances.

The past few decades represent the latest "slack wind" period and once again the question is raised as to why the opera has fallen on hard times. In the People's Republic, analysts point to the competition from new media. Whereas before the reform era the only two public entertainment forms were the movies and *Yuet kek*, nowadays the possibilities are far wider. Disco dancing, pool, the radio, *karaoke*, *ma jiang*, and television offer alternatives that were simply not available a few years ago.

Television is held to be the main culprit. Why is it so popular? Just as its predecessor medium, the motion picture, was held to be a "more lively" art form with greater attraction for all but especially for the young, so is television today seen as the great competitor. Wang Jianxun (1986: 65), however, does not see this necessarily as a fight to the finish. He points out that television has appeared in other societies without wiping out rival entertainment forms; China's opera can likewise recover from the initial challenge. In both the United States and the Soviet Union, movies and drama lost out to television but then experienced a boom. In the United States, movies and drama diversified and kept pace in the entertainment field, while in the Soviet Union, theater and drama attendance increased to levels ten times that of the pre-TV period. To Wang this suggests that the excitement of a new medium temporarily crowds out older and more established entertainment forms, but that given time the old forms will make a comeback. *Yuet kek*, he believes, will do precisely that.

Change, Condemnation, and More Change

Increased competition from other media dimmed the popularity of *Yuet kek* during the 1920s and 1930s and during the post-1950 decades, but such times also gave rise to reform, as the entertainment form and its practitioners struggled to retain their audience. So the opera changed, just as the rest of society changed. Given the outward orientation of the province both then and now, it is not surprising that many of those changes were West-inspired and Hong Kong–mediated.

The increased commercial competition from movies a half-century ago brought a number of innovations to *Yuet kek*, and in fact inspired a renewed "Golden Age of *Yuet kek*." Many foreign tales became the bases for new operas while playwrights also made great use of traditional folk tales and short stories. Even contemporary social commentary was absorbed into the plays of the 1930s and 1940s (Wang, 1986: 65).

Yuet kek absorbed more foreign influences than any other Chinese dramatic form in its music, dance, and acting style. Guangdong saw the first operatic use of the violin (instead of the *er hu*); the pioneering playwrights Shi Juexian (Sit Kok-Sin in Cantonese) and Ma Shizeng introduced instruments, plays, and acting styles from both Beijing opera and foreign drama; and new singing styles captivated audiences, as even the musicians developed their own virtuosi. Other innovations included new types of stage lighting and, significantly, singing and talking in the Guangzhou vernacular, as opposed to the stage speech that had long characterized the drama (Wang, 1986: 66).

The revolution that attenuated Guangdong's ties with Hong Kong also made foreign innovations seem culturally and politically suspect. In the 1950s Guangdong's *Yuet kek* was deliberately shorn of some of the foreign influences, especially the use of foreign instruments and musical styles and the choice of plays written and performed.[18] The art still thrived, though, with official government subvention and support as a people's art.

The Great Proletarian Cultural Revolution that began in 1966, however, was another story. The Cultural Revolution was a disaster for *Yuet kek* in a number of ways. First, the political leadership in Beijing insisted on reforming the opera by making it more like Beijing opera, or more precisely, Beijing *Revolutionary* opera. *Yuet kek* was denounced as feudal and reactionary and overly fond of outside influences. It was under such circumstances that *Yuet kek* was more or less shelved for a decade, as its performers, if they performed at all, put on non–*Yuet kek* pieces.

The effect on the opera's development was longlasting. Revolutionary operas reduced the number of major classical stage characters from sixteen to only two; recent reopenings have featured more than such anemic fare, but hardly the dozen-plus roles of the past. One interesting aspect of these changes, it should be noted, is the greater number of female roles employed.

Although applications to join operatic troupes increased during the Cultural Revolution (as a way to avoid being sent down to the countryside), the decade-long ban on traditional *Yuet kek* meant that nearly an entire generation was raised with little exposure to the opera, its musical style, and its standards of quality. Even as audiences, they have limited appreciation, for their lack of schooling means that they do not understand the artistic, historical, geographical, and cultural references of the plays.[19] Such audiences thus have very low performance standards; half the audience is not sure what a good performance is, and the other, older aficionados are just happy once again to hear and enjoy their favorite art form. Thus it is not surprising that young people consider *Yuet kek* a low form of entertainment.

Aside from the occasional television broadcast, these days it is not as easy as it was to actually take in a performance. Before the Cultural Revolution many theaters were expressly reserved for *Yuet kek*, but now many of these are gone. Even those that remain have major problems, for they have not been renovated for over thirty years, creating insufferable conditions for both troupes and their would-be audiences.

An even more fundamental problem is a sense of lassitude which many claim has enveloped the opera. Some people say the waxing and waning of an opera troupe's strength is natural, that the art form is popular with the masses and will never fade. But this ignores the ill effects the "iron rice bowl" system had on deadening creativity and encouraging few people to perform or raise their level of performance or even to enter the profession (Wang, 1986: 66). Thus one hears complaints that playwrights are not ambitious or creative enough, and that the provincial and city troupes perform too little and have not maintained the high standards of the past.

Despite such criticisms, we should note that since 1978, governments have renewed their support of the opera by subsidizing troupes. This parallels actions taken by the Hong Kong government a decade earlier. In today's Guangdong there are a couple of provincial-level troupes, while Guangzhou itself has three or four, and other cities, municipal districts, and counties have one or two.

Nan Hai county has one troupe today, although it had two in the 1950s as well as during the first flush of reform and prosperity in the early 1980s. The Nam Hoi Yuet Kek Tuen (Nanhai Yuejutuan, South Sea Cantonese Opera Troupe) has a staff of over thirty, twenty-seven of whom are performers and three of whom are managers. The county pays all salaries and much of the expenses, enabling the troupe to put on more than two hundred performances a year. They try out innovations, and a very popular one is to sing pop songs both in their original melody and style as well as a *Yuet kek* version. Although they had to abandon their training classes when their budget was cut, the troupe does manage to tour throughout the county and beyond, often making it to nearby Guangzhou.

Not all *Yuet kek* troupes, though, are based in Guangdong. Perhaps the second most well-known troupe in the People's Republic after the Guangzhou-based Guangdong Yuet Kek Tuen (Guangdong Yuejutuan, Guangdong Cantonese Opera Troupe), is the Wuzhou City troupe. Hailing from the Cantonese-speaking eastern part of Guangdong's neighboring province of Guangxi, the troupe was set up on January 1, 1951, and has since expanded to include ninety people, including sixty or so performers. With support from the city's Cultural Affairs Bureau (See Munfa Guk, Cantonese for Wenhuaju), they make extensive tours of eastern Guangxi and western Guangdong.

Recruitment for this and other troupes, though, has become a problem. With the rural prosperity of the 1980s, fewer young people were drawn to the opera. Traditionally, it attracted people who either had family connections to the opera or who were too poor to take a more socially respectable job and were not averse to undergoing years of rigorous and difficult training. After 1949 and before the Cultural Revolution, government subvention meant that both the salaries and social prestige of *Yuet kek* rose, and thousands attempted to join. In 1957, the provincial training school received more than ten thousand applications for its fifty openings! By 1984, the number of applications for the same fifty openings had dropped to three hundred.

Some *Yuet kek* people point to the training period in school—six to seven years—as too long an apprenticeship for today's youth; few young people want to put up with the hard work and lack of a salary for so long, only to join a profession that keeps you moving constantly around the countryside but pays you only modest wages. New graduates in 1986 were receiving only 39.5 yuan each month and could look forward to a second-year increase to 47 yuan. Even with bonuses of 20 to 30 yuan, monthly pay scales for troupe members at all levels of age and experience were low, with 120 yuan the average. Opportunities outside the profession seem increasingly more lucrative.

Such is the case with Hong Kong's *Yuet kek* scene as well. There the opera has long ceased being a financially remunerative occupation for all but the most renowned stars. There too the opera is no longer an outlet for the poor; in fact, *Yuet kek* has to some degree been converted into a high art form with attraction either for those with a family background in the opera or for well-to-do students whose families can afford the low salaries and frequent expenses nowadays associated with opera work (Guldin, 1992b). Training schools for amateurs and professionals have also opened to train formally those interested in the craft. It seems that in both societies, then, despite difficulties with low salaries, recruitment for the opera has undergone parallel shifts away from the pre-1949 reliance on performers' relatives and the poor to an increasing reliance on school training, with family ties a secondary avenue of entry.

Operatic Reform

Some maintain that just as commercial competition in the prerevolutionary period saved the opera by reinvigorating it, the socialist arts of today can also benefit from competition (Wang, 1986: 66). Many changes have been proposed and some have already been implemented, with music changing the most. Compositions are more elaborate now and new instruments have been added experimentally, such as the electric guitar and the jazz saxophone. One actress pointed out, however, that modernization goes beyond adding instruments, for changes are needed in all aspects of *Yuet kek*, such as performance quality, makeup, musical composition, and the scripts themselves. She believes scripts are the key, and a male colleague of hers was quick to point out approvingly that some new plays of the mid-1980s call for characters to wear Western clothes and perform *Yuet kek* versions of Western plays like *The Merchant of Venice*, because "*Yuet kek* doesn't have to deal with old things and topics."

Still others make more specific recommendations for reviving the art form. He (1986: 66–69) called for resuming the once-a-year gathering of all opera performers for a friendly competition, for this would allow isolated local, district, and provincial troupes an opportunity to interact. He's other suggestions call for (1) resuming the practice of the troupes annually dispersing into smaller groups to create new techniques and to concentrate on skill development, (2) having opera stars cultivate their fans by giving regular performances, (3) encouraging the training of new generations of performers by extending the network of opera schools from the current three to a far larger number, and (4) reviving the connections between troupes and particular theaters.

Other suggestions for operatic resuscitation abound. Just as occurred in Hong Kong during the 1950s, Guangzhou also saw the closing of its *Yuet kek* theaters, so this trend must be turned around. With new theater bases, the troupes could give morning, afternoon, and evening performances, and would have the time, venue, and enthusiasm to develop new angles on their craft. Other ways to increase the exposure of today's Cantonese to the opera might include developing operas for television and the movies, thus giving the other media competitors some competition on their own turf.

Yet another suggestion is to arrange for more low-cost shows on a fee-free performance basis. In the pre-1949 past, business companies sponsored performances in amusement areas; today this should be the government's responsibility, "as it is in Hong Kong" (to a degree).[20] By trying all the above suggestions, *Yuet kek* could once again revive as one of the major artistic forms of southern Chinese society.

However, there are those who warn that implementing too many reforms can threaten the integrity of the art form. Pointing to failed experiments, like Ma Shizheng's attempt to have overseas opera troupes in America sing *Yuet kek* in English, these critics warn against denuding *Yuet kek* of any *Guangdong mei*

(*Guangdong wei*, Cantonese flavor). Many feel that the opera can go only so far in adapting to current conditions without ceasing to be *Yuet kek*; one cannot limitlessly absorb elements of other provincial opera traditions or of Western entertainment forms. Efforts to standardize the twelve-note scale are therefore misguided because they strike at the unique characteristics of Cantonese music. Nor should playwrights continue to ignore the military form (*mo hei*, Cantonese for Wuxi) in favor of the civil (*mun hei*, Cantonese for Wenxi); both are necessary to the future rounded development of *Yuet kek*. Reformers should remember that the less *Yuet kek* sounds and looks like *Yuet kek*, the less its older audience will appreciate it; so in an effort to appease the tastes of the untutored young, permanent damage may be inflicted upon a beautiful art form.

Whereas some (Wang, 1986: 67) believe the key to the opera's popular revival will be in making its themes reflect contemporary life by writing in a more realistic vein, others (Mo, 1986: 70–71) believe that this emphasis is misguided. They resent the implication that, as some leaders charge, *Yuet kek* is the most conservative of all Cantonese art forms and is nearly impervious to change. Such defenders of the opera point out that all art forms change, and so has *Yuet kek*. Realism, furthermore, is not the only artistic form available to a writer, and like the freehand style of painting, one can make powerful statements about life without writing in a realistic vein. When reforming the opera, artists must be careful neither to purge all local flavor (a goal of the Cultural Revolution) nor to resist all innovation. To reform *Yuet kek*, a balance must be struck using the internal rules of *Yuet kek*.

A rise in the social prestige of the opera, paralleling such an increase in Hong Kong, would occur when and if intellectuals and leaders paid more attention to the art form. Opera officials are thus pleased to report enthusiastic receptions from university and middle school students of their performances and hope this anticipates new social attitudes and support. For an art form quite reliant on government support, however, the attitude of party and government cadres is crucial. Discussing the proposed reforms in the opera, one actor explained: "Some people worry that this means 'commercialization,' but I think that is a product of being overly afraid of rightist tendencies. We just need to strengthen and reform the party leadership of *Yuet kek* and then competition will enable us to produce good material, personnel, and popularity." Thus the shifting fortunes of the opera rely very much on changing party attitudes, for only such a changed view of the opera will enable it to capture the funds necessary to popularize it in the late twentieth century.

Even countryside performances require big money in today's China. It takes 1,200 yuan to rent an open field for a week's performances, and if you have eighty or so people in a troupe, the costs of room and board and transportation for a week (including seven or eight trucks) will come to about 10,000 yuan. Who will put up the money? In the city troupes can charge admission—in Guangzhou's Culture Park (Munfa Gongyuen, Cantonese for Wenhua gongyuan) tickets sell briskly for upward of 40 yuan a seat—but the countryside needs sponsors even when local demand is strong. Law Ga Bo, one of the star performers of the Guangzhou stage, reported his frustration with the leadership when, after his return from a very successful tour abroad, one of the province's leaders asked why there was such a big audience for *Yuet kek* abroad and so little demand for it in Guangzhou. "I felt like shouting at him, 'if the leadership would support us more, we could preserve and develop this art as it should be developed!' "

For its part, the leadership reminds opera people that China is a poor country and local governments can ill afford continuing large-scale subsidy of the opera. To cut costs, one performer has suggested that troupes cut down their size so that they will need less financial support.

Learn from Hong Kong

Without a doubt, many in the Guangdong *Yuet kek* world look to the enhanced status and salaries of *Yuet kek* performers in Hong Kong with envy. Performers who have performed in both places will animatedly describe the differing conditions: "Compared to Hong Kong, performing in Guangzhou is like performing in the 1940s. No air conditioning, terrible bathroom facilities, inadequate acoustics. During the summer the entire troupe has to suffer through a performance. By contrast, Hong Kong is heavenly."

To many Guangdong *Yuet kek* people, the question is how to emulate the Hong Kong model. They see that in Hong Kong *Yuet kek* has become a "high art" form, with the intelligentsia and the social elite giving it official sanction and support (Guldin, 1992b). If even colonial Hong Kong can so appreciate such a Chinese art form, What can we do to reach the same goal? they ask.

In Hong Kong today, *Yuet kek* is being popularized, with schools introducing it to their pupils from elementary school to college. People are writing M.A. and Ph.D. theses on it and these efforts should be supported. Finally, if we want to promote *Yuet kek*, we must raise the form's artistic competitiveness (Wang, 1986: 67).

To many in the *Yuet kek* world of the People's Republic, these then are the symbols of sophisticated elite approval in Hong Kong: young people going to the opera wearing Western suits and dresses and then attending classes on the opera in the Chinese University of Hong Kong.

The differences between the locales can also be seen in audience–performer interaction. Poon Choiwa (Pan Caihua), female star of the Wuzhou troupe, pointed out that Hong Kong audiences are more polite, more enthusiastic, and more reverent during performances. By contrast, Wuzhou audiences may also be very appreciative of the opera, but they do not behave like the Westernized Hong Kongers. An air of informality surrounds the performances, while the often standing-room-only crowd mills around, eats, and talks. Rural fans in the

People's Republic often show their appreciation by inviting *Yuet kek* people to their homes to drink tea or by washing their clothes or performing other small services; in Hong Kong *Yuet kek* stars are treated by their wealthy fans and patrons to lavish meals and expensive gifts. Although People's Republic performers do not feel that everything is better in Hong Kong,[21] clearly the attentive audiences and superior material conditions of Hong Kong make proud artists feel that they are finally getting the recognition long due them.

Throughout the 1980s the *Yuet kek* circles in Guangdong and Hong Kong have gradually begun to overlap. As they did before 1949, troupes now travel all around the province and the delta—and Hong Kong is once again a delta performance venue. Joint performances with stars from both operatic circles have been held in Guangzhou and Hong Kong before sold-out crowds of enthusiastic fans. One commentator (He, 1986: 67) thinks the time is right to reintroduce formally the Saang-Gaang Baan (Shenggang ban, Provincial–Hong Kong Troupe), which plied the delta before the Chinese Revolution split the area apart. Another suggestion is to resume as well the Saang-Gaang Hung Leng Daiwooi Kuen, so as to have performers from both sides of the border meet regularly. And perhaps they could take a lead from the soccer world and have a province–Hong Kong awards competition with the proceeds from the extravaganza donated to *Yuet kek* support activities.

"Modernizing" Yuet Kek

In the middle and late twentieth century *Yuet kek*, an art form with hundreds of years of continuous development from the Song and Yuan dynasties to the Ming and Qing, came to symbolize unchanging "tradition" in both Hong Kong and Guangdong. During the 1950s and 1960s xenocentric Hong Kong had its own cultural revolution as it substituted many Western standards for Chinese. Continuing the tendency of many twentieth-century Chinese to assume that what was Western was "modern," Hong Kong came to view much of Chinese culture as "traditional" customs that would inevitably be replaced by the culture of the "modern" West. Of course, there was no room in such an evaluation for the "backward" and "traditional" *Yuet kek*, and its popularity ebbed rapidly.

Beginning in the 1950s but developing with a vengeance in the 1960s and 1970s, the modernizers of the Cultural Revolution also attempted to cast aside *Yuet kek* as a relic of the old "traditional" society that was to be replaced. In such a xenophobic and "antifeudal" atmosphere, *Yuet kek* nearly suffocated. Even today, there are many who say the only way to "save" the opera is to "modernize" it.

In responding to the puzzle of why an art form that is highly flexible and adaptive to new cultural items and that has repeatedly remade itself over the years can suddenly appear to be conservative and traditional, some scholars of the opera point to the increased rate of cultural change. Today's rapid cultural changes outrun the ability of art forms like *Yuet kek* to adapt to the vastly changed conditions of contemporary life. In the past this was certainly not the case, with *Yuet kek* reflecting life even more accurately than novels. By the May Fourth Movement of 1919, however, *Yuet kek* and other regional operas were criticized as backward when compared with spoken plays as introduced from the West (Mo, 1986: 69–70). This appears to have been a reaction to their seeming lack of social commentary relevant to China's twentieth-century plight, as well as a product of the philo-Westernism of many of the critics.

In the 1980s this attitude continued to hold sway among many intellectuals and other Westernizers. As more than one *Yuet kek* aficionado bitterly commented, many of the reporters, scholars, and *ganbu* (cadres) who are most caustic in their remarks about the opera "don't even bother to see it themselves. And those so-called scholars dare to criticize something they have never studied!" There may also be a class bias operating here on the part of intellectuals who consider the opera boorish entertainment of the ignorant masses.

Thus the irony of Hong Kong—the Westernized, modern, and prosperous locus of Cantonese modernity—experiencing a *Yuet kek* revival in the late 1970s and 1980s! Such a development should surely give pause to those who make facile formulas with "Chinese" equaling traditional and "Western" equaling modern. The Hong Kong model for Guangdong is how to be both Chinese *and* modern, and if *Yuet kek* goes in Hong Kong, then should it not be revived in Guangzhou as well?

Certainly, the *Yuet kek* revival has forced people to reconsider some basic cultural assumptions. It may be that *Yuet kek*'s decline was exaggerated, for it might be more accurate to say that *Yuet kek* experienced a significant decline in popularity in the major urban areas of the delta (both Guangzhou and Hong Kong included) but that elsewhere the opera continued to exert a strong hold on its audience. With the greater vision that a pan-delta perspective gives us, we can see that perhaps the intellectuals and newspaper reporters have been noting, cheering, and decrying a basically *urban* phenomenon.

Indeed, many observations seem to bear out this conclusion. We can note, for example, that throughout the 1950s and 1960s *Yuet kek* continued to flourish in Hong Kong's semirural New Territories, while in the People's Republic *Yuet kek*, before and after the Cultural Revolution, had sunk deep roots into the soil of western Guangdong and eastern Guangxi. Local troupes in Zhanjiang and Wuzhou, and in Taishan and Nanhai counties in the delta, have all established reputations for quality performances and have audiences to match. It may very well be that the oft-noted decline of the opera has more to do with urban dwellers' consideration of what is faddishly "modern" than with any fundamental realignment of Chinese culture.

What is also striking about discussions of the "fate" of *Yuet kek* in both Guangdong and Hong Kong is the relative optimism of the opera people in the People's Republic about the future of the opera, even as they admit that things were better in the past and are better now in Hong Kong. They exude self-confidence when they discuss their level of competence as compared with other regional opera forms.[22] Despite the blows they suffered during the Cultural Revolution, *Yuet kek* people readily take a long view of the situation, offering their perspective of how art styles and tastes run in cycles: Now Western arts are popular, but after the novelty wears off, then interest in things Chinese will return. Like the craze for Western clothing and Western suits, this too will pass. The Chinese people will survive and so will Chinese culture, including calligraphy, Chinese painting, and the opera. These new cultural influences may not last. Chinese culture, including the opera, has great strength, so we are not worried about the opera's future.

Of course, one reason the People's Republic opera performers do not worry as much about the future is that they are salaried workers for the most part, and so their personal economic futures are fairly secure. By contrast, it is quite often difficult if not impossible for Hong Kong people to rely on working in the opera to make a living. Such a difference would naturally give one varying orientations about the future. Yet there may also be another quite relevant factor underlying the greater optimism of the Guangdong people. Perhaps people in colonial Hong Kong, long accustomed to considering Hong Kong as if it developed in splendid isolation from the rest of China, forget that Hong Kong and its institutions do not exist in a vacuum, that Hong Kong is actually a part of a larger cultural area. This is something people in Guangzhou and Guangdong seem to understand intuitively and it enables them to see that even though certain areas may experience a dip in popularity for the opera, the countryside is so vast and the combined cultural heritage so ingrained, that long-standing cultural patterns—and art forms—are not so easily consigned to the dust bin of history. Given the revival of *Yuet kek* in Hong Kong, furthermore, it seems that the optimists may be right.

Namyuet (Cantonese for *Nanyue*, Southern Guangdong) Culture

The 1980s saw the functional reintegration of Hong Kong with Guangdong as the region was transformed into an economic powerhouse for southern China and world markets. Political reintegration was also proceeding apace as the People's Republic's representatives and their opinions increasingly held sway in Hong Kong governmental and private councils. Kinship, language, and other cultural ties, moreover, were holding the region ever closer. And now, in the mid-1990s, it is time for us to ask if we are already seeing the outlines of a new Cantonese cultural area.[23]

Perhaps we should more accurately say a *reunified* Cantonese cultural area, for both Hong Kong and the delta have been Cantonese areas even while they pursued very different paths for forty years. Often there were many similarities in their development despite many differences. Take, for example, the fate of *Yuet kek*, that quintessential Cantonese art form, for *Yuet kek*'s ups and downs show some interesting parallels on both sides of the border. As we have seen, the 1940s were a boom period for the opera throughout the entire delta area, including Hong Kong. This was followed by a period of decline in Westernizing Hong Kong, while the opera continued to develop in revolutionary China. Then came the 1960s and the increasing Westernization of Hong Kong and the ultraleftism of the Cultural Revolution in Guangdong. Under both waves, *Yuet kek* was submerged. Then in the 1970s in Hong Kong and later, in the 1980s, in Guangzhou, *Yuet kek* made a comeback. By the 1990s, their fates seemed to be joined once again. This time, however, the cultural milieu in which the new regional *Yuet kek* develops will be radically different from that of the past.

The Emergence of Namyuet *Culture*

Despite the many continuities of today's reintegration of the delta with the pre-1949 past, we would be wrong to imagine that the old patterns have simply reemerged unscathed from the twists and turns of a half-century of history. The emerging culture of the post-1997 period will incorporate two very different versions of Cantonese culture, neither of which existed in the 1940s. This future culture of southern Guangdong—what the ethnologist Chen Qinghua suggested I call *Namyuet* (*Nanyue* in Cantonese) culture—is comprised on the one hand of Guangdong's socialist People's Republic culture and on the other of Hong Kong's capitalist and Western-influenced culture (Zhou, 1990: 38).

Such a culture would not be historically unique, for Chinese culture in general has a history of incorporation of foreign elements, and Guangdong in particular has been at the forefront of many a foreign-born innovation. *Namyuet* culture would encompass Hong Kong's vibrant cultural model of modernity and sinicize and socialize it to the point where it could realistically guide the way for Cantonese in the delta and beyond to reformulate their society. The 1980s and 1990s revival in Hong Kong of interest in things Cantonese can be seen as a cultural turning back toward Chinese origins as well as a testimony to the endurance of regional ties. The emergence of *Namyuet* culture signifies the historical maturation of an integrated southern Guangdong society.[24]

Namyuet culture also promises to play a large role in the formulation of China's twenty-first-century culture. Already, the innovations of the Pearl River Delta and Guangdong are stretching beyond the provincial borders as Hong Kong investors sink their money into the Xiamen Special Economic Zone in Fujian[25] and the provinces of Hunan, Guangxi, and Jiangxi surrounding Guangdong. These regions experience boom trade on their borders, and Guangdong television programs are bought up by the broadcasting stations of the same three provinces (Leeming, 1989: 272–73; Vogel, 1989: 447; Zhou, 1990: 40).

Furthermore, *Namyuet's* cultural innovations in dress, speech, communications, music, and lifestyle are fast becoming the national rage. Cantonese entrepreneurs sell stylish fashions to those up north, while businessmen in the north take classes to learn Cantonese. It has even been reported that customers in search of better treatment in shops north of the Yangzi attempt Hong Kong accents for their *putonghua*, and people throughout the country talk of the *nanfeng* (south wind) blowing from Hong Kong and of its influence on the country.

In the context of 1997, furthermore, we must wonder what political coloration that wind will have during the next few years. In all the talk of Hong Kong's political future the speculation has rested on what China will do to Hong Kong. Little has been said by those outside the People's Republic of China about Hong Kong's political influence on the rest of the country. What strikes this observer is the repeated hope of PRC commentators that Hong Kong will be allowed to keep its international links and its open society after it becomes the Hong Kong Special Administrative Region (HKSAR). Perhaps the hope is that Hong Kong's open and dynamic society—and by extension *Namyuet* culture—will transform China into a more dynamic and democratic society in the second half-century of the People's Republic.

Yuet kek—as an embodiment of the Chinese and Cantonese heritage of the region—serves as a splendid wind vane to show the movements of these future cultural currents. Art forms reflect the social formations of the societies of which they are a part, and so our tracing of the vicissitudes of the opera during the twentieth century shed light on the shifting ideologies and political economies of Guangdong and Hong Kong society. Charting the opera's future will likewise tell us much about the emerging culture of the area, for it will give us insights into the synthesizing, revitalizing, or nationalistic tendencies of *Namyuet* culture.

The Hong Kong SAR: Toward a Pearl River Delta Megalopolis

Namyuet culture is emerging against the backdrop of an increasingly integrated urban zone. The outlines of a highly urbanized zone, a megalopolitan triangle, stretching from Hong Kong and Shenzhen in the southeast of the delta to Guangzhou and Foshan in the north and then to Macao and Zhuhai Special Economic Zone in the southwest, have already appeared. What seems to be developing is a classic megalopolitan cluster, for the physical distance between Guangzhou and Hong Kong, 130 kilometers, fits the pattern for other megalopolises: New York and Philadelphia, the core pivots of the original Boston–Washington, D.C. megalopolis, are 150 kilometers apart, while Beijing–Tianjin, Osaka–Hiroshima, Tokyo–Nagoya, Taibei–Taizhong, Milan–Turin, and Amsterdam–Antwerp are all about 130 kilometers distant from each other (Leeming, 1989: 273–74; Xu and Li, 1990: 65; Zheng, 1989: 255). The Pearl River Delta would thus form a distinct urban area in southern China, while both Guangzhou and Hong Kong would maintain their separate identities and political-economic functions as the twin poles of a common sociocultural entity.

Guangzhou and Foshan would likely specialize in heavy industry and continue to be a center for research and development. The Hong Kong–Shenzhen subregion would continue to be a "window" to the outside through which "information about the latest developments in technology, design and world market trends" would be disseminated to the rest of the country (Xu and Li, 1990: 65–66). Hong Kong's preeminent position as an international hub for finance, insurance, and shipping would continue, and it would serve as the major transshipment point for an ever-greater volume of the People's Republic's international trade (Xu, 1988: 37; Zheng, 1989: 255).

In this integrated greater delta region, the counties (*xian*) located between the Guangzhou and Hong Kong poles would continue their rapid strides toward becoming a developed area far ahead of the rest of the nation. With the "Four Little Tigers" of Guangdong—Nanhai, Shunde, Dongguan, and Zhongshan counties—leading the way, it is also likely that the delta counties will soon overtake Guangzhou in population and industrial output totals (Luk, 1989: 209; Zheng, 1989: 255).

History teaches us that such developments in the delta are usually accompanied by greater inequalities throughout the province (Luk, 1989: 211). With provincial and central government commitments to balanced growth mostly abandoned, the delta has been left to resume its traditional position as the most prosperous area of coastal Guangdong. Yet even within the delta region, there will be uneven movement toward economic and cultural flowering.

Despite the functional differentiation pointed to above, there is no doubt that competition among the three legs of this Pearl River Delta society will continue to influence their development. Guangzhou may be the biggest loser in the equation as its economic preeminence is further eroded by both the delta and Hong Kong and as it competes politically with Hong Kong for provincial leadership. Ever since the founding of Hong Kong in the 1840s, the colony has represented a threat to Guangzhou's supremacy in the area, and the reincorporation of this dynamic international city into the China body politic may cut into Guangzhou's reputation and clout in both the province and nation (Vogel, 1989: 198).

Thus, the twenty-first century will dawn on a Hong Kong Special Administrative Region that will be functionally part of a wider People's Republic entity. In all ways but the political-administrative, Hong Kong will be a part of the delta, and it will be a leading element in the People's Republic. Whichever way the larger societal, political, and economic winds blow during the next century, it is clear that a dynamic and innovative *Namyuet* culture will greatly influence the direction that China and Chinese life take in the years to come.

Notes

1. We should, at the start, note the presence of a third entity here, the Portuguese colony of Macao on the west side of the mouth of the Pearl River. Analysts and official

People's Republic spokesmen are careful to talk about "*sheng-gang-ao*" (Guangdong–Hong Kong–Macao) ties or relations, but this is mostly political ritual. Everyone knows that it is the Hong Kong–Pearl River Delta connection that is central, with Macao usually merely an afterthought (Vogel, 1989: 59).

2. Some of these Hong Kong–sent materials went north; informants tell me they sent many a tin of cooking oil to Beijing and environs. Others noted ironically that much of the foodstuffs from Hong Kong originated in the People's Republic.

3. For a more detailed consideration of the subsidiary role Guangdong played in the development and prosperity of Hong Kong, see Guldin (1989).

4. Zheng estimates that of these millions of border crossings by Hong Kong residents, over 90 percent had the delta as their destination.

5. Zheng (1989: 258) reports that in Guangzhou in the late 1980s only three telephones were available for every hundred residents. Work on telephone expansion since then, combined with the increase in cellular phones, led to the change from six to seven telephone digits in Guangzhou in June of 1991.

6. By 1990, People's Republic residents could make tourist visits to Southeast Asia as well.

7. One should be careful, though, about exaggerating Hong Kong's influence on the delta. Chan (1988: 12–13) makes the point that the expansion in the delta's export production was more an outcome of industrial growth than the opposite. In other words, Hong Kong's China industries were only part of the picture and not the whole scene. As Zheng cautioned us, we must avoid thinking about the Pearl River Delta as *merely* Hong Kong's hinterland and recognize the *limits* of its impacts as well.

8. Hong Kong Chinese insist that their clothes, furniture, and other consumer items all be imports, rejecting out of hand any Chinese-made goods. Then when they move abroad, the same Hong Kong Chinese will wear Chinese cloth slippers, hang Chinese paintings, buy Chinese red wooden furniture for their homes, and do their best to recover their Chineseness! See Guldin (1980, 1992a) for discussions of Hong Kong's model of modernity and its influence on the People's Republic.

9. The *nanfeng qang* ("south wind window") of popular expression can actually refer not just to Hong Kong but to Southeast Asia, Japan, Europe, America, and the overseas Chinese as well. Nevertheless, Hong Kong still remains the source of most of the eddies whirling over the delta.

10. Below the *zhongxin*, furthermore, is another network of village-based *wenhua shi* (culture rooms) which have not yet spread to every area. Some of the *wenhua zhan* were set up with funds from overseas *tongbao* (compatriots).

11. Or at least that is the impression my Nanhai county hosts gave me as we attended more than a few dance halls in the small towns of the county.

12. Not counting, of course, the two "patriotic," or leftist, newspapers in Hong Kong usually sympathetic to the People's Republic, *Ta kung pao* and *Wen wei pao*. Some magazines that are often hand-carried into China by Hong Kong compatriots are *Ming bao*, *Xin bao*, *Tian tian ribao*, and *Xianggang dianbao* (Zhou, 1990: 39).

13. Zhou (1990: 40) also makes the interesting observation that another reason the printed media's effect on the delta is not as great as it could be is the successful competition of the electronic media. His data show the delta per capita monthly expenditure on books and newspapers combined to be not quite 40 fen (cents).

14. This is an old idea in Chinese society, going back at least to the turn of the century, when Chinese reformers sought to change selectively some aspects of Chinese society by utilizing the "best of both East and West."

15. The possibility also exists, however, for *putonghua* exposure to increase in the Guangdong countryside as the now ubiquitous television sets bring the foreign tongue

into everyone's home. Even Hong Kong television, looking toward 1997, has begun to undergo its own limited "*putonghua*-ization."

16. For a discussion of the sociocultural status of *Yuet kek* in Hong Kong, see Guldin, 1992b.

17. As they are today, then too it was young people who were in the vanguard of those abandoning older entertainment forms.

18. The Revolution also looked down on what it dubbed "feudal superstition," and so "spirit performances," the already fading practice of first performing a play for the local village or clan spirits, complete with incense burning, prayer, divination, and chicken-blood sacrifice, were banned after Liberation. In Hong Kong, by contrast, such performances have continued to be a major revenue earner for troupes there (Guldin, 1992b).

19. Even students admitted into *Yuet kek* training schools display an appalling lack of understanding of the scripts due to their low educational levels, especially in Chinese history. This is said to hinder their acting ability.

20. The Hong Kong government (especially the Urban Council) does indeed sponsor some free and open-air performances throughout Hong Kong, mostly in urban areas. Despite the implication of this opera fan's comments, though, these government-sponsored shows are a minority of the total.

21. Certain skills—acrobatics and acrobatic dance, for example—are considered to be on a higher performance level in the People's Republic.

22. For example: "Beijing Opera is far more conservative than *Yuet kek*. Our people are far more open to innovation and always have been. Our people are more enthusiastic about their work and even our male actors spend a great deal of time applying performance makeup."

23. Not everyone was equally enthusiastic about the possibilities of reintegration, however. People on both sides of the border are already voicing worries as to who will take advantage of whom after 1997. Thus some Guangzhou commentators worry about the delta becoming merely a hinterland appendage of Hong Kong rather than an equal partner (Zheng, 1989: 255), while others grumble about People's Republic performers in Hong Kong being more concerned with promoting Guangzhou artists in Hong Kong than local Hong Kong people (Ng, 1987: 5).

24. There are those in Guangdong, however, who fear that Hong Kong will dominate the future Cantonese world. They call for People's Republic Cantonese to adapt judiciously from Hong Kong and its culture only those elements worthy of emulation (Vogel, 1989: 424; Xu, 1987: 298; Zhou, 1989: 237).

25. The anthropologist Chen Guoqiang reported (personal communication) that 70 percent of the investment in the Xiamen SEZ derives from Hong Kong. He and others also report that Hong Kong is now no longer the only outside cultural influence in Fujian. Taiwan, across the narrow Straits of Taiwan, is becoming a cultural model for Fujian similar to what Hong Kong has been to Guangdong.

References

Chan, Anita, Richard Madsen, and Jonathan Unger (1984), *Chen Village*, Berkeley: University of California Press.

Chan, Thomas M.H. (1988), *The Development and Prospects of the Zhujiang Delta Open Zone*, Shanghai: Friedrich Ebert Foundation, China Economic Papers Series.

Guldin, Gregory Eliyu (1980), "Multilineal Modernity: Ideologies of Modernization in Hong Kong," in *Proceedings of the 2nd International Symposium on Asian Studies*, Vol. I, pp. 69–86.

——— (1989), "The Invisible Hinterland: Hong Kong's Reliance on Southern

Guangdong," *City and Society*, Vol. 3, No. 1, pp. 23–39.

———(1992a), "Cantonese Opera in a Colonial Context," *CHINOPERL Papers*, No. 16, pp. 65–94.

———(1992b), "Urbanizing the Countryside: Guangzhou, Hong Kong and the Pearl River Delta," in *Urbanizing China*, ed. G. Guldin, Westport, CT: Greenwood Press, pp. 157–84.

He, Jianqing (1986), "Xiangei yueju jiede 'Sufang gufang' " (Presenting to *Yuet kek* Circles: Quickly transform old ways), *Guangzhou Yanjiu* (Guangzhou Studies), No. 2, pp. 67–69.

Johnson, Graham E., and Yuen-Fong Woon, n.d., "The Impact of Rural Reform in an Overseas Chinese Area: Examples from Two Localities," typescript.

Kristof, Nicholas D. (1991a), "Chinese Taking Hard Line to Guard Linguistic Purity," *New York Times*, February 4.

———(1991b), "A Pop Singer Shows Taiwan's Domination of Mainland Culture," *New York Times*, February 19.

Leeming, Frank (1989), "The Pearl River Delta, Hong Kong and the Guangdong Hinterland," in *Zhujiang sanjiaozhou huanjing yu kongjian fazhan* (The environment and space development in the Pearl River Delta), ed. Xueqiang Xu, Jiann Ye, and Changen Wen, Beijing: Xueshu shukan chubanshe (Science Books Press), pp. 263–75.

Li, Si-ming (1989), "Labour Mobility, Migration and Urbanization in the Pearl River Delta Area," in *Zhujiang sanjiaozhou huanjing yu kongjian fazhan* (The environment and space development in the Pearl River Delta), ed. Xueqiang Xu, Jiann Ye, and Changen Wen, Beijing: Xueshu shukan chubanshe (Science Books Press), pp. 148–71.

Luk, Chiu-ming (1989), "Zhujiang Delta in Guangdong's Regional Development," in *Zhujiang sanjiaozhou huanjing yu kongjian fazhan* (The environment and space development in the Pearl River Delta), ed. Xueqiang Xu, Jiann Ye, and Changen Wen, Beijing: Xueshu shukan chubanshe (Science Books Press), pp. 200–12.

Mo, Rucheng (1986), "Xiquhua yu xiandaihua, Shenghuohua bu ying huxiang duili" (Revising the opera and modernization need not be in opposition), *Guangzhou Yanjiu* (Guangzhou Studies), No. 2, pp. 69–72.

Ng, Sau-fong (1987), "Tuiguang yueju" (Promoting *Yuet kek*), *Dianshi ribao* (Television Daily), August 7.

Vogel, Ezra F. (1989), *One Step Ahead in China: Guangdong under Reform*, Cambridge, MA: Harvard University Press.

Wang, Jianxun (1986), "Yao zai jingzhengzhong qiu fazhan" (Development must be sought in the midst of competition), *Guangzhou Yanjiu* (Guangzhou Studies), No. 2, pp. 64–67.

Wickberg, Edgar (1992), personal communication, January 22.

Xu, Xueqiang (1987),"Duiwai kaifang yu zhujiang sanjiaozhou chengshihua" (Problems and countermeasures on the open policy and urbanization in the Pearl River Delta), *Ridai dili* (Tropical Geography), Vol. 7, No. 4, pp. 293–301.

Xu, Xueqiang, et al. (1988), *Zhujiang sanjiao zhoude fazhan yu chengshihua* (Development and urbanization in Pearl River Delta), Guangzhou: Zhongshan daxue chubanshe (Zhongshan University Press).

Xu, Xueqiang, Jiann Ye, and Changen Wen, eds. (1989), *Zhujiang sanjiaozhou huanjing yu kongjian fazhan* (The environment and spatial development in the Pearl River Delta), Beijing: Xueshu shukan chubanshe (Science Books Press).

Xu, Xueqiang, and Si-ming Li (1990), "China's Open-Door Policy and Urbanization in the Pearl River Delta Region," *International Journal of Urban and Regional Research*, Vol. 14, No. 1, pp. 49–69.

Zheng, Tianxiang (1989), "Gangau wu zhujiang sanjiaozhou kongjian guangxi moshi"

(The spatial relationships model of Hong Kong, Macao and the Pearl River Delta), in *Zhujiang sanjiaozhou huanjing yu kongjian fazhan*, ed. Xueqiang Xu, Jiann Ye, and Changen Wen, Beijing: Xueshu shukan chubanshe (Science Books Press), pp. 253–62.

Zhou, Daming (1989), "Guangzhou dushi wenhua fushe wenti lun" (A discussion on the radiation of Guangzhou's urban culture), *Dongnan wenhua* (Southeast Culture), No. 4, pp. 234–37.

———— (1990), "Zhujiang sanjiaozhoude dazhong quangbo yu dazhong wenhua" (Mass communications and mass culture in the Pearl River Delta), *Shehuixue yanjiu* (Sociology Studies), No. 5, pp. 38–44.

Zhu, Moke (1991), personal communication, August 4.

5

Community and Identity in Transition in Hong Kong

Ming-kwan Lee

The identity problem of the Hong Kong Chinese—critical self-reflections of who they are, where they belong, to which government should they pledge allegiance and loyalty, wondering about options and agonizing over choices—is not new. It is perhaps as old as the colony of Hong Kong. But the quest for answers to the problem has never been as intense and extensive as in this period of Hong Kong's political transition. The prospect of Hong Kong returning to China has reinvigorated old concerns, and, as I intend to argue later on, how the Hong Kong Chinese address these concerns will have important implications for the process and outcome of reintegration.

To put this discussion in some comparative perspective, let me perhaps begin by quickly drawing attention to the identity problems experienced by peoples elsewhere: the peoples in the developing countries and the Southeast Asian, or *Nanyang*, Chinese.

Identity crisis is not uncommon among new nations. It often accompanies the process of nation-building: when emerging from the legacy of colonial rule a people awaken to the new reality that they now have a government of their own and that within the territories defined for them they and their destiny are now bound together. This new reality is unsettling because—to quote Lucian Pye (1971: 111)—"a community finds that what it had once unquestionably accepted as the physical or psychological definitions of its collective self are no longer acceptable under new historic conditions." Perforce they have to redefine who they are and how they are to relate to one another and to the new governing authority. This has often meant that subnational groups have to learn to place their loyalties to the nation-state higher and above their commitments to primordial and communal identities. As has been proven by experience time and again, this is a very difficult process.

The *Nanyang* Chinese have been caught in both the nation-building drama of their host countries and in their predicament as ethnic and cultural minority groups (Gosling and Lim, 1983; Cushman and Wang, 1988; Wang, 1991). Seen from the perspective of the indigenous elites, the identity problem of the overseas Chinese is essentially one of "vertical identification"—of questioning their avowed and actual loyalty to the new nations, and of suspecting that they are still more loyal to the Chinese homeland than to the countries that have adopted them. The display of Chinese nationalism in the early decades of the century, the rallying calls on *Huaqiao* to contribute to China's nation-building efforts, the rise of the Chinese Communist state in 1949, the *de jure* recognition of *Huaqiao*'s Chinese citizenship by the Nationalist government in Taiwan, the holding power of Chinese culture, and the tenacity of Chinese communal solidarity have all to varying extents in different Southeast Asian countries contributed to this suspicion and distrust.

Seen from the perspective of the overseas Chinese, the identity problem has revolved around the interplay of two sets of factors—the "pull" of Chinese identities, be these racial ethnicity, culture, nationalism, or social ties, and the "push" from forces, which could be discriminatory policies and practices, political pressures, or religiocultural obstacles on the way to assimilation, that hold them back from undivided loyalty and commitment to the local societies. The last forty years have seen the increasing weakening of the "pull" factors, but this has not always been matched by a corresponding change in either the Chinese people's actual or attributed identification with *Nanyang* societies. Distancing from China is one thing; whether the overseas Chinese can then gain the acceptance and trust of the host countries is another thing; and whether they are prepared to relinquish communal Chinese identities to gain such acceptance is yet another thing. Assimilation into the national culture is not always possible. In some countries it is nearly impossible. Where assimilation is difficult, the Chinese have often resorted to the adoption of "intermediate identities" as flexible ways to cope with cross-pressures and competing demands, stressing different identities for different purposes (Gosling, 1983). In other instances, they have opted for either "forced retreat" into communal Chinese identity or the exit option, out-migration. Both options, obviously, work against their integration into the national culture, society, and polity.

There are apparent broad parallels in the identity problems posed to the Hong Kong Chinese and to the peoples of the new nations. Like the new nations, an aspect of the identity problem of the Hong Kong Chinese has to do with the impending end of colonial rule. The reality has been forced on them that, like it or not, their status as British subjects will end by June 30, 1997. Like the new nations they will soon have a government of their own. The new reality upsets taken-for-granted identities. Perforce the Hong Kong people will have to redefine who they are and how they are to relate to one another, to the outgoing colonial authority, to the incoming Chinese government, to the Chinese across the border, and to neighboring countries. The experience reinvigorates old questions weakened by one hundred and fifty years of colonial rule, questions like: Who am I? Am I Chinese or Hongkongese? What kind of Chinese am I? What will happen to my Chinese identity if I acquire a Canadian or British passport? What will happen to my children if they become Canadian?

Unlike the new nations, however, decolonization is not going to lead to independent statehood. To the new nations the central issue regarding identity concerns how to integrate various subnational communities—whether these be geographically dispersed groups or ethnic-cultural minorities—into one single system and, on top of parochial attachments and primordial ties, construct a pattern of loyalty and identification that is higher and above particularistic attachments, that is, identification and loyalty to the nation-state. To Hong Kong, however, the identity problem is at once more complex. It concerns first of all the cultivation of a sense of attachment to a new political arrangement, the Hong Kong Special Administrative Region (HKSAR), which is to replace the colonial government after June 30, 1997. It has taken the Chinese government over five years to draw up the miniconstitution, or the Basic Law, for the HKSAR. The process has involved numerous visits of teams of mainland basic-law drafters to Hong Kong, rounds and rounds of meetings and talks among Hong Kong basic-law drafters and members of a Hong Kong–based Basic Law Consultative Committee, and heated debates among them over the pace and direction of political change beyond 1997. But very few people have actually read through the document. And except for some vague notions of "one country, two systems," few people know exactly, in institutional terms, what the future government will be like. The government beyond 1997 remains, to many, a mysterious entity.

The second aspect of Hong Kong's identity problem has to do with the quintessential fact that Hong Kong, instead of gaining independence, will be reintegrated with China. The questions immediately arise of whether the Hong Kong people are prepared to pledge their loyalty and commitment, as Chinese citizens, to the government of the People's Republic, whether they take pride in this new identity, whether they are ready to accord to national political leaders, institutions, and symbols the respect expected from them, and whether they are prepared to identify with the Chinese across the border.

Seen from the perspective of national political leaders, the identity problem of the Hong Kong Chinese is one of vertical identification—of questioning their loyalty to the Chinese state. On top of perennial "center" fear of "peripheral" autonomy and disobedience, there is also apprehension that Hong Kong might become an outpost for "democratic" activities backed by Western powers, aimed at undermining, if not immediately overturning, the Communist regime. These fears are not entirely ungrounded. During the months of May and June in 1989, huge numbers of Hong Kong people (estimated to be near 1 million on each occasion) showed up at rallies and marches in support of Chinese democratic activists and, after June 4, in defiant denunciation of Beijing leaders responsible for the crackdown. The humiliating defeat of all pro-China candidates in Hong Kong's first direct elections to the Legislative Council, held in September 1991, was an unambiguous message, again, that anti-Communist sentiments were pervasive and unyielding. And, despite mounting pressures, the Alliance of Hong Kong People in Support of Democratic and Patriotic Activities in China, the organization behind continuing protest activities and secretive operations to rescue Chinese dissidents, has rejected repeated calls to disband and dissolve. It stays there, a thorn in China's side. The huge donations raised by local organizations to help flood victims in China in the summer of 1991 helped the strained relationship. But the tension remains.

There are also parallels as well as differences in the identity problems posed to the Hong Kong and *Nanyang* Chinese. In the formal sense, the parallels are striking: just as, in the case of the *Nanyang* Chinese, the ultimate and the only true option for the great majority of them is their assimilation as a minority group into the national culture, society, and polity of their respective host countries, so it is also true that, in the case of the Hong Kong Chinese, the root problem and perhaps also its ultimate solution lie in the irrevocable reintegration of capitalist Hong Kong with socialist China. Both involve a minority group agonizing over the destiny of forfeiting its proud identity as it dissolves into a greater but, in many respects, alien whole. Both raise questions not just of whether the minority group is willing but also of whether the receiving host is trusting and accepting.

The parallels perhaps end here. For the *Nanyang* Chinese, assimilation represents perhaps the final leg of a long journey to desinicization. Legal-political links to China, long epitomized in the rights and status extended to *Huaqiao*, have largely been severed. According to the Nationality Law first passed by the Qing government in 1909, Chinese, wherever they were and wherever they were born, remained Chinese as long as they were children of Chinese parents. The Nationality Law passed by the Nationalist government in 1929, which remained unchanged after it moved to Taiwan, also held to the rule of *jus sanguinis* in determining nationality. The rule maintained that a child's citizenship was determined by his parents' citizenship. Many host countries of the overseas Chinese have, however, adopted the rule of *jus soli*, that is, the position that the citizenship of a child is determined by his place of birth. Hence "the national status of those who were born of Chinese parents domiciled in those (respective host) countries was contested and many complicated problems arose from their dual nationality" (Uchida, 1960: 13). The need to adopt a new position, however, did not go unrecognized. At the Asian-African Conference at Bandung in 1955, Premier Zhou Enlai took the opportunity to spell out China's new position on nationality. Zhou declared that the problem of dual nationality was something left behind from Old China, and that the People's Republic of China was ready to solve the problem with the governments of the countries concerned (Li and Shang, 1985). During the conference, a treaty was signed between Indonesia and China. A main provision of the treaty was that all persons holding dual nationality must choose one citizenship within a certain time period. In 1980, a new Nationality Law of the People's Republic of China was adopted at the Fifth National People's Congress. The law specifies that Chinese citizens are not allowed to hold dual citizenship. According to the law, any Chinese national who has settled abroad and has been naturalized there or has acquired foreign nationality of his own free will automatically loses Chinese nationality (Gong, 1980). Accordingly, the term *hua ren* is now used to refer to overseas Chinese who have been naturalized by their host countries and the term *Huaqiao* to refer to overseas Chinese still retaining their Chinese nationality (Wen, 1985).

For the Hong Kong Chinese, Hong Kong's reintegration with China is supposed to put an end to the century-old anomaly of a distorted Chinese identity—Chinese as subjects of a British colony. It enables them to rehabilitate fully their tainted identity and regain the dignity and rights befitting citizens of a sovereign state.

However, in contrast to the desinicization that has befallen the *Nanyang* Chinese, the last thirty years have seen a reverse process, deanglicization, applied to the Chinese in Hong Kong. Successive measures enacted by the British government since the 1960s have the *de facto* effect of stripping their British identities. Until 1962 all Chinese born in Hong Kong were entitled to full British passports with the right to settle and live permanently in Britain. In 1962 this right of abode was abolished for all except "patrials," that is, those who had at least one grandparent born in Britain. In 1982 Britain again changed its nationality law and created a new category of British Dependent Territory Citizens. This change of name made no real difference to the rights of Hong Kong residents, since British Dependent Territory Citizens would still be entitled to call on the assistance of British consular staff when traveling in foreign countries and, as before, had no right of abode in Britain. "But this new type of passport was widely seen in Hong Kong as creating a new and inferior category of British citizenship and as a sign of Britain's desire to distance itself from any obligations to Hong Kong, particularly when the inhabitants of Gibraltar and the Falklands were given full British citizenship with the right of abode in Britain under the same Act of Parliament that made people born or naturalized in Hong Kong merely British Dependent Territory Citizens" (Miners, 1986: 27). The Sino-British Agreement on Hong Kong's future concluded in 1984 introduced a new type of passport that will allow Hong Kong residents born in the territory before July 1, 1997, to travel abroad for the rest of their lives, but this right will not be transmissible to their children born after July 1, 1997. Holders of this new type of passport are described as "British Nationals (Overseas)." The new document is essentially a traveling document: it neither confers upon its holder the right of abode in

Britain nor affords him British consular protection while traveling in third countries. Following the events of June 4, 1989, unofficial members of OMELCO (Office of the Members of the Executive and Legislative Councils) led a "right of abode" campaign to ask the British government to return to the territory's 3.25 million British subjects the right of abode in Britain as a measure to stall the territory's collapsing confidence. The result: the 1991 British Nationality (Hong Kong) Act. Instead of granting the right of abode to all 3.25 million British subjects, the act makes available full British passports to fifty thousand families screened by an elaborate points system. The scheme attracted 63,592 applications, a figure far below the three hundred thousand predicted by Hong Kong officials.

Beijing was naturally outraged by the abode scheme. According to the Nationality Law of the People's Republic of China, no Hong Kong Chinese can assume a non-Chinese identity unless he or she has settled abroad and acquired foreign nationality, or has successfully renounced Chinese nationality. Also, according to the Joint Declaration between the two governments signed in 1984, Chinese residents in Hong Kong holding the British Dependent Territories passports will give up these passports, acquire PRC-HKSAR passports, and, if they still want British passports, be allowed to acquire British National (Overseas) passports purely for traveling purposes after 1997. The abode scheme has the practical effect of transforming two hundred thousand future residents of the HKSAR from Chinese into British citizens. Besides damaging the good will between the two governments, the scheme also complicates the identity profile of the Hong Kong Chinese and sows seeds of division and mutual distrust in the Hong Kong community. As Skeldon (1991: 242) perceptively points out, the scheme could be seen by some as "a reluctant handout from the departing colonial power and, as such, was an insult to the dignity of Hong Kong people." The question, "Are they as loyal and committed as we?" will inevitably be raised at some stage by those in the population who are proud of their Chinese identity and who scorn those who give up this identity for the "reluctant handout from the departing colonial power."

Lest there should be the misconception that by July 1, 1997, Hong Kong is simply to dissolve into China, it must be pointed out that this will not be the case. According to the Joint Declaration of the Chinese and British governments on the question of Hong Kong, and according to the Basic Law of the Hong Kong Special Administrative Region promulgated on April 4, 1991, China will resume the exercise of sovereignty over Hong Kong in 1997 but Hong Kong will enjoy, for the next fifty years, the status of a special administrative region with its own constitution in which is embodied the principle of "one country, two systems." The Basic Law promises a high degree of autonomy for the Special Administrative Region and allows it to retain its capitalist system and current lifestyle. There will be a fully elected legislature and a locally selected chief executive. The Basic Law also guarantees that there will be fundamental rights and freedoms for the SAR residents.

These arrangements would seem to have offered to the Hong Kong Chinese the best of both worlds—they can be Chinese without having to live under Chinese communism. The "one country, two systems" package is, objectively, too good an offer to decline. But it is apparently not the sufficient panacea for a population that has too much distrust in Chinese communism and is too distraught to find faith in much of what is promised to them. At the base of their identity problem are, it seems, certain attitudes and perceptions that cause anxieties, disorientation, and distress. How they see the future and how they see themselves, their identities, and community in relation to the future is therefore the subject to which we must next turn. In introducing this subject, I will draw upon findings from three surveys conducted in Hong Kong in 1988 and 1990.[1]

It has taken Hong Kong forty years to emerge from World War II to become a major economic power in the Pacific Rim. Economic success aside, what was truly remarkable about this period of development was Hong Kong's transformation from a haven for refugees to a place many would call home. The past forty years have seen the gradual shedding of a refugee mentality, the acquisition of a sense of commitment to the place, and the emergence of a strong local identity, the "Hong Kong Man." In very broad terms, these are significant developments in terms of community and identity. Against this background, the prospect of China resuming sovereignty over the city could not have been more inopportune.

The Hong Kong government estimates that in the early 1990s, about 62,000 people have been leaving the territory every year compared with 20,000 who left annually in the early 1980s (Table 5.1). Of these, a great number must have left because of their common concern for an uncertain future beyond 1997. Our 1988 survey found that across the board Hong Kong people foresaw deterioration in every front after 1997. They anticipated curtailment of civil rights (76 percent), reduction of personal liberties (73 percent), deterioration of the legal system (61 percent), and a stagnation or lowering of living standards (67 percent). Over two-thirds did not believe that living conditions would be better after 1997. The statement that "Hong Kong people will enjoy greater happiness after 1997" was flatly rejected by 16 percent of the respondents as an impossibility, while 37 percent thought it unlikely.

This pervasive sense of foreboding was inseparable from the respondents' distrust of the Chinese government (Table 5.2). In our 1988 survey only one-fifth (21.0 percent) of the respondents said they had trust in the Chinese government. The level of trust diminished to less than 10 percent in 1990.

Accompanying this pervasive feeling of worry and distrust is a strong sense of political helplessness (see Table 5.3 on page 127). More than two-thirds (67.8 percent) of the respondents in the 1990 survey agreed with the view that "over many public matters there is simply very little that one can do." For most people, the most sensible strategy in coping with an uncertain future is simply "work hard and save for the rainy days." Eighty percent of the respondents to the 1990 survey agreed with the statement that "it is of utmost importance to make as

Table 5.1

Official Hong Kong Government Estimates of Emigration, 1980–1991

Year	Number of Emigrants
1980	22,400
1981	18,300
1982	20,300
1983	19,800
1984	22,400
1985	22,300
1986	19,000
1987	30,000
1988	45,800
1989	42,000
1990	62,000
1991	60,000 (provisional)

Source: Skeldon, 1991: 235.

Table 5.2

Trust in Governments (%)

	1988 Survey			1990 Survey		
	Hong Kong Government	British Government	Chinese Government	Hong Kong Government	British Government	Chinese Government
Strongly distrust	0.9	4.2	6.7	1.1	5.9	16.7
Distrust	17.3	25.3	37.1	15.7	34.6	43.2
Average	27.5	26.9	23.3	36.0	33.2	21.3
Trust	45.1	29.1	19.6	37.5	14.3	8.6
Strongly trust	3.4	1.4	1.4	2.3	0.7	0.4
Don't know/ no answer	5.7	13.2	11.9	7.4	11.3	9.8
(N)	(1,662)	(1,662)	(1,662)	(1,957)	(1,957)	(1,957)

much money as possible in preparation for the future." For many (40 percent), the best strategy would be to care less about public affairs and just attend to their private lives. One-third of the respondents preferred the retreatist strategy: "Enjoy life and forget about the future." These responses configurate a pattern of values and attitudes reminiscent of the refugee mentality that characterized sojourners in the early postwar days.

Emigration, the exit option, is this refugee mentality in action (see Table 5.4 on page 128). One in five respondents (21 percent) to the 1988 survey and more than one-quarter of the respondents (27.5 percent) to the 1990 survey had either acquired some overseas residential rights or had some such plans in mind. This

Table 5.3

Perception of Hong Kong Community (%)

	Disagree	It Depends	Agree	Don't Know/No Opinion/No Answer	N
1. I will not leave Hong Kong under any circumstances.	23.5	34.8	38.0	3.8	(400)
2. In the last years before 1997, it is most important to take care of oneself and one's family. Don't get too much involved in public matters.	35.1	21.0	40.6	3.6	(400)
3. It is of utmost importance to make as much money as possible in preparation for the future.	10.8	6.3	80.0	3.1	(400)
4. In the last few years before 1997, there are bound to be many problems. Hong Kong people should try to be more altruistic to give help to each other.	15.1	28.8	50.1	6.3	(400)
5. About many public matters there is simply very little that one can do.	13.8	14.8	67.8	3.8	(400)
6. Government policies are all for the wealthy people and the big bosses.	14.1	15.8	59.1	11.3	(400)
7. The wealthy people and the big bosses have already had their safety exits arranged; they are here only to make the last killing.	6.5	9.8	74.8	9.0	(400)
8. Disagreements so often heard among different groups are well motived.	13.1	19.8	51.5	15.8	(400)
9. Public figures are motivated by selfish interests.	27.5	28.5	26.5	17.6	(400)
10. Senior government officials too are making arrangements for exits, and will not be around for too long.	11.3	13.3	50.8	24.9	(400)
11. Enjoy life and forget about the future.	44.8	16.8	33.6	5.1	(400)
12. Holders of foreign passports should be treated just the same as the rest of the Hong Kong population.	40.0	17.0	28.6	14.6	(400)
13. In the last few years before 1997, law and order are bound to deteriorate.	20.6	18.5	44.8	16.3	(400)

Table 5.4

Attitudes Toward Emigration (%)

	1988 Survey					1990 Survey				
	No	Yes	Don't Know	N/A	(N)	No	Yes	Don't Know	N/A	(N)
Overseas residential rights	94.7	4.8	0.5	—	(1,662)	94.7	4.4	0.8	—	(1,957)
Emigration plan	74.3	17.6	2.8	5.3	(1,662)	69.4	23.1	7.4	—	(1,854)
Will emigrate before 1997	70.4	8.5	15.8	5.3	(1,662)	68.4	11.1	17.4	3.2	(1,854)

Note: N/A = Not Applicable.

Table 5.5

Sense of Belonging to Hong Kong (%)

	1988 Survey	1990 Survey
Low	8.9	7.9
Somewhat	25.4	30.6
Strong	63.5	59.2
Don't know/No answer	2.1	2.3
(N)	(1,662)	(1,957)

pervasive inclination to quit Hong Kong gives some good indication of the extent to which the sense of commitment to the community has eroded (Table 5.5). About one-tenth (9 percent and 8 percent) of the respondents to the 1988 and 1990 surveys reported little or very little sense of belonging. When asked to react to the statement, "If one truly loves Hong Kong, one and one's family should stay in Hong Kong and be ready to make sacrifices," half (51 percent) of the professional respondents to our third survey replied in the negative. Perforce, the bodies are around, but the minds have already gone—"the body stays but the identity migrates" (Maines, 1978: 251)—and before they board the planes and go, the almost-emigrants, caught in the painful process of "role exit" (Ebaugh, 1988), are *in* but not *of* the community.

There is also some indication that the process of exodus has disturbed the basis of trust in the community (see Table 5.3). As sociologist Wong Siu-lun

Table 5.6

Claimed Identity, 1990 Survey (%)

Hongkongese	56.6
Chinese	25.4
Both	13.8
Neither	1.2
Don't know/No opinion/No answer	3.0
Total	100 (N = 1,957)

describes it, "The wealthy may be looked on more and more with suspicion and ill feeling."[2] The overwhelming majority (75 percent) of the respondents to the 1990 survey agreed with the view that "the wealthy people and the big bosses have already had their safety exits arranged; they are here only to make the last killing." Such feelings of suspicion and distrust are also harbored against senior government officials. The majority (51 percent) of the respondents agreed with the view that these leaders were not immune from the exodus fever. "They too are making arrangements for exits, and will not be around for too long." Trust in the Hong Kong government also declines (see Table 5.2). While in 1988 nearly half (48.5 percent) of the respondents said they had trust in the Hong Kong government, in 1990 only 39.8 percent said so. There is also the widely shared (59.1 percent) perception that "government policies are for the wealthy people and the big bosses." Subtly and certainly, worries over the future have disturbed the mood and eroded the sense of community.

To stay or not to stay? At the root of this question troubling nearly everyone in Hong Kong lies the more fundamental question of identity. In theory, the end of one hundred and fifty years of colonial rule should be a welcome opportunity for the Hong Kong people to discard their anomalous status and regain their lost identity as Chinese citizens. In practice, this opportunity has been looked at with highly conflicted thoughts and feelings. Underpinning these thoughts and feelings are, it seems, two perspectives or views. The first draws a distinction between "being Hongkongese" and "being Chinese" (Table 5.6). More than half (56.6 percent) of the respondents to the 1990 survey, for example, regarded themselves as "Hongkongese," and only 25 percent as "Chinese."

The second view holds that one does not have to be pro–People's Republic to be Chinese. Indeed less than 10 percent of the respondents to the Survey of Professionals were prepared to regard "political allegiance with PRC" as a necessary criterion for defining Chineseness. Issuing from these two views are, on the one hand, an inclination to assert a Hong Kong identity against a Chinese identity and, on the other hand, a disposition to reconcile with a less-than-full-blown Chinese identity, one that does not have a place for the PRC government. The impending reality of a Communist regime taking over has forced many Hong Kong people to rethink these views and make up their minds on what kind of Chinese they want to become. The impact on them of these thoughts and decisions amounts to nothing less than an identity crisis. To be or not to be Chinese? What kind of Chinese? These are questions with no simple answers, and understandably answers are very varied. The majority are prepared to stay; many are prepared to go and assume alternative identities; many, while staying, are prepared to express their worries and distrust of the Chinese government through the "voice" (Hirschman, 1970), or the political option. A strong indication of the voice option was the wide support given to the liberal candidates standing for direct elections to the Legislative Council in September 1991. Led by prodemocracy activists critical of the Beijing government, the United Democrats and their liberal allies took sixteen of the eighteen available seats, a victory widely believed to be a reflection of the voters' support for their nonreconciliatory approach to China–Hong Kong relations. My own analysis (Lee, 1992) of the positions adopted by all fifty-six candidates running for Legco seats also shows that while the liberal and pro-China candidates were almost equally liberal regarding their positions over social policy issues, the pro-China candidates were indeed most, and the liberal candidates least, pro-China.

At the collective level, individual approaches and solutions to identity crises will add up to yield outcomes with major political implications. An SAR population that becomes too conscious and proud of its local Hong Kong identity, or one that is reluctant to be loyal, will be certain to invite distrust, suspicion, and even interference from the central government. A strong local political identity is never welcomed by the center in China's political tradition. But it has become more upsetting because the display of this identity has occurred at a time when, following the collapse of East European communism, China has become more suspicious of whatever might undermine its rule. A strong local identity is, in Beijing's view, bad enough. A strong local identity seen to be linked politically to Western capitalist powers is even worse. How to articulate an identity that is at once welcomed by the Hong Kong Chinese and acceptable to the central government remains then a most challenging task posed to Hong Kong's political and community leaders.

Another intriguing problem likely to arise in Hong Kong's reintegration with China is the strong possibility that the Hong Kong Chinese are not ready to identify with their counterparts across the border. Lau and Kuan's study (1988: 178–87) has noted that people claiming the Hong Kong identity were both more likely to find it difficult to get along with and less inclined to be affectively related to the mainland Chinese. Wang's (1992) study also reveals that Hong Kong Chinese were prone to attribute a string of negative characteristics to the mainland Chinese: poor, superstitious, lazy, coarse, unfriendly, uncultured, and dumb. Mainland Chinese, on the other hand, were prone to find the Hong Kong Chinese hypocritical, arrogant, and unfriendly. The same study also discovers that the more they came into contact, the more likely they were to have negative impressions of each other. These findings point to a sensitive issue in Hong

Kong's reintegration with China: political reintegration may be inevitable; reintegration at the social level—mutual identification of the Hong Kong and mainland Chinese—may not.

Notes

1. These include: Social Indicators for Development 1988 (sample size 1,662); Social Indicators for Development 1990 (sample size around 1,957; the findings reported in this study are also derived from a subsample to the size of 400); Survey of Professionals 1988 (sample size 2,238). The first two studies are collaborative projects among the Hong Kong Institute of Asia-Pacific Studies at the Chinese University of Hong Kong, the Social Science Research Centre at the University of Hong Kong, and the Department of Applied Social Studies at Hong Kong Polytechnic. The third study is a collaborative work between the author and Professor Wong Siu-lun of the Department of Sociology at the University of Hong Kong.

2. Quoted in *Time*, May 13, 1991, p. 19.

References

Basic Law of the Hong Kong Special Administrative Region of the People's Republic of China (1990), Hong Kong: Consultative Committee for the Basic Law of the Hong Kong Special Administrative Region of the People's Republic of China.

Chutung, T. (1910), "The Chinese Nationality Law, 1909," *The American Journal of International Law*, Vol. 4, pp. 160–66.

Cushman, J., and Wang Gungwu, eds. (1988), *Changing Identities of the Southeast Asian Chinese Since World War II*, Hong Kong: Hong Kong University Press.

Draft Agreement Between the Government of the United Kingdom of Great Britain and Northern Ireland and the Government of the People's Republic of China on the Future of Hong Kong (1984), Hong Kong: Government Printer.

Ebaugh, H.R.F. (1988), *Becoming an Ex: The Process of Role Exit*, Chicago and London: University of Chicago Press.

Gong, Q.X. (1980), "On the Nationality Law," *Beijing Review*, November 10, 1980, pp. 24–25.

Gosling, Peter L.A. (1983), "Changing Chinese Identities in Southeast Asia: An Introductory Review," in *The Chinese in Southeast Asia*, ed. Peter L.A. Gosling and Linda Y.C. Lim, Singapore: Maruzen Asia, Vol. 2, pp. 1–14.

Gosling, Peter L.A., and Linda Y.C. Lim, eds. (1983), *The Chinese in Southeast Asia*, Singapore: Maruzen Asia, Vol. 2.

Hirschman, Albert O. (1970), *Exit, Voice, and Loyalty*, Cambridge, MA, and London: Harvard University Press.

Lau, Siu-kai, and Kuan Hsin-chi (1988), *The Ethos of the Hong Kong Chinese*, Hong Kong: The Chinese University Press.

Lau, Siu-kai, Lee Ming-kwan, Wan Po San, and Wong Siu Lun, eds. (1991), *Indicators of Social Development: Hong Kong 1988*, Hong Kong Institute of Asia-Pacific Studies, Chinese University of Hong Kong.

Lee, Ming-kwan (1992), "Issue-positions in the 1991 Elections," paper presented at the *Workshop on 1991 Elections*, Political Development of Hong Kong Research Program, Hong Kong Institute of Asia-Pacific Studies, Chinese University of Hong Kong, December 13, 1992.

Li, S.Z., and Y. Shang (1985), "The Day Zhou Enlai Spoke at Bandung," *China Reconstructs*, May, pp. 14–16.

Maines, D.R. (1978), "Bodies and Selves: Notes on a Fundamental Dilemma in Demography," in *Studies in Symbolic Interaction*, ed. Norman K. Denzin, Greenwich, CT: JAI Press, pp. 241–65.

Miners, Norman (1986), *The Government and Politics of Hong Kong*, Hong Kong: Oxford University Press.

Nationality Law of the PRC (Adopted at the Third Session of the Fifth National People's Congress, Promulgated by Order No. 8 of the Chairman of the Standing Committee of the National People's Congress on and effective as of September 10, 1980).

Purcell, V. (1965), *The Chinese in Southeast Asia*, London: Oxford University Press.

Pye, Lucian W. (1971), "Identity and the Political Culture," in *Crises and Sequences in Political Development*, ed. Leonard Binder et al., Princeton: Princeton University Press, pp. 101–34.

Skeldon, Ronald (1991), "Emigration, Immigration and Fertility Decline: Demographic Integration or Disintegration?" in *The Other Hong Kong Report 1991*, ed. Yun-wing Sung and Ming-kwan Lee, Hong Kong: Chinese University Press, pp. 233–58.

Uchida, N. (1960), *The Overseas Chinese: A Bibliographical Essay Based on the Resources of the Hoover Institution*, Stanford: Stanford University Press.

Wang, Gungwu (1991), *China and the Chinese Overseas*, Singapore: Times Academic Press.

Wang, Shung-in (1992), "Images of Self and Others Among the Chinese in Three Cities: Peking, Taipei and Hong Kong," *China Times Weekly*, No. 27, July 5–11, pp. 8–14; No. 28, July 12–18, pp. 72–76.

Wen, C.Y. (1985), "The Definition of Overseas Chinese and the Stage of Overseas Chinese History," *Guangzhou Study*, Vol. 2, pp. 34–35.

Part III
Economic Restructuring

6

Production Change in Guangdong

Xueqiang Xu, Reginald Yin-Wang Kwok,
Lixun Li, and Xiaopei Yan

Since Economic Reform in 1978, the Open-door Policy has produced fast, continuous, and comprehensive economic growth in Guangdong. As its economy has been steadily diversifying and expanding, the province's national position has been raised substantially. There are two main reasons for Guangdong's success. First, it has been designated as a experimental region for the Open-door Policy. Second, the province is adjacent to Hong Kong. In this chapter, we attempt to review and analyze the province's growth and its progress toward a mixed economy under these conditions.

The purpose of this chapter is to examine the Guangdong–Hong Kong relationship in the province's growth process. We begin by reporting the extent of the enormous gains in the province since 1978 and where it stands in the national economy. As a result of the Open-door Policy, the economic link to Hong Kong has been made possible and this has had a tremendous impact in the province's industrialization and production restructuring. We examine the growth process in greater specificity by monitoring the changes in both the industrial and agricultural sectors.

Because the increasingly outward-looking economy is due entirely to Guangdong's connection with Hong Kong, we investigate the various roles of the metropolis in this regard. As the province grows, its production structure and economic orientation transform and adjust, as do the employment pattern and population movement. The shifts in employment and population are limited not only to within and between the two territories, but also between the territories and other provinces. Thus, the province generates further interregional economic relationships.

Table 6.1

Pre- and Post-reform Annual Growth Rates of Guangdong

	Guangdong		China
	Pre-reform 1952–1980	Post-reform 1981–1990	Post-reform 1979–1988
GVSP	7.0%	15.8%	11.2%
NI	5.8%	11.4%	9.2%
GDP	5.6%	12.3%	9.6%

Sources: Guangdong tongji nianjian 1991: 48, 55–57; Zhongguo tongji nianjian 1989: 21.

Notes: GVSP = Gross Value of Social Product
NI . = National Income
GDP = Gross Domestic Product

Moreover, in Guangdong, we discover, in conjunction with the state system, a newly formed structure of nonstate production—an independent triple system of agricultural and industrial production, but all connected to Hong Kong. Lastly, we summarize the current thinking in China, both from policy makers and academics, the unusually consensual view on the province's and the metropolis's future development.

General Growth Pattern

Let us first review the nature of economic growth since Economic Reform. This section will give a general picture of the province's achievement and its national standing by presenting a survey of official statistics.

Before 1978, the state concentrated development in the northern provinces where most of the national investment for industry and infrastructure was injected. Being a southern province, Guangdong received little national allocation. The shortage of investment, coupled with a lack of raw material, caused its growth to be severely curtailed. After Economic Reform, the province's growth has been spurred by foreign investment, mainly from Hong Kong and more recently from Taiwan, and by a rapid industrialization process linked to both the international and the domestic market. Table 6.1 shows a doubling of the growth rate since 1978. Since 1985, Guangdong's growth rate ranks as the highest of China's provinces.

Guangdong's economic growth is associated with four discernible characteristics. The first characteristic is the fast pace of growth. The average annual growth rate of the postreform years, whether measured by gross value of social product (GVSP), gross domestic product (GDP), or national income (NI), is

Table 6.2

Comparative Annual Growth Rates of Guangdong and the Nation in Selected Post-reform Years

	GVSP		GDP		NI	
	Guangdong	China	Guangdong	China	Guangdong	China
1980	12%	8.4%	15%	7.9%	16%	6.4%
1985	19%	17.1%	18%	12.8%	17%	13.5%
1988	30%	15.8%	26%	11.1%	24%	11.1%
1990	14%	N.A.	12.2%	5.2%	9.4%	N.A.

Sources: Zhongguo tongji nianjian 1991: 27, 31, 46; *Guangdong tongji nianjian 1990*: 22, 47.

Notes: N.A.   = not available
    GVSP = Gross Value of Social Product
    NI   = National Income
    GDP   = Gross Domestic Product

more than double those of the prereform years. Table 6.1 illustrates the different growth rates of the periods before and after reform.

The second characteristic is the steadiness of the growth. In Table 6.2, the various annual growth rates demonstrate, first, that the province grows every year. Although there are some short-term fluctuations, the general growth trend is strong and firm. The short-term fluctuations are consistent with the national fluctuations, indicating that the province's economy responds to that of the nation, as they are still tied closely through the large state sector. These growth variations merely reflect the regular and normal pattern of major development periods in developing economies—one or two years of high growth followed by one or two years of lower growth. A spurt of fast growth is succeeded by an adjustment period of moderate growth. More significantly, all provincial growth rates, with the exceptions of 1983 and GVSP in 1979, are higher than the corresponding national rates, especially so in recent years. Guangdong is taking off and is steadily and significantly widening the growth gap between itself and the nation.

The third characteristic is the comprehensiveness of development. As shown in Table 6.3, there has been marked growth in all major sectors of the economy since 1979. The sectorial growth rates distinctly exceed those of the prereform period. Economic growth has not concentrated in industry alone but has dispersed to other production sectors as well as to retail. The comprehensive growth in all sectors signifies a well-linked economic network capable of generating a high multiplier effect. This sectorial growth also induces an increase in the province's revenue and exports. Again, Guangdong's growth can clearly be seen to be higher than the national average in every sector. The present growth ensures

Table 6.3

Selected Pre- and Post-reform Growth Rates of Guangdong

	Guangdong		China
	Pre-reform 1952–1980	Post-reform 1981–1990	Post-reform 1979–1987
1. GDP	5.6%	12.3%	13.9%
Primary Sector	3.2%	6.9%	12.3%
Secondary Sector	10.5%	14.4%	13.5%
Tertiary Sector	5.4%	13.8%	17.0%
2. Revenue	6.0%	13.8%	10.0%
3. Retail Sales	7.0%	18.3%	15.8%
4. Exports	10.9%	17.0%	27.4%

Sources: Zhongguo tongji nianjian 1988: 28, 600, 633, 657; *Guangdong tongji nianjian 1991*: 57, 229, 303, 339.

Note: GDP = Gross Domestic Product

the future economic potential and the province's possible contributions to China.

The fourth characteristic is outward orientation. As an Open-door Policy experimental laboratory, Guangdong operates under a series of special policies designed to accommodate the market and foreign investment. Three of the four designated Special Economic Zones (SEZs)—Shenzhen, Zhuhai, and Shantou—are located in the province, two of the fourteen Open Coastal Cities are in the province, and the Pearl River Delta Open Economic Region is designated for foreign investment and trade. For opening up the market, relaxation of selective commodity prices is tried, tested, and adopted. Furthermore, a host of trial regulations for foreign investment was established in Shenzhen. They have furnished conditions conducive to attracting and assuring overseas producers, and they are models for other open cities and regions. These institutional arrangements have prepared the province for the inflow of a burgeoning transnational development. Apart from these institutional innovations, the adventurous, eager, and risk-taking populace, in no small measure, contributes to a welcoming and flexible business and production environment that is unequaled in the nation.

The proximity to Hong Kong, Taiwan, and Southeast Asia gives the province an advantageous position for international investment, particularly from overseas Chinese, and convenient access to international markets. Hong Kong and Taiwan, experiencing the common production dilemma of the Asian Newly Industrializing Economies (Asian NIEs)—labor shortage and excessive financial capital—have found the province an ideal location for offshore production. Hong Kong entered the province first and has become its most important production partner. But Taiwan followed, first through Hong Kong, and has increasingly

Table 6.4

Selected Annual Growth Rates in Guangdong and the Asian NIEs: 1987

	Economic Growth Rate (1987)
Guangdong (1988)	26.0%
Hong Kong	13.9%
Singapore	9.4%
South Korea	12.0%
Taiwan	12.3%

Sources: Guangdong tongji nianjian 1990: 47; *Guangdong tongji nianjian 1991*: 479.

Note: NIEs = Newly Industrializing Economies.

Table 6.5

External Economic Indicators of Guangdong and the Nation: 1990

	Guangdong	China	Guangdong as Percentage of China
	(in billions of U.S. dollars)		
Total Import	5.75	53.33	10.8%
Total Export	10.56	62.06	17.0%
Realized Foreign Investment	2.02	10.10	20.0%
Tourism & Remittance	0.72	2.22	32.4%

Source: Guangdong tongji nianjian 1991: 71.

invested directly in the province. The external input of technology, finance, management, and trade, together with the provincial government's cooperative attitude and the local willingness to provide infrastructure, allows for speedy spread of industrial and trade development. Consequently, the growth performance compares favorably with those of the Asian NIEs (see Table 6.4).

As the province's economy improves, it has taken on a major economic role in the nation. Figures in Table 6.5 show that Guangdong has taken on a disproportionately large share of all foreign-related economy. Much of its economy is externally connected overseas. It is now the most powerful province for foreign trade and foreign investment. For the national economy, the province broadens national production, particularly in the south, into the international market. By assimilating foreign investment and market information, the province has quickly developed light industries, such as household electronics, clothing, foods, and beverages (*Guangdong tongji nianjian*, 1991: 70, Table 1–27). By improving the quality and styling, these products are not only sold in the domes-

Table 6.6

Major Economic Indicators of Guangdong and the Nation: 1978 and 1990

	1978		1990	
Indicators	Guangdong	China	Guangdong	China
Population (in million)	50.64	962.59	62.83	1,143.33
GVSP (in billion yuan)	35.03	684.6	309.39	3,799.6
NI (in billion yuan)	16.08	301.0	113.22	1,442.9
GDP (in billion yuan)	18.47	358.8	147.18	1,768.6
per capita GVSP	695	711	5,034	3,323
per capita GDP	367	373	2,395	1,547
per capita NI	319	313	1,842	1,262

Sources: Zhongguo tongji nianjian 1991: 14, 28, 29, 44, 87; *Guangdong tongji nianjian 1991*: 55, 56, 57, 106, 109.

Notes: GVSP = Gross Value of Social Product
NI   = National Income
GDP   = Gross Domestic Product

tic market, but also exported increasingly into the international market.

With this impressive growth, the general living standards have improved. Previously, Guangdong's various per capita product indicators, which signify living standards, were below or just matching the national average before Economic Reform. The postreform years have seen them rising well above the national norms. Table 6.6 shows the quantitative increase of these indicators relative to the national average. Economic growth has successfully transformed a backward province into an advanced one. Guangdong's economic performance in the postreform years far exceeds that of the nation and, although it has now become the richest province, it is not entirely free of economic problems.

As per capita national income increased, so did consumption. The rising demand for household goods gave incentives to local producers. This local multiplier would produce further growth, particularly beneficial to the locality. Between 1978 and 1990, Guangdong workers' wages increased 6.3 times, at an average annual growth rate of 18 percent (*Guangdong tongji nianjian*, 1991: 347, Table 13–1). With a rapid growth in disposable income, the higher demand, however, increases faster than the supply. The new market did not immediately yield a new economy, but instead inflation ran rampant. For the same period, the social retail indicator rose 2.66 times, at an average annual growth rate of 8.1 percent (*Guangdong tongji nianjian*, 1991: 283, Table 10–1). Still, the gain between wage increase and price increase implies that there has been a real improvement of living standard.

The province's economic growth relies mainly on the increase of input and on the expansion and extension of existing production. The pattern of the economy has depended on high input, but there has been relatively low output because of low efficiency. The fast growth has been accomplished by much waste of social resources, as it has not been supported by the upgrading of production conditions and processes. The outmoded institutional relationship between the private producers and the government, the rigid management system, the low quality of machinery, and the shortage of skilled labor are the main causes for the inefficient production, which requires comprehensive institutional restructuring (Zeng, 1992) and technological renewal.

The state recognized these attendant economic difficulties. In order to combat the overheated economy and inflation, the government cut back on investment in capital construction, thus suppressing demand. Another measure was to relax price controls and let the market set and adjust prices on selected nonessential consumer goods. The market now regulates demand and supply not for all goods but at least for part of the consumption package. The private producers, with access to overseas management methods and production techniques, imported from nearby Hong Kong, gradually learn new ways to improve efficiency, quality, and variety, also to fulfill and match market demand. Reading price as the demand signal, they can now produce to fill the territorial market gaps.

Increasing the range and speed of production is the key to remedying inflation and inefficiency. The maintenance of rapid growth and the effective improvement of living standards depend on the market system for production and trade. The expansion of the market is seen as the way to sustain and expand real economic growth (Zeng, 1992). As Guangdong moves away from a command economy to a mixed economy, it merges closer to the Hong Kong system of development.

Indirectly, Beijing has demonstrated its support to the province in accommodating this form of economic transition, especially in the case of the Shenzhen Special Economic Zone (SEZ), which is located between Guangdong and Hong Kong and is the largest and most developed SEZ experiment in China (Chu, 1983). There were two significant changes in the Shenzhen SEZ that occurred during 1981–82 and 1985–86. In 1981–82, the government of the SEZ went through a major institutional reform. The state production units attached to ministries were detached from the government. These local state units were to operate independently as individual firms responsible for their economic survival. In actuality, these nonstate enterprises are run as private firms. This administration reform drastically separated the government and production into two different systems and introduced market economy into the production sector (Castells, Goh, and Kwok, 1988: 436–40).

In 1985–86, after extensive policy review, Shenzhen recognized that it had not developed into an export-processing economy, but had been dependent on import trade for its development. Several major economic rules and regulations were introduced by the state in order to reduce capital investment, restructure industry, and curb import trade. These measures were forcefully implemented and successfully turned the economy within two years (Chan and Kwok, 1992). The administrative reform and industrial restructuring showed the determination and the effectiveness of the state's intention of making the mixed-economy experiment workable. These efforts are more impressive in view of the massive economic and social investment in Shenzhen. The domestic investment in the SEZ would take twenty to thirty years to recover in full (Wu, 1990).

There are many institutional modifications specifically designed for Shenzhen in order to improve the Guangdong–Hong Kong relationship. Tax, business, and trade laws modeled on those in Hong Kong were formulated and foreign financial institutions were set up specifically to expedite market practice (Hong Kong Trade Development Council, 1990). Stock market and land sales by auction, not previously practiced in socialist China, were adopted. Simplification and improvement of the immigration process to ease travel for Hong Kong residents, businessmen, and tourists alike was another measure pragmatically introduced. All these institutional innovations were made in order to facilitate Hong Kong and overseas investment and market. From Shenzhen's experiment, the move to mixed economy, particularly in Guangdong, can be seen as a serious long-term commitment.

Production Restructuring

In order to sustain the impressive growth and to produce the institutional transformation that would facilitate the movement toward a mixed economy, Guangdong's own production has gone through fundamental structural adjustment. This section concentrates on the restructuring in two major production areas—ownership structure diversification, and a shift within the agricultural and industrial sectors.

The mode of ownership has broadened. Since 1978, the unitary model of state ownership in industrial production has been relaxed to permit nonstate-sector participation. There are many forms of production under nonstate ownership, including rural enterprise, urban-rural cooperative enterprise, individual enterprise, household enterprise, joint enterprise with foreign investors, and enterprise with sole foreign ownership. Although the state sector still dominates the economic landscape, there has been a strong movement toward the nonstate modes, as illustrated in Table 6.7. Whereas the state sector has remained constant, the nonstate sectors have expanded gradually and steadily. The joint enterprise and the foreign sole-ownership enterprise modes have been growing especially fast because of the flow of Hong Kong investment.

Even though the majority of urban workers are still employed by the state, there has been a substantial swing to the nonstate sector. The nonstate sectors attract workers by offering higher wages, greater job variety, and better promo-

Table 6.7

Indicators of State and Nonstate Sectors of Guangdong: 1978 and 1990

	Labor Force (in 1,000)			Labor Force in Retail and Food Business (in 1,000)			Retail Sales (in billion yuan)			Industrial Production (in billion yuan)		
	Total	State Sector	Nonstate Sector	Total	State Sector	Nonstate Sector	Total	State Sector	Nonstate Sector	Total	State Sector	Nonstate Sector
Absolute Number												
1952	2,304.1	494.8	1,809.3	728.9	41	687.9	2.02	0.18	1.84	1.04	1.02	0.14
1978	518.45	369.04	149.41	44.62	175.6	270.6	9.34	4.16	4.73	18.76	13.54	5.22
1990	853.42	528.43	325	247.25	483.5	1,989.0	73.23	29.15	44.07	119.59	50.12	69.47
Percentage												
1952	100	21.5	78.5	100	5.6	94.4	100	8.9	91.1	100	98.6	1.4
1978	100	71.2	28.8	100	39.4	60.6	100	49.3	50.7	100	72.2	27.8
1990	100	61.9	38.1	100	19.6	80.4	100	39.8	60.2	100	41.9	58.1
Annual Growth Rate												
1952–1978	3.2	8.0	-0.7	-1.9	5.8	-3.5	6.1	13.3	3.7	11.8	10.4	25.6
1979–1990	4.2	3.0	6.7	15.3	8.8	18.1	18.7	16.6	20.4	17.0	11.5	24.1

Source: Guangdong tongji nianjian 1991: 114, 153, 229, 245.

Table 6.8

**Employment in the Three Sectors of Economy in Guangdong:
1978 and 1990**

Year	Labor Force (in millions)				Percentage			
	Total	Primary	Second-ary	Tertiary	Total	Primary	Second-ary	Tertiary
1978	22.76	16.77	3.13	2.86	100	73.7	13.7	12.6
1990	31.18	16.43	7.78	6.97	100	52.7	24.9	22.4
1978–1990 Difference	8.42	–0.34	4.65	4.11				

Source: Guangdong tongji nianjian 1991: 114.

tion prospects, but they demand efficiency and discipline, both of which are generally lax in the state sector. That the pull of the nonstate sector has been relatively slow is due to the many health, education, and other social benefits as well as the job security attached to all state firms. When switching from state employment, the worker has to forgo all these guarantees, assistances, and indirect subsidies, as they are largely absent in many of the nonstate sectors.

In value creation from retail and industrial production, the province is, however, mainly upheld by the nonstate sectors. The state sector contributes less than half of these values. Among the various modes of enterprises in retail, the fastest growth occurs in joint enterprise and individual enterprise. Because the initial capital investment is comparatively low, the private entrepreneurs find this sector easier to enter. Compared with the state enterprises, the nonstate enterprises are generally small but more efficient and robust. In contrast, the state-run firms are less efficient and, with underutilized labor, are ineffectual and languishing. In order to maintain economic development, the expansion of the nonstate sectors in number and scale seems desirable.

Similar to the general pattern in the Asia-Pacific economies (Kwok and Au, 1986), there is a major restructuring in production. The substantial reduction in agricultural employment has been complemented by an almost equal growth in industrial employment and service employment, with the former taking a larger share. Table 6.8 records these employment changes. Before Economic Reform, there was an enforced division of production between the city and the countryside. Agriculture was exclusively in the rural areas, while industry was in the urban places—the "dualist structure," as it is referred to in China. Rural enterprise, revived and encouraged since 1978, has caused a growth and diversification of nonfarm sectors, thus largely changing the economic landscape (Chang and Kwok, 1990). Guangdong is no exception, as is evident in Table 6.9—the

Table 6.9

Rural Social-Product Value in Guangdong: 1978 and 1990

	Total	Agriculture	Industry	Con-struction	Transpor-tation	Commerce
1. Absolute (in billion yuan)						
1978	12.5	8.6	2.6	0.5	0.1	0.8
1990	130.4	60.0	49.9	7.5	4.4	8.6
2. Percentage						
1978	100	68.4	20.6	4.1	0.9	6.1
1990	100	46.1	38.3	5.7	3.4	6.6
3. Average Annual Growth Rate						
1978–1990	21.5%	17.6%	28.0%	25.0%	35.7%	22.3%

Source: *Guangdong tongji nianjian 1991*: 128.

rural annual growth rates in the nonfarm sectors hover around 20 percent. By 1990, agriculture produced less than half of the social-product value, with industry alone taking close to 40 percent. Rural industrialization has indeed arrived in the province.

In Guangdong's agricultural sector, crop production, in accordance with the Cultural Revolution policy of self-sufficiency, was converted to mainly food grains, even though the province is climatically suitable for and traditionally had produced cash crops. The removal of this policy restriction has allowed for crop diversification. The effect of opening up export opportunities is to give new incentive to revive the traditional cash-crop cultivation, such as vegetables, pigs, poultry, fruits, flowers, and fish for Hong Kong consumers.

The effect of Economic Reform was the diversification of the entire agricultural production structure. By 1990, the nonfarm sectors—forestry, livestock, handicrafts, and fishery—together exceeded the production of crops, which formerly dominated agriculture (see Table 6.10). By 1988, agricultural export increased 1.9 times from that of 1978, and consisted of 27.2 percent of the province's total export of that year. The transformation in the structure of agricultural production was due to policy change, but the Hong Kong market has been instrumental in making this possible.

Guangdong's industrial production is held back by the lack of mineral resources, but the province is well endowed with agricultural input. It has the advantages of an agricultural processing type of light industrial development. Because of the pre-1978 policy emphasizing heavy industrial development nationwide, Guangdong complied. Even as the growth rate of heavy industrial production in the pre-1978 period was higher and the share of light industrial production was slowly decreasing, heavy industrial output was always lower

Table 6.10

Agricultural Production Value in Guangdong: 1978 and 1990

	Total	Agriculture	Forestry	Husbandry	Handicraft	Fishery
1. Absolute (in billion yuan)						
1978	7.4	4.9	0.4	1.1	0.7	0.3
1990	22.1	10.7	1.3	4.1	3.9	2.1
2. Percentage						
1978	100	66.2	5.5	14.8	9.7	3.8
1990	100	48.5	5.7	18.7	17.6	9.6
3. Average Annual Growth Rate						
1978–1990	9.5%	6.7%	9.8%	11.6%	15.1%	18.2%

Source: Guangdong tongji nianjian 1991: 129.

than light industrial output. With the change of policy, coupled with the advent of foreign investment, the post-1978 period has witnessed the renewed growth of light industry. The province, since 1978, has consistently geared its industrial production in this direction.

Industrialization in the province started in earnest in the late 1980s. Before that time, the investment from Hong Kong was small and the province's economy was dependent on trade, both foreign and with other provinces. After 1984, credit was given liberally nationwide to the extent that the existing consumer-goods industries were unable to keep up with the new demands created by the subsequent surge in investment and consumption. The improving living standard of the urban population broadened its purchasing power. The exposure to foreign consumption patterns through visitors, media, and advertisements diverted the demand to foreign consumer durables. Sensing the vast domestic market, Guangdong embarked on production to substitute for imports. Financed by overseas sources, surplus savings from other provinces, and profits from sales, the nonstate enterprises seized the opportunity and oriented their production for the Chinese market. Convinced of China's commitment to capture foreign investment, the Hong Kong entrepreneurs actively relocated labor-intensive export production, which was floundering due to escalating labor costs. Taking advantage of the large pool of low-cost labor and land availability, these transplanted productions regeared themselves for the large and expanding northern inland market (Chan, T., 1992).

Past industrial production was made up of food, textiles, pottery, silk, folk arts, and light machinery, which were the traditional cottage industries. Because of the new domestic market, the postreform industrial structure went through a radical change. Now, it is headed by electronics, followed by household durables, construction materials, high-grade foods, and high-grade household chemicals—all of which are new industries. The total reordering is aided essentially by external investment. The branch operations relocated from Hong Kong have brought with them financing, technology, design, equipment, management, and public relations. These offshore branches lead and become examples of Guangdong's modern industrialization. The import-substitution industries, in order to satisfy the domestic demand for foreign goods, have been heavily dependent on the importation of components and technology, for which Hong Kong is the necessary conduit. The traditional industries, however, still remain in operation but now have to enter into the export market domestically and internationally. Gearing toward the new markets and new tastes, the indigenous production processes too have been given fresh impetus for technological renewal, design innovation, and new product creation.

Their contacts with the domestic market and the overseas firms inform the province's producers of international fashions and trends, and induce a series of commercial undertakings that are entirely based on market demand. The foreign investors started the new industrial production process and market orientation. For the local producers, imported industrial methods have offered the possibility to adopt these production techniques for the vast market in other provinces. With superior manufacturing and marketing skills, together with access to foreign-supplied parts, Guangdong controls the domestic market to great advantage.

The province's industries still have to overcome the lack of locally endowed industrial resources. This has limited production, which has to rely heavily on labor-added processes, as reflected in the present industrial structure. There are three possible options and each has its own bottleneck. The most obvious alternative is to deepen the labor-added process, but this requires large-scale upgrading of labor skills and technology. The next choice is to import industrial raw material from other provinces, with improvement of regional infrastructure and communication as the necessary condition. The last possibility is to enter into the global production network in which Guangdong has already started to participate. In the short term, the province has been limited in adopting the first two options, because of insufficient capital to embark on the necessary human and infrastructure investment. The province is now concentrating on the last alternative. As part of the transnational network, the province is still at the lower end of the global hierarchy and its production is intricately tied to that of Hong Kong. Guangdong's development, at least in the foreseeable future, has to rely on Hong Kong.

Hong Kong Connection

The most prominent consequences of the Open-door Policy in Guangdong have been the renewed economic, social, and cultural links with Hong Kong and through the metropolis with Taiwan. Let us now turn to a discussion of how this external cause influences the province's recent growth.

The spatial division in the production process between Guangdong and Hong Kong is generally characterized as "front shop, back factory" (*qiandian houchang*). Marketing, design, and administration take place in Hong Kong, the front shop, while manufacturing and assembly are done in Guangdong, the back factory. Capital, technology, machinery, and management come from the international metropolis, and the province supplies labor and land (Lu, 1992). This form of production cooperation propels Guangdong's recent speedy growth and maintains Hong Kong as a world city. For the province, the metropolis's entrepreneurship, investment, transportation, and finance make it the indispensable "bridge"; its trade and communication, the expedient "window" to the international market. Guangdong, however, is not the sole beneficiary from this process, since it contributes significantly to the growth of Hong Kong's information sector and the restructuring of its economy.

For Guangdong's development, Hong Kong has taken on seven crucial roles. The first role is as the instigator of a mixed economy. With the opening of the province, the market system has filtered in from the metropolis. Investment from Hong Kong brings with it the free enterprise mode of production and trade. By necessity, the new mode is quickly adopted by the provincial firms that have business deals with outside investors. Those parts of the state administration that have dealings with foreign investment also have to learn the rules of the market, make accommodation to the nonstate enterprises, and invent new regulations for the imported mode of production. Both the provincial enterprise and government participate and support in developing the mixed economy.

Second, Hong Kong investment brings in, apart from new financial capital, economic stability. Some comes from remittances to family and friends. Other sources include investment and business loans from the metropolis's business associates. These liquid funds work as a reserve to moderate exchange and saving. As the value of the Hong Kong dollar is set in the metropolis's market and is pegged to the United States dollar at a fixed rate, this foreign currency source acts as a buffer in slowing down inflation and leveling out fluctuation in Guangdong. Compared with northern China, the province has a lower rate of inflation. The steadier Hong Kong economy has a stabilizing function for Guangdong's economy (Zheng et al., 1991: 28).

Third, the metropolis is the agent for industrialization. Investment from Hong Kong is directed to industrial production and fills in the province's deficiencies in industrialization—raw material, technology, finance, and market. The offshore branches absorb the rural surplus labor and reduce agricultural employment. Apart from raising the industrial share in the total agricultural and industrial value from 57.8 percent in 1978 to 86.24 percent in 1988, the Hong Kong investment brings about the dominance of the industrial sector, and speeds up rural industrialization and urbanization (Zheng et al., 1991: 27).

Guangdong's industrial output is attributed largely to the growth of the foreign invested sector. In 1989, more than 97 percent of foreign investment was vested in export industries, which include the technologically more advanced production of automobiles, chemicals, and computers. Hong Kong accounted for approximately 90 percent of direct foreign investment (Hong Kong Trade Development Council, 1990) and provided employment for an estimated 3 million workers (Zheng, Lei, and Li, 1992). One major source of capital, which cannot be estimated, is the remittances. These are the informal but significant form of economic support from Hong Kong to households and social services all over the province (Kwok, R., 1986).

Clearly, Hong Kong as the economic core and Guangdong as its hinterland have many mutual advantages in this form of economic cooperation. The international trade access and the know-how of modern production and commerce in the metropolis combined with the available provincial land, labor, and mineral resources from other provinces enhance the production capacity and international competitiveness of the region. A regional transportation network largely dependent on inland water, supported by fairly well-developed railway and highway links to other provinces, opens up the import of raw materials and labor from, and export of products to, other parts of China.

The metropolis's investment concentrates spatially in the adjacent Pearl River Delta. Although located mostly in cities, there is substantial investment in rural enterprises in the countryside. Working with imported machines, and financed with rural household savings, the locally set-up rural enterprises are small and are mainly labor-added manufacturing plants, but producing for export. Their growth has been steady and their industrialization process is deepening (Chan, W., 1992; Huang, 1992). They have started up the initial stage of rural industrialization and employment transfer from agriculture.

Fourth, Hong Kong changes Guangdong's closed economy into an open economy. The province has deliberately and successfully adopted the outward-oriented economic strategy. Externally, the province opened up its borders for international investment and trade. Internally, it encouraged industrialization for export production. For the international market, the proximity to Hong Kong provided the conduit and the informational and financial supports, making it possible to reach beyond to overseas markets. For the domestic market, the Hong Kong–relocated industries set themselves up as the prototypes, demonstrating how to exploit market opportunities and install modern production techniques.

With the Hong Kong link, the province's economy has taken off and has become export-oriented. For trade with the outside world, the metropolis serves as a convenient place for meeting, exchange, and negotiation between the local and foreign businessmen. With superior infrastructure and expertise, Hong Kong is an excellent transshipment point for import and export freight. Guangdong now has the highest export value among China's provinces and over 80 percent goes to Hong Kong, some for reexport to other parts of the world. Among the exports, which are mainly agricultural and textile products, there are processed industrial materials and manufactured products (*China Economic News*, 3–11–1991).

Through production for the domestic and international market, the province begins to forge links with the global economy. With the outward-looking economy, the province is now subjected to competition with the metropolis. Aside from introducing the necessity for efficiency in the domestic and international markets, the Hong Kong business penetration shows the relative ineffectiveness and inflexibility in the province's state and nonstate sectors, challenging both to renovate and improve. By introducing the international economy, Hong Kong has become the conduit that guides and directs Guangdong's outward economy. The provincial capital, Guangzhou, which was the economic center of south China, has relinquished its regional leadership to Hong Kong. With advanced infrastructure, information, markets, and entrepreneurship, Hong Kong has become the center of Guangdong's open economy and the international entrance to China.

Fifth, the Guangdong–Hong Kong connection also has major effects in the metropolis's economy. By transplanting labor-intensive production to the province, a deindustrialization process takes place in the metropolis. With the decline in manufacturing, the service, trade, and information sectors grow in its place. The restructuring process sets up a distinct division of function in the production process between Guangdong and Hong Kong (Chan, T., 1992)—the "front shop, back factory" phenomenon mentioned earlier. That Hong Kong specializes in production planning, financial management, new product design and development, marketing, and business negotiation, and that Guangdong concentrates on manufacturing, capital- and technology-intensive industries, in fact, is integrating the two territories economically, making them increasingly interdependent on each other.

Sixth, Hong Kong has become the top-ranking central city in the Guangdong urban hierarchy. Through its international economic network, the metropolis has integrated the central part of the province, the Pearl River Delta, into transnational production and international trade. The delta's spatial economy continues to expand outward to other parts of the province. Within the delta itself, the urban places have formed a hierarchy, joined by production and trade linkages. Each city has its specific economic function and position, determined by the outward-oriented economy. With Hong Kong being the center for international trade, production management, transportation, finance, information, and tourism, Guangzhou, the provincial capital, will become the cultural, political, and economic core of south China and the exchange node between the province and other provinces. Other lower-level and smaller cities have production and administrative functions, mainly in maintaining transnational and domestic production (Zheng et al., 1991: 111–12). Internal to the region, Hong Kong, despite its present separate political status, is already economically integrated into the greater Guangdong region.

Seventh, Hong Kong has another indirect but important role in the province's development—as the intermediary for Guangdong–Taiwan trade. Since 1988, when the Taiwan government tacitly allowed investment in China, Taiwan entrepreneurs first targeted Fujian, which is across the strait, as the region for offshore production. Because of the conservative administration's attitude toward foreign investment, Fujian stalled its plan to upgrade infrastructural facilities (*Far Eastern Economic Review*, 8–27–1992: 25). Taiwan investment has migrated to Guangdong, which offers a better investment environment and greater production convenience. The relocation of its labor-intensive export industries to Guangdong and the subsequent trade are conducted indirectly, mostly transshipped or reexported through Hong Kong. The Taiwan economy, thus, is going through a similar restructuring process as that of Hong Kong, but its deindustrialization is probably more severe. As a result, there is another long-term economic effect to the province. Taiwan industries in Guangdong produce finished goods for the export market, but their upstream industries are usually at home. Inputs have to be shipped and so production costs increase. As these backward-linked intermediate industries feel forced to follow their clients, they move to Guangdong in order to protect their market outlets. This movement would take place if and when the Taiwan government approves the outward move of this capital- and technology-intensive sector to China (Chan, T., 1992). For this industrial movement, which depends heavily on outside contact and inputs, the position of Hong Kong, as the transitional point, will be pivotal.

Employment and Movement of Labor

What is the impact of the Hong Kong–Guangdong connection on the population and the implications for human resources? How may the province's labor market, which is one of the major attractions for the Hong Kong and Taiwan producers, affect the future relationship of the two territories and regional cooperation?

As stated in earlier chapters, Guangdong, and the Pearl River Delta in particular, has been a source of labor to Hong Kong since its formation. Table 6.11 shows the population flow between China and Hong Kong. These are official figures, thus they undercount, because there has been constant illegal migration from China. Although these figures represent movement to and from China as a whole, most of the origins and destinations are in Guangdong. The absolute statistics, therefore, can be misleading, but the table can be used as a reference to indicate the trend of population movement between Guangdong and Hong Kong. What is shown is that migration from China had been quite substantial from 1978 to 1982. Since strict immigration control was imposed by Hong Kong in 1982, the flow has been stabilized.

The migrants from China, typically, are manual laborers who come to fill industrial jobs. In the 1960s and 1970s, the period of export production in Hong Kong (Taylor and Kwok, 1989), industrial labor was in high demand. Relaxed

Table 6.11

Population Flow Between China and Hong Kong: 1978 and 1990

Year	1978	1979	1980	1981	1982	1983	1984	1985	1986	1987	1988	1989	1990
Legal Immigrants to HK (in thousands)	67.5	70.5	55.4	54.0	54.0	27.0	27.0	27.0	27.0	27.0	27.0	27.0	27.0
HK Residents' Travel In and Out of China (in millions) Depart from HK	1.29	3.20	3.92	4.54	4.62	5.72	8.04	10.96	11.87	14.09	16.51	15.21	16.69
Arrive in HK	1.32	3.20	4.06	4.59	4.60	5.59	7.97	11.00	11.86	13.98	16.21	15.12	16.55

Source: Interview, Immigration Department, Hong Kong Government, 1991.

immigration policies allowed for an ample inflow of labor supply and a low level of wages. With reduced production costs, the metropolis's industrial exports were kept competitive in the international market. Out-migration from Guangdong has been a traditional way of releasing surplus rural labor and supplying industrial labor to the metropolis. By the 1980s, when Hong Kong entered the international business phase (Taylor and Kwok, 1989), its labor demand shifted from the industrial sector to service and information sectors. Remaining local industries were compelled to move into higher value-added products, which require less labor with higher skills. The need for migrant labor receded and the continuous human influx began to pose a social burden to the densely populated metropolis. Immigration policy has been tightened and enforcement has been rigorously executed. Still, illegal migration has been reported sporadically but frequently whenever short-term manual labor shortages occur.

By 1982, the mutually beneficial liberal labor policy had become obsolete in Hong Kong. The traditional surplus rural labor solution by emigration, which had partially served Guangdong, was restricted and the province had to find another way to provide new employment opportunities. The postreform economic growth rescued the province's excessive labor pool. The Hong Kong–led industrialization in the Pearl River Delta opened up many forms of nonfarm jobs, including, apart from manufacturing, service and professional jobs. The new industrial employment has been most effective not only in absorbing the surplus rural labor, but also in transferring the farm labor. The expansion of labor-intensive industry has exhausted the local labor supply. Labor shortage brings forth two new phenomena—labor migration from other provinces, and high employment aspirations among the local labor (Zhou, 1992; Li and Li, 1992).

Because of the relative attraction of industrial work, transfer of agricultural labor was immediate. The first round of labor shortages was the depletion of farm labor, which was filled by contracted migrant farmers. Soon, the high demand for industrial labor surpassed the local supply pool and workers had to be imported from other provinces. With a supply shortage, the local labor began to be selective in employment and to avoid the undesirable "Three-D" (dirty, difficult, and dangerous) jobs. Most of the service sector, which is labor-intensive, is in this category and carries some social stigma, providing another area of work for the migrants. The migrant workers usually take lower-wage, less skilled, and unwanted jobs. From 1978 to 1990, the number of migrants from other provinces in Guangdong was estimated at 4.17 million (Zhou, 1992).

Through this domestic migration, Guangdong is establishing a social and economic relationship with the other provinces, similar to that between the metropolis and itself. This network extends its economic and cultural influence and increases its dominance beyond the province. In China, this southern province is not only the fastest-growing area, but also an attractive place to seek employment and settle. Moreover, for other provinces, linking up with Guangdong will bring economic benefits.

Guangdong's human resources, while adequate in this early stage of industrialization, are less adept for more advanced levels of development. Labor training has been insufficient for the more skilled positions. Comparatively, the province has a lower number of persons with higher education than in the nation at large—13.38 per 1,000 population for Guangdong and 14.22 per 1,000 population for the nation (Li and Li, 1992). For Guangdong's outward-oriented development, there is an acute shortage of skilled technicians and managers. The current demand for these posts is filled through outbidding other provinces for their professionals by offering better rewards and fringe benefits (Zhou, 1992). There is a conspicuous need for producers and entrepreneurs who are familiar with international business operations and socialization, language and jargon (Tu, 1992). For these international businessmen, Guangdong, without any human-resource plan, has to rely on Hong Kong.

Fueled by the inflated labor demand, local labor increasingly has higher expectations for status jobs, but there are real technical limits for advancement. Nevertheless, managerial-level positions are often occupied by untrained and inexperienced personnel (Tu, 1992). Guangdong now has a development dilemma. If the present labor condition persists, wages will increase and inefficiency will rise. Both will weaken the province's competitive edge and subsequently dampen growth. The low level of labor resources is recognized as the major developmental bottleneck. Labor training and upgrading are urgently needed, but there is no policy or program nor is there the capability to train in the province. To resolve this problem, Guangdong probably has to seek a remedy from Hong Kong for some time to come—either by training the province's labor or by importing professionals to fill the vacant posts.

Structure of Nonstate Production

As the market component of the economy is externally induced, is Guangdong's new production purely reactive and is it random and formless? How are nonstate productions organized in response to the market? Are they interlinked? In this section, we explore the structure of the province's nonstate production systems, which are in tandem with but separated from the state system. Following the accepted convention, we divide nonstate production into the two major sectors— industry and agriculture. We then use the market as a criterion for categorization, since it is the prime force in shaping the nonstate sector. In reviewing Guangdong's current economy, we propose that there are three identifiable nonstate production systems.

For nonstate overseas-export industrial production, Hong Kong or Taiwan normally supplies the investment. Combined with external inputs of market, information, design, technology, management, and finance, these producers organize production by assembling land and labor. Production inputs are supplied mainly by the overseas partners, with a smaller amount of input purchased from

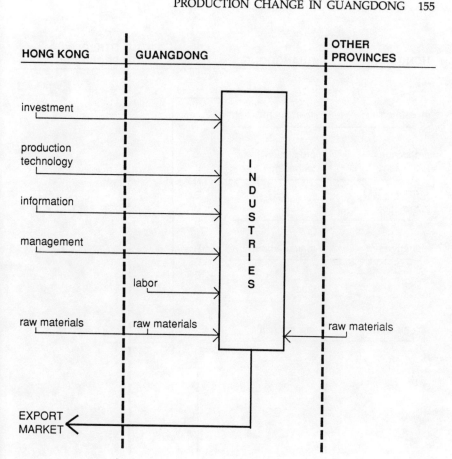

Figure 6.1. **Nonstate Overseas Export Industrial Production**

local firms and firms from other provinces. This is essentially labor-added production for export to Hong Kong for assembly or reexport. This system tends to be enclave industry. Except for food-related production, which receives local farm inputs, firms supported by foreign investment have weak local linkage. The local economic effect is through labor wages. The system of the overseas export industry is shown in Figure 6.1.

Nonstate domestic-export industrial production markets its products to household consumers in other provinces and is essentially internationally and domestically financed and locally manufactured and assembled. By locating in the Pearl River Delta, these firms take advantage of overseas information on marketing and production as well as foreign-made parts obtained through Hong Kong. With improved and fashionable products and higher efficiency, they capture the do-

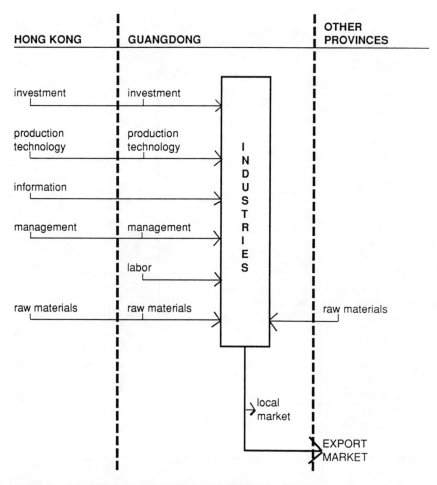

Figure 6.2. **Nonstate Domestic Export Industrial Production**

mestic market. These enterprises import inputs from the province, other provinces, Hong Kong, and Taiwan, and their products are sold within the province and in other parts of the nation. The domestic export industry has strong provincial, national, and international linkages, as illustrated in Figure 6.2.

These two export industrial systems have no common linkage and are independent from each other, unless they manufacture the same products. Spatially, they agglomerate in the Pearl River Delta, as they share the locational advantages in labor market, infrastructure, information, and the Hong Kong–Taiwan connection.

The nonstate agricultural production, despite its diminishing share in the province's production, has the broadest market. Except for the migrant labor

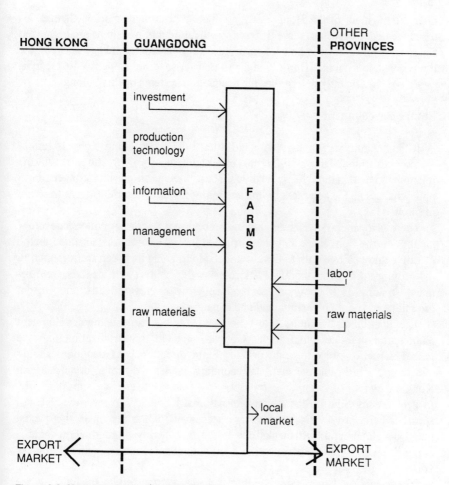

Figure 6.3. **Nonstate Agricultural Production**

from other provinces, production imports are local. Products are exported to Hong Kong and other provinces. They are sold to the cities in the province and they are inputs to the province's food industry. The production system, aside from migrant labor, is internal to the province. Figure 6.3 illustrates this system.

The striking features of the nonstate production systems are that they are dissimilar and are independent of each other. Within their production and marketing processes, all three systems have considerable exchanges with the neighboring metropolis. These extensive attachments to Hong Kong should provide a common ground for some continuity, consistency, and linkage among the province's production systems. However, each type of production responds to a different segment of the Hong Kong production process or market, themselves disconnected. Because of these differences, the production systems are organized separately. Thus, there is no economic reason for horizontal linkage between the three nonstate systems. Hong Kong, through its specific economic links, indirectly but significantly determines the production systems in Guangdong.

Future Development

Will Guangdong's growth be affected after 1997 when Hong Kong is reintegrated with China? How will the province maintain its growth and how will the relationship with Hong Kong evolve? These are questions that concern both policymakers and academics. In this section, we summarize the current thinking in China.

There is a general consensus that the present trend of the province's development is on the right track. Outward-oriented industrialization is accepted as the effective and positive path to development. Hong Kong has been instrumental in the province's growth; therefore, its roles as the catalyst and leader should remain, so long as it continues to produce growth. Pragmatically, the current growth trend should be maintained and expanded.

The position on the future is to follow and continue the existing development path, and not to deviate from it. Outward-oriented industrialization into the global market is agreed to be the primary future direction, but Guangdong should aim to rise within the transnational economic ladder. To move forward, Hong Kong, being part of Guangdong by 1997, will continue to play an important role, as it is already high on the Asian transnational hierarchy. In the future, it will spearhead the province's international ascension. In the province, there exist many developmental bottlenecks due to the low quality of production factors. Hong Kong, being more advanced in international development, will fill in these voids.

The views on Hong Kong's future role in relationship to Guangdong are positive but varied—from a partnership role with greater regional coordination (Tong and Wu, 1992), to a leadership role with the metropolis heading the urban hierarchy (Lu, 1992), to a dominant role with the metropolis directing the regional growth (Wang, 1992). The general tenet is to develop a spatial division of function based on the "front shop, back factory" model, but with a more sophisticated shop and a more high-tech factory. The metropolis will concentrate on marketing, information, trade, transportation, and service, while the province will conduct technological research and development, and upgrade and diversify production. With mutual coordination of existing strengths, the entire region is expected to be able to penetrate deeper into the global economy, capture a larger share of the domestic market, and escalate economic growth.

Moving in this direction, the market sector has to expand and dominate, with concurrent reduction in the state sector. In order to enlarge the domestic market, quick and fluid reaction to the inland market depends on the expansion of the nonstate sector. The international economy operates with the market principle. Guangdong's system has to be consistent with the economic system that it intends to join. The market component of the economy must be allowed to broaden. Otherwise, outward-oriented development will be impeded. With the intensive international competition in the Asian Pacific, where most nations are already practicing market economy, the province's transformation into a mixed economy must quicken its pace. Major institutional restructuring must be in place to facilitate and support the market (Zeng, 1992).

Would this policy direction be accepted by and beneficial to the society? So far, outward-oriented development with foreign investment and a mixed economy has proved capable of producing fast growth and visible improvement of living standards. Both the state and the civil society are convinced and confident that the policy is beneficial and will bring greater prosperity. Guangdong people have developed a strong sense of commitment to commercialization and profit making (Bo and Wu, 1992). The many social and individual benefits and gifts from Hong Kong residents and overseas Chinese migrants convince the local population that internationalization often brings favorable returns (Kwok, 1986). The proposed policy direction fulfills these social expectations and it should be welcome and supported in the province.

For the state, labor surplus is a historical problem relieved only by emigration, and it is still a perpetual social economic problem in the nation. The current development policy has been successful in absorbing the province's rural labor surplus. More than that, it improves the general standard of living at the same time. The key to the labor solution is through industrial growth that generates new nonfarm employment. Without growth, labor surplus will reemerge. This is a hidden threat that necessitates constant industrial growth. Given Guangdong's endowment and historical condition, alternatives to the present proven policy are not so easy to find. The rational development is to reinforce the workable policy by widening and deepening export industrialization.

The optimism for this developmental direction received a strong endorsement when Deng Xiaoping held up Guangdong as a development model for the entire nation after a visit in January 1992 (*Far Eastern Economic Review*, 4–23–1992: 21). With this positive outlook for the future, Guangdong–Hong Kong integration will facilitate the growth of the region even further. The future of the reunification project looks promising and positive to both territories.

References

Bo, Miaojin, and Peiguan Wu (1992), "Zhujiang sanjuezhou juminde shangye yishi" (Commercialization concept of Pearl River Delta population), paper presented at the Conference on Pearl River Delta Economic Development: Review and Prospect, Research Center of Pearl River Delta Economic Development and Management, Zhongshan University, Zhongshan, May 7–11, 1992.

Castells, Manuel, Lee Goh, and R. Yin-Wang Kwok in association with Lap Kee To (1988), *Economic Development and Housing Policy in the Asian Pacific Rim: A Comparative Study of Hong Kong, Singapore, and Shenzhen Special Economic Zone*, Monograph 37, Institute of Urban and Regional Development, University of California at Berkeley.

Chan, Thomas M.H. (1992), "Economic Development and Its Impact on Hong Kong and Taiwan," paper presented at the International Sociological Association, Research Committee 21 on "A New Urban and Regional Hierarchy? Impacts of Modernization, Restructuring, and End of Bipolarity," Lewis Center for Regional Policy Studies, University of California at Los Angeles, Los Angeles, April 1992.

Chan, Thomas M.H., and R. Yin-Wang Kwok (1992), "Economic Development in Shenzhen Special Economic Zone: Appendage to Hong Kong?" *Southeastern Asian Journal of Social Science*, Vol. 19, Nos. 1, 2, pp. 180–205.

Chan, Wenxue (1992), "Yikao keji jinbu, zaizao xinyoushi—Zhujiang sanjuezhou xiangzhen gongye fazhan wenti sikao" (Relying on technological progress, developing new advantage: Thoughts on development problems of rural industry in Pearl River Delta)," paper presented at the Conference on Pearl River Delta Economic Development: Review and Prospect, Research Center of Pearl River Delta Economic Development and Management, Zhongshan University, Zhongshan, May 7–11, 1992.

Chang, Sen-dou, and R. Yin-Wang Kwok (1990), "The Urbanization of Rural China," in *Chinese Urban Reform: What Model Now?* ed. R. Yin-Wang Kwok, William L. Parish, and Anthony Gar-On Yeh in association with Xueqiang Xu, Armonk, NY: M.E. Sharpe, pp. 140–57.

China Economic News, Mar. 11, 1991.

Chu, David K.Y. (Zhu, Jianru), ed. (1983), *Zhongguo zuidade jingji tequ—Shenzhen* (China's largest Special Economic Zone—Shenzhen), Xianggang (Hong Kong): Guangjuejing chubanshe (Guangjuejing Publishing Co).

Far Eastern Economic Review, Vol. 155, No. 16, April 23, 1992, No. 34, August 27, 1992.

Guangdong tongi nianjian 1990 (Guangdong Statistical Yearbook 1990) (1990), Guangzhou: Guangdong Tongjiju.

Guangdong tongi nianjian 1991 (Guangdong Statistical Yearbook 1991) (1991), Guangzhou: Guangdong Tongjiju.

Hong Kong Trade Development Council (1990), Recent Investment Environments of Guangdong, Fujian and Hainan, Hong Kong: Hong Kong Trade Development Council.

Huang, Zhuliang (1992), "Xiangzhen qiye shi jianshe you Zhongguo tese shehui zhuyide zhongyao zucheng bufen—qianshi Guangdong xiangzhen qiye" (Rural enterprise is an important component of Chinese socialist construction: Brief analysis of Guangdong's rural enterprise), paper presented at the Conference on Pearl River Delta Economic Development: Review and Prospect, Research Center of Pearl River Delta Economic Development and Management, Zhongshan University, Zhongshan, May 7–11, 1992.

Immigration Department, Hong Kong Government, 1991.

Kwok, R. Yin-Wang (1986), "Regional Relationship and Interaction Between Hong Kong and China," in *Planning and Development of Coastal Open Cities: Part II Hong Kong Section*, ed. P.L. Choi, P.K. Fong, and R.Y. Kwok, Hong Kong: Centre of Urban Studies and Urban Planning, University of Hong Kong, pp. 159–73.

Kwok, R. Yin-Wang, and Brenda K.Y. Au (1986), "Information Industry, Multinational

Corporations and Urbanization in the Pacific Asian Countries: A Research Agenda," *Habitat International*, Vol. 10, No.1/2, pp. 115–31.

Li, Huajie, and Yongjie Li (1992), "Zhujiang sanjuezhou laodongli shichang fazhan yanjiu" (Study of labor market in Pearl River Delta), paper presented at the Conference on Pearl River Delta Economic Development: Review and Prospect, Research Center of Pearl River Delta Economic Development and Management, Zhongshan University, Zhongshan, May 7–11, 1992.

Lu, Ping (1992), "Fahui gezi youshi, baochi gezi tese, gongtong changzao fanrong (Exploit local advantages, preserve local characteristics, jointly create prosperity), paper presented at the Conference on Pearl River Delta Economic Development: Review and Prospect, Research Center of Pearl River Delta Economic Development and Management, Zhongshan University, Zhongshan, May 7–11, 1992.

Taylor, Bruce, and R. Yin-Wang Kwok (1989), "From Export Center to World City: Planning for the Transformation of Hong Kong," *American Planning Association Journal*, Vol. 55, No. 3, pp. 309–22.

Tong, Da-lin, and Mingyu Wu (1992), "Xianggang–Zhujiang sanjuezhou: xinde jingji lianmeng" (Hong Kong–Pearl River Delta: New economic alliance), paper presented at the Conference on Pearl River Delta Economic Development: Review and Prospect, Research Center of Pearl River Delta Economic Development and Management, Zhongshan University, Zhongshan, May 7–11, 1992.

Tu, Lizhong (1992), "Dali kaifa rencai, maishang jingji fazhan xintaijie—Zhujiang sanjuezhou jingji kaifanqu rencaide hongguan kaocha" (Vigoriously develop human resource, step up to a new economic development platform—Macro survey of human resource in Pearl River Delta Open Region), paper presented at the Conference on Pearl River Delta Economic Development: Review and Prospect, Research Center of Pearl River Delta Economic Development and Management, Zhongshan University, Zhongshan, May 7–11, 1992.

Wang, Zhuo (1992), "Lun 'Da Xianggang' kaifang jingjiquan" (Discussion of "Great Hong Kong Circle"), paper presented at the Conference on Pearl River Delta Economic Development: Review and Prospect, Research Center of Pearl River Delta Economic Development and Management, Zhongshan University, Zhongshan, May 7–11, 1992.

Wu, Wai Man (1990), "China's Shenzhen Special Economic Zone—A Social Benefit–Cost Analysis," Ph.D. diss., University of Hawaii at Manoa.

Zeng, Guangcan (1992), "Zhujiang sanjuezhou jingji tizhi gaigede jinzhan yu shenhuade fangxiang" (Direction for improving and deepening institutional reform in Pearl River Delta), paper presented at the Conference on Pearl River Delta Economic Development: Review and Prospect, Research Center of Pearl River Delta Economic Development and Management, Zhongshan University, Zhongshan, May 7–11, 1992.

Zheng, Tianxiang, et al. (1991), *Yi Sui Gang Ao wei zhongxinde Zhujiang sanjuezhou jingji dili wangluo* (Economic geography network of Pearl River Delta: With Guangzhou, Hong Kong, and Macao as centers), Guangzhou: Zhongshan daxue xuebao bianjibu (Zhongshan University Journal Editorial Bureau).

Zheng, Tianxiang, Qiang Lei, and Xiyuan Li (1992), "Zhujiang sanjuezhou jingji fazhan yu Xianggang guodu shiqi jingji guanxi" (The economic relationship of Pearl River Delta and Hong Kong during the transitional period), paper presented at the Conference on Pearl River Delta Economic Development: Review and Prospect, Research Center of Pearl River Delta Economic Development and Management, Zhongshan University, Zhongshan, May 7–11, 1992.

Zhongguo tongji nianjian 1988 (Statistical Yearbook of China 1988), (1988), Beijing: Zhongguo tongji chubanshe (State Statistics Press).

Zhongguo tongji nianjian 1989 (Statistical Yearbook of China 1989), (1989), Beijing: Zhongguo tongji chubanshe (State Statistics Press).

Zhongguo tongji nianjian 1991 (Statistical Yearbook of China 1991), (1991), Beijing: Zhongguo tongji chubanshe (State Statistics Press).

Zhou, Daming (1992), "Zhujiang sanjuezhou weilai renkou fenbu tezheng ji yidong qushi fenxi" (Analysis of migrant labor in Pearl River Delta: Characteristics and trend movement), paper presented at the Conference on Pearl River Delta Economic Development: Review and Prospect, Research Center of Pearl River Delta Economic Development and Management, Zhongshan University, Zhongshan, May 7–11, 1992.

7

Industrial Transformation of Hong Kong

Victor F. S. Sit

Since its founding as a British colony, Hong Kong's development has been based on dynamics often at loggerheads with the conditions of its immediate hinterland—Guangdong Province. Growth and development of this British enclave in the post–World War II period had further drawn it away from its nearby Chinese province. However, a major reversal of the long historical trend has been moving toward an integrated economic development, and each territory is, more than ever before, exploiting and complementing the other in a new partnership forged by market forces. With the coming of 1997, the date set for Hong Kong's return to China as a Special Administrative Region (SAR), economic integration of the two has been spurred.

The purpose of this chapter is to review these developments from Hong Kong's perspective and to assess Hong Kong's prospects in remaining a dynamic export-oriented free economy in the post-1997 years.

Hong Kong–Guangdong Before World War II

Events leading to the ceding of Hong Kong Island and Kowloon to Britain in 1841 and 1860, and the leasing of the New Territories in 1898, have been well documented by historians (Endacott and Hinton, 1962; History Society of China, 1954; Yao, 1984; and chap. 2 in this volume). It is not the purpose here to argue the right and wrong in effecting the formation of the British colony. It is the fact of the post–World War II economic development of Hong Kong that has staggered the world, not *how* it evolved. Once again, Hong Kong has attracted worldwide attention through the agreement between Britain and China that promises Hong Kong, by 1997, a peaceful transformation into the new political status of a Special Administrative Region (SAR) under Chinese sovereignty. A lot of things will happen in Hong Kong after the change, not least in the realms of politics and social change. Economics, being the mainstay of Hong Kong's existence since its founding, and the raison d'être for its acceptance as a special region within China, is the subject I propose to look into in this chapter.

The choice of Hong Kong in the mid-nineteenth century by the British as their China trade base was obvious, as foreign trade in China was then confined to Guangdong, particularly to the city of Guangzhou. Yet very soon, with the opening of Shanghai as a treaty port that commanded a much larger hinterland and cheaper water transport through the Yangtze River (*Changjiang*) system, Guangzhou lost its predominance in China's foreign trade. Look, for example, at the record of trade between Britain, China's major trading partner, and Guangzhou and Shanghai. In 1844, Guangzhou's total trade with Britain was 33.4 million yuan, compared with Shanghai's meager 4.8 million yuan. By 1852, the trade volumes of the two with Britain were equal. By 1856, Shanghai had surged ahead as the predominant port in China, with a trade volume of 32 million yuan, whereas Guangzhou trailed behind with 17 million yuan. The decline of Guangzhou was due partly to the rise of the new treaty ports; the other significant cause was the creation of Hong Kong. In spite of Guangzhou's downward slide as China's base for foreign trade, Hong Kong rose in importance as a new trading base. Yet Hong Kong differed from the foreign quarters in the treaty ports by being completely isolated from Chinese influence and directly under British rule. It soon provided the headquarters for important merchant houses that preferred to control their agents from the safety of Hong Kong. It also developed shipping and other services to support the transshipment business. Gradually it became the center of supply of British goods to China.

The trade that passed between Hong Kong and China by no means all originated in Guangdong for sale in Guangdong. For example, in 1939, only 19.3 percent of the China trade that Hong Kong handled originated and went south to market in China (probably Guangdong), whereas 75 percent was with north China. Two reasons may be advanced for the relative insignificance of south China in Hong Kong's trade. The larger source of Chinese exports and the larger market for China's imports lay in northern China rather than in Hong Kong's immediate hinterlands. Additionally, coastal transport and river transport were much cheaper and more convenient than the land route from Guangzhou. This was so even compared with rail transport. Despite the British having obtained the right to build a railway from central China through Guangzhou to Hong Kong, the Guangzhou–Hong Kong segment was delayed for quite a long time. Even after its opening, the Guangzhou–Hong Kong line (Kowloon–Canton Railway) did not become an important stimulant to Hong Kong's trade relations with Guangdong. The province's more intensive Nationalist sentiment often proved to

Table 7.1

Trade with China, 1931–1956 (selected years)

Year	Export to China as % of total HK exports	Import from China as % of total HK imports
1931	52.3	27.0
1936	42.2	33.6
1940	24.9	34.1
1946	39.3	35.1
1949	25.2	21.5
1951	36.2	17.6
1952	18.3	21.9
1954	16.2	20.2
1956	4.2	22.7

Source: Szczepanik, 1958: 158.

be a liability to Hong Kong–Guangdong relations. The events surrounding the implementation of the lease of the New Territories in 1898–99, and the boycott of British trade in 1925–26 were clear cases of the hostile relationship (see Chapter 2 of this volume).

However, in the pre-1949 era, the boundary between Hong Kong and Guangdong did not form a major political and economic divide. There had been a free flow of goods and people. Guangdong's share of trade with Hong Kong was based on the size of the market, but was chiefly in food. Of some significance was the ebb and flow of Chinese migration to Hong Kong caused mainly by political unrest and economic circumstances in the neighboring counties in Guangdong (Davis, 1949).

Hong Kong–Guangdong, 1949–1978

After the establishment of the People's Republic of China (PRC) in 1949, Hong Kong's main economic role as an entrepôt of China survived for a few years, but then it went into a sudden downturn in 1952 (Table 7.1). Hong Kong's exports to China dropped precipitously as a result of the United Nations embargo on China. Reexports, which had been about 80 percent of Hong Kong's total exports before 1952, dwindled to only 20 percent. While such a turn of events affected all of China, the impact on Guangdong was not entirely negative. In its drive to compensate for some of the loss of foreign currency due to the lack of foreign trade, China stepped up its efforts to exploit Hong Kong's growing urban market. Hong Kong responded positively to a new, cheap source of food, water, and consumables, since it was unable to produce them domestically and could not afford to import them from other sources. Throughout the 1960s and 1970s, Hong Kong effectively became the largest source of China's foreign currency. For example, the trade balance between Hong Kong and China was HK $0.28 billion in 1970, HK $0.79 billion in 1977, HK $1.57 billion in 1980, and HK $1.85 billion in 1981, all in China's favor (Sit, 1982: 182). This, together with profits from direct investment by Chinese enterprises in Hong Kong and remittances by Hong Kong residents to relatives in China, contributed to about 40 percent of the total annual foreign currency it earned. Guangdong province, due to its proximity to Hong Kong, was the production base for most of the consumables for the Hong Kong market, particularly in food. The province also netted the largest proportion of Hong Kong remittances, as most Hong Kong Chinese originated from the province and still had close kinship ties with it.

In this period, Guangdong also supplied Hong Kong with a much-needed resource—working hands, demanded by the rapid growth of its labor-intensive industries. Szczepanik (1958: 154) estimated a net immigration of 1.25 million people into Hong Kong in the period 1945 to 1956. Probably as many as a million of these could be returnees who were forced to leave Hong Kong during the Japanese occupation from 1942 to 1945. Nevertheless, among the immigrants were Shanghai entrepreneurs and their skilled workers who in the late 1950s made Hong Kong's debut into export-oriented industrialization a success. In the period 1961 to 1979, despite a generally closed border, an estimated 444,376 legal and 447,547 illegal immigrants arrived in Hong Kong from China (Sit, 1988: 5). The bulk of added labor, as most of them were of working age, was important in fueling the growth of Hong Kong's labor-intensive industries, and it provided a continual supply of entrepreneurs to Hong Kong. A study of local small- and medium-scale industries discovered that 71.3 percent of the 415 industrialists surveyed were immigrants from China, of whom 51.4 percent arrived before 1951 and 48.6 percent between 1952 and 1977 (Sit et al., 1980: 266–67).

Because China pursued a different ideology and economic system after 1949, the border between Guangdong and Hong Kong divided the region into two different ideologies and economic systems. North of the border, China based its economy on a revised version of Marxism, with strong central planning emphasizing an inward-looking strategy of self-contained economic development. On the other side of the border, Hong Kong continued to practice capitalism laissez-faire.

The immediate economic environment for Hong Kong after 1949 was harsh. The colony's population was swelling due to immigration from Guangdong, and it had lost most of the China market, the mainstay of its entrepôt economy. This was due to the Cold War and the new economic strategy of China that opposed the importation of Western consumables and relied instead mostly on imports from the Eastern European bloc. Hong Kong, since the 1950s, was forced to shift economically away from being China's entrepôt to seek a future as a newly emerging center of light manufacturing for export markets in the West. There were a number of favorable factors, including the transfer of capital, equipment, entrepreneurs, and expertise from Shanghai in the early 1950s. Besides its good geographical location and well-developed infrastructure and banking support, there were also tariff advantages offered by the Commonwealth Preferential System and the later General System of Preferences (GSP). Hong Kong, therefore, was quick in moving toward export-oriented industrialization, that is, industrial development driven by exports of labor-intensive goods such as textiles, clothing, and toys (Sit and Wong, 1989). Of course, other than those mentioned above, Hong Kong's successful industrial growth between 1950 and 1980 was also based on efficient exploitation of human and infrastructure resources within its boundaries, promoted to some extent by effective policies that gave free rein to entrepreneurship and market forces.

The new phase of economic development in Hong Kong may be gauged by the rapid growth of its domestic exports and the contribution of its manufacturing sector to employment and gross domestic product (GDP). Domestic exports replaced reexports as the predominant element (80 percent) of total exports, which to a large extent financed the importation of food, raw materials, and capital goods demanded by the resource-scarce economy. Manufacturing employed 478,930 persons in 1961 and 990,365 persons in 1981, or 39.5 percent and 41.2 percent of total employment, respectively. Its contribution to GDP rose to a peak of 30 percent in 1971 and stabilized at 21.8 percent in 1981. Growth of the industrial sector in the various stages of industrialization was, at an annual average rate, 8 percent for 1954–62; 15 percent for 1962–70; and 9 percent for 1970–81 in real terms (Sit and Wong, 1989: 18–22).

A few notable features of the post-1949 industrialization need to be spelled out. First, manufacturing growth had ties to and a positive impact on other economic sectors such as banking and finance, shipping, insurance, and tourism. It had directly and indirectly promoted the growth and development of these activities. Second, the export industry relied heavily on "price competitiveness" and a high degree of flexibility in meeting rapidly changing market demands in terms of consumer tastes and seasonality. Such a feature was made possible by Hong Kong's superb international telecommunications and shipping, free-port status, lack of red tape, and an orderly division of labor in the form of an efficient but complex subcontracting system. Timely delivery and the ability to meet rush orders with a competitive price made Hong Kong an outstanding international supplier of ready-to-wear garments, toys, and watches. Third, those products and their processes fit the prevailing production conditions and content of Hong Kong's industrialization. Moreover, Hong Kong was successful in keeping abreast with the latest technology and equipment available. However, to remain "price competitive," local firms were deeply involved with only short-term interests and largely neglected research and development (R and D) and quality development. The government was and still is content with the policy of "positive nonintervention," which is not conducive to research and development or to high-tech and capital-intensive industries.

Thus, in spite of Hong Kong's early success in export-oriented industrialization, there has not been, even today, visible deepening of the process into the making of parts and components and the making of related capital good—that is, development of heavier high-tech industries characteristic of a further stage of industrial growth. Judging from the nature of production, Hong Kong industries have changed little in the past three decades. Their factor inputs remain almost the same. The equipment, technology, raw materials, and other intermediate inputs are largely imported, mainly from the neighboring, more industrialized nations, such as Japan, and more recently, Taiwan and South Korea (Sit and Wong, 1989).

Part of the explanation for Hong Kong's almost stagnant record in the industrial upgrading process lies in its small internal market and the need to maintain a free trade policy for the benefit of other economic sectors such as finance, trade, and tourism. Thus the government is unwilling to abandon its noninterventionist stance, and avoids actively directing industrial upgrading. Another possible reason may be the general short-term view of local entrepreneurs. The perception that Hong Kong is a transient place, on borrowed time, creates a bias against investments for the long-term development that high-tech industries often require.

The last feature that needs to be pointed out is that the post-1949 industrial success can be attributed only partially to China's supply of cheap food, immigrants, and some initial equipment and capital. Hong Kong has created its success mainly through the exploitation of international markets and efficient utilization of its human resources and geographical and infrastructural assets. For the first time in its one hundred fifty years of existence, it was able to develop during these three decades without relying too much on China. In short, Hong Kong in the 1960s and 1970s had an economy mainly dependent on Western economies and had largely turned its back on China.

Hong Kong's development separate from China could be reflected in its trade composition. In 1978, of its HK $53,908 million in total exports, domestic exports (basically of local manufactured goods) formed 75.5 percent. The share of reexports was 24.5 percent. China was the second largest source of imports, by contributing 16.7 percent of Hong Kong's total imports, but took a very meager 0.2 percent of its domestic exports (amounting only to HK $81 million). China was an insignificant receiver of Hong Kong's reexports, that is, 1.6 percent, or HK $214 million. Yet China accounted for 27.7 percent of Hong Kong's source for reexports (*Hong Kong Annual Report*, 1979: 254). Such a situation represented the general picture of Hong Kong–China trade relations in the period 1952 to 1978, but with some temporal fluctuations.

While Guangdong had the lion's share of China's exports to Hong Kong, benefited from being the site of the biannual China Trade Fair, and received a substantial amount in remittances from Hong Kong relatives, its economic relationship with Hong Kong was limited and its pace of economic development constrained to only those roles assigned by the central government. In short, the province was pursuing a strategy and development path largely unrelated to that of Hong Kong; its foreign trade and investments were also not related to those of Hong Kong. In 1978, Guangdong's per capita gross domestic product (GDP) was 364 yuan, or about U.S. $234, whereas Hong Kong's was U.S. $3,046. Guangdong was indeed a long distance behind Hong Kong in economic development. Its foreign trade amounted to only U.S. $1.39 billion, or 11.7 percent of its GDP, and the amount of foreign capital actually invested in the province was only U.S. $91 million, demonstrating a primarily inward-looking, self-contained economy (*Guangdong Yearbook*, 1989: 484).

Hong Kong–Guangdong Relations after 1978

By the end of the 1970s, Hong Kong's industrial economy started to feel an increasing threat from two sides. Internally, the new immigration policy of 1979 (tacitly agreed upon with China) meant a stop to new inflows of labor. This happened at a time when the finance, business, trade, and tourist sectors were experiencing new impetus for growth. It meant substantial job-movement to the rapidly expanding service sectors, which offered better pay and working conditions. Subsequently, labor shortage for manufacturing caused a decline in the price competitiveness of locally manufactured products in the international market. Externally, Hong Kong faced increasing competition from its arch rivals, South Korea and Taiwan. The latter had developed an edge over Hong Kong as a result of efforts to deepen its industrialization and become more self-sufficient in the intermediate- and capital-goods industries. Increasingly stringent protectionist policies in Hong Kong's major markets of Canada, the United States, and Western Europe also put constraints on the expansion of Hong Kong's traditional industrial exports. By the late 1970s, Hong Kong's industrial sector started to go downhill in terms of its share in employment and its contribution to the gross domestic product in the local economy. In 1980 its total employment hit the peak of about 1 million persons but slid gradually to less than 800,000 in 1990.

Significant changes in China at the end of the 1970s bred new opportunities for Hong Kong entrepreneurs and fostered new forms of cooperation between Hong Kong and Guangdong. The downfall of the Gang of Four and rise to power of Deng Xiaoping led China to a new Open-door Policy as well as political liberalization. As the only sizable free-trading base, well connected to the West, located along the China coast, with excellent shipping, telecommunications, and air links to most of the world, Hong Kong's significance was recognized by the new Chinese leadership. A rational settlement with London over the future of Hong Kong was achieved in 1984, promising Hong Kong a high degree of autonomy and the continuance of its present capitalistic social and economic systems for another fifty years after the transfer of sovereignty back to China in 1997. The "Hong Kong" factor was also one of the reasons why Shenzhen, Zhuhai, and Shantou were chosen as three of the four Special Economic Zones

(SEZs), vanguards of the new Open-door Policy. Shenzhen, in particular, was the earliest and largest SEZ, and it shared a border with Hong Kong. Guangdong was also made one of the first two Open Economic Regions, which enjoy an exceptional degree of economic self-determination. The exercise of economic freedom in wooing foreign investment, the movement of goods and personnel between Guangdong and the outside world, and the installation of new measures and management practices that are conducive to the market mechanisms have resulted in rapid entrepreneurial interest from Hong Kong to exploit the resources of this immediate hinterland. The former economic backyard, in terms of Hong Kong's development, had suddenly turned into Hong Kong's new frontier of growth. I shall portray the decade of swift economic integration and growth between Hong Kong and Guangdong in 1979 to 1989 through the perspective of trade, Hong Kong investment, industrial development, and infrastructure development.

A New Trade Pattern

The impact of the new China factor on Hong Kong's economy could be reflected in the revival of its role as China's entrepôt. In the 1970s, reexports were growing more rapidly than domestic exports, at 22.3 percent per annum. The gap of growth sharpened markedly in the 1980s, with reexports growing by 33.9 percent per annum and domestic exports by 15.5 percent. By 1988, the value of reexports exceeded domestic exports. In the past two decades, the ratio of reexports to domestic exports rose from 19 : 81 in 1970, to 31 : 69 in 1980, and to 65 : 35 in 1990 (*Hong Kong Bank Economic Report*, 1–1991). The significant turn in reexports was reexports to China, with 1978 marking an obvious turn. With the Open-door Policy, there was a rapid increase in the purchase by China of equipment, raw materials, and consumer goods from the outside world, and Hong Kong stood to gain (Table 7.2). As a destination for Hong Kong's reexports, China at first had little trade with Hong Kong in 1978, but emerged as the most important destination by 1980. Thus the revival of Hong Kong in reexports was indisputably due to the new Open-door Policy of China. In 1978, 2 percent of Hong Kong's reexports went to China and 28 percent originated there. By 1989, 30 percent of the reexports went to China and 54 percent originated there.

Spatially, a substantial part of the reexport trade with China was originated in and marketed in Guangdong, particularly the Pearl River Delta where Hong Kong's out-processing activities were concentrated. Trade records show that 43 percent of Hong Kong's reexports to China were for out-processing. In the opposite direction, 55 percent of reexports originating from China were for Hong Kong's out-processing. I shall discuss further the nature and extent of out-processing as a feature of the Hong Kong–Guangdong economic integration in a later section. Here, it serves to indicate that up to half, and possibly more, of the reexport trade of Hong Kong came from the new economic relationship with Guangdong.

Table 7.2

Hong Kong–China Trade (in million HK dollars)

	1970	1977	1978	1979	1980	1985	1990
Export to China	30	31	81	603	1,605	15,189	43,452
Reexport to China	34	115	214	1,315	4,642	46,023	110,907
Subtotal	64	206	295	1,918	6,247	61,212	154,359
Import from China	2,830	8,082	10,550	15,130	21,948	93,591	476,543
(Reexport from China)	687	2,492	3,659	5,663	8,394	34,628	240,410
HK-China Trade Balance	−2,766	−7,876	−10,255	−13,212	−15,701	−32,379	−322,184
China's contribution to HK's*							
Imports	16/2	16/2	16/2	17/2	19/2	25/1	36.8/1
Exports	0.2/–	0.1/–	2/–	1.1/–	3.6/5	11.7/2	21/2
Reexports (destination)	1.1/–	1.8/–	1.6/–	6.6/6	15.4/1	43.7/1	26.8/1

Source: Hong Kong External Trade, Census and Statistics Department, various dates.

* Figure to right of slash (/) is rank as a trade partner. Figure to left of slash is the actual percentage contributed. Where the rank is lower than 10, a dash is used.

China also increased its imports to Hong Kong and in the 1980s became Hong Kong's number one import source, surpassing Japan, which had long held that position. China's percentage share of Hong Kong's total imports soared from around 16 percent in the 1970s to 36.8 percent in 1990. For exports, the China factor worked in a similar way, boosting China to Hong Kong's second largest export destination after the United States. These dramatic changes clearly started around 1978–79 (Table 7.2).

New Industrial Division of Labor

As previously stated, the new trade pattern between Hong Kong and China means more than a revival of the pre-1949 entrepôt trade. The intensive economic cooperation between Hong Kong and China is deeper than the sheer flow of goods.

Of the total domestic exports and reexports from Hong Kong to China, 49 percent and 47 percent were used by out-processing facilities that were set up either solely with Hong Kong capital or by Hong Kong–China joint ventures. Of China's exports to Hong Kong, 33 percent were finished and semifinished products for these out-processing facilities. By June 1990, the proportion of Hong Kong's trade with China related to out-processing had grown to 78 percent of domestic exports to China, 49 percent of reexports to China, and 64 percent of imports from China (*Hong Kong Bank Economic Report*, 1–1991).

Out-processing, known in Guangdong as "processing of imported materials," started to appear in the province in 1979. It was and still is the major form of foreign participation and manufacturing investment in China. In this type of cooperative project, China or the Chinese partner provides the plant, labor, water, electricity, and other basic facilities. The foreign investor is responsible for marketing the product and supplying the machinery, material, and product design. The foreign investor pays the Chinese partner a "processing fee" that covers workers' wages and sometimes also the above-mentioned expenses incurred on the Chinese side. A slight variation of this arrangement is compensation trade. Yet the term "out-processing" is so loosely used that it also includes manufacturing for exports by solely foreign-owned and joint-venture enterprises (Sit and Wong, 1989: 220).

An overwhelming proportion of processing was the result of Hong Kong's northward shift of most of its export-oriented manufacturing activities into Guangdong, particularly in the Pearl River Delta next to Hong Kong. At the end of 1988, Guangdong registered 7,377 "foreign" and joint-venture enterprises (*sanzi qiye*), 93 percent of them using capital from Hong Kong and Macao. This source of capital represented about 85 percent of the total invested capital in these enterprises. In the province, about twenty thousand enterprises were engaged in out-processing for Hong Kong and Macao, employing about 2 million workers. The value-added generated by these activities in Guangdong was estimated to contribute to 30 percent of Hong Kong's annual industrial value-added. In some industrial branches, such as leather goods, electronics, and plastic products, as much as 70 to 80 percent of the value-added of the Hong Kong industries was created by out-processing in China (*Hong Kong & Macao Economies*, 4–1990: 5).

Detailed investigation by individual industrial branches showed a massive shift of Hong Kong's predominant manufacturing activities into Guangdong. For example, it was claimed that by 1987, 90 percent of plastics factories had moved north of the border. Hong Kong's export of plastic goods continued to drop from HK $13.9 billion in 1987 to HK $11.9 billion in 1988 and HK $9.1 billion in 1989, yet its reexport of plastic goods grew by 50 percent during those years. By 1989, domestic exports were largely replaced by reexports. However, if we consider the "reexports" as Hong Kong–based, then the spatially extended Hong Kong production system (incorporating Guangdong) had successfully expanded its sales overseas substantially over the two-year period.

Recent Hong Kong–based surveys have confirmed and shed light on the reasons behind and the significance of the northward shift of activities by local manufacturers. A 1990 survey by the Industry Department assessed the reasons for relocation. Of 1,954 factories, 532 had set up out-processing facilities and named location as the factor—with 175 pinpointing Guangdong as the choice of location. Of the factories surveyed, 40.9 percent identified labor cost and 34.8 percent identified cost of premises as prime limiting factors for factory operation in Hong Kong (*Economic Reporter*, 1–1991: 62). In another 1990 survey by the Federation of Hong Kong Industries, 199 reported branches overseas, of which 155 or 79 percent were located in China. These enterprises set up a total of 211 establishments in China, of which 90 percent were in Guangdong (Federation of Hong Kong Industries, 1990). Whereas the respondents' Hong Kong factories had an average employment size of 83 persons, the average employment size of their overseas establishments was much larger: 461 persons. Concerning their choice of China, cheap labor (77 of the 107 respondents) and cheap land or premises (49 of the 107 respondents) were the main reasons.

The much lower cost in China for factor inputs, labor, and land is documented in Table 7.3. Except for Shenzhen, costs were much lower in regions of Guangdong (Sit and Wong, 1989). For example Dongguan's labor cost was only about 50 percent of that of Shenzhen.

On the Hong Kong side, the northward move has caused a number of changes. There has been a decline of employment in the manufacturing sector, as most of the unskilled, labor-intensive processes have now moved out of Hong Kong into Guangdong, and as a consequence there has been a significant drop in the local value-added to gross output ratios. These changes are most obvious in the more export-oriented industries such as apparel, fabricated metal products, electrical machinery, and plastic products (*Hong Kong Bank Economic Report*, 4–1991).

Table 7.3

Comparative Cost for Factory Operation

Country/Region	Monthly wage for unskilled worker (U.S.$)	Monthly industry rental HK$/sq.ft
Hong Kong	412	8
Shenzhen	75	0.8–1.5
Thailand	90	1
Malaysia	110	2
Indonesia	60	2

Source: Hang Seng Economic Monthly, 3–1990.

Although the now expanded manufacturing system of Hong Kong–Guangdong bears many of the characteristics of pre-1978 Hong Kong industries, there have been some structural changes for the incorporated subsystems of Hong Kong and Guangdong. For Hong Kong, there has been a movement toward nonproductive, design-oriented, market-oriented, and management activities, whereas Guangdong has successfully leaped into export-oriented industrialization in a matter of a few years. At present this dualist structure seems to have been working well and continues to be competitive internationally.

Hong Kong Investment in Guangdong

Before 1979, China was rarely heard of as a destination for direct foreign investment (DFI). However, since development conducive to DFI began to emerge in China, formal relations were soon established with the World Bank, the International Monetary Fund, and other multinational financial institutions. New foreign investment legislation, for example, the Joint Venture Law, was enacted. Innovative practices such as compensation trade and out-processing were implemented to attract DFI, in addition to the Chinese government's active negotiations to secure official and nonofficial loans from foreign, mostly Western, countries. The post-1978 drive to woo foreign capital has been successful. For DFI alone, China won an inflow of U.S. $2.8 billion in 1986, ranking first among the Third World countries.

DFI, however, formed a minor part of transnational capital flow (TCF) into China. In the decade of 1979 to 1988 it received an actual inflow of U.S.$47.7 billion, equivalent to 60 percent of the average annual flow from all Third World countries in the years 1980 to 1982.

Table 7.4 shows the overall national picture and Guangdong's share for the decade of 1979 to 1988. Overall, official sources contributed only 22 percent of TCF into China, DFI 36 percent, private loans 37 percent, and "other" 5 percent. Throughout the period, the trend was moving toward more private than official

Table 7.4

Flow of Foreign Capital into China 1979–1988 and Guangdong's Share
(Contractual Commitment in U.S. million dollars)

Type	1979–81	1982	1984	1986	1988	1979–88	Actual Investment 1979–88	Guangdong's Share in 1988 Absolute	Guangdong's Share in 1988 %
Foreign Loans	13,600	1,630	1,917	8,407	9,814	46,549 (59)	33,035 (69)	1,108	11.3
Government	1,800	1,030	505	1,444	3,357			165	
International organizations*			970	1,826	1,717			19	
Commercial banks	11,800	600	442	5,138	4,739			924	19.3
Direct Foreign Investment	3,841	530	2,650	2,834	5,297	28,165 (36)	12,102 (25)	2,242	42.3
Equity joint venture	116	24	1,067	1,375	3,134			1,062	
Contractual joint venture	2,430	300	1,484	1,358	1,624			1,046	
Cooperative oil development	950	170	—	81	59	2,896 (37)		N.A.	
Wholly foreign-owned enterprises	345	36	99	20	481			134	
Other	238	170	225	496	894	3,799 (5)	2,589 (5)	477	53.4
Compensation Trade	238	170	162	313	532			177	
Miscellaneous**			63	140	205			197	
Leasing			—	43	156			103	
Total	17,679	2,330	4,791	11,737	16,004	78,513 (100)	47,726 (100)	3,827	23.9

Sources: Compiled from *China Statistical Yearbook*, various dates; *Guangdong Yearbook 1989.*

*Including export credits.

**Mainly equipment related to out-processing contracts; figures in parentheses are percentages.

Table 7.5

Spatial Distribution of Foreign Investment in the Pearl River Delta, 1988

Location	TCF flow (mil. U.S.$) A	Processing fees received (mil. U.S.$) B	Enterprises with foreign participation No. C	Enterprises with foreign participation Export (mil. U.S.$) D	Total exports (mil.U.S.$) E	Total exports B+D as % of E[c] F
Guangzhou	221	82.7	769	11.7	1,077	8.8
Shenzhen	444	149	503	528[b]	1,850	36.6
Zhuhai	218	14	769	51	421	15.4
Jiangmen	103	9.6	600	53.4	362	17.4
Dongguan	130	107	130	41.9[b]	313	47.5
Foshan	218	10.1	253	83.6	624	15
Zhongshan	57	9	88	32.8	303	13.8
Delta total	1,391	381.4	2,702*	802.4	4,950	23.9
As % of province	57	94.6	90*	68.9	66.1	20.9
As % of nation	15.8	73.5[a]	38.6*	33.2	10.8	6.4

Source: Compiled from *Guangdong Yearbook 1989* and others.
Note: All figures have been subject to rounding.

*Only enterprises in operation. The provincial and national totals are 3,000, and 7000.
[a]Estimated; based on Guangdong's 77.8% share of the national total for 1979–86.
[b]Estimated.
[c]This represents underestimates of TCF's contribution to exports, as it does not include exports under compensation trade and uses processing fees instead of exports arising from out-processing.

flows. As of 1978, 78 percent of the private flows were estimated to originate in Hong Kong. It becomes obvious that Guangdong's share in DFI figures prominently. Guangdong netted 23.9 percent of the nation's TCF total in 1988. However, its share in private flows is disproportionately high: 42.5 percent of DFI and 53.4 percent from other sources (Table 7.4). It is reported that over the ten-year period, Guangdong accumulated a sizable total fixed investment, of which about 80 percent or U.S. $6 billion went to the Pearl River Delta. Such data underscore the increasing openness of the province and intensive economic cooperation between Hong Kong and Guangdong. Some analysts even pointed out a general distance-decay rule for concentration of DFI with increasing distance from Hong Kong (Ng et al., 1988).

The Pearl River Delta can be taken as an illustration to map out the pattern of Hong Kong's DFI in Guangdong and to illustrate its major impact on the province. Table 7.5 shows TCF into the delta in 1988. In that year, it amounted to U.S. $1.39 billion, or 57 percent of the province's and 15.8 percent of the nation's

Table 7.6

Agricultural Change in the Pearl River Delta, 1980–1986

Acreage/type of crop	% Change	
	Acreage	Yield
Total farm acreage	−8.24	N.A.
Grains (mainly paddy)	−18.7	−6.9
Sugar cane	37.7	49.6
Mulberry	−81.9	−83.3
Jute	−89.8	−98.7
Fruit	401.7	631.4
Pond fish	N.A.	130.3

Source: Xu et al., 1988.

DFI. Most was concentrated in Guangzhou, Shenzhen, Zhuhai, and Foshan. The breakdown for the provincial TCF shows 49.6 percent in official and private loans, 37.2 percent in DFI, 1.8 percent in foreign aid, and 11.9 percent in investments in out-processing and compensation trade. For the delta, a higher portion of DFI is within TCF, as suggested by its large share in the province's total processing fees (94.6 percent), in the number of foreign and joint-venture enterprises (90 percent), and in the contribution of these enterprises to exports (68.9 percent). This would signify a high dependence ratio on Hong Kong, judging from the size of the delta and its short history of active promotion of DFI.

The influx of DFI into the delta led to drastic changes in many areas. Investments from Hong Kong in agriculture in the form of compensation trade changed the delta's crop structure. For example, in Shajing in Baoan county, in the years 1979 to 1988, the acreage used for cultivation of rice dropped from 80 percent to 20 percent. Most of the former paddy fields were either used for fish farming or vegetable cultivation; 43 percent of the converted fish-farming acreage and 44 percent of the converted vegetable acreage were under compensation trade agreements with Hong Kong (Sit, 1990).

DFI injected into the farm sector led to land amalgamation, farm specialization, and commercialization. The end result is reflected in Table 7.6, which shows the changes in the delta in the period 1980 to 1986. The total acreage had substantially declined (due to urbanization and industrialization led by TCF, which will be discussed later), whereas the crop structure and yield had changed in favor of upper-market products such as fruits and pond fish.

The impact of TCF in the rural economy of the delta was across the board, as illustrated by the case of Shunde county. In the period 1980 to 1986, it experienced a mass out-movement of employment from the primary sector into the secondary and tertiary sectors. The proportion employed in the primary sector dropped from 70.1 percent to 45.8 percent. Within the secondary sector, construction increased from 1.6 percent to 6.7 percent, manufacturing from 19.6 percent to 28.8 percent, commerce and services from 0.6 percent to 3.7 percent, and transport from 0.7 percent to 2.9 percent. For the province as a whole, between 1979 and 1987, 6.7 million former peasants, or 28.1 percent of the total rural labor force, had moved out of the primary sector into the secondary and tertiary sectors (Sit, 1990).

Rapid structural change naturally resulted in accelerated urbanization. Growth was more concentrated in the larger urban centers, particularly the designated Special Economic Zones, which experienced an average annual population growth rate of 30.86 percent between 1978 and 1986. The four small municipalities of Zhongshan, Dongguan, Foshan, and Jiangmen registered an average growth rate varying from 4.03 percent to 10 percent, and the nine county seats, an average growth rate of 7.51 percent. For the 191 smaller urban places in the delta, their aggregated built-up area increased by 40.3 percent between 1980 and 1984 (Sit, 1990).

Cooperation in Infrastructural Development

Historically, Hong Kong has been dependent on Guangdong for over half of its supply of fresh water. In 1990, Guangdong supplied 590 million cubic meters of fresh water to Hong Kong, or 67.5 percent of Hong Kong's total consumption for that year. The supply is channeled from the East River through a series of stage reservoirs. A new plan is targeted for a maximum annual supply of 1,100 million cubic meters after 1994. Cooperation in water supply started in 1960, and it has remained an important and mutually beneficial project.

In electricity, Hong Kong has a surplus, particularly in times of low demand, whereas Guangdong has a serious shortage problem. Some have estimated that the shortfall in the province amounts to 40 percent of demand (Lu and Chen, 1990). The supply system of China Light and Power Co. Ltd. (CLP), the largest electricity company in Hong Kong, is now connected with that of the Guangdong General Power Company through which Hong Kong supplies about 4 million units of electricity to the province each day. CLP also has a running contract to supply electricity to the Shekou Industrial Zone of Shenzhen. A subsidiary of CLP joined with the Guangdong Nuclear Investment Company to develop the Daya Bay Nuclear Power Station in Shenzhen. The station started up operation in the mid-1990s and ultimately have two 900-megawatts pressurized water reactors. About 70 percent of the power from the station would be purchased by CLP to meet Hong Kong's long-term demand. Hong Kong's Hopewell Group also led a consortium in constructing a major coal-fired power station in Guangdong—the Shaijao B Station. In this project, most of the financing comes from syndicated loans from Hong Kong to be repaid by sales of the electricity generated. These are further examples of how Hong Kong entrepreneurship and financial capability play a major role in improving the infrastructure of the province.

Table 7.7

Hong Kong's Foreign-Invested Enterprises' Investment in China, 1989 and 1990 (in billion U.S. dollars)

	1989		1990		
	1st Half	2nd Half	1st Half	1st Quarter	2nd Quarter
Value of agreed contracts					
Country total	3.01	2.58	2.35	0.87	1.48
Hong Kong	1.66	1.50	1.49	0.57	0.92
Value of actual investments					
Country total	1.20	2.19	1.23	0.51	0.72
Hong Kong	0.71	1.37	0.74	0.32	0.42

Source: Hang Seng Economic Monthly, October 1990.

Assessment of the New Relation

Foreign investors have apparently turned more cautious since the Tiananmen Incident on June 4, 1989. New investment from Hong Kong was withheld for the first few months of 1990. The number of contracts and agreed value of new investments in 1990 were down 18 percent and 48 percent, respectively, for the corresponding period in 1989 (Table 7.7). A close analysis of the data for first two quarters of 1990 indicated a swift rebound of Hong Kong investments in the second quarter. The upward trend continued throughout July and August, bringing the cumulative total for the first eight months of 1990 to U.S. $3.6 million—the same level as 1989. The same set of statistics also showed that Hong Kong remained the largest foreign investor in China, accounting for 68 percent of the total number of projects approved and 63 percent of the value of investment pledged for the first half of that year. Statistics for Guangdong also indicated an increased flow of Hong Kong investment for the same period. Most of the newly agreed projects were of small to medium size and 98 percent of them were industrial projects (*Hang Seng Economic Monthly*, 10–1990).

The fact that Hong Kong–Guangdong economic relations continued to surge ahead, despite the political protests in Hong Kong concerning the June 4 Incident, indicates the weight of economic reality. Cheaper factor inputs of labor and land exerted a forceful enough economic pull to lure Hong Kong investments into Guangdong. Compared with competitive hosts in Southeast Asia, the proximity of the production sites across the border also enabled many of the ancillary activities to continue to be performed in Hong Kong; that is, the manufacturing sector's important linkages with other sectors of the economy could largely be undisturbed, an import cost advantage as well as a vital management edge that only Guangdong could provide. Hong Kong's concentration of investment in

China (Table 7.8) in the decade 1980–89 demonstrated the strength of the Hong Kong–Guangdong bond despite the uncertainty of 1997 and the frequent media talk of China's unstable political and economic situation.

To some extent, the rapid recovery of China's economy and its continual process of economic liberalization might have given added assurance to China's claim that it was committed to an Open-door Policy under the Chinese form of socialism. Nevertheless it is a strong assumption that China's pledge of an Open-door Policy and its unchanged policy toward Hong Kong over the last fifty years will be kept. It is with this assumption that this chapter turns to assessing the new Hong Kong–Guangdong economic relationship and its possible future development.

Led by Hong Kong's direct foreign investment and entrepreneurial talents, Guangdong is rapidly transforming its economy. The role of the market has become increasingly significant, and the export component of its manufacturing has grown substantially (to almost one-third of its gross output value). Within Guangdong, the distance-decay in terms of level of development and export orientation in relation to proximity from Hong Kong is obvious (Table 7.9). By 1987, Shenzhen had developed into an export-oriented industrial economy comparable to Macao. Its per capita gross national product (GNP) had reached the lower level of an Asian Newly Industrializing Economy. The economy was dominated by firms with foreign participation (largely from Hong Kong) that accounted for 63.7 percent of its industrial output and 83 percent of its total exports. The Hong Kong factor is envisaged to continue to operate into the mid-1990s in its present form, with Guangdong's growth in GNP projected at a pace of 7 percent to 10 percent per annum in real terms. Continued growth will be driven by the exogenous factors of comparative advantages for the production of labor-intensive light industrial products for export markets to the West. In other words, Guangdong will have a continuing role as the extended workshop of Hong Kong industries. By 1995, Guangdong and Shenzhen will probably have economies equivalent to 150 percent and 10 percent, respectively, of the Hong Kong economy as of 1987. Shenzhen will probably attain a per capita GNP of U.S. $4,000, the lower level of medium-developed countries. With its population of around 1 million, it will become an important adjunct to Hong Kong.

This relationship has given a new lease on life to Hong Kong's export-oriented industrialization. In the past decade, manufacturing's share of industrial exports continued to grow in real terms. Within this macro picture, there has been a realignment of activities within this sector. A movement toward more mechanization and a higher ratio of nonoperatives to operatives, as well as a decline in local value-added to gross output value, are the notable features reflecting the division of labor with Guangdong. The situation is now widely known as "front shop, back factory," meaning that Hong Kong concentrates on marketing, and Guangdong on production. Successful exploitation of Guangdong's labor and land resources has therefore increased the competitive edge of Hong Kong's

Table 7.8

Hong Kong's Direct Outward Investment to Major Asian Countries (approval basis, in million U.S. dollars)

Year	China	Indonesia	Thailand	Taiwan	South Korea	Philippines	Malaysia	Japan	Total (excluding Japan)
1980	N.A.	N.A.	N.A.	40	0	N.A.	N.A.	N.A.	N.A.
1981	N.A.	N.A.	N.A.	35	34	0	15	N.A.	N.A.
1982	N.A.	195	N.A.	41	27	1	2	N.A.	N.A.
1983	642	126	N.A.	24	7	4	21	N.A.	N.A.
1984	2,175	706	N.A.	65	4	10	4	N.A.	N.A.
1985	4,134	53	N.A.	29	13	3	7	N.A.	N.A.
1986	1,449	10	127	76	13	7	11	57	1,693
1987	1,947	135	125	181	43	28	11	36	2,470
1988	3,466	240	451	157	14	27	50	44	4,405
1989	3,160	407	561	248	37	133	42	63	4,588
Total	20,651	2,657	1,264	1,194	225	214	163	453	26,368
	(1979–89)	(1968–89)	(1986–89)	(1952–89)	(1962–89)	(1981–89)	(1981–89)	(1950–89)	(end–1989)

Source: Hong Kong Bank Economic Report, 11–1990.

Notes: Figures for Malaysia cover only manufacturing investment; figures for Singapore are not available; figures for Thailand, Malaysia, and the Philippines were converted into U.S.$ terms by applying the average exchange rates in individual years.

Table 7.9

Basic Economic Statistics of the Major Constitutent Parts of Guangdong and Hong Kong Compared (1987 data)

	Guangzhou	Shenzhen*	Zhuhai*	Pearl River Delta	Guangdong Province	Hong Kong
Area (sq. km.)	1,405	327	15	46,000	178,085	1,070
Population (mil.)	7.35	0.56	0.44	24.11	64.5	5.65
GDP(bil. yuan/HK$)	18.5	4.45	1.4	41.7	86.4	360.2
Per capita GDP(U.S.$)	677	2,150	863	470	360	8,227
Gross Output (bil. yuan)						
Agriculture	16.6	0.1	—	8.6	39.6	—
Industry	21.5	4.9	0.4	57.6	90	—
Exports (bil. US$)	0.9	1.41	0.27	3.5	5.6	25
Foreign Investment (mil. U.S.$)	61	394	57	1,107	1,230	—
Government Revenue (mil. yuan/HK$)	3,480	823	217	4,520	9,597	41,894

Source: Guangdong Yearbook 1987.
* With exception of population and area, the fixtures include the whole municipality.

traditional industries, that is, their price competitiveness. Yet it also means making Hong Kong more dependent on Guangdong. The interdependence goes beyond factor input. Since the largest market for the province's exports through Hong Kong is the United States, a change in China's relations with the United States can affect Hong Kong's economy. So far, the most-favored-nation status, conferred by the United States on China, has been beneficial to Hong Kong. Besides supporting Hong Kong's manufacturing sector, the spatial interdependence in production has led to expansion of activities in other sectors, such as transport, finance, tourism, and business services. The dwindling labor demand by manufacturing in Hong Kong has been compensated for by expanded labor demand in these other sectors.

In the past decade, active cooperation on a broad range of economic activities, involving numerous small to large entrepreneurs and firms across the border, has forged mutual understanding and familiarity between Hong Kong and Guangdong—a good basis for further cooperation.

Implication for Hong Kong's Economic Future

The new relationship between Hong Kong and Guangdong that has developed in the past decade is due to China's Open-door Policy. It is fueled by the Hong Kong government's permissive attitude, by the efforts of Hong Kong's entrepreneurs, and by Guangdong's drive for economism. Of course, the adjustment in Guangdong's regulations and the improvement in its infrastructure have provided the basic conditions for such economic changes to occur. On the Hong Kong side, the basic driving force has been the singular profit motivation of entrepreneurs. There is no direct official involvement, but there is some indirect support and a permissive attitude, at best. The new relationship, from the Hong Kong perspective, is one of scale and spatial expansion of its production system.

The opening up and expansion of Hong Kong industrialization not only extends industries across the border, but also restructures the economy. The spatial extension enlarges the scale of production and output. Moreover, local firms with headquarters in the metropolis and branch plants in the province are now transformed into transnational enterprises. This fundamental organizational change leads to labor restructuring. The headquarters require office workers, while manual workers are rapidly replaced by Guangdong's labor, as demonstrated by a labor composition that is biased toward service workers. Also, cross-border intra- and inter-firm freight movement has increased. The demand for information, labor, and freight traffic necessitates new skill training and road networks, forcing the government to improve higher education and transportation facilities. Provision of infrastructure has become the major governmental investment, thus involving the official sector more directly in the production process.

With the increase of local export production and exports from Guangdong, Hong Kong reemerges as an entrepôt. International trade becomes, once again, an important economic sector, further diversifying the economy. Direct foreign investment to Guangdong from other Asian economies, notably from Taiwan, is routed mostly through Hong Kong. The transnational corporations generate a flow of goods, technology, finance, and labor. Hong Kong, with abundant expertise in Guangdong investment, is able to provide information and managerial services to the overseas investors. Besides benefiting from these TNC flows, the metropolis takes on an additional "comprador" role for the province's external trade.

The new relation with Guangdong, thus, is beneficial to Hong Kong—broadening existing production, restructuring labor, offering new investment possibilities, diversifying the economy, strengthening international trade, and providing a variety of opportunities to entrepreneurs and professionals.

For the future, economists and planners on both sides of the border are aware of the need for cooperation and coordination in order to maintain and deepen the relationship. As suggested by such terms as "Guangdong–Hong Kong–Macao Economic Integration," or "South China Economic Ring," there is a degree of unanimity that Guangdong and Hong Kong (to some extent incorporating Macao) have evolved a new economic bond.

The economic characteristics of the present bond may be summarized as: (1) biased toward processing of light industrial goods, (2) highly labor-intensive, (3) dependent for exports on price competitiveness, (4) market-responsive, and (5) lacking in long-term planning. Many analyses indicate that the future for both territories lies not only in maintaining the bond, but in developing it further through guidance and planning (Stanford Research Institute, 1990; Cheng, 1990). Deng Xiaoping has suggested four major targets to further deepen the relationship:

1. Both sides should cooperate in developing new and improving existing basic infrastructure such as energy supply, transport, and communication.
2. Both sides should cooperate in setting up intermediate industries to produce parts, components, and raw materials for existing light industries.
3. Both sides should collaborate in research and development and the marketing of new products.
4. Both sides should cooperate in new agricultural development.

To achieve these goals, new intergovernmental agencies have to be set up to create mutually agreeable infrastructure development plans and a coordinated sectorial investment program. In addition, new institutions for high technology, product development, market information, and marketing have to be set up (Deng, 1990). Such views represent some of the wishes of the Guangdong authority. The Hong Kong authority has yet to respond.

The rapid development of the past decade, instigated by China's new Opendoor Policy and economic realism, has produced a workable cooperative relationship between Hong Kong and Guangdong. Such integration has solved some of the economic problems with which Hong Kong was confronted in the 1980s. Simultaneously, it has unified Hong Kong with its natural hinterland. Even with Hong Kong's political integration with China in 1997, there is still much worry that further development in this direction will increase Hong Kong's dependence on China, and may undermine Hong Kong's political autonomy and the economic system on which its previous growth was based. The evidence so far is that the province–metropolis connection has been well received and is supported by the Chinese leaders, and especially enthusiastically in Guangdong where the change has directly increased employment and income as well as improved the standard of living. Direct foreign investment and entrepreneurship from Hong Kong extend the unique metropolitan approach, style, and philosophy into the actual implementation of the development. Maintaining Hong Kong as a reservoir of these critical factors and utilizing its infrastructure and geographical advantages will be of primary significance for deepening Hong Kong–Guangdong relations and achieving economic development for the region for many years to come.

The unresolved issue at present is how to upgrade the cooperation at an intergovernmental level, which seems to be the precondition for the next stage of Hong Kong–Guangdong economic integration and development.

References

Cheng, T.C. (1990), "Some Thoughts on Economic Integration of Hong Kong–Macao–Pearl River Delta," *Hong Kong & Macao Economies*, No. 6, pp. 3–6.
China Statistical Yearbook, China National Statistical Bureau.
Davis, S.G. (1949), *Hong Kong in Its Geographical Setting*, London: Collins.
Deng, L.C. (1990), "Guangdong–Hong Kong's Structural Cooperation Is a Must," *Hong Kong & Macao Economies*, No. 9, pp. 5–6.
Economic Reporter (Hong Kong), January 1991.
Endacott, G.B., and A. Hinton (1962), *Fragrant Harbor: A Short History of Hong Kong*, Hong Kong: Oxford University Press.
Federation of Hong Kong Industries (1990), *Hong Kong's Offshore Investment: A Survey of Hong Kong's Industrial Investment in Overseas Countries*, Hong Kong: Federation of Hong Kong Industries.
Guangdong Yearbook 1987 (1989), Guangzhou: Guangdong People's Press.
Hang Seng Economic Monthly, March, October 1990.
History Society of China, ed. (1954), *The Opium War*, 6 vols., Shanghai: History Society of China.
Hong Kong & Macao Economies, April 1990.
Hong Kong Annual Report, 1979, Hong Kong: Hong Kong Government.
Hong Kong Bank Economic Report, November 1990; January, April 1991.
Hong Kong External Trade, Hong Kong: Census and Statistics Department, Hong Kong Government.
Lu, X., and C. Chen (1990), "Promoting Basic Infrastructure Development to Aid Development of Guangdong–Hong Kong–Macao," *Hong Kong & Macao Economies*, No. 5, pp. 9–12.

MOFERT (Ministry of Foreign Relations and Economic Trade).

Ng, Y.T., et al. (1988), "Foreign Direct Investment in China—With Special Reference to Guangdong Province" in *Perspectives on China's Modernization,* ed. Y.K. Wong, C.C. Lau, and B.C. Li., Hong Kong: Chinese University of Hong Kong, pp. 187–210.

Sit, Fung Shuen (1982), *Hong Kong, China Economics and the Future of Hong Kong,* Hong Kong: Wide Angle Press.

——— (1988), "Post-war Population and its Spatial Dynamics," in *Urban Hong Kong,* V.F.S. Sit, ed., Hong Kong: Summerson, pp. 2–25.

——— (1990), "Impact of Transnational Capital Flows on Urbanization in Developing Countries" (mimeograph).

Sit, Fung Shuen, and S.L. Wong (1989), *Small and Medium Industries in an Export-Oriented Economy: The Case of Hong Kong,* Hong Kong: Centre of Asian Studies, University of Hong Kong.

Sit, Fung Shuen, S.L. Wong, and T.S. Kiang (1980), *Small-Scale Industry in a Laissez-faire Economy,* Hong Kong: Centre of Asian Studies, University of Hong Kong.

Standard Research Institute (1989), *Tasks for the 1990s: Implementing Hong Kong's Strategy for Building Prosperity,* Hong Kong: Standard Research Institute.

Szczepanik, E. (1958), *The Economic Growth of Hong Kong,* London: Oxford University Press.

Xu, Xueqiang, et al. (1988), *Collected Works on Research on the Pearl River Delta,* 4 vols., Guangzhou: Zhongshan University Press.

Yao, W. Yuan (1984), *Investigating the Historical Facts of the Opium War,* Beijing: People's Press.

Part IV
Partnership in Flux

8

Political Transformation in Hong Kong: From Colony to Colony

Ian Scott

The political dimensions of the Hong Kong–Guangdong nexus need to be seen in the wider context of relationships among the central Chinese government, Britain, and the territory. There are, of course, political implications arising from the rapid growth of Hong Kong's economic links with Guangdong. But increased investment and output in Guangdong in the 1980s does not in itself constitute grounds for the assumption that these developments will lead to a semiautonomous Hong Kong after 1997 or for the belief that economic prosperity will significantly change the central government's attitudes toward future political control over the territory. The main thrust of the present Chinese government's policies in the region is to ensure that Hong Kong is compliant with central directives after 1997; economic development along capitalist lines in southern China is subsidiary to that aim.

To understand what this means for Hong Kong, it is necessary, first, to distinguish the formal provisions for the transfer of sovereignty, contained in the Sino-British agreement of 1984 and the Basic Law of 1990, from the reality of how power is actually changing hands. The agreement and the Basic Law have been used by the Chinese and British governments to attempt to legitimize a new political order after 1997. On the surface, they speak to four sets of central concerns—the autonomy of the post-1997 government, the development of representative institutions, the maintenance of civil liberties, and continued economic prosperity—that are appropriately regarded as critical to the Hong Kong people's acceptance of the future regime. However, the actions of the respective governments have been so far removed from the promises made in the agreement and in the Basic Law that they have rendered those promises largely implausible. Despite the solemn commitments given in the agreement, two of the pillars on which reluctant local acceptance of the accord were based—the autonomy of the Special Administrative Region (SAR) and the development of representative government—were rapidly renegotiated by the Chinese and British governments after 1984. A third, China's commitment to the preservation of existing civil liberties in Hong Kong, was generally regarded as worthless even before, but especially after, the Tiananmen Square massacre.

It is this erosion of the provisions of the agreement, as much as the agreement itself, that explains the substantial emigration of the middle class, the search for foreign passports, the relocation of some major companies, aspects of civil service unrest, and the general malaise over the future of the territory.[1] If there had been more congruence between the promises made in the agreement and the later provisions of the Basic Law, it is possible that some of the major problems of political stability and legitimacy now facing Hong Kong would not have arisen. As it stands, the task of the Chinese, British, and Hong Kong governments is to attempt to persuade the people of Hong Kong that they have a free and autonomous future in a situation in which there is little credible evidence to support such a conclusion.

The approaches of the respective governments to their self-inflicted predicament have been long on rhetoric and short on substance. The British government has stressed the commitments made in the agreement and the Basic Law, China's record in observing international treaties, and the continuing, but increasingly discredited, view that China's economic need for Hong Kong will act as a constraint preventing violations of the formal constitutional provisions.[2] The Chinese government has issued bland assurances about its future intentions for Hong Kong, mixed with occasional threats about the consequences of noncompliance with its aims.[3] Most problematic of all has been the position of the Hong Kong government, whose legitimacy, already shaken by the advent of 1997, has been further damaged by its inability to give any guarantees on future autonomy, democracy, or civil liberties. Aside from the enactment of a Bill of Rights, which Chinese officials promptly implied would be repealed after 1997 (*South China Morning Post,* 6–4–1991), the Hong Kong government had only one remaining argument to preserve stability in the transitional period and beyond. That argument was that the constitutional arrangements provided a basis for the continuing economic prosperity of the territory. More specifically, Hong Kong's centrifugal role in promoting the greater affluence of the southern China region would confer economic benefits on its citizens. And, although this could only be hinted at, there were political advantages, particularly greater autonomy from Beijing, that might be derived from an economically dynamic Cantonese-speaking regional association.

In this scenario, Hong Kong would act as the technological, financial, and export center for southern China. High-technology industries and superior infrastructural facilities would ensure that the territory retained its position of economic dominance in the region. Labor-intensive manufacturing industries would gradually be relocated to Guangdong Province to take advantage of cheaper labor and rents. China would continue to supply to the territory water and agricultural products and eventually energy from the Daya Bay nuclear plant. The Hong Kong government's efforts to encourage this outcome have had important policy implications in the field of infrastructural development, such as the plan to build a new airport and improve port facilities, educational policy, support for technological development, and industrial incentives. It is too soon to judge whether the government's policy will facilitate long-term economic growth. Politically, however, it must already be regarded as a failure. It has not met the two political ends at which it was aimed. It has not bolstered support for the colonial regime in the transitional period, for there is no evidence to suggest that the chimera of a coprosperity region has succeeded in persuading the people of Hong Kong that they are likely to enjoy an untroubled, economically buoyant future.[4] And it has not won Chinese support for the Hong Kong government's actions. On the contrary, it has enabled the Chinese government to extract further concessions, notably on the question of autonomy. This chapter examines the reasons for the failure of the policy in the wider context of Hong Kong's transition from British to Chinese control.

The Negotiation of the Sino-British Agreement

The political difficulties that Hong Kong faces owe something to the peculiar colonial history of the territory.[5] But they are probably rather more the result of recent British diplomatic blunders, Chinese intransigence, the political naivety of Hong Kong's leaders and entrepreneurs, and the absence of representative institutions through which the Hong Kong people might express their views.

The British government has a rather different view. Since the signing of the agreement, it has taken the position that it was required by the terms of the lease over the New Territories to return sovereignty over the whole of Hong Kong to China.

> Whether or not there is an agreement between Her Majesty's Government and the Chinese Government, the New Territories will revert to China on 1 July 1997 under the terms of the 1898 Convention. The remainder of Hong Kong .. . would not be viable alone. . . . The choice is therefore between reversion of Hong Kong to China under agreed, legally binding international arrangements or reversion to China without such arrangements. This is not a choice which Her Majesty's Government have sought to impose on the people of Hong Kong. It is a choice imposed by the facts of Hong Kong's history. (*Draft Agreement*, 1984: para. 29)

This was in fact not a choice at all—it was an ultimatum—but to the extent that there is truth in this assertion, it is a political rather than a legal or historical truth. The Chinese government certainly has the military power to retake Hong Kong at any time, and it has consistently maintained that the territory was part of China. But the British government's contention that the 1898 convention required it to return Hong Kong to China is pure rationalization.[6] The Chinese government did not recognize the convention. And much of the British government's effort in the years before the signing of the agreement had been directed at rewriting the convention to ensure a continued British presence after 1997.

British diplomatic efforts to secure the future of Hong Kong began in 1979 with a visit by the governor, Sir Murray (later Lord) MacLehose, to Beijing. With the accession of Deng Xiaoping and a program of economic reforms under way in China, the British government believed that the time was propitious to resolve the issue of the New Territories lease. They were under some pressure to do so from Hong Kong businessmen and bankers who wanted to consolidate politically the dramatic economic growth that the territory had experienced in the 1970s. And there was also the prospect of long-term trade and investment opportunities for British firms as a possible outcome of a successful agreement. Prevailing opinion in Hong Kong in 1979 was that China would see the economic advantages of maintaining the status quo and that life would go on under a British administration much as it had in the past. MacLehose apparently took with him to Beijing a proposal that might have been interpreted as an attempt to retain British control over Hong Kong beyond 1997. According to Munro (1990), this decision set in train a series of events that led directly to the political problems the territory now faces.[7]

The Chinese view was that they did not recognize the British occupation of Hong Kong. By this token, the date for the handback of the New Territories was not, as the British Foreign Office was subsequently to maintain, of any special significance. The Hong Kong question, according to the Chinese, would be resolved at the appropriate time. This position maintained maximum flexibility while retaining the essential criterion that sovereignty over Hong Kong rested, as it always had, with China. MacLehose's visit served at the public level to confirm this view, for Deng Xiaoping was widely quoted as telling Hong Kong people—or perhaps, more specifically, investors—that they should put their hearts at ease.[8] Munro maintains that MacLehose did not raise the proposal with Deng except, perhaps, in passing. However,

> British diplomats went back to the Chinese in the following weeks to explain the proposal and to press the Chinese for their approval. Chinese officials were mystified, then flustered, and finally alarmed. . . . Ultimately, the Chinese concluded, the British wanted them to endorse the continuation of the "unequal treaties"; for the prickly and nationalistic Chinese, this was equivalent to implying that Hong Kong was sovereign British territory. And this was one thing that no Chinese leader could ever accept. (Munro, 1990: 33–39)

The negotiations over the future of Hong Kong came about because the British pressed for them. When the Chinese reluctantly agreed, they were determined that the question of sovereignty should be at the core of the discussions. The negotiations lasted for two years between 1982 and 1984. For the first part of this period, which began with Prime Minister Margaret Thatcher's visit to Beijing in September 1982, the British position was that the treaties ceding Hong Kong island and Kowloon to Britain were valid. Thereafter, from about October 1983 onward, with the Foreign Office increasingly determining British policy, the British government conceded sovereignty and worked on securing an agreement that, it was hoped, would have binding international effect (Scott, 1989: chap. 5). The formal provisions of the agreement take, as their starting point, Deng Xiaoping's slogan "one country, two systems." By this is meant the coexistence of socialism in China with capitalism in Hong Kong under the rubric of Chinese sovereignty. The capitalist system in Hong Kong is to persist for fifty years and the territory, as a Special Administrative Region (SAR), is to enjoy "a high degree of autonomy" in most matters except defense and foreign affairs. Extensive rights and freedoms are guaranteed including

> freedom of the person, of speech, of the press, of assembly, of association, to form and join trade unions, of correspondence, of travel, of movement, of strike, of demonstration, of choice of occupation, of academic research, of belief, inviolability of the home, the freedom to marry and the right to raise a family freely. (*Draft Agreement,* 1984: Annex I, XIII)

There were even signs of progress toward representative government. In an annex to the agreement elaborating the Chinese government's basic policies toward Hong Kong, it was specified:

> The legislature of the Hong Kong Special Administrative Region shall be constituted by elections. The executive authorities shall abide by the law and shall be accountable to the legislature. (*Draft Agreement,* 1984: Annex I, I)

Critically, however, the future political system after 1997 was left to the Chinese government to define through the promulgation of a Basic Law.

The Agreement and the Political Values of the Hong Kong People

Throughout the negotiations, there was virtually no consultation with the people of Hong Kong on their political future. The Chinese government did not recognize their right to negotiate on the grounds that they were Chinese subjects; consequently, there were no Hong Kong representatives at the discussions.[9] The British government paid lip service to the notion of consultation by keeping the appointed members of the Executive Council informed of developments. But those members were sworn to an oath of secrecy and, in any case, they had little popular support in the community. The British government had done nothing to develop representative institutions in Hong Kong, so there were no channels through which local views could be expressed. Every opinion poll—then as now—showed that the Hong Kong people overwhelmingly favored the status quo.[10] Predictably, the British and Chinese governments refused to permit a referendum on the agreement.

Instead, an Assessment Office was established and charged with the task of gauging opinions on the agreement from individuals, representative bodies, survey findings, and the media. The assessors believed, rather curiously, that

> people would not write in if they found the draft agreement acceptable; nor would they find it necessary to write in if their views had already been reflected in the media or by organizations or groups to which they had access. (Assessment Office, 1984)

Silence, in other words, meant consent. An equally plausible explanation, of course, was that people did not write to the Assessment Office because they had been told that there was nothing in the draft agreement that they could change (Scott, 1989: 13–14).[11] There were only 2,494 responses to the call for views on the agreement's acceptability. Yet the assessors were able to reach the conclusion that "most of the people of Hong Kong find the draft agreement acceptable" (Assessment Office, 1984: 15).

Accompanying the Assessment Office report were two volumes of evidence from legislative councilors, urban councilors, and district board members. These volumes were not widely circulated but they are of interest for two reasons. First, aside from the opinion polls, they are the only picture we have—albeit an incomplete and impressionistic one—of the feelings of the Hong Kong people and their representatives toward the agreement at that time. Second, there is some discrepancy between the raw material published in these volumes and the detailed findings of the Assessment Office on particular clauses of the agreement. It is probably true that those who did bother to write found the agreement acceptable. However, if we break the content of the raw material down by critical issues, there are anomalies.

The respondents chose to express their views predominantly in four major areas of concern: the autonomy of the post-1997 government; representative government; civil liberties (including the important subcategory of nationality); and the economy. Less frequently mentioned but still important matters included the stationing of People's Liberation Army troops in Hong Kong after 1997, educational policy, and recognition of professional status. The four principal sets of concerns were not self-contained. Those who believed, for example, that the agreement would result in "a high degree of autonomy" tended also to believe that this would help to preserve the economy. Conversely, those who did not believe that the agreement would promote "a high degree of autonomy" tended

Table 8.1

Summary Data of Submissions Made by Political Leaders and Representative Organizations to the Assessment Office on the Draft Agreement on the Future of Hong Kong

Would the agreement facilitate:*		Yes	No	Total	As a percentage of all sub-missions**
The maintenance of autonomy	I	35	5	40	
	II	22	10	32	
	Total	57	15	72	26.87
The development of representative government	I	22	14	36	
	II	7	17	24	
	Total	29	31	60	22.39
The protection of civil liberties	I	16	10	26	
	II	13	20	33	
	Total	29	30	59	22.01
Continued economic growth	I	29	5	34	
	II	22	3	25	
	Total	51	8	59	22.01

Source: Assessment Office (November 29, 1984).

*The material is treated as an open-ended question on the assumption that the area of concern would not have been mentioned unless it were regarded as important.

**There were 268 submissions from political leaders and representative organizations. Most either did not indicate precisely why they supported or opposed the agreement or focused on a particular area of concern other than the principal areas listed here. Submissions from individuals were not reproduced in these volumes.

Key

I: Submissions by Legislative councilors, urban councilors, and district board members.

II: Submissions by representative organizations such as trade unions, business associations, voluntary organizations, and mutual aid committees.

to doubt whether there would be much progress toward representative government or much protection of civil liberties. Nonetheless, as Table 8.1 shows, there were significant differences in the attitudes of respondents to the four major areas of concern and whether the agreement would facilitate their attainment.

An initial difference, which is shown clearly in Table 8.1 but which is not mentioned in the Assessment Office report, is that political leaders were more positive toward the agreement than were the representative organizations. The explanation seems to be that many political leaders were government appointees and were reflecting official thinking whereas the representative organizations were rather more independent. Both groups, however, placed considerable stress on autonomy, seeing local control over Hong Kong affairs as the best defense for the protection of civil liberties, economic growth, and representative government. A considerable majority believed that this could be achieved through the agreement and the implementation of the "one country, two systems" concept. But it soon became clear—as shown by the drafting of the Basic Law, by repeated Chinese government statements that implied control over Hong Kong rather than autonomy, and by the second airport agreement—that the formal provisions of the agreement would largely be ignored after 1997 (*Renmin ribao,* 4–17–1991).

On the question of representative government, the Assessment Office (1984: 22) found:

> The provision for the legislature of the Hong Kong SAR to be constituted by elections was hailed by many including members of the District Boards and the Urban Council as "far-sighted and progressive."

Some believed that:

> the new political structure should be established by the late 80s or early 90s, so as to practice self-administration before 1997. (Assessment Office, 1984: 22)

The raw data summarized in Table 8.1 suggest that there were many others who did not believe that the agreement would lead to more representative government. They were concerned about the drafting of the Basic Law, the composition of the post-1997 legislature, and China's power to appoint the chief executive of the SAR. In the event, they were proven correct: the British, Chinese, and Hong Kong governments made concerted efforts to slow the pace of the development of representative government after the signing of the agreement.

Civil liberties were equally contentious. There was strong condemnation of the British government's decision to change, without their consent, the nationality status of those who had been born in Hong Kong. And there was alarm over China's human rights record and its implications for Hong Kong. The Assessment Office (1984: 27) report is misleading in this respect. It notes:

> The minority who opposed the draft agreement because they objected to the reunification of Hong Kong with the communist PRC (People's Republic of China) expressed concern at the possibility that the communist government in China would not respect individual rights and freedoms; but the majority who accepted the draft agreement found the provisions in the section comprehensive.

In fact, a majority of the representative organizations that responded did not believe that the agreement would serve to protect civil liberties. The Assessment

Report is also misleading because it draws a false dichotomy: many of those who accepted the comprehensive nature of the declaration on human rights did not believe that rights had been adequately defined or that they would be respected. The evidence for the importance Hong Kong people attached to civil liberties is that this became an issue of domestic importance after 1984 and, of course, of central significance after the Tiananmen Square massacre.

On the fourth central area of concern—the economy—there can be little doubt that the agreement, in the words of the Assessment Office, was "warmly welcomed." It had, after all, been negotiated with the interests of Hong Kong businessmen firmly in mind. The three major business associations—the Hong Kong General Chamber of Commerce, the Chinese Manufacturers Association, and the Hong Kong Federation of Industries—jointly stated that the agreement could be "widely accepted by businessmen and industrialists as providing the best possible basis for continued economic prosperity" (Assessment Office, 1984: 24). Businessmen saw the agreement as a means of enabling them to exploit investment opportunities in China. The Hong Kong government soon proved receptive to the same argument and sought to reap political benefits from closer economic links with China. The provisions in the agreement that were attractive to the majority of Hong Kong's population—autonomy, the development of representative government, and the protection of civil liberties—were soon sufficiently under threat that the government had little option but to advance the notion that Hong Kong would become the economic dynamo for the whole of southern China. Once the other pillars on which the agreement had been founded began to crumble, the legitimacy of the Hong Kong government in the transitional period was in considerable jeopardy. Pushing the economic argument for the settlement soon came to be seen as the sole available credible means of bolstering political support.

The Renegotiation of the Agreement

Following the signing of the agreement, the British and Chinese governments reached a series of compromises and accommodations that essentially undermined the spirit in which the agreement had been accepted by the Hong Kong people. The effect of these accords was to reinterpret and renegotiate the meaning of autonomy and of representative government.

The Erosion of Autonomy

Autonomy is very closely linked with the issue of representative government, but it is possible to separate the two concerns because they were supposed to fall under different jurisdictions in the transitional period. Autonomy after 1997 was to be guaranteed by the Basic Law, which was to be drafted by the Chinese government in consultation with the people of the territory; the development of representative government, at least theoretically, was expected to be the responsibility of the British and Hong Kong governments. In practice, the drafting of the Basic Law was used as a pretext to prevent the development of representative government.

For the Chinese government, the drafting process, which lasted from 1985 to 1990, served two important political purposes. First, it enabled the Chinese government to participate in Hong Kong's political affairs. As a former member of the Basic Law Consultative Committee Secretariat puts it, the Chinese government learned

> who could be included in its united front and who should be expelled from it . . . which groups of people should be incorporated or liaised with more closely; and which groups should be granted recognition through the appointment to the NPC (National People's Congress) or CCPC (Chinese Communist Party Congress) or through the future allotment of functional constituencies. (Tang, 1990: 172)[12]

Second, the drafting of the Basic Law gave the Chinese government the opportunity to devise the conditions under which it might intervene in Hong Kong after 1997. Instead of guaranteeing autonomy, as promised in the agreement, the Basic Law permits the Chinese government to administer the territory directly, should it wish to do so.

The Basic Law Drafting Committee consisted of fifty-nine members of whom twenty-three came from Hong Kong. Two of the Hong Kong members, the democratic activists Martin Lee Chu-ming and Szeto Wah, were expelled from the committee following their protests over the Tiananmen Square massacre. The remaining Hong Kong members were largely drawn from business and the professions, although there were also representatives from the media, labor, and religious groups. The Drafting Committee was to be assisted by a Consultative Committee composed of Hong Kong people from all walks of life. In practice, the Consultative Committee was soon factionalized and played only a limited role in the production of the final document.[13]

The Basic Law was supposed to reflect the provisions of the Sino-British agreement and many of its clauses do repeat the words in the agreement. The freedoms mentioned in the agreement are guaranteed, the economy is to remain capitalist, the judiciary is to be independent, and the laws of Hong Kong are to apply, except in certain matters, the most important of which are the laws of the sea and nationality, where Chinese law will prevail (Basic Law, 1990: Annex III). The critical differences with the agreement are in the political realm, where it is clear that control is vested in the Chinese government. The contradiction between the requirements of autonomy and the Chinese intention to control the post-1997 SAR government is immediately apparent in Article 12:

> The Hong Kong Special Administrative Region shall be a local administrative region of the People's Republic of China, which shall enjoy a high degree of

autonomy and come directly under the Central People's Government. (Basic Law, 1990: art. 12)

Other provisions in the Basic Law leave little doubt that the operative phrase is "come directly under the Central People's Government." The direction of the Chinese government in foreign affairs and defense, as provided in the agreement, is spelled out (art. 13). Chinese troops are to be stationed in Hong Kong and, if requested by the SAR government, may assist in the maintenance of public order (art. 14). The Chinese government appoints the chief executive and the principal officials (art. 15). High Court judges, who must be Chinese citizens with permanent residence in the region and no right of abode elsewhere, are appointed by the chief executive and endorsed by the Legislative Council (art. 90). The appointment is then reported to the Standing Committee of the National People's Congress. The provision in the agreement that provides that the executive should be accountable to the legislature is essentially turned around. It is the legislature that owes its existence to the executive, for it may be dismissed if it fails to endorse the executive's policies (arts. 49, 50). The powers of the legislature are very weak and it could not be entirely directly elected until 2007 at the earliest (Annex II). Interpretation of the Basic Law itself rests with the National People's Congress.

The final constraint on any autonomy that Hong Kong might have enjoyed after 1997 is provided in Article 18, which states:

> In the event that the Standing Committee of the National People's Congress decides to declare a state of war or, by reason of turmoil within the Hong Kong Special Administrative Region which endangers national unity or security and is beyond the control of the government of the Region, decides that the Region is in a state of emergency, the Central People's Government may issue an order applying the relevant national laws in the Region.

Given the other provisions for control with which the Chinese government has armed itself, it is to be hoped that this article will prove unnecessary. But legally it would provide the central government with the powers to impose a state of emergency in Hong Kong on July 1, 1997, and to administer the territory directly.

The British government had a responsibility to ensure that the Basic Law, as the then foreign secretary, Sir Geoffrey Howe, put it, "conforms fully with the spirit as well as the letter of the Joint Declaration" (House of Commons, 1989: 249–50). According to Howe, the British government did raise concerns relating to Article 18 and the stationing of troops in Hong Kong after 1997 and the interpretation of the Basic Law with the Chinese government. But this appears to have had absolutely no effect. By conceding that the Chinese government had the sole untrammeled right to draft the Basic Law, the British government effectively foreclosed on any chance of autonomy after 1997. The Basic Law does not conform with what the Hong Kong people thought the Sino-British agreement meant. It represents an implicit agreement on the part of the British government to recognize virtually direct rule over Hong Kong after 1997. In this context, the Memorandum of Understanding, which was agreed by the British and Chinese governments in July 1991 and which provided for a greater say for the Chinese government in Hong Kong's internal affairs *before* 1997, is not a particularly radical development but merely a way station along the road to the complete erosion of autonomy (Memorandum, 1991).

Constraints on the Development of Representative Government

The development of representative government was a political concession extracted by the British government in the last few months of the negotiations. The reaction to the announcement in May 1984 that China would station troops in Hong Kong after 1997 was almost entirely adverse. If the agreement was to receive even reluctant acceptance, it was necessary to provide a sweetener. In July 1984, the Hong Kong government produced a green paper entitled "The Further Development of Representative Government in Hong Kong." This promised a more accountable government, the introduction of functional constituencies, and an electoral college composed of District Board members but no direct elections because

> direct elections would run the risk of a swift introduction of adversarial politics, and would introduce an element of instability at a crucial time. (Green Paper, 1984: 9)

There was some modification of this position in a subsequent white paper that was released in November 1984 at the same time as the Assessment Office report. The white paper suggested that there could be "a very small number of directly elected members in 1988 . . . building up to a significant number of directly elected members by 1997" (White Paper, 1984: 8). Even more important perhaps was the promise that there would be a review of public opinion in 1987 on attitudes toward the development of representative government.

In the interim, however, the Chinese government made it clear that it did not wish to see any development toward representative government. This was phrased in terms of opposition to changes in the transitional period that might potentially be in conflict with the still-to-be-drafted Basic Law. Xu Jiatun, then director of the New China News Agency, suggested that the provisions of the Sino-British agreement would be violated if direct elections were considered seriously in the 1987 constitutional review (*Far Eastern Economic Review,* 12–12–1985: 21). The agreement stipulated that there would be elections to the legislature, but the Chinese view was that these need not be direct elections and could even include the possibility of appointed members. This explains, in part, the Chinese government's fondness for functional constituencies and for the disproportionate representation of such constituencies in the post-1997 setup. Members from functional constituencies are generally selected by small electorates that are organizationally based; the prospect of controlling such electorates and elections is much higher than that of controlling a large electorate on a wide franchise.

There was nothing in the agreement that prevented the British government from introducing a more representative government in the transitional period. However, the Foreign Office conceded almost immediately to the Chinese position that there should be "convergence" between constitutional developments in the transitional period and the Basic Law. Timothy Renton, the British minister of state in charge of Hong Kong affairs, said in November 1985 that the present system of indirect elections should be allowed to settle and that Britain had no moral commitment to the establishment of a Westminster system of liberal democracy in the territory (*South China Morning Post*, 12–1–1985). The deal was sealed during Renton's visit to Beijing in January 1986. This was, in effect, a renegotiation of the agreement and it left the Hong Kong government in a very embarrassing position. It was no longer possible to make significant constitutional advances. Yet a commitment had been made to a constitutional review that would consider the question of the introduction of directly elected members to the legislature in 1988.

What followed was one of the least savory episodes in a decade that had not been kind to the political aspirations of the people of Hong Kong. Although every opinion poll had shown that at least a plurality favored the introduction of direct elections in 1988, a government-conducted review found that there was no case for change.[14] The findings were flagrantly biased by the exclusion of a signatory campaign that contained 220,000 signatures in favor of direct elections but that allowed the inclusion of cyclostyled forms, many of which came from Communist-dominated organizations. Further, AGB McNair Hong Kong Limited, who conducted the poll on behalf of the government, managed to produce a questionnaire that was so confusing that respondents could not opt unequivocally for direct elections in 1988 (Public Response to Green Paper, 1987: 55). The result was very damaging for the credibility of the Hong Kong government, whose autonomy to decide on constitutional affairs in the transitional period was now severely circumscribed.

The white paper produced in February 1988 predictably made few changes to the composition of the legislature. Two additional functional constituencies were created and the number of appointed members was reduced from twenty-two to twenty. The government justified the slow pace of constitutional reform on the grounds that most people believed in "a prudent and gradual evolution" of representative government (White Paper, 1988: 22). The only concession to popular sentiment was the decision to allow ten directly elected seats to the legislature in 1991.

The government's caution was quickly shown to be out of step with the aspirations of the people. The events in Beijing leading up to the suppression of the students and workers on June 4, 1989, drew strong support from those in Hong Kong who saw their own future liberties and chances for democracy closely linked to the success of the demonstrations. At one point more than 1 million people took to the streets to protest the actions of the Chinese government.

Coincidentally, the House of Commons' Foreign Affairs Committee was discussing Hong Kong when the Beijing massacre took place. Their report, compiled at a time when the Chinese government was distracted by this severe challenge to its authority, was the last window of opportunity for the development of representative and democratic government in the territory. The committee's critical recommendations were that full democracy should be introduced before 1997, that the legislature should be sovereign, that 50 percent of the members should be directly elected by 1991, and that the whole legislature should be directly elected by 1995 (Foreign Affairs Committee, 1989: XXVII, XXVIII). This would have gone a long way to meet the demands of the majority. But it was too radical a step for the British, Chinese, and Hong Kong governments and for the local legislature, many of whose members would have lost their seats if the committee's proposals had been implemented. It was eventually announced that, after the September 1991 elections, the Legislative Council would consist of sixty members, eighteen of whom would be directly elected, seventeen appointed by the government, twenty-one elected from functional constituencies, three officials from the Hong Kong government, and an appointed president (*South China Morning Post*, 3–21–1990). The timing of the announcement, just two weeks before the promulgation of the Basic Law, suggests the explanation for the timidity of the British and Hong Kong governments: the notion of "convergence" with the Basic Law was still central to official thinking. As the Foreign Affairs Committee (Foreign Affairs Committee, 1989: XXVII) pointed out, however, the Basic Law should have been framed in the spirit of the Sino-British agreement, not, as essentially happened, as a subsidiary clause to the constitution of the People's Republic.

The Basic Law is a profoundly antidemocratic document. As Table 8.2 shows, there is little prospect that the legislature will ever be directly elected. Even in the third term of the legislature of the Special Administrative Region, the thirty elected members and the thirty functional constituency members vote as a block, each holding a veto. It need hardly be stated that these provisions were introduced without the consent of the people of Hong Kong. Their support for the liberal parties in the September 1991 elections and the evidence of the opinion polls suggest that a majority remain committed to a directly elected legislature. But the British and Hong Kong governments had already reached their accommodation with the Chinese authorities. It matters little what the Hong Kong people want in the transitional period, for the Hong Kong government will

Table 8.2

Evolution of the Legislative Council 1984–1991 and under the Basic Law

	Officials	Appointed unofficials	Electoral college	Functional consti- tuencies	Directly elected	Total
1984	17*	30	—	—	—	47
1985	11*	22	12	12	—	57
1988	10*	20	12	14	—	56
1991	3	18*	—	21	18	60
1995 (First Term)**	—	—	10***	30	20	60
Second Term (1999?)	—	—	6***	30	24	60
Third Term (2003?)	—	—	—	30	30	60

Sources: Basic Law (1990): Section 3, Arts. 66–79; White Paper (1988): Chapter 4, para. 43; *Hong Kong Hansard* (10–4–84): 8–9; *South China Morning Post* (3–21–90).

*Includes the deputy president of the council.

**The British and Chinese governments reached an understanding that there would be a "through train" from 1995 to 1999 if the 1995 legislature was constituted according to the Basic Law. Since Patten's proposals are apparently unacceptable to the Chinese, it is now unclear what will happen after 1997.

***Under Patten's proposal, the Election Committee that will select these members will "draw all or most of its members from the directly elected District Boards" for the 1995 elections.

continue to bend the constitutional provisions in accordance with the Basic Law. The secretary for Constitutional Affairs admitted as much at a conference in May 1991 when he noted that "careful consideration will have to be given to the creation of nine more new functional constituencies before the 1995 elections" (Suen, 1991). All other options were seen to be precluded by the Basic Law.

There is, of course, a price to pay for the blatant disregard of popular opinion. The Hong Kong government's legitimacy has declined markedly; it has effectively retracted its promise that the government would become more accountable. In 1997, it will hand over to the Chinese government an institutional framework that will be simple to control and manipulate but will bear little resemblance to a representative government.

Civil Liberties

The third pillar on which Hong Kong support for the Sino-British agreement was based was the protection of civil liberties. There was always great mistrust of Chinese intentions after 1997, even before the events in Tiananmen Square. But, even without an adverse political environment, the issue of civil liberties poses particularly intractable problems because it involves different cultural interpretations of the meaning of rights. The Chinese government's view is that personal liberties stem from, and are granted by, the state (Edwards et al., 1986; Lee, 1987). The traditional Western view, which is formally embodied in the agreement, is that rights are inherent in the individual and may not be alienated by governments. Rights are comprehensively listed in the agreement and are strengthened by the proviso that the International Covenant on Civil and Political Rights, which was the basis for the passage of the Hong Kong Bill of Rights in June 1991, and the International Covenant on Economic, Social, and Cultural Rights, will continue to apply to the territory after 1997 (*Draft Agreement, 1984*: art. 13). The problem, of course, is that high-sounding promises often run into practical political difficulties. The first of these, which arose from the agreement itself, was the nationality issue.

The agreement changed the nationality of people born in Hong Kong from that of British Dependent Territories citizens to that of British Nationals (Overseas) (Council, 1985; White, 1988). One result of this was that children born to such citizens after 1997 were no longer entitled to British passports. The change in nationality status also detrimentally affected minorities, such as Indians, whose children might be rendered stateless with the resumption of Chinese sovereignty. There was little demand for the new British National (Overseas) passport. Most Hong Kong–born people kept their British Dependent Territories passports or actively sought a more reliable alternative from Canada, Australia, or the United States. The British government did grant fifty thousand "genuine" British passports with right of abode after Tiananmen Square in the hope that this would persuade key people to stay in Hong Kong after the takeover. But it persistently refused to accept responsibility for those people whose nationality had been changed without their consent. The nationality issue raised the question of whether other rights would also be subject to arbitrary change in the future.

The Hong Kong government did not help matters. Legislation introduced shortly after the signing of the agreement served to fuel concern that rights might soon be treated in a cavalier fashion. The Legislative Council (Powers and Privileges) Ordinance gave certain immunities to legislative councilors; the Public Order (Amendment) Bill made it an offense to publish "false news," and the Trial of Commercial Crime Bill sought to abolish juries in complex commercial cases (Chen, 1989; Scott, 1989). There were protests or demonstrations over all these bills and they were all subsequently withdrawn or repealed. In one case— the Public Order (Amendment) Bill—the Hong Kong government actually sought to amend the ordinance to take potentially repressive legislation off the books, but it violated other civil liberties in the process. In a climate of sensitivity and suspicion, these disputes reduced the credibility of the government and made it difficult to sustain subsequent assurances on rights.

The events in Tiananmen Square and the subsequent arrests of political dissidents dispelled any notion that the Chinese government would protect civil liberties in Hong Kong after 1997. A government that was prepared to use troops against unarmed civilians was clearly not going to be receptive to arguments about the niceties of personal freedoms. In the aftermath of the massacre, the Hong Kong government failed to respond adequately to the fresh anxieties that had been raised by the Chinese government's actions. The first reaction was to give greater priority to the introduction of a Bill of Rights. In his testimony to the Foreign Affairs Committee in March 1989, the British foreign secretary, Sir Geoffrey Howe, suggested that there was a case for such a bill (Foreign Affairs Committee, 1989: 20). The Committee reported in June, shortly after the massacre, and strongly endorsed the idea. It also recommended that the British government should make clear to China the strength of feeling against any stationing of People's Liberation Army in the territory, noted the implications for civil liberties of Article 18 of the Basic Law, and concluded that there were considerable possibilities of unlawful arrest and political persecution after 1997 (Foreign Affairs Committee, 1989: XI, XX).[15] None of this had any effect on the Chinese government, whose leaders viewed many political activities in Hong Kong after Tiananmen Square as "subversive, particularly the rallies and demonstrations held by the Hong Kong Alliance In Support of The Prodemocracy Movement in China. When the Bill of Rights passed the legislature, the Chinese government issued a statement regretting its enactment, warning that it would adversely affect the implementation of the Basic Law and noting that it might be reviewed after 1997 (*South China Morning Post*, 6–7–1991).

The Bill of Rights has something in common with the Sino-British agreement and the Basic Law. It contains promises in its formal provisions that are not in fact being implemented (Wacks, 1990). The Immigration Department, for example, possibly on orders from the Political Adviser,[16] consistently violates the spirit of the bill, which provides for freedom of movement. The department made it difficult to extend the visas of Chinese students studying in Hong Kong after the Tiananmen Square events had placed them in some jeopardy. It also imprisoned a Chinese swimmer who had applied for political asylum, and threatened to deport him to the mainland. And after the Bill of Rights had passed, it refused entry to Chinese students who had been given valid visas to attend a conference on democracy in the territory (*South China Morning Post*, 7–15,16–1991). Police action has also occasionally been heavy-handed. A demonstration held against the Chinese government in October 1989 was broken up with excessive use of force. Subsequently, the police seized tapes from a television studio in an attempt to identify the demonstrators. The Hong Kong government has already distanced itself from the Bill of Rights by refusing to entrench it to make it superior to other legislation. This means that it may be repealed at any time by a simple majority of legislative councilors. The senior unofficial legislative councilor, Allen Lee Peng-fei, himself predicted that civil liberties would be curtailed after 1997 (*South China Morning Post*, 8–7–1990).

A New York–based civil liberties organization, Freedom House, probably accurately assessed the state of political and civil liberties when, on a scale of 1 to 7, where 1 represented the most free, they gave the territory a 4 for political liberties and a 3 for civil liberties (*South China Morning Post,* 4–9–1990). There is every indication that freedom in Hong Kong will decline until 1997 and that it will be significantly reduced thereafter, the glowing promises in the Sino-British agreement and the Basic Law notwithstanding.

Economic Integration and Political Legitimacy

There are profound moral and political implications that flow directly from the renegotiation and reinterpretation of the agreement. Even assuming—and it is a highly dubious assumption—that the majority of the 2,494 respondents to the Assessment Office who supported the agreement can be construed as having provided the consent of the Hong Kong people to the future political arrangements, the conditions of the contract have not been met. If their submissions to the Assessment Office are anything to go by, what the Hong Kong people wanted, and may have thought the agreement guaranteed, was "a high degree of autonomy," a representative government, and full protection of their civil liberties. What they appear to be getting is close control by the Chinese government, an authoritarian political system, and paper assurances about civil liberties that are simultaneously being violated by the very governments that claim to preserve them. Such disparity between promises and reality does not bode well for the legitimacy of either the present or the future government. It raises questions about whether the citizen has any obligations to the polity under such circumstances. And it suggests to governments that if support cannot be generated on the premises for which it was originally asked, then other arguments and means of persuasion must be found.

Most of the Assessment Office respondents agreed that the one aspect of the accord that could not be faulted was the handling of the economy. The protection of the capitalist system for fifty years and the prospects raised for mutual benefits for trade and investment to complementary economies were intrinsically appealing. In the immediate aftermath of the signing of the agreement, it appeared that these hopes were fully justified. There was a relocation of labor-intensive manufacturing industry to Guangdong and the Shenzhen Special Economic Zone, more Chinese investment in the territory, and more Hong Kong investment—by 1987, of 7,800 foreign enterprises in China, 6,600 were from Hong Kong (*Hang Seng Economic Monthly,* 10–1989). There was a logic to these developments that had the support of all three governments. It was good for the Hong Kong and Chinese economies and the British benefited from contracts awarded for such projects as the Daya Bay nuclear power station.[17] Economic cooperation with China also had the important political advantage of securing support from the Hong Kong government's most favored constituency, business people and bankers.

It is not entirely clear when this generally laissez-faire approach to development became translated into an official policy that sought not only to transform the economy but also to rationalize the agreement and win political support for the government. As early as 1985, the Hong Kong government must have been aware that advances toward representative government and autonomy would at best be token and would never meet the promises contained in the agreement. It must have expected to lose support on those issues and from its own poor handling of civil liberties questions. The temptation to turn the one remaining asset—the success of the agreement in promoting regional economic growth—into political capital must have been very great. The policy that eventually emerged was premised on a variant of the "golden goose" argument that had been used during the negotiations by those who supported the agreement. According to this view, which is still occasionally heard, the Chinese will do nothing to harm Hong Kong's economy because it is in their own best interests that the territory should flourish and prosper. In the post-1984 setting, the new version of this argument is that Hong Kong will act as the economic dynamo for southern China, that it will provide capital and financial expertise for Chinese economic development, that labor-intensive industries will be relocated to Guangdong province, and that the government will encourage infrastructural projects that will aid economic integration. China was expected to endorse these developments because they would be seen to be consistent with its modernization policies. The Hong Kong government's view, I shall argue, did not remain simply at the level of rhetoric. It made quite conscious policy decisions to attempt to create a new role in China for the future Special Administrative Region, the most dramatic, but not the only, example of which was the decision to expand port facilities and to build a new airport.

One of the first indications of the government's perspective on the future came in an article by Piers Jacobs, the financial secretary, in 1986 (Jacobs, 1986).[18] He begins by restating the "golden goose" argument:

> One of the reasons that has been put forward for believing that the PRC will faithfully implement the Sino-British Declaration . . . was that Hong Kong and its future stability and prosperity were important to the successful implementation of the "four modernizations" program.

However, he then moves the argument forward to take account of Hong Kong's future role and of the necessity to transform the economy to maintain the territory's leading technological and financial edge in the best interests of China's modernization policies.

> Hong Kong's ability to make a significant contribution to the modernization of the PRC depends on its remaining a successful autonomous commercial, industrial, and financial center in its own right, with markets in the developed world. The pressure from rising costs and competition from newly-industrialized

countries means that Hong Kong's industry will have to move forward into new and more sophisticated products and production processes for Hong Kong's export performance to be maintained. Only by this process will Hong Kong acquire the techniques and the expertise which will be of value to officials and managers in the PRC. Only by this process will Hong Kong retain and increase the purchasing power to buy industrial and consumer goods from the PRC, thereby representing a valuable source of foreign exchange earning to the PRC.

Jacobs felt that Hong Kong's position as a regional center would be maintained because of its location and languages, its ability to provide for technology transfer, its financial and related services, and its investment in manufacturing, trade, and tourism. Perhaps significantly, Jacobs's journal article followed one by Rong Yiren, the chairman of CITIC, China's investment arm in Hong Kong, which stressed the mutual benefits to China and Hong Kong of the PRC's modernization policies (Rong, 1986).

Jacobs's article might simply have been taken as an expression of goodwill that did not involve any particular course of action by the Hong Kong government. But, as we shall see, the government did provide resources to back its view of the future role of Hong Kong. The policy itself was implicitly endorsed in Governor Sir David Wilson's annual "state of the territory" addresses to the Legislative Council in 1989 and 1990. In 1989, in an address called "A Vision of the Future," Wilson promised a number of new developments, including the Port and Airport Development Strategy (PADS), which were entirely consistent with the financial secretary's earlier views. Wilson said:

> We can strengthen *the basis of our special future political status* by the contribution that we can make to the modernization of the Chinese economy and by the access to world markets, advanced technology and expertise that we can provide for China. (*Hong Kong 1990,* 1990: 5) (Italics mine.)

In 1990, Wilson said that without the airport it would be difficult to maintain Hong Kong's role as a regional business center and warned:

> This is not something which just affects Hong Kong. The new airport will make a significant contribution to the economic development of south China in general and Guangdong in particular. In turn, economic expansion will generate more than enough business for the existing and the proposed airports in the vicinity of Hong Kong. (Wilson, 1990: 24)

Subsequently, a former high-ranking official, Dennis Bray, writing in the government's yearbook, expressed the policy in its most optimistic form:

> The national capital of China will be at Beijing but financial, stock and commodity exchanges, media headquarters, advertising and other business services

now in Hong Kong would come to serve not only the region but also China. (*Hong Kong 1991*, 1991: 13)

Such a view does not involve the economic integration of Hong Kong and Guangdong province so much as it involves the maintenance and development of Hong Kong's special and privileged position vis-à-vis China.

There was reason to assume that such policies would be welcomed by China; they were, after all, consistent with the modernization policies and promised the People's Republic ready access to capital and new technology. The sticking points focus principally on what kind of relationship the Chinese government anticipates will exist between Hong Kong and the mainland after 1997. First, if the objective is seen to be a genuine integrated Pearl River estuary economy, then local interests in Guangdong could well object to policies that turn the people of the province into hewers of wood and drawers of water for the coming Hong Kong technological revolution. There have been, of course, important economic benefits for Guangdong from Hong Kong investment in manufacturing concerns. The pressures for more sophisticated forms of investment will undoubtedly build and were in evidence to some extent on the question of the location of the airport (*Hong Kong's Manufacturing Industries 1989*, 1991; *Hong Kong's Manufacturing Industries 1990*, 1991; Survey 1991a). Second, the developments proposed are very much seen to be in the hands of the Hong Kong government and Hong Kong businessmen. There are questions— again very much to the fore on the airport issue—as to how far the Chinese government will allow such policies to be pursued without extracting other political and economic concessions from the British and Hong Kong governments. Nonetheless, since 1986 the Hong Kong government has actively intervened in pursuit of this policy in a number of different areas. We may examine its role in the three related fields: the relocation of the manufacturing industry to Guangdong province; the attempts to create a new technological base; and, most important of all, the decision to expand the port facilities and build a new airport.

The Relocation of the Manufacturing Industry

In recent years, the Hong Kong government has closely monitored industrial development, including the relocation of the manufacturing industry to Guangdong province. The development of an industrial policy up to the year 2011, which is currently in hand, is seen to be directly related to the PADS project and involves collecting information from manufacturers about their future intentions (*Hong Kong's Manufacturing Industries 1989*, 1991; *Hong Kong's Manufacturing Industries 1990*, 1991; Survey 1991a). The results of the surveys suggest that manufacturers do not intend to expand as rapidly in China as they have in the past. The government, however, has been entirely positive about the relocation of the labor-intensive manufacturing industry, citing the figure (probably an overestimate) of 2 million people who are employed in Guangdong as a result of Hong Kong investments, and noting the benefits of relief for Hong Kong's labor shortage and the creation of more sophisticated technological jobs in the territory. As the Hong Kong government explained it while speaking on the 1991 budget:

> With a relocation of the more labor-intensive manufacturing processes to Guangdong and elsewhere, our own workers have often been able to move to more rewarding jobs in both the manufacturing and nonmanufacturing sectors. There has also been substantial investment in new machinery and equipment, which in turn has raised productivity. (Financial Secretary, 1991:12)

In common with many academic commentators (e.g., Vogel, 1989), the Hong Kong government has tended to believe that this process is linear and that it will eventually lead to an industrial belt stretching from Hong Kong to Guangzhou. The surveys indicate, however, that, while manufacturers certainly appreciated the advantages of cheap labor and rents in China, a majority would be happy with a capitalist system that provided and protected infrastructural and financial facilities rather than a system that encouraged greater integration with Guangdong.

The results of the 1989 and 1990 surveys were based on the responses of manufacturers from all major Hong Kong industries. They were asked to identify their reasons for investing in Hong Kong (see Table 8.3) and their plans for expanding production outside the territory. It is notable that the uncertain political future (ranking second in 1989 and seventh in 1990) is regarded as a major drawback to investing in Hong Kong and an important constraint on growth (*Hong Kong's Manufacturing Industries 1989*, 1991: 223). While Hong Kong's location as a gateway to China was regarded favorably, it was not seen as a factor of major importance (see Table 8.3). Of the 1,832 manufacturers in 1989, 422 had plans to expand production outside Hong Kong. Of these, 315 intended to locate to China with 103 choosing Guangdong.[19] In the 1990 survey (as reported in Table 8.3), 353 of 1,954 factories had plans to expand outside Hong Kong with 69 percent (244) choosing China. This may be taken to represent a wider spread than earlier in the 1980s when the vast majority of Hong Kong investment was in Guangdong. There are also some indications of sectoral differences in future investment plans. For example, in 1989, over 40 percent of the electronics firms intended to expand elsewhere, but only fifty-six of the eighty-six companies expected to expand production in China (*Hong Kong's Manufacturing Industries 1989*, 1991: 252). Household electrical appliances and the plastics industry still overwhelmingly favored China as the first choice.

Table 8.3

Opinion of Companies* on the Importance and Favorability of Investment Factors in Hong Kong

Factors	Ranking of Impor- tance**	Favorability		
		Favorable	Neutral	Unfavorable
Labor cost	1	413 (21.1)***	284 (14.5)	1,257 (64.3)
Labor productivity	2	1,126 (57.6)	390 (20.0)	438 (22.4)
Political stability	3	587 (30.0)	472 (24.2)	895 (45.8)
Infrastructure	4	1,565 (80.1)	278 (14.2)	111 (5.7)
Cost of factory space	5	451 (23.1)	369 (18.9)	1,134 (58.0)
Banking and financial facilities	6	1,530 (78.3)	321 (16.4)	103 (5.3)
Political future	7	299 (15.3)	659 (33.7)	996 (51.0)
Availability of technical skill	8	966 (49.4)	343 (17.6)	645 (33.0)
Government economic policy	9	1,322 (67.7)	482 (24.7)	150 (7.7)
Labor–management relationship	10	1,109 (56.8)	635 (32.5)	210 (10.7)
Gateway to China	11	1,164 (59.6)	639 (32.7)	151 (7.7)
Supporting industries	12	1,153 (59.0)	550 (28.1)	251 (12.8)
Regional location	13	1,301 (66.6)	571 (29.2)	82 (4.2)
Availability of managerial skill	14	898 (46.0)	633 (32.4)	423 (21.6)
Business laws and regulations	15	1,101 (56.3)	635 (32.5)	218 (11.2)
Pegging HK dollar to U.S. dollar	16	1,077 (55.1)	804 (41.1)	73 (3.7)
Local market potential	17	768 (39.3)	698 (35.7)	488 (25.0)
Corporate taxes	18	1,007 (51.5)	733 (37.5)	214 (11.0)
Exchange controls	19	924 (47.3)	866 (44.3)	164 (8.4)
Government bureaucracy	20	578 (29.6)	881 (45.1)	495 (25.3)

Source: Hong Kong's Manufacturing Industries 1990, 1991: 275.

*The industries surveyed were clothing, electronics, watches and clocks, textiles, plastics, toys, jewelry metal products, household electrical appliances, photographic goods, optical goods, printing, industrial machinery, and food and beverages.

**The twenty factors used in this survey of 2,976 companies, conducted between June and August 1990, were ranked in order of their importance by each of the responding companies and then averaged by the Industry Department to produce the overall ranking of importance.

***Figures in parentheses denote the respective percentage shares of the total number of respondents.

Another survey conducted by the Industry Department in November and December 1990 provides the broader picture. In 1990, there were 45,492 manufacturing establishments in operation in Hong Kong (Survey 1991a: 9). The survey puts the figure of manufacturing plants in Guangdong with Hong Kong investment at 6,289 with over 75 percent of those being located in Shenzhen, Dongguan, or Guangzhou (Survey 1991a: 39). Perhaps most significant, of the 6,289 establishments that owned plants in Guangdong, 26 percent had plans to expand their operation in Guangdong in the coming year, 12 percent in the coming five years, and 1 percent beyond five years. However, of the 39,203 establishments that did not own plants in Guangdong, only 5 percent had plans to expand in China in the coming year, another 5 percent in the coming five years, and 1 percent beyond five years (Survey 1991a: 42–43). Since we do not know the monetary value of the investments planned, it is necessary to be cautious about these figures. The magnitude of the figures, however, does suggest that it is existing firms that will continue to expand in Guangdong, presumably in the same line of business. New types of manufacturing plants—at least insofar as they originate from Hong Kong companies—will not be created in Guangdong province in great numbers in the 1990s; rather, the emphasis will be on expanding existing plant and production lines. As the Industry Department survey points out, "most Hong Kong manufacturers who had plans to expand production in China have in fact done so and, . . . given the right conditions, the bulk of the remaining manufacturers would prefer to stay in Hong Kong rather than move into China" (Survey 1991b: 12).

All this is entirely consistent with the Hong Kong government's economic vision of the future. It supports the idea of a Pearl River estuary economy, but it would also prefer that the Chinese side of that economy should be composed of labor-intensive manufacturing concerns. There is no doubt about its commitment to this process. In July 1991, at a cost of between three thousand and ten thousand jobs, an amendment to the Trade Descriptions Act, passed largely without consultation with labor groups, effectively moved parts of the garment and knitwear manufacturing process to China. There is equally no doubt, as we shall see, about the Hong Kong government's commitment to keeping and attracting high technology to the territory. And it is here that two economic visions of the future collide. It is stated Chinese policy that the country should seek the most modern technology to improve its industrialization.[20] The best immediate source of intermediate technology is Hong Kong. It is not unreasonable to suppose that Chinese leaders might begin to look to Hong Kong to seek high-technology investments in China and to spread wealth and employment opportunities. But there are many high-technology industries in Hong Kong that could not relocate to China and still remain profitable. If the vision of an economically integrated southern China, with investments spread more generously in high-technology fields, is to be realized, it will require more direct political intervention and control by China.

Technology and Industrial Promotion

The Hong Kong government's policy on technology has two important themes. First, it seeks to attract firms that use sophisticated new technologies to Hong Kong. Second, it has sought to build a base in Hong Kong through the development of tertiary and other institutions to assist in the provision of trained manpower for industry and the creation of appropriate technology for local industrial needs. The effects of these policies have been to lay the groundwork for the high-technology industries the Hong Kong government hopes will dominate the economy in the future.

The government has increasingly abandoned a laissez-faire approach toward technological development and industrial promotion. The policy is defined as "maintaining an infrastructure which enables manufacturing businesses to function efficiently, and providing services which enable industry to become more competitive through productivity growth, quality improvement and product innovation" (*Hong Kong 1991,* 1991: 84–85). In practice, government and industry work hand in hand to promote economic growth. The principal advisory body for this purpose is the Industry Development Board, which is chaired by the financial secretary and includes some leading industrialists.[21] The board has a number of subcommittees, including an Industrial Technology Subcommittee, which monitor developments in particular industries, publish reports, and make recommendations to the government for improvements. The Industry Department usually implements the recommendations of the board, which itself is serviced by Industry Department personnel.

Over the past five years, the Development Board has been especially active in the fields of technology and industrial promotion. In February 1990, the government agreed, on the advice of the board, to establish a technology center—eventually to be known as the Hong Kong Technology Center—at a cost, of approximately $450 million. The objective of the center is to encourage "the growth of technology based firms" (*Hong Kong 1991,* 1991: 86). The board has also been involved in productivity-enhancement services and in moves toward creating a Science Park. In addition to the work of the Development Board, a Committee on Science and Technology was established in 1987 "to seek out and develop new scientific ideas of relevance to Hong Kong and [study] how they might best be applied" (*Hong Kong Hansard,* 10–7–1987: 21).[22]

The concern for developing high-technology industries extends to promoting overseas investment in Hong Kong. High-technology firms are given preference on industrial estates. Hong Kong government officers in New York, San Francisco, Tokyo, London, and Brussels actively seek suitable candidates. The government believes that this has been responsible for an increase in overseas investment from $26,172 million in 1988 to $29,734 million in 1989 (*Hong Kong 1991,* 1991: 87). The 1991 Hong Kong annual report remarks:

> Many of these investments are from world leaders in their respective fields and have contributed significantly to upgrading the level of technology and exper-

tise of the local manufacturing sector. *All projects completed in 1990 were of a technology level comparable with or superior to that of the best Hong Kong companies.* (Italics mine.)

Clearly, it is government policy, backed by its own resources and those of local industrialists, to move Hong Kong's manufacturing sector up-market and into the realm of high technology.

Government has bolstered this industrial policy by seeking to direct higher education toward a more technological curriculum. The creation of a third university for science and technology, the expansion of the other universities and the polytechnics, the growth of the Hong Kong Productivity Center and the Vocational Training Council have been quite consciously aimed at the task of producing trained manpower to staff the high-technology industries of the future. However, while the government is likely to be successful in establishing a trained work force, the policy depends in the long run on a continued flow of high-quality overseas investment into Hong Kong. It means that Hong Kong must be seen to be a better investment than its regional competitors. While the territory does have locational advantages, political factors could clearly easily dissuade investors from choosing Hong Kong.

The Hong Kong government has so far successfully managed to attract high-technology investment to the territory and to keep it there. As far as can be judged, the situation regarding technology transfer to China seems to remain much as Jacobs (1986) described it:

> As an access point for technology transfer, Hong Kong's main contribution has been in the areas of construction, hotel management, and catering trades. . . . For capital-intensive projects involving more sophisticated technologies, direct contacts between the PRC and the advanced developed countries are more usual. But in respect to managerial and production skills and technology for light manufacturing industries, Hong Kong remains a significant contributor. (See also Lai, 1984.)

The pressure from China to change this situation seems sure to increase, particularly in areas where it can see immediate advantages. One of these, for example, may be the chemical industry, where Hong Kong seems likely to attract high-technology multi-national investment. However, there are problems with transferring high technology, aside from the Hong Kong government's desire to keep those industries in the territory. In some cases there are bans on transferring technologies to China. Some believe that these technologies may not be exported to Hong Kong after 1997 because of concern that they could immediately be acquired by China (Mok, 1991: 263). In addition, most of the technologies require trained manpower and may be dangerous if operated by people with little experience. Hong Kong's fears over the Daya Bay nuclear plant seemed well founded when it was discovered that it was not being built to proper specifications (Yee and Wong, 1987). Finally, some high-technology industries require a well-developed supplementary infrastructure if they are to be profitable. Hong Kong has such an infrastructure; China does not.

Despite these limitations, the Chinese government remains committed to obtaining modern technologies. It is a logical outcome of this policy that Hong Kong should serve the motherland's modernization after 1997 by establishing high-technology industries more evenly throughout China. But this is a view that clearly runs counter to the Hong Kong government's present policy.

The Port and Airport Development Strategy (PADS)

The Port and Airport Development Strategy (PADS) is clearly part of a wider policy to move Hong Kong into a position where its technology and infrastructure guarantee the territory a high degree of economic leverage and autonomy. But PADS has had many objectives, and much wishful thinking, attached to it, and it is important to distinguish those that might be achieved from those that are beyond the realm of the possible. The origins of PADS is political, although it has been camouflaged to some extent by studies purporting to show that the existing Kai Tak airport will be saturated by 1997, if not earlier. Three critical points are germane to such studies. First, since they tend to represent projections on future use based upon current economic conditions, whether the study is undertaken in a time of recession or a time of economic boom inevitably affects the results and consequently the estimated saturation date of the airport. The five major studies on Kai Tak all reflect this tendency; those that were completed in recessions estimate a much longer life for the airport (Leung, 1991: 48).[23] Second, the crucial factor bearing upon saturation is the number of aircraft movements. A reduction in the number of smaller airplanes using an airport could mean increased capacity without leading to saturation. This is relevant to the life of Kai Tak because smaller airports are now being built in China and Macao. Third, such studies rarely explore in detail the kinds of improvements that could be made to existing facilities, a consideration that only became evident when the Hong Kong government thought that it might not be able to build a new airport. It is quite possible, then, to argue vehemently both for and against plans for new airports. Estimates of saturation are not objective and quickly become associated with discussions about political, economic, and social costs and objectives.

The decision to proceed with PADS was announced by the governor, Sir David Wilson, in his "Vision of the Future" speech to the Legislative Council in October 1989, two months before he received the consultant's final report on the airport (Leung, 1991: 48). PADS was projected to cost HK $127 billion, a figure which no one, including the financial secretary, seemed inclined to believe. Many were skeptical, too, of the notion that PADS would attract private investment, expecting instead that the burden would fall on Hong Kong government reserves and on the taxpayer. This sentiment became even more pronounced when the Chinese government expressed its opposition to PADS on the grounds that it would drain the reserves of the Special Administrative Region after 1997. The timing of the announcement to build the airport was itself overtly political. It was designed to restore confidence after the Tiananmen Square massacre. Whose confidence was to be restored was not entirely clear. Decisions to build airports do not in themselves create optimism about the future, except perhaps in those contractors and business people who stand to profit from the venture. Rather, it seems from the "Vision of the Future" speech that PADS was part of a grander strategy, one that anticipated a vibrant new Hong Kong after 1997 (*Hong Kong 1991*, 1991: 21). The airport was the cornerstone of that strategy, not simply, as some saw it, a memorial to British rule or an attempt to internationalize the Hong Kong issue; rather, it was a necessary condition for Hong Kong to thrive and direct economic development in southern China.

It was believed to be important for Hong Kong's political autonomy that the decision to build the airport should be seen to be made by the Hong Kong government without the need to ask permission from either the British or the Chinese government. This was consistent with the allocation of powers in the Sino-British agreement, and initially the Hong Kong government did not expect an adverse reaction from the Chinese. The plans to build the airport were sent to the Chinese government through the New China News Agency in Hong Kong but, beyond this, there seems to have been little consultation in the period following the announcement (*South China Morning Post*, 4–20–1990). Even if there had been consultation, it is likely that the Chinese government would have seen the airport issue as a means of exerting political and economic leverage over the territory in the transitional period.

Events thereafter mirrored the Sino-British negotiations over the agreement. The Hong Kong and British governments continued to insist on their legal rights. Wilson was quoted as saying, "It's a decision to be taken in Hong Kong. I would like them (the Chinese authorities) to look favorably at it but the decisions are Hong Kong decisions, they don't depend on . . . formal approval from elsewhere" (*South China Morning Post*, 9–2–1990). The chief secretary, Sir David Ford, reportedly said, "There is no question of China vetoing these projects. To do so would be contrary to the Basic Law" (*South China Morning Post*, 9–15–1990). As if to underline the government's determination, Ford announced in October 1990 that the Lantau Fixed Crossing, a suspension bridge estimated to cost $6 billion, would be built without support from private investors.[24]

For their part, the Chinese relied legally on the argument that the agreement gave them the right to be consulted on all matters that straddled 1997. They complained, with some justification, that the airport represented a financial burden that would fall on the SAR government and would seriously deplete Hong Kong reserves. Lu Ping, the director of the Hong Kong and Macao Affairs

Office, called on the government to stop deceiving the people and tell them what the airport would cost (*South China Morning Post*, 12–12–1990). This was later extended to embrace the view, which had little justification or support in Hong Kong, that the Chinese government had the right to speak for the Hong Kong people in the transitional period. What the Chinese government wanted, it eventually became clear, was a say, perhaps a veto, in the decision-making process and some guarantees on the use of the reserves.

The war of words, reminiscent of the "megaphone diplomacy" during the Sino-British negotiations, continued during the first half of 1991. What was required were British concessions that essentially abrogated the right of the Hong Kong government to make independent decisions on the airport. Chinese support ultimately was viewed as more important than the autonomy guaranteed in the agreement. The Memorandum of Understanding provides that

> the British side will consult the Chinese side within the Airport Committee before the Hong Kong government grants major airport-related franchises or contracts straddling 30 June 1997 or guarantees airport-related debt straddling 30 June 1997. (Memorandum, 1991)

The Hong Kong government is committed to retaining fiscal reserves of $25 billion until 1997 and may not borrow more than $5 billion without the consent of the Chinese government. Chinese involvement in the financing and construction of the project is virtually guaranteed and will be ensured through the Chinese presence in a cumbersome committee structure that will be set up to deal with airport matters. In addition, both governments agreed to intensify "consultation and cooperation" on Hong Kong issues through twice-yearly meetings of the foreign ministers (Memorandum, 1991). Finally, the British prime minister was to travel to Beijing to sign the memorandum. On all major points at issue the Chinese view prevailed. That the pattern of diplomacy closely matches that of the Sino-British negotiations is not entirely surprising. It reflects a particular Chinese approach to diplomacy and the fact that those responsible for the airport talks on the British side—Percy Cradock, Sir David Wilson, MacLaren, and Donald—were the same Foreign Office China experts who had been involved in the negotiations (Scott, 1989: chap. 5).

For the purposes of the present analysis, the airport issue has important repercussions for the political and economic autonomy of the territory and, by implication, for a strategy that seeks to make Hong Kong central to the future development of Southern China. The Memorandum of Understanding was criticized for compromising the autonomy of the future Special Administrative Region and the ability of the Hong Kong government to function in the transitional period.[25] As far as political autonomy is concerned, however, the passage of the Basic Law already effectively meant that there would be no autonomy, in any meaningful sense of the word, after 1997. The Memorandum of Understanding set the seal on the loss of autonomy and represented a further abrogation of the 1984 agreement. No doubt, more accords will be reached in the transitional period that will serve to entrench Chinese control.

As far as economic autonomy is concerned, the Memorandum of Understanding did break new ground. By providing a structure that gave the Chinese government an institutional role in decision making on the airport, the agreement created precedents for Chinese intervention on all issues straddling 1997, which means all matters of importance, and for significantly affecting the direction of economic policy making. Until the Memorandum of Understanding, Chinese leverage on the economy had been restricted to the use to which it put its substantial investments in the territory; it did not have a direct voice in decision making. Now that it has, there is no valid reason why the Chinese government should not argue, by precedent and analogy, that it should participate in many other advisory committees and decision-making bodies.

The advantage of the Memorandum of Understanding is that it preserves, at least temporarily, the Hong Kong government's economic strategy and the centrality of the territory in the region. Although never publicly raised by the Chinese, the implicit question about the airport was always whether it should be built in Hong Kong or whether it might not be built, much less expensively, in China. Answering this question, Mrs. Anson Chan, the secretary for Economic Services, argued that the airport must be located within the geographical limits of Hong Kong because the Sino-British agreement required that the territory remain a center of international and regional aviation (*South China Morning Post*, 11–1–1990). The niceties of this argument might well be lost if the question comes down to whether future large capital projects should be located in the territory or in China. If there are Chinese government representatives on important economic decision-making bodies in future, the answer might not always be in favor of the territory.

Conclusions

The argument to this point has been that three central features of the 1984 Agreement that had support in Hong Kong—the promises of a high degree of autonomy, the development of representative government, and the preservation of civil liberties—have all been eroded to the extent that few believe there is any prospect of their implementation after 1997. The fourth pillar of support—policies aimed at economic growth—has survived in the form of government and industrial efforts to move Hong Kong up-market and to develop an infrastructure that will make the maintenance of an advanced form of capitalism vital for the economy of Guangdong, if not for China. There are signs that this policy may eventually come under threat from Chinese officials who would prefer to see Hong Kong's wealth spread more widely. To change the direction of Hong Kong's economic policy to ensure that it complies more closely with the needs of China's modernization policies would, however, require political control. This is already provided for in the Basic Law and may be extended by analogous agreements along the lines of the Memorandum of Understanding.

Hong Kong has been ruled for the past one hundred and fifty years by a colonial regime which did nothing to encourage the development of a representative and democratic government. For a brief period in Hong Kong in 1984, the governments of Britain, China, and Hong Kong made promises that such a form of government would be permitted to develop. Those promises have been broken. The overwhelming evidence is that in 1997 one form of authoritarian government will be replaced by another.

Notes

1. These are aspects of the political transformation of Hong Kong that can only be mentioned in passing. For more detail, see Chiu et al. (1987); Miners (1991); Scott (1989); Skeldon (1990–91); and Wesley-Smith and Chen (1988).

2. See, for example, White Paper (1990: 2); and the testimony of the then foreign secretary, Sir Geoffrey Howe, in Foreign Affairs Committee (1989: 14–89).

3. This was particularly so after June 4, 1989, when Hong Kong people were warned of the dangers of "subversion." For the more common Chinese response to the problems of the transitional period and beyond, see *Beijing Review* (1991: 8). See also Li (1991).

4. An opinion poll conducted by the government in May 1991 found that economic problems were a major source of concern. The respondents seemed to feel, however, that attention should be concentrated on the local economy. There is no mention of future economic integration with China, and views on the new airport were very mixed. When asked what the government should do to boost public confidence, the largest number of respondents (24 percent) suggested that the government should improve communications with the public, while 23 percent opted for improving the local economy. Information supplied by Government Information Services.

5. On the historical background of the problem, see Scott (1989) and Wesley-Smith (1984).

6. The official position of the Foreign Office now is that "the British side initially argued hard for the retention of British administration in Hong Kong after 1997 as the surest way of maintaining the prosperity and stability of the territory. After protracted discussion, however, it became clear that the continuation of British administration in any form was unacceptable to the Chinese Government and that the talks would break down if the British Government continued to insist on it. Since most of Hong Kong would in any case under the Treaty pass under Chinese jurisdiction in 1997, the only way forward was to explore the possibility of negotiating arrangements under Chinese sovereignty . . ." Memorandum submitted by the Foreign and Commonwealth Office to Foreign Affairs Committee (1989).

7. Munro's conclusions are based in part on interviews with MacLehose and the former British foreign secretary, David Owen.

8. The accepted version seems to be that he told Hong Kong investors to put their hearts at ease. See *Far Eastern Economic Review* (April 20, 1979: 42–43).

9. "No three-legged stool," said Deng Xiaoping, who insisted that the negotiations should be bilateral. The then governor of Hong Kong, Sir Edward Youde, argued that he represented the people of Hong Kong but this was rejected by the Chinese. "China rejects Britain's secret proposal over Hong Kong's future," (trans.) *Hong Kong Economic Jour-*

nal (April 19, 1983); *South China Morning Post* (April 20, 1983).

10. See, for example, *Far Eastern Economic Review* (July 21, 1983); *South China Morning Post* (April 11, 1982); and *Hong Kong Standard* (September 22, 1983). See also Cheng (1984). In 1991, respondents to the question, "If you were controlling history, what would you most like to have happened to Hong Kong in 1997?" gave the following replies: independent, 29 percent; part of Britain, 26 percent; part of the Commonwealth, 19 percent; part of China, 21 percent; no opinion, 5 percent. The poll, which was conducted by Asian Commercial Research, appeared in the *Sunday Morning Post* (June 30, 1991).

11. Some people wrote in to make this point.

12. Tang (1990: 172). On the Basic Law, see also Cheng (1991); Davis (1990); Clark (1989); Chan and Clark (1991); Lee and Wah (1988); *Journal of Chinese Law* (1988: No. 1); McGurn (1988); and Wesley-Smith and Chen (1988).

13. For a different view, see *Beijing Review* (March 19–25, 1990).

14. The government documents that relate to this phase of constitutional development are: Green Paper (1987); Public Response to Green Paper (1987); and White Paper (1988). For commentary, see Miners (1989) and Scott (1989: 284–98).

15. It should be noted that this report contains the committee's recommendations. The citations in footnotes 2 and 53 are the collected volumes of evidence to the committee.

16. A mysterious letter, leaked from the office of the Political Adviser, implied that the Hong Kong government was quite willing to go along with the concerns of the Chinese government even if this meant violating rights. As a *South China Morning Post* (10–26–1989) editorial put it, "the arrest of members of the group [which demonstrated in October 1989 against the Chinese leadership] may have been motivated by more than normal police concern to maintain public order."

17. This project, however, caused considerable local consternation over the ability of China to manage a nuclear power plant only fifty kilometers from Hong Kong. See Yee and Wong (1987).

18. An earlier, equally buoyant version is Dunn (1985). Dunn was senior unofficial member in the Legislative Council at the time. Her version does not, however, envisage the economic transformation of Hong Kong, which is the distinguishing feature of Jacobs's commentary. For a further highly optimistic view of the economic effect of Hong Kong on China, see Scobell (1988).

19. Thailand was in second place, with forty-three companies choosing to expand production there.

20. This is clear from the laws governing joint ventures, which pay great attention to technology transfer. See, for example, Ministry of Foreign Economic Relations and Trade (1983: arts. 43–46), and Simon (1989).

21. This high-powered committee includes not only the financial secretary but also the secretary for Trade and Industry, the secretary for Economic Services, the secretary for Planning, Environment and Lands, the director of Industry, the president of the Chinese Manufacturers' Association, the chairman of the Hong Kong Federation of Industries, the chairman of the Hong Kong Productivity Council, the chairman of the Vocational Training Council, the chairman of the Hong Kong Industrial Estates Corporation, two representatives from tertiary institutions, and prominent industrialists appointed in their own right (*Government Gazette*, January 4, 1991). The terms of reference of the board are "to advise the Government on all matters affecting Hong Kong's manufacturing industry which the government may refer to it."

22. On the government's role in encouraging the development of high-technology industries up to 1986, see Hong Kong Society of Scholars (1986).

23. The studies were conducted in 1974, 1979, 1982, 1985, and 1988. Leung (1991:

48) notes: "As the forecasts were based on the trends of air traffic demand growth rate of the time, the most optimistic forecast was made in 1974, the second being that of 1988 and 1979 and the most pessimistic were made in 1982 and 1985, that is, at the times when Hong Kong was suffering from an economic recession or the economic consequences of political turbulence."

24. The price of the bridge has risen, and will continue to rise. Latest estimates put it at $10 billion.

25. The leader of the United Democrats, Martin Lee, raised this point even before agreement was reached. See his article in the *South China Morning Post* (March 2, 1991).

References

Assessment Office (Report of the Assessment Office) (1984), *Arrangement for Testing the Acceptability in Hong Kong of the Draft Agreement on the Future of Hong Kong,* Hong Kong: Government Printer.

Basic Law of the Hong Kong Special Administrative Region of the People's Republic of China (1990), Hong Kong: Consultative Committee for the Basic Law of the Hong Kong Special Administrative Region of the People's Republic of China.

Beijing Review, Vol. 33, No. 12, March 19–25, 1990, pp. 9–10; Vol. 34, No. 15, April 15–21, 1991.

Chan, Ming K., and David J. Clark, eds. (1991), *The Hong Kong Basic Law: Blueprint For 'Stability and Prosperity' under Chinese Sovereignty?* Armonk, NY: M.E. Sharpe; Hong Kong: Hong Kong University Press.

Chen, Albert H.Y. (1988), "Civil Liberties in Hong Kong: Recent Controversies, Evolving Consciousness and Future Legal Protection," *Journal of Chinese Law,* Vol. 2, No. 1, pp. 137–51.

Cheng, Joseph Y.S. (1984), "The Future of Hong Kong: Surveys of Hong Kong People's Attitudes," *Australian Journal of Chinese Affairs,* No. 12, pp. 113–42.

——— (1991), "The Basic Law: Messages for Hong Kong People," in *The Other Hong Kong Report,* ed. Richard Wong and Joseph Y.S. Cheng, Hong Kong: Chinese University Press, pp. 29–64.

Chiu, Hung-dah, Y.C. Yao, and Yuan-li Wu, eds. (1987), *The Future of Hong Kong: Towards 1997 and Beyond,* New York: Quorum.

Clark, David (1989), "A High Degree Of Autonomy under the Basic Law: An Analysis," in *Hong Kong: The Challenge of Transformation,* ed. Kathleen Cheek-Milby and Miron Mushkat, Hong Kong: Centre of Asian Studies, University of Hong Kong, pp. 153–88.

Council (Joint Council For the Welfare of Immigrants) (1985), *A Question of Belonging: British Nationality Law and the Future of Hong Kong,* Hong Kong: The Council.

Davis, Michael C. (1990), *Constitutional Confrontation in Hong Kong,* Basingstoke: Macmillan.

Draft Agreement Between the Government of the United Kingdom of Great Britain and Northern Ireland and the Government of the People's Republic of China on the Future of Hong Kong (1984), Hong Kong: Government Printer.

Dunn, Lydia (1985), "Hong Kong after the Sino-British Declaration," *International Affairs,* Vol. 61, No. 2, pp. 197–204.

Edwards, R. Randle, Louis Henkin, and Andrew J. Nathan, eds. (1986), *Human Rights in Contemporary China,* New York: Columbia University Press.

Far Eastern Economic Review, December 12, 1985; April 20, 1979.

Financial Secretary (*The 1991–1992 Budget,* Speech by the Financial Secretary, moving the second reading of the Appropriation Bill, 1991) (1991), Hong Kong: Government Printer.

Foreign Affairs Committee (1989), *Second Report: Hong Kong,* Vol. II, London: HMSO.

Government Gazette (Hong Kong), January 4, 1991.

Green Paper (1984), *The Further Development of Representative Government in Hong Kong,* Hong Kong: Government Printer.

Green Paper (1987), *The 1987 Review of Developments in Representative Government,* Hong Kong: Government Printer.

Hang Seng Economic Monthly, October 1989.

Hong Kong Economic Journal, April 19, 1983.

Hong Kong Hansard, October 7, 1987, p. 21; October 15, 1984.

Hong Kong 1990: A Review of 1989 (1990), Hong Kong: Government Printer.

Hong Kong 1991: A Review of 1990 (1991), Hong Kong: Government Printer.

Hong Kong Society of Scholars (1986), *The Role of High Technology in Hong Kong's Industrial Development,* Hong Kong: Hong Kong Society of Scholars.

Hong Kong Standard, September 22, 1983.

Hong Kong's Manufacturing Industries 1989 (1991), Hong Kong Government Industry Department: Government Printer.

Hong Kong's Manufacturing Industries 1990 (1991), Hong Kong Government Industry Department: Government Printer.

House of Commons (House of Commons Debate on China and Hong Kong) (1989), in *The Hong Kong Basic Law,* ed. Ming K. Chan and David J. Clark, Hong Kong: Hong Kong University Press, pp. 248–58.

Jacobs, Piers (1986), "Hong Kong and the Modernization of China," *Journal of International Affairs,* Vol. 39, No. 2, pp. 63–75.

Journal of Chinese Law (1988), Vol. 2, No. 1.

Lai, Kwong-tak (1984), "Transfer of Technology Between Hong Kong and the People's Republic of China: A Case Study of Daning Brigade in Guangdong," Master's diss., University of Hong Kong.

Lee, Martin, and Szeto Wah (1988), *The Basic Law: Some Basic Flaws,* 2nd ed., Hong Kong: Kasper.

Lee, Ta-ling (1987), "Hong Kong: The Human Rights Dimension," in *The Future of Hong Kong,* ed. Hung-dah Chiu, Y.C. Yao, Yuan-li Wu, New York: Quorum, pp. 115–38.

Leung, Jonathan Man-ho (1991), "An Analysis of the Decision to Build Hong Kong's Second International Airport," Master's diss., University of Hong Kong.

Li, Peng (1991), "Reunification to Ensure Hong Kong Stability," (trans.) in *Foreign Broadcast Information Service, Daily Report: China* (Washington), April 4, 1991.

McGurn, William, ed. (1988), *Basic Law, Basic Questions: The Debate Continues,* Hong Kong: Review Publishing.

Memorandum (Memorandum of Understanding Concerning the Construction of the New Airport in Hong Kong and Related Questions) (1991), mimeo, July 4.

Miners, Norman (1989), "Moves Towards Representative Government, 1984–1988," in *Hong Kong: The Challenge of Transformation,* ed. Kathleen Cheek-Milby and Miron Mushkat, Hong Kong: Centre of Asian Studies, University of Hong Kong.

———— (1991), *The Government and Politics of Hong Kong,* 5th ed., Hong Kong: Oxford University Press.

Ministry of Foreign Economic Relations and Trade (1983), *Guide to Foreign Economic Relations and Trade in China,* Hong Kong: Economic Information Agency.

Mok, Victor (1991), "Trade and Industry," in *The Other Hong Kong Report 1991,* ed. Richard Y.C. Wong and Joseph Y.S. Cheng, Hong Kong: Chinese University Press, pp. 241–66.

Munro, Ross H. (1990), "Who Lost Hong Kong?" *Commentary,* December, pp. 33–39.

Public Response to Green Paper (1987), *The 1987 Review of Developments in Representative Government*, Hong Kong: Government Printer.

Renmin ribao (1991), (trans.) in *Foreign Broadcast Information Service, Daily Report: China* (Washington), April 17, 1991.

Rong, Yiren (1986), "China's Open Policy and CITIC's Role," *Journal of International Affairs*, Vol. 39, No. 2, pp. 56–61.

Scobell, Andrew (1988), "Hong Kong's Influence on China: The Tail that Wags the Dog?" *Asian Survey*, Vol. 28, No. 6, pp. 599–612.

Scott, Ian (1989), *Political Change and the Crisis of Legitimacy in Hong Kong*, Hawaii: University of Hawaii Press; Hong Kong: Oxford University Press.

Simon, Denis Fred (1989), "Technology Transfer and China's Emerging Role in the World Economy," in *Science and Technology in Post-Mao China*, ed. Denis Fred Simon and Merle Goldman, Cambridge, MA: Council on East Asian Studies, Harvard University.

Skeldon, Ronald (1990–91), "Emigration and the Future of Hong Kong," *Pacific Affairs*, Vol. 63, No. 4.

South China Morning Post, April 11, 1982; April 20, 1983; December 1, 1985; October 26, 1989; March 21, 1990; April 9, 1990; April 20, 1990; August 7, 1990; September 2, 1990; September 15, 1990; November 1, 1990; December 12, 1990; March 2, 1991; June 4, 1991; June 7, 1991; July 15–16, 1991.

Suen, Michael M.Y. (1991), "The Hong Kong Electoral System and Its Future Development," speech at seminar *Democracy and Political Development—Hong Kong Characteristics*, Hong Kong, May 19, 1991.

Sunday Morning Post, June 30, 1991.

Survey (1991a) (Survey on the Future Development of Industry in Hong Kong), Hong Kong: Hong Kong Government Industry Department, Census and Statistics Department: Government Printer.

Survey (1991b) (Survey on the Future Development of Industry in Hong Kong: Executive Summary), Hong Kong: Hong Kong Industry Department.

Tang, Karen Tak Shuk (1990), "An Analysis of the Basic Law Consultative and Drafting Process," Master's diss., University of Hong Kong.

Vogel, Ezra (1989), *One Step Ahead in China: Guangdong under Reform*, Cambridge, MA: Harvard University Press.

Wacks, R., ed. (1990), *Hong Kong's Bill of Rights: Problems and Prospects*, Hong Kong: Faculty of Law, University of Hong Kong.

Wesley-Smith, Peter (1984), *Unequal Treaty 1989–1997: China, Great Britain and Hong Kong's New Territories*, rev. ed., Hong Kong: Oxford University Press.

Wesley-Smith, Peter, and Albert Chen, eds. (1988), *The Basic Law and Hong Kong's Future*, Singapore: Butterworths.

White, Robin (1988), "Nationality Aspects of the Settlement," *Journal of International Law*, Vol. 20, No. 1, pp. 225–51.

White Paper (1984), *The Further Development of Representative Government in Hong Kong*, Hong Kong: Government Printer.

White Paper (1988), *The Development of Representative Government: The Way Forward*, Hong Kong: Government Printer.

White Paper (1990), *White Paper on the Annual Report on Hong Kong 1989 to Parliament*, Hong Kong: Government Printer.

Wilson, Sir David (1990), *Address by the Governor, Sir David Wilson, to the Legislative Council October 10, 1990*, mimeo.

Yee, Herbert S., and Yiu-chung Wong (1987), "Hong Kong: The Politics of the Daya Bay Nuclear Plant Debate," *International Affairs*, Vol. 63, No. 4, pp. 617–30.

9

Economic Integration of Hong Kong and Guangdong in the 1990s

Yun-wing Sung

The inauguration of the People's Republic of China's Open-door Policy in 1978 has led to the rapid integration of Hong Kong with China, especially with Guangdong Province. As wages have risen rapidly in Hong Kong, its labor-intensive industries have moved to the mainland on a large scale. The synergy of China's cheap labor with Hong Kong's know-how and capital was the main factor behind China's spectacular export drive, as acknowledged in earlier chapters.

Economic statistics are more available on a national level. This is especially true of Hong Kong trade statistics, which are classified by country of origin or destination but not classified by province. China's trade statistics are disaggregated by province, but provincial trade statistics are much less detailed than national trade statistics. Whenever statistics are not available for Guangdong, this chapter will describe the integration of Hong Kong with China rather than with Guangdong. This is not a serious drawback, as Guangdong accounted for the bulk of trade and investment between Hong Kong and China, and Hong Kong–China links in trade and investment tend to reflect Hong Kong's trade and investment with Guangdong.

There is no doubt that the economies of mainland China and Hong Kong are highly integrated. The mainland is Hong Kong's foremost trading partner and vice versa. In 1991, China's exports to (imports from) Hong Kong accounted for 45 (42) percent of China's exports (imports), whereas Hong Kong's exports to (imports from) China accounted for 27 (38) percent of Hong Kong's exports (imports). Hong Kong and the mainland are the foremost investors in each other.

To understand China's statistics on foreign investment, it is necessary to distinguish between direct foreign investment and "other foreign investment," which includes foreign funds involved in processing/assembling operations, compensation trade, and leasing. "Other foreign investment" constitutes commercial credit, while direct foreign investment does not, since the Chinese partner theoretically controls the operation and usually pays for foreign machinery and technical assistance with labor services used in making goods for the foreign partner. In this chapter, the term "foreign investment" includes both direct foreign investment and "other foreign investment." In terms of contribution to capital formation, "other foreign investment" is relatively small because processing/assembling operations are labor-intensive rather than capital-intensive. From 1979 to 1990, the cumulative stock of "other foreign investment" was only 10.7 (14.6) percent of contracted (utilized) foreign investment in China. However, processing/assembling operations are very important in China's exports because they tend to be export-oriented. In 1990, exports from processing/assembling operations amounted to U.S. $25.4 billion or 40.9 percent of China's exports (Sung, 1991c: 23). In comparison, exports from enterprises with direct foreign investment amounted to only U.S. $7.8 billion or 12.6 percent of China's exports. In other words, foreign investment (both direct foreign investment and other foreign investment) accounted for 54 percent of China's exports in 1990, or for 64 percent of the *increase* in China's exports from 1978 to 1990. As Hong Kong's cumulative contracted investment in China from 1979 to 1990 amounted to U.S. $26 billion or 59 percent of the national total, the crucial role of Hong Kong in China's export drive is evident.

Hong Kong is also the pivot of China's economic links with the outside world, especially with Taiwan. In late 1987, Taiwan lifted its ban on travel to the mainland and also started to ease its restrictions on trade and investment with the mainland. Since then, Taiwan's trade with the People's Republic of China (PRC) and Taiwan's investment in the People's Republic have increased very rapidly. After Hong Kong, Taiwan has become the mainland's second most important economic partner, albeit a distant second. Taiwan still stipulates that all trade with China and all investment in China have to be conducted indirectly, most often through Hong Kong. The growth of trade and investment between the People's Republic and Taiwan has further strengthened the position of Hong Kong as China's middleman.

The economic ties of the mainland with Hong Kong and Taiwan have become especially important since the Tiananmen Incident of June 1989. Since Tiananmen, China has become more isolated, but China's economic links with Hong Kong and Taiwan have strengthened. Since June 1989, investment and tourism from developed countries have declined, but investment and tourism from Taiwan have increased sharply, and investment and tourism from Hong Kong (for investments, see Chapter 7) rebounded rapidly in 1990 after sharp declines in the second half of 1989. Thanks to investment from Taiwan and Hong Kong, total contracted foreign investment in China grew from U.S. $6.2 billion in 1988 to U.S. $6.3 billion in 1989 and grew further to U.S. $6.9 billion in 1990. China's tourism earnings decreased from U.S. $2.2 billion in 1988 to U.S. $1.9 billion in 1989, but recovered to U.S. $2.2 billion in 1990 largely due to the continuing surge of tourists from Taiwan, Hong Kong, and Southeast Asia. In a nutshell, Hong Kong and Taiwan are essential to the success of China's Open-door Policy.

The nature of the economic ties between the mainland and Hong Kong and Taiwan is qualitatively different from China's ties with the developed countries. China's commodity trade with the latter is mostly interindustry trade, whereas its trade with Hong Kong and Taiwan includes substantial intraindustry trade. This is because China, in the aspect of development, is closer to Hong Kong and Taiwan than to the developed countries. Moreover, Hong Kong and Taiwan have invested heavily in outprocessing operations in China, giving rise to thriving intrafirm trade. Hong Kong and Taiwan have less of the advanced technology of the developed countries, but their medium-level technology may be more suited to China's level of development and could enhance China's bargaining power in acquiring technology from the developed countries. The investment from Hong Kong and Taiwan tends to be in export-oriented processing/assembling operations, whereas Japan and the United States tend to invest in import-substitution enterprises. The investment from Hong Kong and Taiwan is the most significant factor behind China's successful export drive.

After the Tiananmen Incident, the prestige and authority of Beijing and the Communist Party suffered severely. Meanwhile, Guangdong and Fujian have continued to gain in economic strength, thanks to their links with Hong Kong and Taiwan. China's economy has become increasingly regionalized and southeast China is emerging as a dynamic and distinct economic entity.

Hong Kong's ties with Guangdong are particularly strong. Table 9.1 shows the importance of Hong Kong's investment in Guangdong. From 1979 to 1990, contracted foreign investment in Guangdong amounted to U.S. $20 billion or 45 percent of the national total. Hong Kong's contracted investment in Guangdong amounted to U.S. $15 billion, accounting for 75 percent and 34 percent, reespectively, of total foreign investment in Guangdong and in China, or equal to 57 percent of Hong Kong's investment in China. However, statistics of contracted investment are likely to exaggerate Guangdong's share because many contracted investment projects in Guangdong in the early years of the Open-door Policy never materialized. Figures on utilized investment would be a better indicator of Guangdong's share. From 1979 to 1990, utilized foreign investment in Guangdong amounted to U.S. $8 billion or 37 percent of the national total. Utilized investment from Hong Kong in Guangdong amounted to U.S. $5 billion, accounting for 64 percent and 23 percent, respectively, of total foreign investment in Guangdong and in China, or equal to 40 percent of Hong Kong's utilized investment in China. Figures for the period 1985 to 1990 tell roughly the same story. We can conclude that while Hong Kong accounted for the bulk of foreign

Table 9.1

Cumulative Foreign Investment in China and in Guangdong
(in U.S. million dollars)

		National Total	In Guangdong	From Hong Kong	From Hong Kong in Guangdong
1979–90 Foreign Investment	contracted	45,245 (100)	20,332 (44.9)	26,480 (58.5)	15,208 (33.6)
	utilized	22,219 (100)	8,132 (36.6)	12,888 (58.0)	5,180 (23.3)
1985–90 Direct Foreign Investment	contracted	33,454 (100)	11,484 (34.3)	18,415 (55.0)	8,652 (25.9)
	utilized	15,922 (100)	5,307 (33.3)	9,657 (60.7)	4,239 (26.6)

Source: Data for the national total, and for investment from Hong Kong, are obtained from the *Almanac of China's Foreign Relations and Trade* (1984–91); data for investment in Guangdong and for investment from Hong Kong in Guangdong are obtained from the *Guangdong Statistical Yearbook* (1983–91).

Note: Figures in parentheses represent percentage share of the national total.

investment in Guangdong, Guangdong accounted for less than half of Hong Kong's investment in China.

Hong Kong's trade with Guangdong is also very important. In 1990, Guangdong's exports amounted to U.S. $10,560 million or 19 percent of the national total, and Guangdong's exports to Hong Kong amounted to U.S. $8,543 million, accounting, respectively, for 81 percent of Guangdong's exports and 46 percent of China's exports to Hong Kong. These statistics were collected by China's Ministry of Foreign Economic Relations and Trade (MOFERT), and they grossly understated Guangdong's exports because the MOFERT included in its statistics only the processing fees of processing/assembling operations instead of the value of goods exported from such operations. Processing fees are usually only 10 percent of the value of goods exported, and exports from processing/assembling operations have been very important in Guangdong. China's Customs Statistics, which consistently value exports by the value of goods exported, would give a more accurate picture of Guangdong's exports. Unfortunately, China's Customs Statistics are not available in great detail at the provincial level. It is known, however, that the China's Customs Statistics for 1991 exports of goods made in Guangdong was U.S. $22,800 million[1] or 32 percent of the national total, whereas the corresponding MOFERT figure was only U.S. $13,548 million.

Hong Kong accounts for the bulk of investment in processing/assembling operations in Guangdong, and the overwhelming portion of the output of such operations is exported to Hong Kong. Guangdong's 1990 share of 46 percent in China's exports to Hong Kong calculated from MOFERT statistics is thus a gross underestimation. Exports of Guangdong goods to Hong Kong were also not published in China's Customs Statistics. However, Guangdong's 1990 exports to Hong Kong can reliably be estimated to be U.S. $16,697 million,[2] accounting for 86 percent and 27 percent, respectively, of Guangdong's and China's exports, or 73 percent of China's exports to Hong Kong. In a nutshell, Hong Kong accounted for the bulk of Guangdong's exports, and Guangdong also accounted for the bulk of China's exports to Hong Kong. Unfortunately, statistics on Guangdong's imports were less useful because they included only imports handled by provincial authorities, excluding the substantial imports handled by Beijing. Guangdong imports from Hong Kong in 1990 amounted to U.S. $4,116 million or 72 percent of Guangdong's imports.

The rest of this chapter is organized as follows. Section two discusses the degree of economic integration between China and Hong Kong. Section three covers trade and investment between Hong Kong and China. Section four evaluates the prospect of Hong Kong as a middleman for China. Section five analyzes the impact of China's opening up to Hong Kong manufacturing. Section six concludes the chapter.

The Degree of Economic Integration Between Hong Kong and China

Economic integration means the lowering of barriers to economic interactions across countries or regions, thereby facilitating trade and investment. Economic integration can occur through institutional channels such as the establishment of a free trade area or granting mutual discriminatory preferences to the parties involved. It can also occur naturally without the establishment of a formal institution, as in the case of a fall in transportation costs as a result of technological advancement.

Despite intense trade and investment flows, there is an obvious lack of institutional integration between Hong Kong and China. The three important institutional barriers to economic integration often listed in textbooks are tariffs, controls on factor movements, and exchange risks. On these three counts, the barriers to economic integration between Hong Kong and China are still very high. Even though China will resume sovereignty over Hong Kong in 1997, it is specified in the Sino-British agreement on Hong Kong that Hong Kong will remain a separate customs territory and will continue to have its own currency. Migration from China to Hong Kong will be strictly controlled. It can be argued, therefore, that even after 1997 Hong Kong and the mainland will be less institutionally integrated than, say, Greece and Ireland, which are both members of the European Economic Community (EEC); there is complete freedom of movement of goods and factors between these two countries. Moreover, both countries are members of the European Monetary System and have pegged exchange rates. As

China is not a member of the GATT (General Agreement on Tariffs and Trade) and the Chinese currency is not convertible, Hong Kong is institutionally more closely integrated with most of the economies of the free world than it is with China.

Though economic theory concentrates on tariffs, controls on migration, and exchange integration, the effect of geographical and cultural distances may be even more important. Hong Kong is only a half-hour's train ride from China, and Taiwan is quite close to China in terms of geography. The importance of cultural affinity is quite evident; Guangdong has received the bulk of Hong Kong's investment in China; Taiwan's investment is similarly concentrated in Fujian.

Geographic and cultural proximity can enable businesses to evade the formal barriers to trade and investment. Tariffs can be evaded through smuggling, and there is rampant smuggling from Hong Kong to China. The movement of people from Hong Kong and Taiwan to China is relatively free, though movement in the other directions is highly controlled. However, illegal immigrants from the mainland are quite common in Hong Kong. Though the Chinese yuan is not convertible, the Hong Kong currency has circulated widely (and unofficially) in Guangdong, especially in the Shenzhen Special Economic Zone (SEZ). It has been estimated that the amount of Hong Kong dollars circulating in China amounts to HK $6,300 million (U.S. $808 million) or 16 percent of the total supply of the Hong Kong currency (*Hong Kong Economic Times*, 3–21–1991).

The foremost barrier to economic integration between Hong Kong and China is the command economy in China. It is inherently difficult for a command economy to benefit from international trade and investment, because a command economy is designed to insulate itself from the world market. A command economy tends to have an overvalued and inconvertible currency, which is a big obstacle to international economic integration. Moreover, it is extremely difficult for the planner of a command economy to know what goods should be exported or imported because the economy tends to have a highly distorted and arbitrary price system. East–West trade is characterized as "asymmetric integration" because it involves the interaction of two economic systems that are functionally very different. It is no accident that the partial marketization of the Chinese economy is the single most important factor in the promotion of economic integration between Hong Kong and the mainland, and this integration will inevitably be limited unless China can further marketize its economic system.

In the era before the Open-door Policy, the economic ties linking the mainland and Hong Kong were quite strong, but the relationship was asymmetric and one-sided. Hong Kong was open to China's export and investment, but China was closed to Hong Kong's export and investment. Large numbers of Hong Kong people were able to visit their relatives on the mainland, and remittances from Hong Kong residents to their mainland relatives were quite large, but mainland Chinese could not visit Hong Kong. In the 1960s, Hong Kong was the foremost market for the mainland. China's trade surplus with Hong Kong was around one-fifth of China's total exports, and China used the hard currency thus earned to finance its imports of grain, industrial raw materials, and capital goods from developed countries. With the inauguration of economic reforms and the Open-door Policy in the mainland in 1978, the economic relationship between the mainland and Hong Kong has become much more balanced and multifaceted.

China has tailored its Open-door Policy to build closer links with Hong Kong and Taiwan. In 1979, Guangdong and Fujian were given authority to operate Special Economic Zones that have autonomy in trade and investment. Guangdong operates three such zones: the Shenzhen and Zhuhai zones, which are adjacent to Hong Kong and Macao respectively, and the Shantou zone, which has close links to overseas Chinese populations, including a community in Hong Kong that originated in Shantou. Fujian operates the Xiamen Special Economic Zone, which is across the strait to Taiwan and only a few miles from the two coastal islands controlled by Taiwan.

Hong Kong businesses receive no favorable concessions in China over other overseas businesses. In reality, due to geographical proximity and kinship links, Hong Kong businesses have a significant advantage. Hong Kong investors have been able to obtain favorable concessions from local authorities in Guangdong as a result of the kinship network. It is also easier for Hong Kong Chinese than it is for foreigners to visit the mainland, as visas are not required by Hong Kong Chinese. China is thus more open to Hong Kong than it is to other economies. Hong Kong, as a free economy, is open to the whole world including China. It should be noted, however, that, as a result of the fear of illegal immigrants from the mainland, Hong Kong's controls on visitors from the mainland are stricter than its controls on visitors from other places. In cooperation with Hong Kong, Beijing also imposes strict controls on visits to Hong Kong. Mainlanders often complain that it is easier for them to visit foreign countries than to visit Hong Kong. There are few restrictions against mainlanders entering Hong Kong on official passports, however, and it is estimated that more than sixty thousand mainland cadres are working in mainland companies in Hong Kong. Due to kinship links, a substantial number of mainlanders, especially those from Guangdong, have been able to settle in Hong Kong and some of them function as business representatives of local authorities or enterprises. Guangdong has concluded a special agreement with Hong Kong whereby the Guangdong government can issue special passes to its personnel, enabling them to enter Hong Kong without a visa or passport as long as their trips last no more than seven days. Such passes have greatly facilitated the integration of Hong Kong and Guangdong.

Trade and Investment Between Hong Kong and China

As a large fraction of China's trade is conducted via Hong Kong in the form of entrepôt trade, the statistics on China's trade by country are very misleading. In trade statistics, exports are classified by country of destination whereas imports are classified by country of origin. For example, in United States–China trade, both countries regard their exports to each other through Hong Kong as exports to Hong Kong. Both countries thus understate their exports to each other. Imports are not understated because they are traced to the country of origin. Both countries thus overstated the bilateral trade deficits or understated the surpluses. In 1990, according to statistics published by the United States, it had a deficit of U.S. $11.5 billion in its trade with China, whereas China claimed a deficit of U.S. $1.4 billion in its trade with the United States!

While the value of Hong Kong's reexports of Chinese goods can be obtained from *Hong Kong Trade Statistics,* the value of Hong Kong's imports from China for reexport is unknown because the importer usually cannot ascertain whether a certain import is destined for reexport at the time of importation. To obtain the value of Hong Kong's imports from China for reexport, we have to subtract an estimated reexport markup (usually obtained from sample surveys) from the value of Hong Kong's reexports of Chinese goods.

To obtain the value of China's indirect exports via Hong Kong from the value of Hong Kong's imports from China for reexport, we have to subtract from the latter the cost of transporting and insuring the goods between China and Hong Kong, which is equal to the difference between the cost, insurance, and freight (c.i.f.) price of Hong Kong's imports and the free-on-board (f.o.b.) price of China's exports.

While the difference between the c.i.f. and f.o.b. prices are usually quite small (a few percentage points of the value of the goods traded), the reexport markup, which is earned by the Hong Kong middleman, is very substantial. The reexport markup includes profits and the cost of transportation, storage, insurance, packaging, and minor processing that is not substantial enough to confer country of origin. The reexport markup for Chinese goods is estimated to be 25 percent, whereas that for non-Chinese goods is 15 percent. The reexport markup for Chinese goods is much higher because a lot of Chinese goods are packaged or processed in Hong Kong before exportation (Sung, 1991e: 480–82).

In this, all statistics on China's trade by region include the direct trade as well as the indirect trade via Hong Kong. The reexport margin is netted out of indirect exports because exports should be reported on an f.o.b. basis. However, the reexport margin is not netted out of indirect imports because imports should be reported on a c.i.f. basis. The procedure used in this chapter should give the best estimates of trade with China.

Using the above procedure, the true United States–China trade balance can easily be calculated. In 1990, 62 percent of China's exports to the United States were reexported through Hong Kong, whereas the corresponding percentage for the United States was 20 percent. The United States' deficit should be U.S. $10.3 billion whereas China's surplus was U.S. $7 billion. The difference between the two figures largely represents Hong Kong's reexport markup.

The high reexport markup for Chinese goods implies that Hong Kong earns a lot from reexporting Chinese goods, and Hong Kong would lose heavily if the United States were to revoke China's most-favored-nation (MFN) status. In 1990, 62 percent of China's exports to the United States went through Hong Kong in the form of reexports. If China loses its MFN status, China's exports to the United States will decline substantially, and Hong Kong will lose considerably in the reexport margin as well as in the profits of its investment in China. Though China's loss of exports would be substantial, most of these exports would be from processing/assembling operations that have a low value-added margin and a high import content. The wages (processing fees) that China earns from such operations are usually no more than 10 percent of the value of the exports. This implies that Hong Kong's loss is likely to be as large as that of China in absolute terms if China loses its MFN status (Sung, 1991d: 15.6–15.9).

China's Commodity Trade with Hong Kong

In analyzing China's trade with Hong Kong, we must distinguish between China's trade with third countries via Hong Kong, and China's trade with Hong Kong itself (Table 9.2). For China's exports, we distinguish between China's goods retained in Hong Kong for internal use and those reexported via Hong Kong. For China's imports, we distinguish between China's imports of Hong Kong goods and imports of third-country goods via Hong Kong.

To estimate China's exports to Hong Kong for internal use, we first subtract the value of Hong Kong's imports of Chinese goods for reexport from the value of Hong Kong's total imports from China to calculate the value of Hong Kong's retained imports (that is, imports retained for internal use) from China. Then we form the ratio of Hong Kong's retained imports from China to Hong Kong's total imports from China. In 1990, the ratio was 16 percent, showing that the bulk of China's exports to Hong Kong was reexported. Lastly, we multiply China's exports to Hong Kong (obtained from China Customs Statistics) by this ratio.

China's statistics of imports from Hong Kong are highly misleading. China's imports from Hong Kong in 1990 amounted to U.S. $14 billion according to China Customs Statistics, while Hong Kong's trade statistics show that Hong Kong's domestic exports (that is, exports of Hong Kong goods) to China amounted to only U.S. $6 billion, though there was another U.S. $14 billion of third-country goods reexported. It appears that China included as imports from Hong Kong some but not all of Hong Kong's reexports. Overinvoicing of imports on the Chinese side would explain part of the discrepancy. We would expect significant overinvoicing of imports in China, as it is a classic means of evading foreign-exchange control. Since China's statistics on its imports from Hong Kong are inaccurate, we take China's imports from Hong Kong to be Hong Kong's domestic exports to China. Time lags and differences between f.o.b. (free on board) and c.i.f. (cost, insurance, and freight) prices are ignored.

Due to the geographical proximity of the mainland and Hong Kong, such differences should be quite minor.

Table 9.2 shows China's trade with Hong Kong. As mentioned previously, in the pre-1978 era, China had a large trade surplus with Hong Kong and most of China's exports were consumed in Hong Kong. China's imports from Hong Kong were negligible. China–Hong Kong trade was transformed in the reform era. Of China's exports to Hong Kong, the reexported portion grew rapidly and exceeded the retained portion by 1986. The share in total Chinese exports of Chinese goods reexported through Hong Kong rose from 6 percent in 1977 to 40 percent in 1991. China's imports from Hong Kong also grew rapidly: From 1977 to 1991, imports via Hong Kong and imports that were of Hong Kong origin grew 517 times and 996 times respectively. The share of indirect imports in China's total imports rose from 0.5 percent in 1977 to 31 percent in 1991. Hong Kong re-emerged as a major entrepôt for China, and China also become a major market for Hong Kong products. Domestic exports from Hong Kong to China have grown from negligible amounts to U.S. $7,001 million in 1991. In 1984, Hong Kong became the third largest supplier of goods to China after Japan and the United States. Part of the reason for the rapid growth of Hong Kong's domestic exports is due to Hong Kong investment in processing/assembling operations in China. Hong Kong firms supply such operations with the required raw materials and components, parts of which are made in Hong Kong.

The share of the Chinese market in Hong Kong's domestic exports had risen rapidly. China became the second largest market for Hong Kong's domestic exports in 1984, with a market share of 8.2 percent, surpassing that of the United Kingdom (7.6 percent), but still much lower than that of the United States (44 percent). In 1991, China's share rose to 24 percent, while the United States' share dropped to 27 percent. China surpassed the latter to become the largest market for Hong Kong products in 1992. It should be remembered, however, that the bulk of Hong Kong's domestic exports to China consisted of semimanufactures that were further processed in China for export, and that the United States was China's foremost market. If we exclude the cross-flow of semimanufactures between Hong Kong and China and just look at the export of finished goods, the United States would still be by far Hong Kong's foremost market.

Hong Kong was the largest final market (that is, excluding Chinese exports via Hong Kong) for Chinese exports in the late 1960s and early 1970s, but the Hong Kong market was overtaken by the Japanese and United States markets in 1973 and 1987 respectively. The Hong Kong market still accounted for 5 percent of China's exports in 1991, however.

China's exports retained in Hong Kong have been stagnating since 1987, and their share of China's total exports has declined sharply. China has been unable to capture the higher end of Hong Kong's market, which was dominated by Japan. Given the increasing affluence of Hong Kong and the Japanese dominance in vehicles, capital goods, and quality consumer durables and consumer

Table 9.2

China–Hong Kong Trade (in U.S. million dollars)

	China's exports to Hong Kong			China's imports from Hong Kong		
	Total	Retained in Hong Kong	Reexported elsewhere	Total	Hong Kong goods	Hong Kong reexports
1931–38 Average	87 (31.5)	16 (6.3)	70 (25.2)	87 (21.3)	9 (2.1)	79 (19.2)
1950	137 (24.8)	—	—	221 (37.8)	—	—
1951	151 (20.0)	—	—	281 (23.4)	—	—
1952	145 (17.6)	—	—	91 (8.1)	—	—
1955	157 (11.1)	—	—	32 (1.8)	—	—
1960	207 (11.2)	—	—	21 (1.1)	2 (0.1)	19 (1.0)
1965	487* (20.5)	399* (16.8)	88* (3.7)	13 (0.6)	3 (0.2)	10 (0.5)
1970	467 (20.7)	376 (16.6)	91 (4.0)	11 (0.5)	5 (0.21)	6 (0.2)
1975	1,378 (19.0)	1,096 (15.1)	282 (3.9)	33 (0.5)	6 (0.08)	28 (0.4)
1977	1,734 (22.8)	1,306 (17.2)	428 (5.6)	44 (0.6)	7 (0.09)	38 (0.5)

Year						
1979	2,139 (15.7)	3,044 (22.3)	905 (6.6)	383 (2.5)	121 (0.8)	263 (1.7)
1981	3,465 (15.7)	5,293 (24.1)	1,828 (8.3)	1,961 (8.9)	523 (2.4)	1,438 (6.5)
1983	3,680 (16.6)	5,818 (26.2)	2,139 (9.6)	2,531 (11.8)	856 (4.0)	1,675 (7.8)
1984	3,979 (15.3)	6,689 (25.6)	2,709 (10.4)	5,033 (18.4)	1,443 (5.3)	3,590 (13.1)
1985	3,746 (13.7)	7,168 (26.2)	3,422 (12.5)	7,857 (18.6)	1,950 (4.6)	5,907 (14.0)
1986	4,734 (15.3)	9,778 (31.6)	5,045 (16.3)	7,550 (17.6)	2,310 (5.4)	5,241 (12.2)
1987	5,710 (14.4)	13,762 (34.8)	8,052 (20.4)	11,290 (26.1)	3,574 (8.3)	7,716 (17.9)
1988	5,579 (11.8)	18,269 (38.4)	12,690 (26.7)	17,030 (30.8)	4,874 (8.8)	12,157 (22.4)
1989	4,599 (8.8)	21,916 (41.7)	17,323 (32.9)	18,816 (31.8)	5,548 (9.4)	13,268 (22.4)
1990	4,361 (7.1)	26,650 (42.9)	22,287 (35.9)	20,305 (38.1)	6,086 (11.4)	14,219 (26.6)
1991	3,687 (5.1)	32,137 (44.7)	28,450 (39.6)	26,631 (41.7)	6,975 (10.9)	19,656 (30.8)

Sources: Hong Kong data for 1931–38 from Tom (1957); 1948 and after, from *Hong Kong Trade Statistics* (1960–91); 1966 and after, from *Review of Overseas Trade* (1966–91). Chinese data for 1931–48 from *Yearbook of International Trade Statistics*, various issues; 1950–79, from *Statistical Yearbook of China* (1981); 1981 and after, from *China Customs Statistics* (1982–92).

Note: Figures in parentheses represent percentage share of China's total exports (imports).

* Export figures are for the year 1966.

Table 9.3

China's Trade by Region in 1990 (in U.S. million dollars)

	Total Trade		Exports		Imports	
	Value	Rank	Value	Rank	Value	Rank
U.S.	20,142	1	13,554	1	6,588	2
	(17.5)		(21.8)		(12.3)	
Japan	18,230	2	10,642	2	7,588	1
	(15.8)		(17.1)		(14.2)	
Hong Kong	10,447	3	4,361	3	6,086	3
	(9.1)		(7.1)		(11.4)	
Germany	6,732	4	4,048	4	2,684	5
	(5.8)		(6.5)		(5.0)	
Taiwan	5,666	5	932	—	4,734	4
	(4.9)		(1.5)		(8.9)	
USSR	4,379	6	2,239	6	2,140	6
	(3.8)		(3.6)		(4.0)	
South Korea	3,652	7	2,099	7	1,553	8
	(3.2)		(3.4)		(2.9)	
Singapore	3,231	8	2,373	5	858	—
	(2.8)		(3.8)		(1.6)	
France	2,897	—	1,234	—	1,663	7
	(2.5)		(2.0)		(3.1)	

Source: Data on China's direct trade are obtained from *China's Customs Statistics* (1982–92), and data on China's indirect trade via Hong Kong are obtained from the Census and Statistics Department of Hong Kong.

Note: China's indirect trade with other countries via Hong Kong is excluded from the Hong Kong figures and included in the figures of other countries. Data for Taiwan are taken from Sung (1992: 39) and include direct trade as well as the indirect trade via Hong Kong. Figures in parentheses represent percentage share of China's total trade/exports/imports.

goods, the future of Chinese products in Hong Kong is not very bright (Sung, 1991a: 119–22). The exports of Hong Kong goods to China has exceeded China's exports retained in Hong Kong since 1989, and Hong Kong has had a surplus in its direct trade with China from 1989 onward.

China's Trade by Country and Region

Given the estimates of China's trade with Hong Kong, we can form an accurate picture of China's trade by country and region in Table 9.3. China's trading activities with third countries via Hong Kong are distributed to their final destinations or initial sources. China's trading partners in 1990, in order of importance, were the United States, Japan, Hong Kong, Germany, Taiwan, USSR, and South Korea. In order of importance, China's major markets were the United

States, Japan, Hong Kong, West Germany, Singapore, USSR, and South Korea, and China's major suppliers were Japan, the United States, Hong Kong, Taiwan, West Germany, USSR, France, and South Korea. China regards Hong Kong as both its largest market and its supplier because in Chinese statistics China's trade with third countries via Hong Kong is regarded as trade with Hong Kong. It should be noted that, in the first half of 1991, Taiwan surpassed both Hong Kong and the United States to become the mainland's second largest supplier after Japan (Sung, 1992: 22–24).

China's Trade with Third Countries Through Hong Kong

Since the inauguration of the Open-door Policy, China has established numerous direct links with the rest of the world, including diplomatic, commercial, and transportation links. Paradoxically, the middleman role of Hong Kong is becoming more prominent, and an increasing share of China's commodity trade is handled through Hong Kong. To explain this paradox, it is worthwhile to construct a theory of intermediation. The theory has strong predictions for entrepôt trade and services trade.

In explaining entrepôt trade, it is important to distinguish transshipment from entrepôt trade. Transshipment means that goods are consigned directly from the exporting country to a buyer in the importing country, though the goods are transported via an entrepôt and may be stored there for onward shipment. Transshipped goods are not regarded as part of the trade of the entrepôt and they do not clear customs because they represent only goods in transit.

Unlike transshipment, entrepôt trade is part of the trade of the entrepôt. Imports for reexport are consigned to a buyer in the entrepôt and the buyer takes legal possession of the goods after clearing customs. These imports may then be processed before being reexported as long as the processing is not substantial enough to confer country of origin.

The usual explanation of entrepôt trade in terms of transportation cost is faulty because it ignores the importance of transaction costs. It is useful to distinguish processed reexports from pure reexports. *Processed reexports* are those that have been physically treated (packaged, sorted, and so on), whereas *pure reexports* have not been changed in any physical way.

Pure reexports are difficult to account for theoretically because reexports involve higher costs than transshipment (other things being equal) owing to two factors: one, reexports have to clear the customs of an entrepôt twice, whereas transshipped goods do not have to clear the customs of the entrepôt at all, so fewer delays and lower storage costs for transshipment are involved; and, two, transshipped goods are insured and financed just once, whereas reexports have to be insured and financed twice—first when they are imported into the entrepôt, and second when they are reexported. While transportation costs determine transshipment, pure reexports are determined by both transportation costs and transaction costs, and processed reexports involve processing costs as well.

Since China's adoption of an Open-door Policy in 1978, it has been easier to trade directly with China. The transaction cost of establishing a direct trade link has gone down and this should lead to a rise in direct trade relative to indirect trade. However, China started to decentralize its foreign trade system in 1979, replacing vertical channels of command with horizontal links. The number of trading partners and trade links multiplied rapidly, creating a huge demand for intermediation. Before 1979, establishing trade links with ten state trading corporations would have ensured a complete coverage of China trade. By 1984, however, the number of trading corporations increased to more than one thousand. It is very costly for an individual firm to establish trade links with the mushrooming number of Chinese trading corporations, intermediation has emerged as a more economical way to facilitate the process, and this demand for intermediation has been channeled to Hong Kong due to its comparative advantage in trading. China's foreign trade decentralization came in four waves: 1979, 1984, 1988, and 1991. The share of China's trade through Hong Kong jumped after each wave of decentralization (Table 9.2).

The market composition of China's indirect trade via Hong Kong and the change over time of these markets in dependency on Hong Kong's entrepôt trade confirm the overwhelming importance of trade decentralization on intermediation (Sung, 1991a: 141–43). Countries with a long history of trading with China have found it worthwhile to pay the fixed cost of establishing trade links, and they are less dependent on Hong Kong than are the new entrants. Political recognition and trade pacts also lower dependency on Hong Kong. However, the decentralization of China's trading system in 1979 and 1984 increased the dependency of both old China hands and new entrants on Hong Kong's entrepôt trade. For instance, the dependence of Canada and the United States on Hong Kong for China's exports decreased in the early 1970s as they established political and commercial links with China, but this trend was reversed in 1979. Starting from 1984, the dependence of all of China's major markets (Japan, United States, Singapore, West Germany, United Kingdom, Canada, and Australia) on Hong Kong for China's exports increased substantially. Similarly, starting from 1979, all of China's major suppliers (Japan, United States, West Germany, United Kingdom, France, Italy, and Singapore) became more dependent on Hong Kong for their exports to China.

China's Service Trade with Hong Kong

Trade in services between the mainland and Hong Kong is extremely important. Conceptually, the reexport margin that Hong Kong earns through entrepôt trade in fact represents the export of services. Such services are embodied in the goods sold, however, and are usually recorded in trade statistics as export of goods rather than export of services.

For tourist services, Hong Kong visitors accounted for 66 percent of tourist arrivals as well as tourist expenditure in China in 1990. Hong Kong also exports transportation services, trading services, construction services, financial services, and business services to China. However, besides the data on entrepôt trade and tourism, only some data are available for shipping, trading, and financial services. Reliable data are lacking for the other categories. Hong Kong's export of financial services to China will be discussed in the section below on investment. Though Hong Kong's export of construction services and business services to China is very important, there are very little data to go by. Hong Kong is the foremost base for China consultancy services. According to *Intertrade* (10–1984: 2), half of the foreign law firms in Hong Kong provide legal advice on China's trade.

Hong Kong is also the foremost gateway for foreigners touring China. Many foreigners also join package tours of China that are organized in Hong Kong. Though China has established more and more direct air links with other countries since 1978, the percentage of foreign tourists leaving (visiting) China via Hong Kong increased from 40 (34) percent in 1982 to 55 (44) percent in 1987. Again this paradox can be explained by the theory of intermediation, as China decentralized part of the authority to organize China tours from the China Travel Service to provincial and local authorities in the early 1980s. Taiwan lifted its ban on travel to the mainland in 1987, and this of course led to another jump in the number of foreigners visiting China via Hong Kong.

In commodity trade, Hong Kong is an important entrepôt as well as a center of transshipment for China. The value of transshipped goods is not available since they do not go through customs, but their weight is known. In 1990, transshipment of goods to (from) China weighed as much as 9 (13) percent of China's imports from (exports to) Hong Kong. If we assume that the value of transhipment to (from) China per ton is the same as China's imports from (exports to) Hong Kong, transshipment of goods to (from) China via Hong Kong would amount to 3.6 (6) percent of China's imports (exports) by value in 1990. Hong Kong trading firms also perform an important brokerage role for China's direct trade, amounting to U.S. $15 billion or 7 percent of China's total trade in 1988 (Hong Kong Trade Development Council, 1988). Lacking data from after 1988, we make the simple assumption that Hong Kong brokers involved in China's direct trade continued to account for 7 percent of China's trade after 1988. The shares of China's exports consumed, reexported, transshipped, and intermediated by Hong Kong were 7 percent, 36 percent, 6 percent, and 7 percent, respectively, in 1990. The total of the four categories was 56 percent. Though there is likely to be some overlap in the last two categories, we can safely conclude that Hong Kong plays an important role in over half of China's exports. On the import side, the shares of China's imports produced, reexported, transshipped, and intermediated by Hong Kong were 11 percent, 27 percent, 4 percent, and 7 percent, respectively, in 1990. The total of the four categories was 49 percent. We can thus conclude that Hong Kong plays an important role in close to half of China's imports.

It should be noted that China's export of services to Hong Kong has increased rapidly in recent years. China's construction firms are active in construction projects in Hong Kong. A large number of mainland Chinese are working in Hong Kong, including manufacturing workers imported to relieve the labor shortage in Hong Kong, and engineers working in mainland-owned factories in Hong Kong. Hong Kong residents have also traveled to China for medical treatment because the price of health care is lower in the mainland.

Investment Between Hong Kong and China

Table 9.4 shows China's inward foreign investment by source. The large share of Hong Kong in China's direct foreign investment conceals the important middleman role of Hong Kong. In China's statistics, investment from Hong Kong includes the investment of the subsidiaries of foreign companies incorporated in Hong Kong. Many multinational companies like to test the Chinese investment environment through investments from their Hong Kong subsidiaries because Hong Kong has the required expertise. If such investment is successful, then the parent company will also invest in China.

The United States and Japan have been significant investors in China. The investment of both countries has decreased appreciably, however, since the Tiananmen Incident. Moreover, the investment of the two countries in China is minuscule compared with their total overseas investment. For instance, Japan's cumulative investment in China was only 29 percent of its investment in Hong Kong and only 0.9 percent of its total overseas investment by June 1990. China had openly complained about the lack of Japanese investment in China and Japanese stinginess in technology transfer. Japan's strategy has been to invest in Hong Kong, since Japanese business regards Hong Kong as the future capital of an industrialized southern China. Similarly, cumulative investment in China by the United States was only 37 percent of its investment in Hong Kong and only 0.57 percent of its total overseas investment by the end of 1990.

Hong Kong's Investment in China

Hong Kong's investment in China is very diversified, ranging from small-scale labor-intensive operations to large-scale infrastructural projects. Though manufacturing in Hong Kong is not as sophisticated as that in South Korea and Taiwan, Hong Kong has considerable expertise in service industries including construction, hotels, and financial services.

The share of Hong Kong in China's external loans was small in the early 1980s, but the share rose from 0.6 percent in 1983 to 9.4 percent in 1989. Hong Kong's share was low partly because Hong Kong does not extend official loans to China. However, China-backed companies registered in Hong Kong began to raise funds in Hong Kong's stock market through share placements in 1987

Table 9.4

Foreign Investment in China by Source, 1979–90 (contracted investment U.S. million dollars)

	1979–84	1985	1986	1987	1988	1989	1990	Total share	Cumulative percentage
National Total	11,791	6,333	3,330	4,319	6,191	6,294	6,986	45,244	100
Hong Kong	6,495	4,134	1,449	2,466	4,033	3,645	4,258	26,480	58.5
United States	1,025	1,152	541	361	384	646	366	4,476	9.9
Japan	1,158	471	283	386	371	515	478	3,662	8.1
Taiwan	—	—	—	100*	420	480	1,000	2,000	4.4
Singapore	117	77	141	80	137	148	107	805	1.8
Canada	66	9	91	34	40	49	21	309	0.7
Australia	91	14	32	47	17	84	18	303	0.7
South Korea**	—	0.1	1.8	6.0	5.4	14.5	57	81	0.2

Sources: Data for Taiwan are obtained from press releases of the Xinhua News Agency. Data for South Korea are obtained from the Korean Overseas Trade Association. Data for other economies are obtained from the *Almanac of China's Foreign Relations and Trade* (1984–91).

*Cumulative total up until 1987.

**Direct investment in China approved by the South Korean Government. Data are obtained from the Korean Overseas Trade Association.

(*South China Morning Post,* 6–18–1987). Due to the differences in accounting systems and company law, it is more difficult for Chinese firms registered in China to raise funds in the Hong Kong stock market. However, many firms in Guangdong are amending their accounting systems to prepare for listing in the Hong Kong stock market.

Hong Kong is the center for raising 80 percent of China's syndicated loans. Loan syndication is an important middleman function performed by Hong Kong. The share of China's external loans (syndicated loans and other loans) syndicated in Hong Kong rose from 6 percent in the period 1979 to 1982 to 31 percent in 1987 and then declined to 14 percent in 1989. Such changes can be explained by the theory of intermediation. The rapid jump of the share of China's loans syndicated in Hong Kong in 1987 was related to the 1986 decentralization of the power to raise foreign loans to selected provincial governments and enterprises. The rapid decline in the share of China's loans syndicated in Hong Kong since 1988 was related to the 1988 recentralization of the power to borrow foreign loans as part of the retrenchment program. Decentralization had a decisive impact on intermediation in the commodity trade and tourist trade, as well as in financial services.

China's Investment in Hong Kong

China's investment in Hong Kong is likely to exceed Hong Kong's investment in China. According to Chinese statistics, Hong Kong's contracted investment in China from 1978 to 90 amounted to U.S. $26.5 billion. However, Hong Kong's utilized investment in China was only around 49 percent of contracted investment. Hong Kong's utilized investment in China from 1978 to 1990 is thus estimated to be around U.S. $13 billion. This is likely to be a gross overestimate, however, as it includes the investment of the subsidiaries of Taiwanese companies and multinational companies in Hong Kong. In fact, mainland companies have also invested in China through their Hong Kong subsidiaries in order to qualify for the concessions granted to overseas investors. From anecdotal evidence, it is known that Hong Kong investors often overstate the value of their investment in China with the connivance of local officials. For example, Hong Kong manufacturers tend to put a high value on the outdated machinery that they move to China. It is well known that government officials in command economies tend to exaggerate economic achievement, resulting in such phenomena as the "success indicator problem."

China's cumulative investment in Hong Kong was estimated to be around U.S. $10 billion, but this is likely to be an underestimate as there is an incentive for China's local authorities and enterprises to establish unofficial subsidiaries in Hong Kong to evade controls on foreign trade as well as foreign-exchange controls. China's investment in Hong Kong is thus likely to exceed Hong Kong's investment in China.

There are no accurate statistics on Guangdong's investment in Hong Kong.

From anecdoctal evidence, however, it is known that many firms backed by Guangdong's provincial government or local authorities are very active in Hong Kong.

China's investment in Hong Kong is very diversified, covering nearly all sectors of the Hong Kong economy, namely banking, insurance, entrepôt trade, shipping, aviation, real estate, and manufacturing. China's investment strengthens the ties between Hong Kong and China and enhances the position of Hong Kong as the gateway to China.

The Prospect of Hong Kong as a Middleman for the Mainland

The role of Hong Kong as a middlemen for China is important both in commodity trade and services trade, including tourist services and financial services. A middleman creates opportunities for trade and investment by lowering transaction costs. An efficient middleman thus enhances the degree of economic integration between different economies. Due to the many rigidities of China's economy and political barriers, the efficiency of Hong Kong as a middleman is crucial for its economic interactions with the world, especially for transactions with Taiwan and South Korea.

The Tiananmen Incident has paradoxically speeded up the reform and decentralization of China's foreign trade, and such reforms have enhanced the middleman role of Hong Kong. After the cutting off of soft loans following the Tiananmen Incident, China was under great pressure to expand its exports to pay off its foreign debt. China devalued the renminbi against the United States dollar in December 1989 and in November 1990 by 21 percent and 9.6 percent respectively. China further decentralized its external sector in early 1991. Provincial governments and export enterprises were allowed to retain 80 percent of their foreign-exchange earnings, and subsidies on exports were abolished. The number of commodities that required licensing for export decreased from 185 categories to roughly 90 categories. China's exports continued to grow at double-digit rates from 1989 to 1991. As expected, the further decentralization of China's trade enhanced the middleman role of Hong Kong. The share of China's exports (imports) reexported via Hong Kong jumped from 36 (27) percent in 1990 to 40 (31) percent in 1991 (Table 9.2, page 234).

As China is likely to further decentralize its foreign trade and investment, the prospect of Hong Kong as a middleman is very bright. There are significant economies of scale and economies of agglomeration in trading activity and it is very difficult for other cities such as Singapore or Shanghai to compete with Hong Kong, because Hong Kong is the established center for China's trade. The existence of economies of scale in intermediation would enhance the demand for the middleman, as small firms will not be able to trade efficiently.

Traders tend to agglomerate in a city, suggesting that there are significant external economies involved. This implies that once a city acquires a comparative advantage in trade, the advantage feeds upon itself, and more trading firms will come to the city, making it even more efficient in trade (Sung, 1991a: 28–42).

Though the greater part of Hong Kong's entrepôt trade is China-related, the non-China component of Hong Kong's entrepôt trade is also thriving, growing faster than world trade. This implies that an increasing share of the trade among market economies is handled through Hong Kong in the form of entrepôt trade, confirming our theory on the efficiency of large trading centers.

Empirical analysis also indicates that Hong Kong's entrepôt trade is much more capital- and skill-intensive than Hong Kong's wholesale trade, retail trade, and exports manufacture. The skills required for international trade include a good knowledge of English, familiarity with modern business practices, the ability to work in different cultural and legal environments, and proficiency with complex contractual forms. The supporting industries of international trade, namely, shipping, air transport, communications, finance, insurance, and business services, are also capital- or skill-intensive. As Hong Kong has a long-run labor shortage due to declining fertility rates and an aging demographic structure, the factor requirements of entrepôt trade are consistent with Hong Kong's changing factor endowments and dynamic comparative advantage.

It should be noted that economies of agglomeration and economies of scale characterize most economic activities, including agriculture, manufacturing, transportation, trading, business services, and financial services. As business activities agglomerate, land prices and wages start to rise, putting a drag on the tendency to agglomerate. Agriculture will be the first activity to move out of the city because it is land-intensive. Manufacturing will be the second activity to relocate, and a lot of Hong Kong manufacturing firms are moving their land-intensive and labor-intensive processes to China. Transportation will be the next activity to be affected, as ports and airports are also land-intensive. The high cost of Hong Kong's new airport is a testimony to the difficulty of building a big airport in land-scarce Hong Kong. The new Hong Kong airport will be twenty times as expensive as the Huangtian airport in Shenzhen, which will also have two runways when it is fully developed. Were it not for political barriers, it would be more rational to put Hong Kong's new airport in Shenzhen. China's customs administration is not noted for its efficiency, however, and it would be risky for Hong Kong to put its new airport in Shenzhen unless China thoroughly reforms and modernizes its administration. The completion of such reforms cannot realistically be expected in the near future. But when such reforms are completed, and when Hong Kong's new airport also gets congested, it will be rational for Hong Kong to divert a substantial portion of its air traffic to Shenzhen.

Trading, business services, and financial services will be least affected by rising land prices and wages, because such activities are neither land-intensive nor labor-intensive. It should be noted that New York and London long ago lost their comparative advantage in manufacturing, but their positions as centers of trading, business, and finance remain formidable.

In the long run, China is likely to overcome its transportation bottlenecks and acquire modern trading skills. China may even clean up its bureaucracy. But China will still rely on Hong Kong for trade and financial and business services because of the economies of scale and of agglomeration in such activities.

The Chinese themselves are establishing many trading companies in Hong Kong, showing that they recognize the established efficiency of Hong Kong in trading. Some Hong Kong traders fear competition from Chinese trading companies in Hong Kong. The situation is not a zero-sum game, however, because of economies of agglomeration; the arrival of Chinese trading companies further enhances the position of Hong Kong as a trading center.

It is often alleged that if South Korea and Taiwan were to establish direct commercial links with the mainland, the role of Hong Kong as a middleman in China's trade would decline. This view is mistaken, being supported neither by theory nor by empirical evidence.

The combined indirect trade of Taiwan and South Korea with the mainland via Hong Kong was only 13 percent of China's indirect trade via Hong Kong in 1990. As mentioned before, though most countries have direct commercial and diplomatic relations with China, they have became more dependent on Hong Kong for their trade with China since 1979.

Canada, the United States, and Indonesia established direct commercial or diplomatic relations with China only in the 1970s or 1980s, and their experiences again confirm the efficiency of Hong Kong in intermediation. In these four countries, the establishment of direct commercial or diplomatic relations led to a sharp decline in their dependence on Hong Kong, but their dependence on Hong Kong rose again as China decentralized its trading system. For example, in the case of China's exports to the United States, the share of indirect exports via Hong Kong fell sharply from 100 percent in 1970 to 15 percent in 1975. However, the share rose in 1979 with the decentralization of China's trade, and it increased to over 62 percent in 1990. In the case of China's exports to Canada, the share of indirect exports via Hong Kong also fell sharply to as low as 7 percent in 1975, but it also rose in 1979, and increased to 59 percent in 1990. In the case of China's exports to Indonesia, the share of indirect exports via Hong Kong fell to a low of 50 percent in 1988, but it rose slowly thereafter.

Hong Kong–Guangdong Link

The impacts of China's opening on Hong Kong's trade and services have been described in some detail. China's opening also has significant impacts on Hong Kong's manufacturing, as Hong Kong manufacturers have relocated the more labor-intensive part of their production processes into Guangdong on a large scale.

The moving of labor-intensive processes to China has been described negatively in some quarters as the "hollowing out" of Hong Kong manufacturing. This description is misleading in some ways. What has happened is a division of labor between Hong Kong and the Pearl River Delta, with Hong Kong concentrating on the skill-intensive processes (product design, sourcing, production management, quality control, technical support, and marketing) while the labor-intensive and land-intensive processes have moved to the Pearl River Delta (see chapters 6 and 7). The division of labor is beneficial: labor shortage and inflationary pressures in Hong Kong have been alleviated; labor upgrading and employment opportunities in the delta have been introduced.

Though the availability of cheap labor in China has led to high profits in Hong Kong manufacturing, manufacturing investment in Hong Kong in the 1980s was quite modest in light of the colony's past experience. The uncertainty generated by the 1997 issue and the Tiananmen Incident had depressing effects on manufacturing investment in Hong Kong (Sung, 1991b: 10–14). Despite modest manufacturing investment, manufacturing labor productivity had grown at an average annual rate of close to 10 percent in the 1980s. This rate of growth was higher than the historical average in Hong Kong manufacturing and also higher than the rates achieved in the 1980s in Singapore (5.3 percent), South Korea (4.9 percent), and Taiwan (4.8 percent) (Sung, 1991b: 22). The relocation of low-productivity and labor-intensive processes to China has boosted the growth of manufacturing labor productivity in Hong Kong. The latter's manufacturing has remained very competitive due to high rates of growth in labor productivity and moderates rates of growth in wages.

The proximity of Guangdong has enabled many of the ancillary services of Hong Kong's relocated industries to be performed in Hong Kong. The linkages of the manufacturing sector with other sectors have thus been preserved. Demand for ancillary services has increased tremendously due to the expansion of the scale of production after relocation. As mentioned before, China's opening and the decentralization of China's trade and finance have increased the demand for Hong Kong's trading, financial, business, and transportation services, and the industrialization of Guangdong has led to a further increase in the demand for these services. The relocation of Hong Kong industries to Guangdong has accelerated the transformation of Hong Kong into a commercial, financial, and service center. Relocation has increased the demand for services and facilitated the expansion of services by releasing scarce labor for the use of services industries.

The infusion of Hong Kong know-how and capital into Guangdong has led to the economic takeoff of Guangdong. In the reform era (1978 to 1990), Guangdong's real per capita gross domestic product (GDP) has grown at an average annual rate of 11 percent per year, a performance exceeding that of the East Asian Newly Industrializing Economies (NIEs) at the time of their economic takeoff. In his tour of Guangdong in January 1991, Deng Xiaoping affirmed Guangdong's leading status in China's opening and economic reform. Guangdong is trying to vie with Thailand for the title of "fifth little dragon." It should be noted that, in 1991, approvals of foreign investment in Thailand dropped by close to 60 percent while contracted foreign capital in Guangdong jumped by 83 percent. After Deng's tour and Thailand's political disturbances in

1992, Thailand's investment environment deteriorated further while the pace of foreign investment continued to accelerate in Guangdong.

In short, Hong Kong has become the economic capital of an industrialized Guangdong. The region, often called "greater Hong Kong," has a vast development potential. Guangdong alone has a population of 63 million, which is equal to the combined population of South Korea and Taiwan.

The Future of "Greater Hong Kong"

It is clear that China's Economic Reform, especially reform of the external sector, has permitted the synergy whereby Hong Kong's and Taiwan's know-how and capital have combined with Guangdong's labor into a potent force with which to penetrate the world market. The role of Hong Kong is particularly important, not only as financier, investor, consumer, supplier, middleman, and technical consultant, but also as a catalyst in China's Economic Reform and trade liberalization.

Of course, China's export expansion may run into demand-side constraints, and its trade friction with the United States may be a harbinger of an all-out trade war. Trade and investment is not a zero-sum game, however. China can ease trade frictions by liberalizing its imports. Moreover, the U.S. trade deficit with China is partly a statistical artifact. Hong Kong and Taiwan are giving up their labor-intensive industries, making way for the expansion of China's exports. China's Open-door Policy has facilitated the industrial restructuring of the Asian NIEs, since they can move their labor-intensive industries to China.

There have been a number of proposals for promoting the integration of the mainland, Hong Kong, and Taiwan through institutional arrangements such as the formation of a free trade area, or the use of unilateral tariff preferences. Most of these proposals are utopian and counterproductive. The reality is that there are very real political differences dividing the mainland and Taiwan, and such differences are not going to disappear overnight. Moreover, the foremost barrier to economic integration between China and any other economy is the command economy in China, not tariffs or exchange risks. It is not fruitful to concentrate on tariff preferences unless China can further marketize its economy, and that further reform and marketization of the Chinese economy will inevitably be a lengthy process.

Though Hong Kong is irrevocably integrated with the mainland, it must be remembered that Hong Kong can function as the bridge linking the mainland and the world only because Hong Kong is also irrevocably integrated with the world economy. An inward-looking bloc involving Hong Kong and the mainland would be detrimental to both.

Hong Kong is traditionally a free port, and the freedom of movement of goods and capital in Hong Kong is enshrined in the Sino-British agreement on the future of Hong Kong as well as in the Basic Law because all parties involved recognized that such freedom is essential to the future prosperity of Hong Kong. As the free-port status of Hong Kong is guaranteed by constitution and international agreement, the only way that the mainland and Hong Kong can form a trade bloc is for the mainland to abolish all its tariffs. This is obviously ludicrous and utopian.

Even a trading bloc comprising Hong Kong and Shenzhen is utopian. Shenzhen has built a "second line" managing the flow of goods and people between its Special Economic Zone and the rest of China, and Shenzhen has plans for becoming a free trade area. If Beijing allows Shenzhen to become a free trade area, trade between Hong Kong and Shenzhen would be similar to trade between Hong Kong and any other free trade area (between Hong Kong and Kaoshiung, for example). There are obstacles to the formation of a trade bloc. If Hong Kong and Shenzhen were to become a trade bloc such as a customs union, the two would have to bargain as a single entity in world trade and also agree on the sharing of textile quotas. A prerequisite for that is Shenzhen acquiring autonomy in external economic affairs. This implies that Beijing would have to relinquish control of Shenzhen's external economic affairs and China would have to enter the General Agreement on Tariffs and Trade (GATT) as the mainland minus Shenzhen, because the bargaining position of Shenzhen in world trade may differ from that of Beijing. Another problem is that the union would undermine Hong Kong's autonomy. Hong Kong's autonomy in external economic affairs is guaranteed by both the Sino-British agreement and the Basic Law, and Hong Kong is a member of the GATT. A trading bloc of Shenzhen and Hong Kong would give an institutional channel to Beijing to encroach on Hong Kong's autonomy and a say over the utilization of Hong Kong's textiles and clothing quotas.

In 1991, some Hong Kong businessmen lobbied for tariff preferences from the mainland. Such preferences, if granted, would be un-GATT-able and also detrimental to both the mainland and Hong Kong. Free competition has long been the source of strength and dynamism in the Hong Kong economy. Such preferences would entice Hong Kong businessmen to spend their energy on lobbying for favoritism instead of concentrating their resources on improving productivity. Moreover, there is no "free lunch," and Hong Kong's seeking of favoritism from the mainland would invite the mainland to ask for reciprocal favoritism from Hong Kong. Given Chinese sovereignty and Beijing's intervention-prone record, Hong Kong would have a hard time preserving the autonomy promised in the Basic Law. The seeking of favoritism from Beijing would further compromise Hong Kong's ability to manage its own affairs. It should be stressed that the erosion of Hong Kong's autonomy and dynamism would also be detrimental to China's long-term interests.

It is often not realized that tariff preferences and institutional arrangements may not be important for economic integration. That goal requires the lowering of transaction costs, and tariffs are often only a small part of transaction costs. Other factors, such as transportation costs, cultural affinity, foreign-exchange controls, and government regulations, may be much more important. The integration of "greater Hong Kong" will continue to be largely market-driven, though consultation to improve information flow and to coordinate policy, especially policies on transportation and infrastructure, will be useful. Bilateral discriminatory preferences are utopian and counterproductive, and unilateral discriminatory preferences are un-GATT-able and detrimental.

Some commentators speak of the tremendous economic potential of "greater China," including the mainland, Taiwan, and Hong Kong. It is more realistic, however, to confine the attention to "greater Hong Kong," as the successful synergy of foreign know-how and capital with China's resources is largely confined to Guangdong. A large part of the Chinese economy, especially the big state enterprises and heavy industries, is still mired in bureaucratic red tape and inefficiency. While China's economic reforms have achieved spectacular success in Guangdong, the national picture is less sanguine.

The dynamic growth of Guangdong is perhaps the brightest spot in China's Open-door Policy and Economic Reform. Though China's Economic Reform has run into many of the same problems of Eastern European reforms, the success of Guangdong has no Eastern European parallel, and the availability of kindred resources in Hong Kong and Taiwan is the obvious factor accounting for Guangdong's success. The dynamism of Guangdong may help China to pull through the long and tortuous process of economic reform.

The future prosperity of "greater Hong Kong" is by no means assured, however, and the Tiananmen Incident has severely tested the confidence of the Hong Kong community. Whether Beijing can honor its pledges to Hong Kong after 1997 is uncertain. The possibility of tensions heightening across the Taiwan Straits cannot be ignored, as the Taiwanese independence movement is becoming more assertive.

The paradox of the future of "greater Hong Kong" is that the political side of the picture looks gloomy but the economic side of the picture looks bright. While the future of "greater Hong Kong" is not assured, it must be stressed that "greater Hong Kong" has tremendous economic potential. The labor force of Guangdong is as large as the labor forces of the four Asian NIEs combined. The exports of "greater Hong Kong" have already led to a lot of trade friction between China and the United States. The world cannot afford to ignore the emergence of "greater Hong Kong."

Notes

1. Information obtained from interview with Guangdong official.
2. The figure is estimated as follows. We add Guangdong's 1990 exports to Hong Kong of U.S. $8,543 million (obtained from MOFERT statistics) to Guangdong's 1990 processing/assembling exports to Hong Kong of U.S. $9,055 million (obtained from China's Customs Statistics). The latter figure was given by Guandong officials to the Hong Kong Trade Development Council. The sum of these two figures is U.S. $17,598 million. Then we have to substract from the total the processing fee of exports from processing/assembling operations to Hong Kong, because the processing fee is included in

both figures. We know from MOFERT statistics that Guangdong's 1990 processing fee amounted to U.S. $990 million, and Hong Kong accounted for 93 percent of Guangdong's investment-related exports (exports from processing/assembling operations and enterprises with foreign investment). Guangdong's 1990 processing fee of exports to Hong Kong from processing/assembling operations was thus estimated to be U.S. $919 million (0.93 × U.S. $990 million). This gives the estimate of U.S. $16,679 million (U.S. $17,598 million – U.S. $919 million).

References

Almanac of China's Foreign Relations and Trade (1984 to 1991), Hong Kong: China Resources Trade Consultancy Co., Ltd., various issues.

China Customs Statistics (1982 to 1992), Hong Kong: Economic Information and Agency, various issues.

Guangdong Statistical Yearbook (1983 to 1991), Beijing: China Statistical Publishing Company, various issues.

Hong Kong Economic Times, March 21, 1991.

Hong Kong Trade Development Council (1988), *Survey on Hong Kong Reexports: Summary Report,* November (mimeo).

Hong Kong Trade Statistics (1960 to 1991), Hong Kong: Census and Statistics Department, various issues.

Intertrade, October 1984.

Review of Overseas Trade (1966 to 1991), Hong Kong: Census and Statistics Department, various issues.

South China Morning Post, June 18, 1987.

Statistical Yearbook of China (1950 to 1979), Beijing: China Statistical Publishing Company.

Sung, Yun-wing (1991a), *The China–Hong Kong Connection: The Key to China's Open-Door Policy,* Cambridge: Cambridge University Press.

——— (1991b), "Competitiveness of Hong Kong Manufacturing Versus Its Major Competitors," paper presented to the *Symposium on Industrial Policy in Hong Kong: An Interdisciplinary Chapter,* organized by the Hong Kong Institute of Asia-Pacific Studies, Chinese University of Hong Kong in Hong Kong, July 12–13, 1991, photocopied.

——— (1991c), "Explaining China's Export Drive: The Only Success among Command Economies," Occasional Paper, Hong Kong Institute of Asia-Pacific Studies, Chinese University of Hong Kong.

——— (1991d), "Foreign Trade and Investment," in *China Review,* ed. Hsin-chi Kuan and Maurice Brosseau, Hong Kong: Chinese University of Hong Kong Press, pp. 15.1–15.22.

——— (1991e), "Hong Kong's Economic Value to China," in *The Other Hong Kong Report 1991,* ed. Sung Yun-wing and Ming-kwan Lee, Hong Kong: Chinese University Press, pp. 477–504.

——— (1992), "Non-institutional Economic Integration Via Cultural Affinity: The Case of Mainland China, Taiwan, and Hong Kong," Occasional Paper No. 13, Hong Kong Institute of Asia-Pacific Studies, Chinese University of Hong Kong, July.

Tom, C.F. (1957), *Entrepôt Trade and the Monetary Standards of Hong Kong, 1842–1942,* Chicago: University of Chicago Press.

Yearbook of International Trade Statistics, United Nations Statistical Office, various issues.

10

Socioeconomic Center, Political Periphery: Hong Kong's Uncertain Transition Toward the Twenty-first Century

Alvin Y. So and Reginald Yin-Wang Kwok

The 1990s will prove to be a turning point in Chinese history. The Hong Kong–Guangdong integration process will have significance not just to Hong Kong and Guangdong, but also to other parts of China, to Taiwan, and even to Korea.

As such, the Hong Kong–Guangdong integration process is bound to be highly controversial. In this volume, there are two sets of contradictory arguments with respect to the future of Hong Kong–Guangdong/mainland integration. Ming K. Chan, Xueqiang Xu, R. Yin-Wang Kwok, Lixun Li, Xiaopei Yan, Victor Sit, Yun-wing Sung, Greg Guldin, and Graham Johnson have presented an optimistic view on the economic integration process. On the other hand, Ian Scott and Ming-kwan Lee have presented a pessimistic view on the political linkages between Hong Kong and mainland China. How then can we explain their differences in interpreting the Hong Kong–Guangdong/mainland China integration? Why do scholars who have been widely published in this field disagree with one another?

The explanation, we argue, is due to the complexity and the indeterminate nature of the integration process. The Hong Kong–Guangdong/mainland China integration is not just economically promising, it is at the same time politically destabilizing. This imbalance between the economy and the polity will have profound implications on the future of the integration process.

In order to analyze this economic-political imbalance, we have adopted a center–periphery framework, as suggested by R. Yin-Wang Kwok and Roger Ames (see also So, 1990). There are several key features of this center–periphery to one another; a center is not a center unless it has a periphery under its control. Second, the center–periphery relationship is highly dynamic. Center always wants to exercise more exploitation on the periphery, while periphery always wants to resist such exploitation. Finally, center–periphery relations are highly complex. They are not confined to the economic sphere, but are extended to the political, social, and cultural spheres as well.

Using such a center–periphery framework, we argue that while Hong Kong has risen to be the socioeconomic center of Guangdong, it has become the political periphery of Beijing since the signing of the Joint Declaration between the British and Chinese governments in 1984.

Hong Kong as the Socioeconomic Center of Guangdong

Following the founding of the People's Republic of China in 1949, as Victor Sit points out, the border between Hong Kong and Guangdong was turned into an effective divide for two different ideologies and economic systems. Hong Kong, forced by the dwindling China market, turned to export-led industrialization and became one of the four "little dragons." The economy of Guangdong grew only slowly, under a new reign of socialist centralism and self-sufficiency.

After China adopted the Open-door Policy in 1978, however, the economy of Hong Kong and Guangdong experienced substantial restructuring and rapid integration into what Graham Johnson calls a "Pearl River Delta region."

On the one hand, Hong Kong is becoming the center of the Pearl River Delta economy. There is a massive northward shift to Guangdong of Hong Kong's labor-intensive, low-value-added manufacturing industries (like the garment, footwear, and plastics industries). Ming Chan points out that over 3 million Guangdong workers are currently employed in Hong Kong–owned and –managed enterprises in the delta. This figure is much larger than the total manufacturing work force in Hong Kong itself (estimated at about 0.74 million in 1991). This shift has released pressure on labor and land resources, which are both short in Hong Kong, and has allowed Hong Kong to concentrate its energy on economic diversification and structural transformation. As a result, the colony has upgraded itself to be the financier, investor, supplier, designer, promoter, exporter, middleman, and technical consultant of the Pearl River Delta economy. Yun-wing Sung asserts that Hong Kong has been the pivot of Guangdong's economic links with the world economy since the 1980s.

On the other hand, Guangdong is turning into the periphery of the Pearl River Delta economy. Xueqiang Xu, et al., report that there is a division of labor in the delta economy through the pattern of "front shop, back factory" (*qiandian houchang*). Marketing, design, financing, and administration take place in the "front shop" in Hong Kong, while manufacturing and assembly are done in the "back factory" in Guangdong. As a result, Guangdong is dependent upon Hong Kong businessmen for capital, technology, machinery, and management;

Guangdong becomes the supplier of labor, land, and raw intensive industries that have little in the way of high-tech components. In addition, Guangdong engages in cash-crop cultivation—such as vegetables, fruit, pigs, poultry, and fish—for the Hong Kong consumer.

Nevertheless, Guangdong is actively resisting the peripheralization of its economy. Since Guangdong is more economically advanced than other Chinese provinces, it is making use of its Hong Kong connections to turn other Chinese provinces into its periphery. Consequently, Xu et al. observed that there is a continuous migration from other provinces to provide cheap, docile labor to the Guangdong economy; that other provinces supplied raw materials and minerals to Guangdong; that other provinces became the domestic market of Guangdong light industries. Due to these domestic linkages as well as to the external linkages with Hong Kong, Guangdong has experienced the highest growth rate of any Chinese province and a very rapid increase of income level, all of which serves to widen the gap between Guangdong and other mainland provinces. In this respect, although Guangdong stands on the economic periphery of Hong Kong, it has become an economic center to other provinces in mainland China (see Kwok, 1992).

On the cultural front, Greg Guldin argues that a Pearl River Delta cultural area (the *Namyuet* culture) has gradually emerged in the last decade. Since Hong Kong represents not only prosperity but also a sinified version of Western prosperity, the "south wind" that blows into Guangdong from Hong Kong thus brings with it a model of modernity that is adjusted for local tastes. From computer links to academic conferences to trade exhibitions, the Hong Kong cultural model has established itself firmly in the minds of Guangdong businessmen and women. Through videos, radio, television, newspapers, and magazines, Hong Kong ideas and lifestyles have found a ready and receptive audience across the Guangdong border. For example, Guangdong residents now spend their evenings glued to television showings of Hong Kong's soap operas, kungfu movies, and variety shows. The reunified Guangdong cultural area also witnesses linguistic changes (the spread of Hong Kong speech styles) and the comeback of opera in Guangdong.

In the Pearl River Delta, therefore, Hong Kong has emerged since 1978 as the center of Guangdong in both the economic and the cultural spheres. With Guangdong providing labor, raw materials, and investment opportunities, Hong Kong's economy is booming. With Guangdong residents aspiring to the Hong Kong cultural model, the Hong Kong people tend to look down on their Guangdong "country cousins." Nevertheless, Guangdong has not suffered from Hong Kong's core domination. In fact, Guangdong's economy has a remarkable growth rate because it has used its Hong Kong connections to dominate other mainland provinces; and Guangdong's residents do not seem to mind Hong Kong arrogance because they are enjoying a more diversified lifestyle than before.

Consequently, economists, urban planners, economic geographers, and anthropologists tend to offer a highly optimistic view of the future: Hong Kong and

Guangdong working harmoniously with one another toward a bright socioeco-nomic integration. Nevertheless, political scientists and political sociologists offer a different, pessimistic, picture of Hong Kong transition.

Hong Kong as the Political Periphery of Beijing

In the political sphere, the integration process is between Hong Kong and Bei-jing, not between Hong Kong and Guangdong. In 1997, the sovereignty of Hong Kong will be resumed by the Beijing government of mainland China, not by the provincial Guangdong government. The negotiation talks and the Joint Declara-tion were conducted and signed by the London and Beijing governments; the people of Hong Kong had little control over these two crucial events that deter-mined their future (So, 1993). In this respect, although Hong Kong is the socio-economic center of Guangdong province, it is merely at the political periphery of the central Beijing government.

Since the signing of the Joint Declaration in 1984, the Beijing government has been actively interfering in Hong Kong politics. Beijing successfully shelved the proposal to have a direct election in 1988, slowed down the democratic reforms through the drafting of the Basic Law, pressured the London government to refor-mulate its Ports and Airports Development Scheme, and heavy-handedly challenged the new Governor's democratic proposal (*South China Morning Post,* 12–23–92).

This being so, Ian Scott is concerned about the political future of Hong Kong. He points out that political legitimacy of the future Hong Kong government depends on three sets of concerns stipulated in both the 1984 Sino-British agree-ment and the 1990 Basic Law: (1) the autonomy of the post-1997 government, (2) the development of representative institutions, and (3) the maintenance of civil liberties. But the Chinese, the British, and the Hong Kong governments have been long on rhetoric and short on substance on the above concerns. Scott contends that it is this erosion of the provision of the Joint Declaration that explains the substantial emigration of the new middle class, aspects of civil service unrest, and the general sense of malaise over the future.

Along similar lines, Ming-kwan Lee's surveys report that anticipation of 1997 has transformed the political culture of Hong Kong. There was distrust of the Chinese government, a strong sense of political helplessness, a carefree attitude toward public affairs, and a shift to such values as "it is of utmost importance to make as much money as possible" and "enjoy life and forget about the future." As a result of this political alienation, sixty thousand persons emigrated from Hong Kong in 1990 alone, because they foresaw deterioration on every front after 1997, including the curtailment of civil rights and the lowering of living standards. Furthermore, there emerged a new political identity among the Hong Kong residents. Lee's surveys show that only 29 percent regarded themselves as "Chinese," with the majority identifying themselves as "Hong Kong persons."

In addition, there is the development of a nascent democracy movement to resist the political peripheralization of Hong Kong (So and Kwitko, 1990; So and Kwitko, 1992). The democrats want direct elections, a fully representative legislature, a highly autonomous government, and an independent judiciary so as to protect Hong Kong from Beijing interference. The democrats began to campaign on an anti-Beijing line in the early 1990s, and many of them have been elected to the legislature council. With Chris Patten, the current Hong Kong governor, echoing the democrats' demand for representative government, the political conflict between Hong Kong and Beijing has become more acute since the early 1990s.

In sum, there is an imbalance between socioeconomic and political integration. On the one hand, Hong Kong has become the socioeconomic center of Guangdong, and the Pearl River Delta economy and culture are flourishing. On the other hand, Hong Kong has become the political periphery of Beijing, and Hong Kong's resistance to political peripheralization is on the rise.

How, then, can this imbalanced integration process between Hong Kong and Guangdong/Beijing be resolved in the near future? What will happen to Hong Kong in 1997?

Hong Kong's Uncertain Transitions

The imbalanced integration helps to explain not just the disagreement between the economists and the political scientists in this volume, but also Hong Kong's uncertain transition toward the twenty-first century. It is possible that Hong Kong will go through one of three scenarios.

The Collapse Scenario

This is the argument of the political pessimists. They predict that if political peripheralization is to be intensified in 1997—that is, if there is prevailing civil alienation, out-migration of professionals, urban riots, political unrest, and the like—then there will be a crisis of confidence among Hong Kong's entrepreneurs, and the economic superiority of Hong Kong will quickly erode. If this happens, there will be large-scale out-migration of capital, depreciation of Hong Kong currency, a downfall of stock and real estate prices, followed by inflation, unemployment, and panic buying at supermarkets. Anticipating that the Hong Kong economy could collapse at any moment, Beijing will then be forced to take over Hong Kong, abolish the capitalist market economy, and impose the Chinese style of socialist economy (Davies, 1991; Hicks, 1987). In this respect, the integration balance is restored when economic peripheralization is followed by political peripheralization.

The False-Alarm Scenario

This is the argument of the economic optimists. They figure that Hong Kong will continue to prosper and play a significant role in China's Four Modernizations.

Hong Kong is the single largest foreign investor in China and its investment is expanding from Guangdong to all over the nation. Hong Kong's expanding higher education is producing a higher level of human resource to replace the migrants, and there is a massive return of migrants to Hong Kong after they have fulfilled residence requirements and cannot find a decent living overseas. Thus the Hong Kong economy will continue to prosper in the late 1990s, and Hong Kong people are just having a false alarm on the 1997 issue. On the other hand, China's economic problems are getting more severe. Market socialism not only does not work, it leads to overheating of the economy accompanied by unemployment, inflation, strikes, and political protests. The Pearl River Delta economy is the only bright spot for the Chinese nation. In gaining economic power, however, the delta region will also grow in political power. By becoming China's most advanced economy and most influential political region, the Pearl River Delta may set itself up as a strong rival to Beijing (Chen, 1991; Hicks, 1987). In this respect, the integration balance is restored when the Delta region is turned into a model for mainland development—acquiring status as both economic center and political center.

The Cyclical Scenario

This is what the realists are hoping for as Hong Kong moves toward the twenty-first century. The realists agree that the few years before and after 1997 will definitely cause political chaos and economic nervousness in Hong Kong, and its economy will suffer. By the first decade of the twenty-first century, however, after the transition is over and after the new Hong Kong government is firmly in place, business confidence will be quickly restored. Capital will return to Hong Kong and continue to invest in the Pearl River Delta region. With the Hong Kong economy booming, the professionals too will seek to return to Hong Kong. Subsequently, Hong Kong will regain its economic prosperity and center status over Guangdong in the Pearl River Delta region, although it will still be politically peripheral to Beijing. In this respect, in the future integration process, there will still be an imbalance. But after the 1997 storm is over, political peripheralization will not cause much harm to the Hong Kong center economy.

Which scenario is more likely to happen in 1997? It depends. History never follows a determined path but is always subject to the intervention of human agency. The future of Hong Kong integration depends on socioeconomic and political changes currently under way in Hong Kong, Guangdong, and Beijing. More studies are needed in order to examine the complexity and the undetermined nature of the Hong Kong integration process. Thus it may be appropriate to end our discussion here by calling for the following research agenda.

Future Research Agenda

First, it is necessary to adopt a multidisciplinary approach that goes beyond the study of either political or economic or sociocultural topics. It is vitally important to examine how politics, economics, and sociocultural values interact and affect one another.

Second, it requires a geopolitical focus that goes beyond the territorial confines of Hong Kong. Instead of studying Hong Kong or Guangdong or Beijing in isolation from one another, it is important to trace the intricate economic and cultural integrations between Hong Kong and Guangdong, to examine the dynamic political connections between Hong Kong and Beijing, and to investigate the profound developmental strategies that bring Hong Kong, mainland China, and Taiwan together (Hsiao and So, 1993).

Third, it is important to take a historical perspective that goes beyond the short-term episodes that make news headlines. It is important to trace and analyze the long-term, complex structural transformations in Hong Kong, Guangdong, and Beijing.

References

Chen, Edward (1991), "Recent Development in Hong Kong and Its Relationship with China," paper presented at the International Symposium on Pacific Asian Business, Pacific Asian Management Institute, University of Hawaii at Manoa, Honolulu, January 6–9, 1991.

Davies, Derek (1991), "Comments on Recent Development in Hong Kong," paper presented at the International Symposium on Pacific Asian Business, Pacific Asian Management Institute, University of Hawaii at Manoa, Honolulu, January 6–9, 1991.

Hicks, George (1987), "Hong Kong on the Eve of Communist Rule," in *The Future of Hong Kong: Toward 1997 and Beyond,* ed. Hungdah Chiu et al., New York: Quorum Books.

Hsiao, Hsin-Huang Michael, and Alvin Y. So (1993), "Ascent Through National Integration: The Chinese Triangle of Mainland–Taiwan–Hong Kong," in *Asia-Pacific and the Future of the World Economy,* ed. Ravi Palat, Westport, CT: Greenwood Press.

Kwok, R. Yin-Wang (1992), "An Overseas Assessment of the Pearl River Delta Development," paper presented at the Conference on Pearl River Delta Economic Development: Review and Prospect, Research Center of Pearl River Delta Economic Development and Management, Zhongshan University, Zhongshan, May 7–11, 1992.

So, Alvin Y. (1990), *Social Change and Development: Modernization, Dependency, and World-System Theories,* Newbury Park, CA: Sage Publications.

———— (1993), "Hong Kong People Ruling Hong Kong! The Rise of the New Middle Class in Negotiation Politics, 1982–1984," *Asian Affairs: An American Review,* Vol. 20, pp. 67–87.

So, Alvin Y., and Ludmilla Kwitko (1990), "New Middle Class and the Democratic Movement in Hong Kong," *Journal of Contemporary Asia,* Vol. 20, pp. 384–98.

———— (1992), "The Transformation of Urban Movements in Hong Kong, 1970–1990," *Bulletin of Concerned Asian Scholars,* Vol. 24, No. 4, pp. 31–42.

South China Morning Post, December 23, 1992.

Postscript

Mid-1992 Toward Mid-1994

Alvin Y. So and Reginald Yin-Wang Kwok

The contents of this volume represent the collective thought of our contributors on the subject of Hong Kong–Guangdong integration up to the first half of 1992. What then has changed after mid-1992? Although the economic integration between Hong Kong and Guangdong has continued unabated through the mid-1990s, there was a sudden intensification of political conflict between London and Beijing following the appointment of Chris Patten as governor of Hong Kong in mid-1992.

Economic Integration Continued

Toward the mid-1990s, Hong Kong manufacturers continued to relocate their businesses to Guangdong. It was estimated that as many as 5 million people in the Pearl River Delta were employed in factories controlled by Hong Kong interests. Subsequently, manufacturing's contribution to Hong Kong's gross domestic product continued to fall while that of the services sector continued to increase. In 1993, manufacturing's share of Hong Kong's work force was only 17.7 percent, while the share of services reached 60 percent (Hong Kong Government, 1994: 2).

Despite the economic integration between Hong Kong and Guangdong manufacturing that has become obvious, their financial integration hardly progressed. Using the colony as their base, Hong Kong businesses in China had built up not only a large trade surplus, but also massive holdings of Hong Kong dollars. In 1992, these overseas holdings totaled some U.S. $807.7 million, or more than the Hong Kong banking system's entire demand deposit base. These Hong Kong dollars were repatriated to Hong Kong through the interbank market, but the local financial system was either unable or unwilling to lend them back to China. Instead, lending remained overwhelmingly concentrated on Hong Kong–based assets, notably mortgage lending. As a result, an overheated and speculative housing market emerged in Hong Kong, with values of small flats rising by some 30 percent in both 1992 and 1993. It was reported that demand for housing was so strong that would-be buyers were willing to put down cash, up to 10 percent of the final price, when the block was nothing more than a hole in the ground (*Far Eastern Economic Review,* 1993; Economist Intelligence Unit, 1994).

This booming housing market was accompanied by a real growth in gross domestic product of 5.5 percent, a very low 2-percent unemployment rate, and a rapid growth of manufacturing wages of 6 percent after inflation in 1993. In order to promote the robust Hong Kong economy further, business interests have pressed for closer ties with Guangdong. Thus the Business and Professional Federation called for an infrastructure plan for the Pearl River Delta that would look at the long-term needs of the entire region (Economist Intelligence Unit, 1994; Burns, 1994).

As such, the present trend of economic integration between Hong Kong and Guangdong will most likely continue toward the twenty-first century. Nevertheless, Sino-British conflict over political reform for Hong Kong has intensified in the midst of the economic boom.

Political Conflict Intensified

In the early 1990s, with 1997 only a few years away, the London government began to feel the pressing need to prepare Hong Kong for the transition from British rule to Chinese rule. Subsequently, London reemerged as a key player in Hong Kong. It is interesting to note that Sino-British relations sharply deteriorated during the last phase of colonial rule. From 1984 to 1991, the London government had generally adopted a policy of cooperation with Beijing toward the political development of Hong Kong. The Hong Kong government in 1988 was willing to postpone the introduction of direct elections in Hong Kong until 1991 (the year after the promulgation of the Basic Law), according to Beijing's demand; it was willing to "consult" Beijing on all major matters straddling 1997 in order to get Beijing's approval for the new airport project; and it even sent Prime Minister John Major to Beijing in September 1991 for the signing of the new airport memorandum. Major must have felt humiliated as the first Western leader to visit Beijing after the Tiananmen Incident, for he soon replaced Sir David Wilson (who was an exponent of the cooperative policy) with Chris Patten as the last governor of Hong Kong, and adopted a less conciliatory policy toward Beijing (Chan, 1994:3).

Without consulting Beijing, Governor Patten sparked the Sino-British conflict in October 1992 with his proposals seeking to increase the pace of democratization for Hong Kong. Patten's strategy was to adhere to the wordings of the Basic

Law (which apportions twenty seats of legislature members to be returned by popular elections, thirty seats to be elected by functional constituencies, and ten seats to be elected by an electoral committee composed of members appointed in the 1995 elections), but he filled in many gray areas in the Basic Law document.

Patten's proposals can be summarized as follows: (1) To lower the voting age from twenty-one to eighteen for the elections in 1994 and 1995. (2) Single vote, single seat: Since the 1991 system of double-member constituencies had been criticized, Patten proposed to give each elector a single vote for a single, directly elected representative in a single-seat constituency. (3) Functional constituency revisions: At present, the thirty functional constituencies in the Legislative Council are decided largely on a corporate basis; that is, each bank has a vote for the financial constituency. Patten proposed redefining the functional constituency so that each includes the entire working population in that sector. This redefinition of the functional constituencies would broaden the voting franchise from a few thousand corporate bodies to around 2.7 million people by giving every worker the opportunity to elect to the Legislative Council a member to represent him or her at the workplace. (4) Strong local administration: Patten proposed abolishing all appointments to local district boards and municipal councils and choosing their members instead by direct election. Those chosen in local elections would then make up the Election Committee, who would elect the remaining ten members of the Legislative Council (Patten, 1992). In other words, under Patten's plan, all members of the Legislative Council would be elected directly or indirectly by the people of Hong Kong in 1995. Thus, Patten could claim that his proposals for constitutional reforms were quite compatible with the provisions of the Basic Law (Patten, 1992).

Patten actively lobbied for his proposals in late 1992. He appeared in town-meeting-style gatherings and participated in radio phone-in programs to explain his political reforms to the public. Forty human rights and service groups in response organized public support for the proposals, through political advertisements, press conferences, public meetings, and demonstrations outside the New China News Agency. Subsequently, opinion polls conducted in Hong Kong in late 1992 showed that a clear majority approved of Patten's proposals and his performance. In addition, Patten flew to London to secure the blessing of Prime Minister John Major. By mid-November, the Canadian, Australian, and United States governments had publicly stated their support for greater democracy in Hong Kong (Luk, 1992).

Beijing's reaction to Patten's proposals was highly negative, however. Patten was given a cold reception when he visited Beijing in October 1992. Beijing demanded that Patten's proposals be withdrawn, or else Beijing would take unilateral drastic action with regard to both the political system and the proposed airport before and after 1997. Specifically, Beijing threatened that "contracts, leases, and agreements" signed by the Hong Kong government would not be honored after 1997 unless they were approved in advance by China (Luk, 1992).

In the British community, former Governor of Hong Kong Lord MacLehose, former ambassador to Beijing Percy Cradock, and former Hong Kong chief secretary David Akers-Jones took a public stance against Patten's proposals. They were joined by British business interests who did not want to risk antagonizing Beijing and losing their privileges. Back in Hong Kong, Patten's proposals were criticized by both conservative business interests and the democrats. On the one hand, the conservative Business and Professional Federation issued a statement in favor of "convergence" with the Basic Law and against the new proposals. On the other hand, the United Democrats complained that Patten's proposals were still too timid to bring real democratic reforms to Hong Kong. In the midst of this political conflict, the Hong Kong stock market experienced violent fluctuations, plunging more than one thousand points, or about 17 percent, in three days in December 1992 (*Economic and Business Report,* 1993; *Far Eastern Economic Review,* December 17, 1992). Patten's tactic was to appeal to Beijing and Hong Kong business interests to make concrete counterproposals so that the citizens of Hong Kong could decide what kind of future government they wanted.

In March 1993, the conflict was intensified as Patten published his proposals in the government gazette. Beijing reacted by stepping up "united front" work in the territory. It appointed a second batch of forty-nine Hong Kong affairs advisors, which included business leaders, retired civil servants, and professionals. However, just before the proposals were to be debated by the Legislative Council for passing into law, Beijing agreed to hold talks after London agreed that the talks should be based not on Patten's 1992 proposals directly, but on the Sino-British Joint Declaration, the Basic Law, and "previous understandings" reached by the two sides.

The seventeen rounds of talks in Beijing from April to November 1993, nevertheless, failed to produce any concrete results. Burns (1994) points out that the two sides disagreed on the following three major issues: (1) The through train: London pressed Beijing to establish objective criteria prior to the 1994–95 elections for determining who could "ride the through train" (i.e., those who were elected to office in 1994–95 elections could finish their four-year term and remain in office until 1998–99) beyond 1997, but Beijing insisted that this was a matter for the Preparatory Committee for the Special Administrative Region to decide in 1996. (2) The functional constituencies: Although London compromised to narrow the scope of functional constituencies to 1 million voters, Beijing still insisted that they should be based on clearly identifiable corporate bodies. (3) The election committee: London and Beijing disagreed on the composition of a committee to elect ten members to the legislature in 1995. London argued that the committee should be made up of locally elected members, while Beijing insisted that it come from functional constituencies and appointed members.

In November 1993, with the two sides still in disagreement over not only the above three "major issues" but also three other "simple issues" (lowering the voting age, the "single-seat, single-vote system" for the election, and abolishing the appointed seats on local councils), the talks broke down. Patten had long warned that time was running out; if the talks led nowhere, he would have to present his proposals to the legislature as soon as possible in order to make preparations for the District Board elections in 1994 and Legislative Council elections in 1995.

In order to discredit Patten's reforms package, Beijing repeated its threat to sack any legislative member elected under a system it does not approve when it resumes the exercise of sovereignty on July 1, 1997, and suggested that it might dismiss the other tiers of government (District Boards and Municipal Council) as well. In addition, Beijing accelerated preparations for a shadow government to be installed in Hong Kong when it reverts to Chinese sovereignty. Thus, the Chinese-appointed Preparatory Working Committee for post-1997 Hong Kong was instructed that its members should immediately embark on plans for an alternative body to the legislature elected under the Patten proposals in 1995 (Economist Intelligent Unit, 1994).

In the midst of Beijing's offensives, Patten's new tactic was to split his election proposals in two. In December 1993, the Legislative Council was asked first to consider legislation for the three "simple issues." When they were passed easily in February 1994, Patten immediately presented the three "major issues" to the legislature for debate, and he declared July as the latest deadline for passing them. In the spring of 1994, only twenty-three legislature members, together with three *ex officio* appointees from the ranks of senior civil servants, could be counted on as firm votes in favor of Patten's "three major issues," while twenty-three legislature members would definitely vote against Patten's proposals (Economist Intelligent Unit, 1994). Given the tightness of the vote, the support of ten independent legislature members was crucial in the passing of Patten's reforms package after a seventeen-hour debate on June 29, 1994.

Whither Hong Kong?

As of July 1994, the conflict between London and Beijing over the political reforms for Hong Kong was yet to be resolved. In mid-July, Governor Patten lashed out again at Beijing's declared intention of scrapping the elected Legislative Council when it takes over Hong Kong in 1997. It seems unlikely that the conflict over political reforms will be settled in the near future.

What is amazing, then, is to observe that the Hong Kong economy has not been adversely affected by the intensification of the Sino-British conflict. Despite the breakdown of the Sino-British talks in late 1993, the stock market in Hong Kong held its own. Despite the government's highly publicized commitment to bring down real estate prices in early 1994, the property market has not significantly cooled down. In fact, Hong Kong may well eventually overtake Tokyo as the most expensive city in the world in which to work. It is estimated that the property market will not collapse in 1997 either, as mainland Chinese (who owned more than U.S. $7.5 billion in real estate assets in the early 1990s) will likely own an even bigger slice of the Hong Kong property market after Beijing resumes sovereignty of the colony (*Economic and Business Report,* 1993; Economist Intelligence Unit, 1994).

In this respect, the future of Hong Kong will depend on whether its robust economic integration with Guangdong and mainland China can withstand the political typhoon in 1997.[1]

Honolulu
July 25, 1994

Note

1. By mid-1994, though, there were signs that the political typhoon in 1997 might be losing force. In late June, the Sino-British Joint Liaison Group (JLG) held a meeting in Hong Kong after a six-month suspension. In addition, just hours after the passage of Patten's democratic proposals, London and Beijing clinched a major agreement on the issue of military lands in Hong Kong, marking the end of a seven-year dispute over the allocation of valuable existing military sites. Further progress had also been made with respect to financing the airport, passport regulations, local laws, and other issues.

References

Burns, John P. (1994), "Hong Kong in 1993: The Struggle for Authority Intensifies," *Asian Survey,* Vol. 34, No. 1, pp. 55–63.

Chan, Ming K. (1994), "Introduction: Hong Kong's Precarious Balance—150 Years in an Historic Triangle," in *Precarious Balance: Hong Kong Between China and Britain, 1842–1992,* ed. Ming K. Chan, Armonk: M.E. Sharpe.

Economic and Business Report (1993), *Asia Pacific Review 1993/94,* London: Kogan Page Limited.

Economist Intelligence Unit (1994), *Country Report: Hong Kong, Macau,* London: Economist Intelligence Unit.

Far Eastern Economic Review, December 17, 1992.

Far Eastern Economic Review (1993), *Asia 1992 Yearbook,* Hong Kong: Far Eastern Economic Review.

Hong Kong Government (1994), *Hong Kong in Figures,* Hong Kong: Government Printer.

Luk, Bernard (1992), "Reaction to Patten's Constitutional Proposals," *Canada and Hong Kong Update,* No. 8, pp. 1–4.

Patten, Chris (1992), "Governor Patten's Policy Speech to Legco," *Canada and Hong Kong Update,* No. 8, pp. 1–4.

Index

Abundance of remittance *(huifeng)*, 38
Africa, 69
Agriculture
  in Baoan, 75, 177
  DFI in, 177–78
  in Duanfen, 69, 71
  in Fucheng, 74–75
  in Leliu, 71–72
  in Luogang, 72
  in Naamshui, 76–77
  in Ngawu, 77
  in Renhe, 72–73
  state policies controlling, 74, 83–84n.11
  in Tsimkong, 75
  in Wantong, 75
  see also Production change
    (Guangdong)
Air traffic, 50, 92
Akers-Jones, David, 262
Alliance of Hong Kong People in Support
  of Democratic and Patriotic Activities
  in China, 122
Analytical framework
  developmental factors of, 13–16
  institutional structure factors of, 10–13
  issues in, 5–6
  political, cultural factors of, 6–10
Anhui, 33
Arrow Incident (Hong Kong), 34, 35, 43
Asia-Pacific region
  off-shore production zones in, 13, 14
  regional economic interdependence in,
    14
Asian Wall Street Journal, 6

Asian-African Conference, 122–23
Australia, 238, 241

Baiyun *qu*, 69, 71
Bandit gangs, 34
Baoan county, 43, 75, 83n.5, 177
Baosai (inner boarder-guarding), 20
"Basic Law" to govern Hong Kong, 64,
  82–83n.1, 121, 124, 189–91, 247–48
  autonomy eroded by, 197–200, 217–18,
    254
  representation eroded by, 200–203,
    254
Beijing (city), Beijing Opera in, 116n.22
Beijing (PRC government)
  Hong Kong negotiations through, 53
  integration impact on, 5
  political, cultural factors in, 6–10
    center vs. periphery in, 8–10, 15
    "One Country, Two Systems" policy
      of, 7, 12, 121, 124–25, 193
    unity vs. diversity in, 7–8
  projections from, 6
  Second Anglo-Chinese War and, 34
  state to market socialism transition in, 5,
    10–13, 15–16
  U.S.-Hong Kong policy and, 56
  see also People's Republic of China
Bonham, George, Sir, 43
Border crossing, 50
  figures on, 90, 115n.4
  illegal immigrants and, 53, 93, 151–53,
    166
  Vietnamese boat people and, 53

Pearl River Delta *(continued)*
conclusions regarding, 80–82
industrial growth, 67, 69, 91, 170, 172
economic statistics of, 182
Hong Kong bond to, 65–69
Hong Kong, Guangzhou economic core, 32, 66, 113–14
Hong Kong population from, 31, 36–37, 65–66
international capital flow in, 12
Macao in, 66, 113
man-land ratio of, 16–17
Open Economic Region of, 67, 83n.5, 138, 170
per capita income growth in, 69, 71
population migration to/from, 6, 9, 16–21, 37, 49, 50, 65–66, 67, 90, 93, 115n.7, 151–54, 165, 166, 169
PRC development strategies of, 65–69
SEZs in, 49–50
smuggling network into, 47–48, 53–54, 90
territorial containment area of, 12
see also Guangdong; Guangzhou; Sociocultural factors
Peihua (Cultivate China) foundation, 94
People's Liberation Army, 194, 205
People's Republic of China (PRC)
Central Broadcasting Station of, 97
Chinese People's Political Consultative Conference of, 51
commune movement in, 10
Cultural Revolution in, 48, 69, 71, 79, 90, 103–104, 109, 110, 111
diversity vs. unity in, 7
Economic Reform, Open-door Policy in, 3, 4, 6, 7, 13, 14, 49, 64, 66, 135–136, 169, 170, 180, 183, 224
economic sanctions against lifted, 55
Great Leap Forward and, 48, 84n.11, 90, 115n.2
Guangdong in, 6
historical perspective of
British recognition of (1949), 47
Convention of 1898 and, 36
Guangzhou Trade Fair and, 48
Korean War involvement of, 47, 90
political conflict (1992–1994), 260–64, 264n.1
Second Anglo-Chinese War and, 34
treaty port system and, 32–33, 65, 138

People's Republic of China (PRC) *(continued)*
Treaty of Shimonoseki and, 36
Hong Kong citizenship and, 119–24, 204
Hong Kong example used by, 54
Hong Kong importance to, 3, 4, 14, 37–39, 40–41, 47–52, 64–65, 68
Hong Kong trade with, 3, 165–69, 170–72
Hong Kong-Guangdong integration and, 4–5
most favored nation (MFN) status of, 55–56, 183, 232
National People's Congress and, 51
Pearl River Delta development strategies of, 65–69
Sino-British Joint Declaration and, 17, 50, 254–55
stock exchange of, 55
"the Basic Law" to govern Hong Kong and, 64, 82–83n.1, 121, 124, 189–91, 198, 247–48
autonomy eroded by, 197–200, 217–18, 254
representation eroded by, 200–203, 254
Treaty of Nanking and, 32–33
UN embargo of, 47, 164
see also Beijing (PRC government); Economic integration; Pearl River Delta; Political transformation (Hong Kong); Production change (Guangdong); Sino-British Agreement; *specific city, province, region*
Philippines, 14, 181
Political factors
center vs. periphery and, 5, 8–9, 15
contention among, 5
democratization movement and, 12–13
self-sufficiency and, 20, 145
unity vs. diversity and, 5, 6–10, 15
see also Political transformation (Hong Kong)
Political periphery
discussion of, 251–52
future research agenda on, 257
Hong Kong in, 254–55
Hong Kong's uncertain transitions in, 255–56